Backpacking in Central America

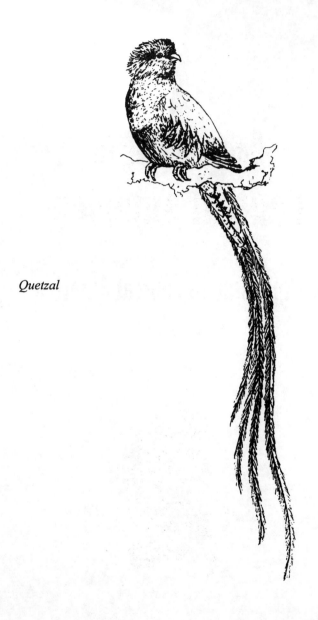

Quetzal

For Lucy Gregory, who should be in hiking boots before long.

Backpacking in
Central America

Tim Burford

Bradt Publications, UK
The Globe Pequot Press Inc, USA

Published in 1996 by Bradt Publications,
41 Nortoft Road, Chalfont St Peter, Bucks SL9 0LA, England.
Published in the USA by The Globe Pequot Press Inc, 6 Business Park Road,
PO Box 833, Old Saybrook, Connecticut 06475-0833.

British Library Cataloguing in Publication Data
A catalogue record for this book is available from the British Library
ISBN 1 898323 25 9

Library of Congress Cataloging-in-Publication Data
Burford, Tim
  Backpacking and hiking in Central America / Tim Burford
  p. cm.
  Includes index
  ISBN 1-58440-817-5 (Globe Pequot Press)
  1. Hiking–Central America –Guidebooks. 2. Backpacking–Central
  America–Guidebooks. 3. Central America–Guidebooks. I. Title.
GV199.44.C43B87 1995
917.28'0452–dc20
                                                                95-48122
                                                                CIP

Cover photos *Front:* Wash day, Santiago village, Lake Atitlán, Guatemala
(John Noble, Wilderness Photography) *Back:* The Darién Gap (Hilary Bradt)
Illustrations Hilary Bradt, Wendy Dison
Maps *Inside covers:* Steve Munns *Others:* Hans van Well

Typeset from the author's disc by Patti Taylor, London NW10 1JR
Printed and bound in Great Britain by The Guernsey Press Co Ltd

INTRODUCTION

This is a great time to visit Central America! Peace and democracy seem to be breaking out everywhere, although of course nothing's perfect and it'll be a long time before Guatemala, El Salvador and even Honduras reach the state of peaceful, prosperous Panamá and Costa Rica. For the 'ecotourist' there are all kinds of attractions, above all some of the most diverse and colourful wildlife in the world. In most of the region hiking is in rainforest and cloudforest, largely on trails in national parks, and in many cases the only way to get clear views above the forest is by climbing a volcano. In Guatemala, however, it's possible to hike on high plateaux where you can find your own route from one colourful village to another.

Note that the order of countries assumes a trip from south to north (or more accurately from southeast to northwest) because this follows the dry season. Readers doing the more conventional route south from Mexico should have no problem.

I am grateful to Mike Shawcross, John Wolff, Bob Carey, Alex Gaertner, Jen Smith, Neil Shook, Mike Costa, William Jackson, Simon Carter and Eric Hansen for their help and information. Also to Peter Sterling and Mark Fischer for use of their material that appeared in the first edition of *Backpacking in Mexico and Central America*.

Tim Burford
October 1995

NOTE FROM THE PUBLISHER

This guide is based on *Backpacking in Mexico and Central America*. The first edition, by George and Hilary Bradt, was published in 1978 and the second, updated by Rob Rachowiecki, in 1982. Some material has been retained from those editions (updated where needed). This means a shift from "I" (Tim or Rob) to "We" (George and Hilary). Just visualise one of those mythical beasts with four heads but one body (with pack and boots) and you'll have no problem!

The beast would like more heads for the next edition, so do report any changes or new hikes that you find. The address is on the opposite page.

Hilary Bradt

Hilary Bradt

CONTENTS

Part One

BACKGROUND
INFORMATION

Chapter One

The Land

GEOLOGY AND GEOGRAPHY

Geologically, Central America is divided into two parts: 'nuclear Central America' from the isthmus of Tehuantepec in Mexico to a line across the centre of Nicaragua; and the 'land bridge' to the southeast, which is a recent addition.

The oldest rocks in Central America are pre-Permian metamorphic rocks, at least 280 million years old, in Guatemala, Honduras and northern Nicaragua. This area has been above sea level since at least the early Mesozoic era, around 200mya (million years ago); from the Upper Jurassic (150-136mya) volcanic cones began to appear above water to the south, along the ridge between the Atlantic and Pacific plates. This produced an arc of islands along which bird species were able to move throughout the Tertiary period. Uplifting in the Miocene (15-20mya) produced continuous land to central Panama, and the last gap (the Bolivar Trench) was closed by the end of the Pliocene (3mya).

South America was isolated from the other continents from the Eocene (38-54mya) to the Pliocene; it's possible that there was species interchange with North America through Africa and Europe when the continents were still rammed together, but there's no evidence of this. Therefore the flora and fauna of Central America were almost entirely North American in origin until around 5mya, when island-hopping across the Bolivar Trench became possible. The land bridge, when it appeared, was ideal for the transfer of savanna species; the Pleistocene ice ages destroyed most tropical forests, so it's only in the last 25,000 years that tropical rainforests developed and montane species were able to move. Animals moving north from South America included the sloth, opossum, capybara, toxodontes (giant hippos), porcupine and anteater, while raccoon, deer, mastodon, sabre-toothed tiger, weasel, tapir, skunk, peccary, dog and bear moved south from North America.

Central America is long and thin and relatively small, only a quarter of the size of Mexico. Both northern and southern parts are dominated by volcanoes, which have produced immensely fertile soil, but on the other hand eruptions and earthquakes have caused immense damage at regular intervals. On either side of the *cordilleras* that run the length of Central America are coastal plains, mostly recent sediments but also fertile and used largely for growing cash crops such as bananas. It's worth noting here that we use the term 'Atlantic', not 'Caribbean', throughout for the eastern coast, as is the practice in most of Central America.

Volcanic activity

There are over a hundred volcanoes in Central America, some of which are still active. Some of these emit highly noxious gases, while others seem inactive but can belch forth lava and rocks without warning — something to consider before hiking to the summit.

So how does a volcano form? The active ingredient is magma, molten gas-charged rock which rises after being liquified by subterranean heat and friction. The various types of magma define the various types of volcano, with soup-like magma spurting over the edge of the volcano in frequent and minor releases of energy, or thick and viscous magma which coagulates and is then blasted violently high into the air — the norm in Central America. If a large quantity of magma emerges it may leave a void into which the top of the volcano topples, turning the summit into a *caldera*. Years later lakes can form in the calderas of extinct volcanoes.

These beautiful lakes can be your reward if you've struggled up a volcano, although chances are slim that you'll be able to drink from them because they're usually at the bottom of a very steep pit, and almost always excessively alkaline. But they catch the light splendidly and the colours can be stunning.

You'll often find your path covered with pumice stone and obsidian. Usually they're found together because they're created together: pumice is the solidified foam on top of molten obsidian. As obsidian cools it inherits those qualities so sought after by primitive people in search of material which could be knapped into broad flat areas and sharp edges: just right for arrow and spear heads.

These are inactive indicators of past volcanic activity, but what about current events? Normally we see little evidence of magma under the earth's surface, but in Central America there's plenty of proof that such stuff actually exists, just as you learned in school. If you visit Rincón de la Vieja in Costa Rica you'll see a terrific area of hot springs, 'porridge pots' and fumaroles, all caused by superheated water vapour created by magma far below the earth's surface and under such pressure that it forces its way to the surface. Of course you can see them in other locations, but nowhere have we ever seen such an array of features so close to each other.

Fumaroles (Latin *fumus*: smoke) are formed by the condensation of super-heated water vapour as it hits the cooler air and turns into steam. We've seen fumaroles puffing from a hole a metre across, and hissing from one as small as a straw. This water vapour, combined with surface water, produces other phenomena such as bubbling porridge pots, paint pots, hot springs or mud volcanoes. For instance, a stream flowing over ground heated by a fumarole will be hot or warm depending on the amount of water and heat. Suppose that stream is dammed up and stops flowing: it will turn into a steaming cauldron, possibly ringed with fantastic colours provided by iron oxides (a 'paintpot'). On the other hand, perhaps the stream has been flowing through a bed of clay: dam it up and you will have a porridge pot.

These phenomena may vary with the season of the year. If it is the wet season chances are that fumaroles will be turned into porridge pots, while the absence of rain will change them back into dry fumaroles. But whatever season you're guaranteed a good show — and possibly a hot bath!

CLIMATE AND WHEN TO GO

To the backpacker accustomed to temperate zone seasons, the Central American climate is confusing. The area is far enough north of the Equator for May-September to be warmer than October-April, but temperature changes affect the walker (and the farmer) far less than do the rainy and dry seasons.

These seasons happen to coincide with the northern hemisphere's summer and winter. The problem is that early settlers nostalgically called the rainy season 'winter' (*invierno*), even though it falls in the summer months, from May to November. So days are actually shorter in the summer (*verano*), although not enough to make a huge difference — it's always dark by about 18.30. The main school holidays are in the *verano*, when the most popular areas can be very busy; equally Easter (*Semana Santa*) can be hectic.

The rains move northwards, so although it will already be unpleasantly wet in the Darién Gap in April, Guatemala may still be awaiting the first rains at the end of May. Generally speaking, they come after hot, humid weather which gets increasingly uncomfortable as the rains approach. They begin erratically, first with brief showers, then with heavy downpours with clear spells in between, and finally prolonged rain and cloudy weather. On the Pacific coast there's all-day rain, the *temporal*, in June and September, and a dry spell, the *canicula* or *veranillo*, in late July or early August. On the Atlantic coast, where far fewer people live than on the Pacific coast or in the central highlands, it rains all year (with total precipitation from 3,500mm to as much as 7,000mm), and indeed the heaviest rainfall may be from November to January. Hurricanes can occasionally strike the Atlantic coast of Nicaragua and Honduras, but are rare to the south.

Global warming may well be disrupting climatic patterns worldwide, but in any case Latin American weather is disrupted at irregular intervals by the *El Niño* current, which reduces rainfall and is blamed for low levels in the reservoirs and consequent power cuts.

The most pleasant months for hiking the trails we describe are from October through to February, and (providing you are prepared to get up early and weather the occasional afternoon storm) July and August. November and December are the nicest months of all, since that's when meadows are ablaze with flowers, rivers are full and the air is crisp and pure. January and February are the coolest months, and you can rely on dry weather in most areas. March, April and May tend to be too dry and hot: except in select areas, the landscape is parched, the rivers dry and the air hazy with smoke from hundreds of fires as farmers prepare their *milpas* for the next planting of corn.

There are many local variations, and where weather is of critical importance for a particular hike, we've described the local conditions.

NATURAL HISTORY

By Hilary Bradt and George Bradt with additions by Rob Rachowiecki and Tim Burford

In its original state Central America was, as you might suspect, almost entirely covered with forest, but this is now reduced to less than 20% of the land area (the same as in Europe); by around 2003 it's likely that the only substantial forest remaining will be in national parks and forestry reserves. Most of the hikes in this book are in those parks and reserves, although a few are in different settings. In the introductions to the hikes we refer to specific 'life zones' as classified according to the 'Holdridge system' (such as 'tropical premontane moist forest'), but here we just give a general overview of what you'll find. Likewise, a general overview of the flora and fauna of the region is all that a book of this kind has space or scope for.

Tropical **rainforests** and **cloudforests** are what most people call jungle. They receive up to 7,000mm of rain annually (yes, that's seven *metres* of rain!), so are very humid, lush and verdant. The forest recycles 50% of the rain that falls on it while absorbing and processing vast quantities of carbon dioxide — one of the reasons deforestation is so disastrous is that this is released, contributing to the greenhouse effect. This great ecosystem, containing more diversity of life than any other, obtains most of its nutrients from the thin layer of soil which it itself produces, as leaves and epiphytes constantly fall and rot. Thus nutrients are continually returned to the soil, only to be immediately taken up again by a plant. Leaf litter that would take a year to rot in temperate climates can be totally broken down and reabsorbed in just six weeks here. Once the forest is felled, this thin layer of soil is rapidly washed away, leaving infertile land that is soon exhausted.

All plant life in the forest competes for sunlight. Trees grow tall and straight, branching out at the top to form the canopy which provides a separate sun-drenched world. Smaller plants (epiphytes or air-plants, including many orchids) grow on these trees, and other seeds wait to grow in clearings where larger trees have died and fallen. Creatures live and breed up there, never descending to the ground. Rain-water gathers in bromeliads (a type of epiphyte with very close fitting bowls of leaves), mosquito larvae hatch in the water and are eaten by the tadpoles of tree frogs, which are themselves fed on by crabs, lizards and snakes. Monkeys, sloths and other arboreal mammals and reptiles also have everything they require. There are even 'arboreal highways' in the canopy where the mosses and bromeliads have been compacted by animal traffic. There is always food here: in particular there are 900 species of fig worldwide (65 in Costa Rica), each fertilised by a different agaonid wasp at a subtly different time of year to provide year-round food for many birds and bats. Indeed fruit is so plentiful that some frugivorous birds can spend 90% of their time singing to attract a mate!

At ground level the forest is far from impenetrable because there is insufficient light for excessive growth; in fact it's only at the forest edge and where large trees have fallen (or where forest has been cleared for slash-and-burn agriculture) that truly 'jungle-like' conditions occur and a machete might be helpful. All tropical forests have a natural cycle, changing from primary or virgin forest to this secondary or succession forest and then gradually reverting to primary forest as the canopy trees grow and plants adapted to lack of light take over below them from the 'jungle'. Palms and treeferns dislike light and are very rare in secondary forest, providing a good indicator of undisturbed forest. It's uncertain how the amazing diversity of tree species of the rainforest develops, but within an area of 1.5 hectares in Panamá scientists have counted 130 different species of tree (not counting the many vines, lianas, shrubs and epiphytes), and a survey of 500 trees revealed 115 different species. (In Amazonia, though, just one hectare can contain 580 trees of 283 species!) However, at ground level many look the same, with broad thick leaves, trunks covered with moss and lichen and vast buttress roots. Because the layer of nutritious soil is thin, trees have shallow root systems and the fin-shaped buttresses have probably evolved to help support them.

Whereas rainforest is found in lowlands with a generous year-round supply of rain, the cloudforest is situated where warm air moving up a mountain mingles with the higher cooler air to condense into almost constant cloud cover (usually at 1,500-plus metres). Water is collected in the sponge-like mosses that proliferate, so that even on a sunny day the air is very humid. Everything here is smaller than in the mighty rainforests, due to the effects of wind and fog. Oak trees are common (it's been said that Central America is the 'headquarters of the world's oaks'), their gnarled limbs bearing such a burden of air-plants that they sometimes break off under the weight. Even the creatures tend to be miniature: toucanets rather than toucans, many species of hummingbird, tiny jewel-like frogs and multi-coloured butterflies.

Perhaps the most majestic tree of the tropical forests is the kapok or silk-cotton tree *ceiba/Ceiba pentandra*, which has soft wood useless except for coffins and so is usually left when forest around it is cleared; increasingly the typical Central American countryside is pasture with isolated ceibas. These have a distinctive wide flat crown on a very tall trunk, and drop their leaves in the dry season before producing white/pink flowers that open in the evening for bats to fertilise them. Perhaps the largest tree in Central America is a ceiba in Corcovado (Costa Rica), 80m tall and 3m in diameter.

Other big trees in primary forest include oaks (*Quercus sp.*; broad-leaved types are known as *roble*, small-leaved types as *encino*), cedars (*cedro/Cedrella sp.* and *Wilsonia pusilla*), mahogany (*caoba/Swietania macrophylla* and *humilis*) and maría (or Santa María: *Calophyllum brassiliense*); smaller trees below the canopy include the avocado and its relatives (*Persea, Nectandra* and *Ocotea sp.*), rosewood (*cocobolo/Dalbergia retusa*), mangabey (*Didymopanax morototoni*), palms (*Chamaedorea sp.*), bamboos (eg: *Chusquea sp.*), treeferns such as *Cyathea arborea* and strangler figs (*matapalo/ Ficus* and *Clusia sp.*), which sprout on a branch in the canopy, then send roots down to the ground, which grow all around the host tree and eventually (after maybe a hundred years) choke it to death. Under these grow dahlias, magnolias, ferns, poor man's umbrella (*sombrilla de pobre/Gunnera*) and cow's tongue (*lengua de vaca/Miconia sp.*).

In secondary forest to 2,000m you'll find large numbers of cecropias (*guarumo/Cecropia sp.*), easily recognized by the bamboo-like rings on its trunk and its large hand-like leaves; the hollow trunk of the *guarumo hormiguero* (*C. insignis*) is inhabited by *Azteca* ants, which protect it from other insects and prune back competing plants, and are rewarded by secretions of nectar — they bite, so take care! Heliconias, recognizable by their huge paddle-shaped leaves and the opposed red or orange lobster-claw bracts that hold the blossoms, *candelillos* (*Piper sp.*), with their candle-like flowers, *capulín* (*Trema micrantha*), balsa (*Ochroma lagopus*) and *papelillo* (*Miconia argentea*) are also common in these areas.

You will also find some **tropical dry forest** (also known as wet season or monsoon forest) described here; mostly on the relatively dry and accessible Pacific coast, the majority of this has now been felled, but what survives is largely protected. This is big, open forest with cacti and deciduous trees evolved to survive a long dry season by shedding their leaves; many are also very spiny to protect them against other hazards.

There's a great variety of species here too: huge trees such as the buttercup-tree (*poro-poro/Cochlospermum vitifolium*), the ear-tree (*guanacaste/ Enterolobium cyclocarpum*), trumpet tree (*corteza/Tabebuia ochracea*), the calabash tree (*jicaro/Crescentia alata*), and *tempisque* (*Mastichodendron capirio*), and smaller species such as gumbo-limbo (*indio desnudo/Bursera simarouba*), sandpaper tree (*chaparro/Curatella americana*), strawberry trees (*madroño/Arbutus sp.*), *ron-rón* (*Astroneum graveolens*), cedars (*pochote/ Bombacopsis sp.*), *madero negro* (*Gliricidia sepium*), frangipani (*Plumeria rubra*), *jocote* (*Spondias sp.*), and acacias. Again there are epiphytes growing on everything.

From northern Nicaragua northwards there are also **pine forests**, mainly a man-made association created by the clearing and regular burning, since pre-Hispanic times, of the original broadleaf forest; a variety of pine trees, each with its specific ecological niche, is associated with a variety of oaks and other broadleaf trees. Liquidambar or sweetgum (*Liquidambar styraciflua*) is widespread, especially in Honduras, in secondary growth and along streams; its rough, grey bark is often cut for resin, used in soaps and expectorants. Its leaves are like maple leaves (although alternate, not opposed), and they also change to marvellous reds and oranges in autumn.

There are various types of open **savanna**: only in Panamá and southern Costa Rica are they even partly natural, with *guanacaste* or eartrees (*Enterolobium cyclocarpum*), Spanish cedar (*Cedrela fissilis*), *nance (Byrsonima crassifolia*), and corozo palms (*Attalea gomphococca*); in the rainy season appears a carpet of dwarf herbs (*Crotolaria, Mimosa, Stylosanthes, Zornia, Borreria* and *Diodia sp.*). Others in Honduras and Nicaragua are the result of clearing forest, grazing and repeated burning; they're now dominated by introduced grasses from Africa and by *Pinus caribaea* and acacia shrubs.

Broadly speaking, as you head towards the Equator, the forest gets denser (and the fireflies get brighter and start flashing earlier in the afternoon). Dry forest is best for seeing animals, while cloud and rainforest are best for seeing birds.

Mammals

Tropical America is home to such a variety of creatures that we can only describe those that you are most likely to see.

Monkeys are the most conspicuous and least shy of the tropical mammals. Three kinds are commonly seen in protected areas in Central America.

Howler monkey
(*mono congo, saraguato/Alouatta palliata, A. pigra*)
Unlike most travellers we saw howlers before we heard them. We were chugging up Colombia's Río Atrato in our banana boat when an astonishing sight met our eyes. A tree covered in yellow blossoms stood near the bank, its boughs festooned with enormous monkeys with rich chestnut-coloured bodies and black limbs. Some were nibbling the blossoms, but most were hanging motionless, like huge toys. We asked the captain what they were. "*Mono congo*", he replied, and illustrated his answer by making an Indian war-cry; a passable imitation of the howl we were to hear later that day. If you camp in tropical forests or by Mayan ruins, you are very likely to hear this unearthly cry, even if you don't see the creatures. The sound carries for miles; from a distance it can be mistaken for the wind in the trees, but close to it defies description. If you're not forewarned you may think the forest is haunted.

Howler monkeys move around in troops, the leader of which is responsible for the dawn and dusk howling concerts, although others join in. The male has a huge voice box, strengthened with cartilage, which enables him to project the sound so impressively. Being the largest of the American monkeys also helps.

Spider monkey
(*mono colorado, mono araña, chango/Ateles geoffroyi*)
Our contact with spider monkeys was early and intimate, since there were two tame youngsters at the ranger station in Los Katios National Park where we stayed on our way to the Darién. They had been raised from infancy by the park personnel, were not caged, and were always in trouble. Judas, the male, was a competent thief, and I'm afraid my appreciation of certain religious works of art has been affected by knowing him. Now, when I hear of Judas, I think of a spider monkey running along on his hind legs, holding half a cooked chicken above his head. The female, less brazen and more vulnerable, had adopted a piglet as a surrogate mother. She would jump on its back when it passed, but was happiest when it was sleeping and she could curl up on top and suck its ear. Spider monkeys have some unusual characteristics. For ages we thought Judas was the female, and vice-versa, because of the female's elongated clitoris which we mistook for a penis.

They have no thumbs but their bodies are beautifully adapted to tree life, where they are the most efficient climbers and swingers of all the New World monkeys. It's a joy to watch them moving effortlessly through the trees, making prodigious leaps, and using their tails as hands; howlers also have prehensile tails, but they're less agile. In fact the spider monkey's tail has a hairless area on the underside which can feel as efficiently as a finger, so it really is a fifth limb.

Spider monkeys come in a variety of colours, black, chestnut, and light brown, but you will always be able to recognize them by their long limbs. They are common in Costa Rica and further north, particularly around the Mayan ruins of Tikal; in Darién and Colombia you may see the rarer brown-headed spider monkey (*mono araña negra/A. fusciceps*).

White-faced or Capuchin monkey
(*mono cara blanca/Cebus capucinus*)
You may well have seen this monkey before you begin your trip, since they make popular pets and are the traditional organ-grinders' monkeys. A troop soon made our acquaintance in Los Katios Park, lined up on a bough to observe us carefully. They are more inquisitive than other monkeys so you can watch them at close quarters. With their pink faces and white 'cowl' they are unmistakeable, and are common in protected areas from Darién to Honduras.

Other animals may be more shy and less inquisitive than the monkeys, but all of the following may be seen in low-lying areas:

Three-toed sloth
(*perezoso/Bradypus variegatus*)
All sloths have three digits on their rear feet, so this animal should really be known as the three-fingered sloth; however, it really does live up to the last part of its name. It sleeps for 18 out of 24 hours, descends to urinate and defaecate just once a week, and is so inactive that algae grow on its fur and beetles and moths live deep in its coat, laying their eggs only in sloth dung. Its maximum speed is about 1km/hour and it is very hard of hearing.

In fact, of course, the sloth is perfectly adapted to its environment, and doesn't need to alter its torpid way of life. It feeds on leaves (not only on cecropia, although it's often invisible in other trees), its algae-covered fur and slow movements make it very inconspicuous and few predators can reach it anyway.

There is also a nocturnal species, the two-toed (two-fingered) sloth *Choloepus hoffmani*, which is larger and faster and likewise is found from Honduras to South America.

It's not easy to spot a sloth in the wild, but there are always some in the trees of Vargas Park in Puerto Limón, Costa Rica.

Nine-banded armadillo
(*cusuco, armado/Dasypus novemcinctus*)
These endearing animals are quite common, and you'll often see them shuffling around in leaves or grass, hunting out insects and other small creatures, then digging frantically to reach their nest. With their noses so often buried deep in the ground, it's as well that armadillos can hold their breath for up to six minutes. They have poor hearing and even poorer eyesight, but an excellent

sense of smell. Less common, and found only from Honduras to the south, is the eleven-banded or naked-tailed armadillo (*Cabassous centralis*).

Agouti
(*tepescuintle/Dasyprocta punctata*)
Agoutis have the misfortune to taste good, so you are unlikely to see one except in well-protected parks such as Santa Rosa or Tikal. Indeed, relentless hunting has turned these diurnal rodents into mainly nocturnal ones in populated areas. Agoutis have two colour phases, reddish brown and black. The related *Agouti paca* is known as the paca; it's nocturnal and bears rows of creamy spots along its flanks.

Raccoon
The raccoon (*mapache/Procyon lotor*), is recognizable by its black face-mask and ringed tail, and is common near beaches and rivers. The crab-eating raccoon (*Procyon cancrivorus*) is found more in mangrove swamps, from southern Costa Rica to South America.

Kinkajou
(*cusumbí* or *mico de noche/Potus flavus*)
With a truly prehensile tail, the kinkajou is as agile as a monkey, and is popular as a pet. Although it is a member of the raccoon family, it looks nothing like a raccoon, but has soft brown fur, large eyes (it is nocturnal) and low set ears.

Coati or Coatimundi
(*gato solo, pizote/Nasua narica*)
You are unlikely to travel far in Central America without meeting a coati, either in the wild or as a pet. They are playful and affectionate pets, but their long whiffly noses get into everything and they are very destructive. Coatis belong to the same family as raccoons and live in tropical forests where they are particularly active in the early morning and evening, foraging in troops of up to 30, although the males may also be solitary. They are excellent tree climbers and may at first glance be mistaken for monkeys as they shin up trees in search of fruit or tasty insects.

Anteaters
(*oso hormiguero/Tamandua mexicana*)
The giant anteater is rare or possibly extinct in Central America. Still relatively common is the northern tamandua (*Tamandua mexicana*), half its size, and the nocturnal squirrel-sized silky anteater (*serafín/Cyclopes didactylus*) can all be found in trees on the forest edge.

Collared peccary
(*chancho de monte, saíno, javalina/Tayassu tajacu*)
Peccaries are related to pigs and live in a variety of habitats in the Americas, up to 2,000m. They are highly gregarious. and you are likely to see groups of

up to 100 of them in many of Central America's national parks, where they are protected from hunters. The slightly larger white-lipped peccary (*jabalí, chancho de monte/Tayassu pecari*) is also found throughout the region, but is very sensitive to environmental disturbance.

Peccaries secrete musk from a gland in the middle of their backs, so you often smell them before you see them. Adults can be aggressive and are capable of inflicting a serious wound with their sharp tusks, but young ones make delightful (if rather smelly) pets. We met one such charmer in Los Katios Park; like all members of the pig family, he loved to be scratched and would roll onto his back, waving his legs in ecstasy and inviting us to tickle his tummy.

Tapir
(danta/Tapirus bairdii)
These are large creatures, related to the horse and weighing up to 300kg. You will be very lucky to see one, as they generally inhabit dense forests, coming out at night to feed; however you may well see their large hoofprints and piles of dung along the trail. They are excellent swimmers and often take to the water to escape their main predator, the jaguar.

Cats
There are six species of cat in Central America: in descending order of size they are the jaguar (*el tigre/Felis onca*), which needs a territory of at least 20km^2 of hot wet forest and is thus suffering badly from deforestation; the puma/cougar (*Felis concolor*), the ocelot or manigordo (*Felis pardalis*), the margay or caucel (*Felis weidii*; the best tree-climber of this group), the tiger cat or tigrillo (*Felis tigrina oncilla*, only from Costa Rica southwards), and the jaguarundi (*Felis yaguarundi*), which looks more like a weasel with its short legs and long slender body. All are largely nocturnal and hard to see, especially as the bigger ones only need to hunt every week or so.

The jaguar (*el tigre*) is the largest of the New World cats. You will read and hear more rubbish about this magnificent and retiring creature than about any other. No description of adventures in the jungle is complete without a hair-raising account of the terrors and dangers suffered by the author on account of 'tigers'. However, while locals used to say, "*Cuidado! hay tigres!*" and shake their heads in disbelief on hearing that you were about to venture into *la selva* (the jungle), nowadays the forest is so disturbed and degraded that the remaining jaguars stay well out of the way.

So let's get a few facts straight about the jaguar, even though you won't see one unless you're incredibly lucky. The jaguar is immensely strong, killing large animals such as the tapir with ease. A good swimmer and fond of the water, it often pursues its prey into rivers. Being such a good hunter, it is self-sufficient in the jungle and very rarely makes an unprovoked attack on a human. There is no authenticated account of one becoming a habitual man-eater, although naturally one will attack if provoked or threatened, or if injured.

Marsupials
For a time the marsupials of the Americas were the only ones known to science (although in fact the Australian marsupials are far better examples of the type). They include opossums (*zariguela, tacuazine*), mouse-opossums (*marmosa*), murine opossums, which no longer have pouches, and the water opossum (*Chironectes sp.*), whose pouch is sealed by a sphincter muscle when the mother swims.

Deer
The most obvious species of deer is *Odoceilus virginianus*, the white-tailed deer (*venado cola blanco*) hunted by the million across North America; you might if lucky also see the red brocket deer (*cabro de monte* or *guizisil/Mazama americana*), a small rainforest deer with short prong antlers.

Bats
At least half of the mammals of Central America are bats — 101 of 186 species in Honduras, 103 of 200 in Costa Rica. Less than half of these are insectivorous, the others eating fruit, fish, animals, nectar, and even, in the case of three species, blood. One of these is the common vampire (see *Health and Safety)*, and the two others are similar but only feed on smaller animals and birds. *Thyroptera tricolor* is the disk-winged bat, which has adhesive pads to allow it to roost on the underside of banana and heliconia leaves; *Ectophylla alba*, a tiny white bat, goes one step further, cutting the ribs of a heliconia leaf so that it droops to make a tent.

Other vaguely familiar mammals include the Eastern grey fox (*gato de monte/ Urocyon cinereoargentus*), otters, rabbits, squirrels (including the flying squirrel *ardilla voladora/Glaucomys volans* and pygmy sqirrels *Microsciurus*). In addition there are plenty of skunks and small rodents such as mice and pocket gophers.

Reptiles and amphibians
You're bound to see plenty of **lizards** wherever it's dry and sunny. These include spiny lizards (sometimes misnamed *escorpión*), skinks and green anole lizards; in addition, above 1,500m you may well see salamanders. Some of them are pretty big, and of course the largest members of the family are the **iguanas**: contrary to what you might expect, these like to live in trees, particularly along rivers, so are suffering from habitat loss. They are also widely hunted for meat, and thus are now threatened with extinction. There are imaginative schemes to breed them commercially in Panamá, Costa Rica, Guatemala and Belize, as they yield three or four times as much meat per hectare as cattle, and the trees can be left standing. The *garrobo* (*Ctenosaura sp.*) is like an iguana but smaller and non-arboreal, and is said to be even tastier. A half-sized iguana, up to a metre long, may be a basilisk (*Basiliscus sp.*); these essentially Central American creatures have dinosaur-like sailfin crests and the smaller ones at least (nicknamed 'Jesus Christ lizards') can run

on water, for up to 400m and at up to 12km/h.

You'll see lots of **frogs**, some of which spend their entire lives in the forest canopy, breeding in pools of water in bromeliads. The most striking species are the bright red, yellow or blue poison-dart frogs; there are 135 species between Nicaragua and Brazil, of which 55 are actually poisonous while the rest merely mimic their coloration. It is the skin which excretes venom, so handling these frogs if you have a sore or cut on your hand is dangerous. Just three species of *Phyllobates* are used by Chocó and Kuna Indians to poison darts fired from blowpipes, simply by rubbing the tip on the frog's back. The glass frog (*ranita de vidrio/Centolenella sp.*) really is semi-transparent!

Watching **turtles** is, unfortunately, a very popular activity among 'ecotourists' in Costa Rica and other Central American countries; female marine turtles come ashore on beaches to lay their eggs, and may be harassed by tourists and egg-stealers to the point where some may return to the sea without laying. There are four main species of *tortuga*: the smallest is the olive ridley (*Lepidochelys olivacea*), found only on the Pacific coast, though very numerous there. The others are found on both coasts: the green turtle (*Chelonia mydas*) can dive to 1,400m, deep enough to escape sharks, and migrates up to 2,000km to nest on a very few beaches, including Tortuguero; the hawksbill (*Eretmochelys imbricata*) is more solitary, nesting on a wider range of sites, and the leatherback (*Dermochelys coriacea*) weighs up to a tonne and nests mainly in November and December. Only 50% of turtle hatchlings make it to the water, thanks to all the predators eagerly waiting; just 0.6% survive to mate, that is, only 0.3% of the survivors (the females) return to lay their eggs. Freshwater turtles are also common, but attract far less interest.

Snakes are dealt with under *Health and Safety*.

Birds

With over 933 species in Panamá alone, it's obviously impossible here to provide more than a peep at Central America's more colourful and interesting birds.

First, the river birds. Since river travel is leisurely and comfortable, there is ample opportunity for birdwatching and you will see far more species than during a walk in the jungle, when they're all out of sight in the treetops and your pack makes it difficult to look above you anyway. Most are migratory, but juveniles may be seen throughout the year. Any marshy area is full of **jacanas** (usually *Jacana spinosa*). Also known as lily-trotters, they're the ones with long toes and yellow wings visible only when they fly. **Anhingas** or snake-birds (*Anhinga anhinga*) are common down some rivers; we saw plenty around the Río Atrato in Colombia. Their long snake-like neck is often the only part visible above the water's surface, but you're more likely to spot them as they stand motionless drying their wings in the sun. **Herons** and **egrets** need no introduction and the various **kingfishers** are easily recognizable. A striking bird you'll see only by the Río Atrato (its northern limit) is the **northern screamer** or black-necked screamer (*Chauna chavaria*). These turkey-sized birds are in the same group as ducks and geese. Mainly black and grey with bright pink legs, they stand along the banks of the river, living up to their name with a piercing cry. The Caribbean coast is barely tidal, so without an inter-tidal feeding zone there are few shorebirds; the Pacific coast, however, is used by many migratory North American species.

Moving on to tropical forest, this is the habitat of a huge variety of birds, but you will need binoculars to spot them in the concealing foliage. **Parrots** (*loros amazona* spp.) can easily be recognized; you are much more likely to see them as they fly home in the evening than in the trees where they noisily prepare for the night. Parrots usually fly in pairs, although larger flocks are also common, and you can recognize them by their rapid wing-beats and their habit of shouting at each other as they fly. All Central American parrots are basically green with other colours on their heads and wings. Similar but smaller are the **parakeets** (*perico*). **Macaws** (*guacamaya, lapa*) are even noisier than parrots, and are unmistakeable with their brilliant colours and long tails.

Dry tropical forests are the home of the bossy and striking **magpie-jay** (*urraca azul/Calocitta formosei*). Like all jays, these birds do not approve of humans intruding into their territory. Quite the opposite are the **mot-mots** (*taragón*) which seem positively to enjoy having people around. The plumage of these beautiful birds is a soft green and chestnut, with brilliant turquoise patches. The blue crowned mot-mot is instantly recognizable by its distinctive tail which has a long bare shaft with a disc near the end, and which it often swings like a pendulum.

Toucans (*tucán*) favour humid tropical forests, whilst their smaller cousins the **toucanets** (*tucancillo* or *araçari*) prefer cloudforests. Toucanets have a finer bill than the true toucan, but are still distinctive, especially in silhouette. **Trogons** (*trogón* or *coa*) are widely distributed, although the most famous of the family, the **resplendent quetzal** (*quetzal real/Pharomachrus mocinno*), lives only in certain cloudforests. Most trogons have bright green plumage and red or yellow breasts, but only the male quetzal has a golden sheen to its green feathers and that magnificent tail.

Most of the other birds in the forests are more drab and hard to spot, but you'll hear them. The most obvious, in its breeding season, is the three-wattled bellbird (*pajaro campana/Procnias tricarunculata*), which sounds more like a hammer striking an anvil than a bell, but is still unmistakeable, as is its appearance, with three black wattles hanging from its beak. The chachalaca (*Ortalis vetula*) is a plain brown-grey bird, but its call is like a rattle or a firework going off. According to legend, the solitaires (*jilguero/Myadestes sp.*) were the last to be given their colours and all the brightest ones had gone, so they were given the best voice instead; they're characteristic of cloudforest, from 1,500m to 2,500m. The cloudforest is also home to several species of guan or *pava*, big ungainly wild turkeys that I'm always surprised to see on a branch rather than the ground, the great curassow (*pajuil/Crax rubra*), a brown bird with a striking black-and-white head and crest which is very sensitive to disturbance and is thus a good indicator of the state of the ecosystem, quail (*codorniz*) and the *tinamou* or *gallinita de monte*, a sort of partridge. There are also many species of woodpecker in the forests, including the flickers and sapsuckers.

Of the many large birds in Central America, the most obvious are the **vultures**. The black vulture (*zopilote cabeza negra/Coragyps atratus*) is relatively small, with a 1.5m wingspan, and is found wherever garbage is dumped. The turkey vulture (*zopilote cabeza roja* or *sonchiche/Cathartes aura*) has a distinctively ugly red head and an incredibly sensitive sense of smell, allowing it to smell carrion up to 20km away. The king vulture (*rey zope/Sarcoramphus papa*), black and white and also with a bare head, is more solitary, living in the tropical forest. A particularly beautiful bird is the **American swallow-tailed kite** (*gavilán tijerilla* or *milano golondrino/ Elanoides forficatus*), a very pure black and white and an immensely graceful flier. It can drink and catch insects on the wing, and also takes lizards, snakes and nestlings from trees; it's usually seen around the forest edge. The most powerful bird of prey in the world is the **harpy eagle** (*aguila harpia/Harpia harpyja*), which can take sloths and small monkeys and has a huge nest 1.5m across set in a ceiba tree 50m above the ground.

Whereas in Europe we have hordes of virtually indistinguishable **LBJs** (little brown jobs), in Central America there's a huge variety of yellow-bellied birds, including kiskadees, orioles, vireos, flycatchers and kingbirds. There are many species of **tanagers**, some resident and some visiting for the northern winter; the males are all brightly coloured while the females tend to be more drab. Tanagers tend to forage in mixed flocks, and for me at least this is the only way to distinguish the scarlet-rumped tanager (*sargento/Ramphocelus passerini*) from the scarlet-rumped **cacique** (*Cacicus uropygialis*) — both very striking black-and-red birds. The yellow-rumped cacique (*turpial/Cacicus cela*) is black with bright yellow on the wings and the base of the tail; it's often found in colonies of nests like footballs hanging from high branches. Similar but even more elaborate nests are built by its relatives, the **oropendolas** (*urapa*), plainer brown and chestnut birds with a distinctively bubbling call. The latter's nests are often parasitized in a cuckoo-like manner by the **giant cowbird** (*Scaphidura oryzivora*); the alien hatchlings may be fed by the oropendolas, and repay the favour by picking botfly eggs and larvae off their young.

One bird that you will see everywhere, in town and country, is the **great-tailed grackle** (*zanate/Quiscalis mexicanus*), somewhat like a blackbird but with a long broad tail; males may be a metallic blue colour, while females are black. The **groove-billed ani** (*talingo* or *tajuil/Crotophaga sulcirostris*) is similar, jet black but wih a large puffin-like beak. The clay-coloured **robin** (*yiquirro/Turdus grayi*) is also very common throughout the lowlands and middle elevations. Another bird that you won't fail to notice is the **cattle egret** (*garza del ganado* or *garcilla garrapatera/Bubulcus ibis*), a white bird always found with cattle, whose ticks it eats: amazingly, this bird has been in the Americas for only about a century, but, as elsewhere (its distribution is more or less worldwide) it has prospered.

ANTS

Though disliked by most travellers, the various species of ant that you'll come across are fascinating and deserve detailed description. The most conspicuous are the leaf-cutter or parasol ants (*Atta sp*). These industrious creatures can be seen in almost any forest in tropical America (up to 2,000m) carrying their neatly shaped pieces of leaf back to the nest. And what do they do with the leaves once they reach the nest? They take them to a carefully cultivated fungus garden, fertilised with faecal droplets. The ants eat the fungus (not the leaves) and the *Basidiomycetes* fungus can only exist in the moist dark atmosphere of the ants' garden. It's a perfect example of a symbiotic relationship. The tree or shrub that the ants are cutting may be over 100m from the entrance to the nest, and this may be just as far from the actual nest. About half their journey is therefore underground so that the leaves do not become too dry in the sun. You will observe that these foraging trails are quite wide and cleared of all debris. The ants know exactly where they're going, because they lay down an odour trail. If you look closely, you'll see the ants constantly touching the ground with their antennae, smelling their way home. This chemical probably also kills off the vegetation on the trail, helping to create that well-swept look.

Other good examples of symbiotic relationships are those between the *Azteca* ant and the cecropia tree and the *Pseudomyrmex* ant and bullhorn or ant-acacias (*cornizuelo*); in both cases the ants protect the tree from predators and prune back nearby seedlings and are rewarded with nectar and a sheltered home.

Talk of beautiful relationships ends here. The army ant (*hormiga arriera*) has no redeeming features (other than its remarkable success as a species) and is the source of all those jungle horror stories. And they're true. Army ants (above all *Eciton burchelli*) really do devour everything they come across, including birds, lizards and small mammals, and deliver very nasty bites to anything bigger that gets in their way.

Army ants have no permanent nests but are constantly on the move. It may take an hour or more for the column (wih 50,000 to a million members) to pass a given spot. First go the foraging soldier ants with their enormous jaws, then the rank and file, the workers, whose job it is to carry the queen and the larvae, while the column is flanked by blind soldier ants who march with their great jaws uplifted and open, ready to deal with any attacker. Each night the ants make a temporary bivouac, with the queen and larvae safe inside a living nest of workers and soldiers. Finally a temporary nest is made in a hollow tree, where the queen lays up to 50,000 eggs. When they hatch, the march begins again; with swollen numbers and voracious appetites, the army spells death to any small creature in its path.

They are accompanied by antbirds, mixed flocks of externally very similar small drab birds — contrary to initial assumptions, these are not eating the ants but other insects flushed from cover by them; they offer a good lesson in ecology, as each has a very precise niche, seeking a specific food at a specific height above the ground.

I say there's no redeeming feature? There is one: the Indians once used soldier ants to suture wounds, squeezing an ant above the cut so that the powerful jaws closed, holding the edges together. Then they simply pinched off the body. Maybe it would still work in an emergency!

Insects

Invertebrates account for more than 90% of known species, and doubtless an even higher proportion of unknown ones, as they're small, hard to distinguish from each other, and usually cunningly disguised or hidden. Most national parks and so on don't even try to quantify them. One tree in Panamá (presumably on Barra Colorado Island) was home to 950 species of beetle alone. The most interesting insects are, alas, detailed in our health section.

Termite (*Nasutitermes sp.*) nests are very obvious in trees in lowland forest, dark brown or black spheres of *carton* or chewed wood. **Pasalid beetles** can be up to 80mm long, and **rhinoceros beetles** (*cornizuelo/Megasoma elephas*) can be as big with their huge horn, used for fighting for food or a mate. The most conspicuous butterflies are the huge and stunning beautiful **morphos**, usually an iridescent blue, although there are also white types.

Spider monkey

Chapter Two

History, Economy and Religion

History

Humans first crossed into North America over the Bering Strait about 60,000 years ago, and headed south, crossing the Central American isthmus around 15,000 years ago and reaching Tierra del Fuego approximately 4,000 years later. Some stopped along the way, living as small nomadic bands until some time between 7,000 and 2,000 BC, when they learnt to farm corn (*Zea mays*) and beans (*Phaseolus vulgaris*), as well as squashes and root crops. This was the key to the development of the settled cultures of Mesoamerica (the region from north-central Mexico to the Nicoya peninsula of Costa Rica), above all the Maya; further south more primitive cultures developed, mostly dependent on yuca (*manihot*) and other tubers.

The Atlantic coast, now seen as impenetrable rainforest, was largely inhabited and cultivated in preHispanic times; with the Spanish conquest (from 1492 to the 1530s) the indigenous population was reduced by as much as 90%, due above all to introduced illnesses, and much territory was abandoned to the jungle, as the Spaniards preferred to settle in the highlands where the weather was cooler and there was the prospect of finding gold. Rape and abduction led in remarkably short order to the growth of a *mestizo* or mixed-race population, perhaps the Spaniards' main achievement in the region. The chief exceptions were Costa Rica, where the indigenous population all but vanished, and Guatemala, where it was large and homogenous enough to resist intermarriage.

Some chocolate and indigo were exported under Spanish rule, but by and large there was little economic development in the colonial period. Independence came first in 1821, as a Central American confederation, and then from 1839 as the present separate states (though not with exactly the current frontiers). Coffee had been introduced in the 18th century, but exports only began in the 1830s; in 1843 a British ship returning home empty managed to procure a load on credit and soon returned to pay and to buy much more. The Central American economies were transformed by a boom which lasted until a crash in 1914; by now bananas were well established as an alternative, but in this case the profits were largely extracted by US companies.

In 1823, just two years after Central American independence, the Monroe Doctrine claimed the Americas as the USA's 'sphere of influence'; already in 1816 the USA had taken Florida, in 1824/25 Texas was taken, and in 1845 the phrase 'Manifest Destiny' was coined in the *Democratic Review*. In 1859 Britain ceded the Moskito Coast and Bay Islands to Honduras, signalling an effective withdrawal from the Central American mainland (although Belize remained quasi-British). It was the Spanish-American War of 1898 that made the Panamá Canal a strategic necessity for the USA and tied it more closely to the region's economies. In 1906 US forces intervened in Cuba for the first time, in 1912 in Nicaragua, in 1914 in Mexico and the Dominican Republic, and in 1915 in Haiti — this was the 'Roosevelt Corollary' to the Monroe Doctrine: if the European powers couldn't intervene in the area, then the USA must. Woodrow Wilson's doctrine was that the USA had a moral duty to teach the Latin Americans 'to elect good men'; but under FDR's 'good neighbour' policy the US Marines were withdrawn from Cuba and Nicaragua and the dictators promptly took over.

Of course, with its close economic ties, the USA remained deeply involved in the region's politics; in 1954 it removed the Guatemalan government, in 1961 it tried to do the same in Cuba, and of course the Reagan government spent a great deal of time, money and energy trying to overthrow the Sandinista regime in Nicaragua by armed force before changing tack and forcing it out through elections. Bananas and coffee continue to be important, but in the 1960s and early 1970s the 'burger boom' in the USA caused the number of beef cattle in Central America to double, from one million to two, and pasture land to increase in area by 62% between 1963 and 1973. This grass-fed beef was, in US eyes, fit only for burgers and pet-food, but even so this set off a process of deforestation which is far from ending, as rapidly growing populations throughout the region demand more and more land.

Integration

In 1960 there was a serious attempt at regional integration, with the creation of the Central American Common Market, which fell apart after the 1969 Soccer War between Honduras and El Salvador. Since 1986 the process has again gathered way, with annual summits producing a Central American Court of Justice, Commission for Environment and Development, and so on; the six countries covered in this book and Belize are all members of the *Sistema de la Integración Centroamericana*, but the core states are Guatemala, El Salvador, Honduras and Nicaragua, known as the CA4. You'll notice the CA4 *tarjeto de control migratorio* whenever you enter one of these countries.

Things like car number plates are being standardised (although these will probably remain optional in Costa Rica), electrical and fibre optic links are planned, and products are increasingly labelled *Producto de Centroamerica*. Many companies can already be seen throughout the region — *Pollo Campero, Mas x Menos, Tropigas, Credomatic*, as well as multinationals such as Shell and Texaco. Conveniently, the states already all have blue and white striped flags. The same sorts of squabbles can be seen as in the European Union: in 1994 the problem was a *Tratado de Integration Social*. However all the Central American states are going through the same process of economic restructuring, with parallel debates about, for instance, privatising telecoms in each one. El

Salvador is the furthest ahead in this process, and is willing to go it alone and enter NAFTA, the North American Free Trade Area, without the others. Likewise in South America, Mercosur (the Southern Cone Market) came into effect in January 1995, but Chile was more interested in NAFTA.

Of more interest to visitors is the increasing cooperation between the region's airlines (TACA, Aviateca, COPA, NICA and Lacsa — the Honduran SAHSA has gone bankrupt) whose Mayan Air Pass is supposedly aimed mainly at ecotourists.

Economy

The region's economies are mostly doing well, with exports rising fast in most countries. In Costa Rica foreign exchange receipts (from exports and tourism) in the first quarter of 1995 were 29% above the same period of 1994 to US$910m, with tourism up 18%. Guatemala's exports were up 57.7% in the first five months of 1995 to US$1.05bn, and El Salvador's exports were up 51% in the first three months of 1995 to US$427m. However, only Costa Rica and El Salvador are seeing export-driven growth in the economy as a whole; in the other countries the population is growing far faster than new jobs can be created. The Nicaraguan economy is growing by just 3% a year, while exports are rising by almost 6%, but even this growth is largely a matter of catching up after years of war. Honduras is in poor condition, with GDP shrinking by 1.4% in 1994 and 25.6% annual inflation, but by 1996 it should have 4% growth and 6.5% inflation; likewise Costa Rica has just 1.5% growth and 20% inflation in 1995. At the opposite extreme Panamá has just 1.3% inflation in 1995. Across the region 70% of the population still live in poverty.

An important trend in the region is a **decrease in militarism**: Costa Rica is well known for having abolished its army in 1949, supposedly (there's a pretty competent para-military force). In 1993 Panamá copied this idea (attributed to H G Wells), abolishing its Defence Forces, and President Aristide of Haiti is keen to do the same. In 1995 Honduras abolished conscription, and even in El Salvador and Guatemala the army is playing a less dominant role in political life. But in 1994 military spending in Central America added up to US$400m, 3.4% more than in 1992, even though armies are smaller. Guatemala, El Salvador, Honduras and Nicaragua accounted for US$358m of this. Salvadoran defence spending rose from US$100m in 1992 to US$142m in 1994, although manpower fell from 60,000 to 34,000. Guatemala's military budget rose from US$109m in 1992 to US$133.3m in 1994, although manpower has fallen to 40,000. This presumably reflects resettlement costs and a move to a more technology-based military.

Religion

The religion of the area is in general Roman Catholicism, but it's worth noting that the indigenous population of Guatemala in particular has grafted its own animistic and shamanistic beliefs onto Catholicism, so that saints have fused with Mayan figures. The best known is Maximon, known as San Simón, or Judas Iscariot, the evil saint who drinks, smokes and grants prayers for revenge.

Catholicism is also being undermined by evangelical faiths from North America, which have in theory converted up to 20% of the population of some countries. Whereas Catholicism was able to incorporate existing social structures to a certain extent, evangelicism tends to disrupt them, partly promoting a free-for-all approach that undermines traditional social and environmental controls.

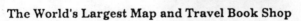

Chapter Three

Preparations

GETTING THERE

Travelling to Central America is inexpensive for North Americans, while Europeans flying from London via Miami benefit from low transatlantic fares. This may change, but the chances are that there'll always be a reasonably cheap flight to one of the American gateway cities. Indeed, in 1995 Monarch Airlines have begun operating charter flights from the UK to San José.

At present the most economical route for Europeans is to fly from London to Miami, and from there to Cancún or Mérida in Mexico's Yucatán or to Belize. It's always worth checking KLM's fares, via either Mexico City or Curaçao; Iberia and Aeroflot are also affordable. If you want to see Mexico, fly to Houston, San Diego or Los Angeles, cross the border, and continue by bus, or by Mexicana Airlines' 'Moonlight Express' from LA to Mexico City. Shop around: wherever you go, there's bound to be a cheap flight to one of the US gateway cities for Mexico. If you're hopping around the region, the five Central American airlines now have a joint airpass, and there's the Latin Pass, involving 14 airlines including them and USAir, Hertz, Avis, Sheraton and Intercontinental.

From the US-Mexican border, there are luxury and second-class buses to Mexico City. It is possible to go straight through from points in the US into Mexico, but it is cheaper to buy a ticket only as far as the border, then get off and buy another ticket south of the border. That way you'll be travelling at Mexican prices, not US ones. You'll need to change again in Mexico City to reach the southern borders, where you'll have to change once more.

In Britain, agencies specializing in travel to Central America include:

Journey Latin America, 16 Devonshire Rd, Chiswick, London W4 2HD (tel: 0181 747 3108), and in Manchester.

South American Experience, 47 Causton St, Pimlico, London SW1P 4AT (tel: 0171 976 5511).

Steamond, 23 Eccleston St, London SW1W 9LX (0171-730 8646)/for tours 278 Battersea Park Rd, London SW11 3BS (tel: 0171 738 0285).

Passage to South America, 41 North End Rd, West Kensington, London W14 8SZ (tel: 0171 602 9889).

Trailfinders, 48 Earl's Court Rd, London W8 6FT (tel: 0171 938 3232/938 3939/ 938 3366.

STA has offices nationwide (London tel: 0171 937 9921).

In North America:

STA, 5900 Wilshire Boulevard, Los Angeles, CA 90036 (tel: 800 777 0112, fax: 213 937 2739).
CIEE/Council Travel Services, 205 East 42nd St, New York, NY 10017 (tel: 212 661 1414, fax: 212 972 3231).
TravelCUTS, 171 College St, Toronto M5T 1P7 (tel: 416 977 3703, fax: 416 977 4796).

From continental Europe a number of companies offer seats on charters to Mexico and Guatemala:

Nouvelles Frontières, across France (Paris tel: 41 41 58 58).
Uniclam-Voyages, 63 rue Monsieur-le-Prince, 75006 Paris (tel: 43 29 12 36).
Hajo Siewer Jet Tours, Martinstrasse 39, 57462 Olpe, Germany (tel: 02761 924 120).
Globetrotter Travel Service, Rennweg 35, Zurich (tel: 211 7780).

The German airline LTU International flies from München and Düsseldorf to San José once a week, with connections from Miami to Guatemala, San Salvador, San Pedro Sula, Tegucigalpa and Managua.

From North America there are frequent scheduled services to all the Central American capitals and other centres, and an increasing number of charters, especially to Costa Rica but also to Honduras and Panamá. This is especially the case from Canada, with companies like Regent, Fiesta and FunSun offering flight-only deals with Air Transat, Canada 3000, Sunquest SkyService and Royal Air (from C$500 plus tax), as well as packages.

Group tours
Few companies offer organized hiking trips, but there's any number of ecotourism packages, above all to Costa Rica, that chiefly involve guided tours and day-walks in national parks. It's worth checking out:

Worldwide Journeys & Expeditions (8 Comeragh Rd, London W14 9HP; tel: 0171 381 8638)
Explore Worldwide (1 Frederick St, Aldershot GU11 1LQ; tel: 01252 319 448, fax: 343 170)
Ramblers Holidays (PO Box 43, Welwyn Garden City, Herts AL8 6PQ; tel: 01707 331 133, fax: 333 276)
Forest Trails (Oakdene, High St, Heathfield, E Sussex N21 0UP; tel: 01435 864 078)
The Imaginative Traveller (14 Barley Mow Passage, Chiswick, London W4 4PH; tel: 0181 742 8612, fax: 742 3045)
GAP (264 Dupont St, Toronto M5R 1V7, Canada; (tel: 416 922 8899, fax: 922 0822)
Himalayan Travel (112 Prospect St, Stamford, CT 06901, USA; tel: 800 225 2380, fax: 203 359 3669)
Reef & Rainforest Tours (3 Moorashes, Totnes, Devon TQ9 5TN, UK; tel: 01803 866965, fax: 865916)
Tread Lightly (1 Titus Rd, Washington Depot CT 06794, USA (tel: 800 643 0060/ 203 868 1710, fax: 860 868 1718).

Wilderness Travel (801 Allston Way, Berkeley, California 94710, USA; tel: 800-368 2794, 510-548 0420, fax: 510-548 0347) offer fairly standard tours of Costa Rica (with Costa Rica Expeditions) and Guatemala, but they also offer the chance to spend 21 days working on research projects — for US$2,000!

For Guatemala (usually combined with neighbouring countries), try:

Journey Latin America, Explore Worldwide, The Imaginative Traveller, GAP, Himalayan Travel (as above), and for classy cultural tours **ACE Study Tours** (Babraham, Cambridge CB2 4AP; tel: 01223 835 055, fax: 837 394). Additionally, **Exodus** (9 Weir Rd, London SW12 0LT; tel: 0181 675 5550, fax: 673 0779) operate an eight-week overland trip from Mexico City to Panamá City (£1,190-1,390).

For hiking, you're pretty much limited to:

Above the Clouds (PO Box 398, Worcester, MA 01602-0398, USA; tel: 800 233 4499, fax: 508 797 4779), who offer an 11-day trip (with five days hiking in Chirripó) from US$1,525, or **Journeys International** (4011 Jackson Rd, Ann Arbor, MI 48103, USA; tel: 800 255 8735, fax: 313 665 2945), who offer a 15-day trans-Darién hike (with Eco-Tours as their ground operator) from US$2,590 — they give a share of profits to an affiliated charity, the Earth Preservation Fund. Both of these companies also do regular tours of Costa Rica with day hikes from comfy lodges.

Journeys International also offer similar trips to Honduras, and a week in Mosquitia. Adventures Unlimited of Toronto, Canada (tel: 800 567 6286) offer 14 different itineraries for walking holidays in Costa Rica. British readers will have noticed that these are all North American companies, but as the rule is to offer land-only prices it's easy enough to make your own way out and join up with the group there. If you have time, it's *far* cheaper to go to San José and see what local ground operators are offering there.

From Britain the only hiking tours to Central America are:

High Places (Globe Works, Penistone Rd, Sheffield S6 3AE; tel: 01142 757 500), who go to Costa Rica, and
Encounter Overland (267 Old Brompton Rd, London SW5 9JA; tel: 0171 370 6845, fax: 244 9737), who offer a Darién Gap trip, 16 days Panamá City to Cartagena for £780-795.

The tour operators are just testing out Honduras with research trips in 1994 and 1995; contact Journeys International, The Imaginative Traveller, or Himalayan Travel. GAP are trying out Honduras, the Darién Gap, and mountain-biking in Costa Rica. The same applies to package holidays, with, for instance, Canadian companies Fiesta and FunSun (well established in Costa Rica) starting up in Panamá and Honduras (7 nights from C$699), and Regent/Canadian Holidays in Nicaragua (at Montelimar, on the Pacific). Most of these packages include an 'Eco-Safari' option, which is more of a bus trip.

Specialist trips for wildlife and bird-watching are easily found in specialist magazines; a few operators are:

Footprint Adventures (5 Malham Drive, Lincoln LN6 0XD; tel: 01522 690 852, fax: 501 392), **Voyagers International** (Box 915, Ithaca, NY 14851, USA; tel: 800 633 0299), **Neotropic Bird Tours** (38 Brookside Ave, Livingston, NJ 07039, USA; tel: 800 662 4852), **Quest Nature Tours** (36 Finch Ave West, Toronto, Ontario M2N 2G9, Canada; tel: 800 387 1483, fax: 416 221 5730) and **Royal Adventures** (tel: 800 453 4754). Botanical trips to Costa Rica are run by **David Sayers Travel** (tel: 0181 995 3642), with Costa Rica Expeditions.

Budget and finance

How much your trip will cost is anyone's guess, but let us reassure you that you can live and travel quite comfortably on US$10 a day, particularly if you're spending time in the wild. Day to day expenses will fluctuate wildly depending on the country you're in (they get more expensive as you head south) and how much time you're spending in towns and cities.

One thing we've learned is that hitting a capital city after backpacking for a couple of weeks can be a pretty heady experience and can blow apart a perfectly good budget. Everything looks so delicious, so comfortable, so splendid, after weeks of rice and beans, thatched shelters and school buses; and after all, backpacking costs next to nothing. So we over-indulge ourselves and money justs spins through our hands. We've made it a rule never to cash more than US$50 on such occasions. When that's gone we usually get a grip on ourselves.

The US dollar is the only currency you need to carry in this part of the world, although you'll find a few branches of Lloyds and other European banks which may change sterling and other currencies. Take your dollars partly in travellers cheques and partly as cash (some in small denominations). If you carry American Express or Thomas Cook travellers cheques you can change them in their respective offices without commission; otherwise you'll pay about 2% (either declared as a commission or just massaged from the exchange rate), as well as the 1-1.5% paid when you bought the cheques. Thomas Cook offices in Britain give a notoriously bad rate.

There are plenty of street changers; take great care using these guys in the cities, but at the borders they're safe enough, though you should have an idea of the exchange rate before getting there.

Cash machines (ATMs) are appearing in most major cities, allowing you to withdraw cash either from your bank account or on your credit card. Both the issuing bank and VISA take a fee of 1-2%. The real advantages are in being able to get cash at any time, without queues and with English instructions, and in small quantities, just to last you to the border.

If you want to have money sent out to you, plan this in advance and talk to your bank. They will have a list of Central American banks with which they have links, and you can select one or two before you go. Then all you have to do is cable your bank and wait for the cash. It will take a few days, and actually collecting the cash is invariably a hassle, but it works. Citibank (US) and Lloyds (British) have quite a few branches in the region, and Western Union can also cable money to branches there.

WHAT TO TAKE

As Saint-Exupéry said, 'He who would travel happily must travel light'; you should take the standard 20kg airline allowance as your absolute maximim, bearing in mind that you gain a kilogram when you put a litre of water into your bottle. Start by disposing of as much packaging as you can before departure; I find that a 60ml plastic bottle carries enough shower gel for a month or two, and if you want soap as well this can be carried in a film canister.

Specifically for hiking, you should remember the six essentials of map, compass, matches (and maybe a firelighter) in a waterproof box, first-aid kit, extra food and extra clothing. A knife, spoon and plastic mug or bowl are also pretty important. Wood fires are becoming environmentally unacceptable nowadays; if you want to cook, take a stove. Kerosene is usually available, and it's getting easier to find Camping Gaz. Personally I don't bother for three to five day trips in warm climes. There's no need to spend a fortune buying special lightweight saucepans for backpacking, as perfectly suitable aluminium ones are sold throughout Central America.

With regard to clothing, you will usually be dressing for hot humid conditions, so won't need heavy clothes unless you plan to go high. Even so, the key principle is that of layering; tee-shirts are light and comfortable but expose you to sunburn, so you should take a bandana and some long-sleeved shirts to protect you from the sun and insects. You should also take an insulation layer (a light pullover or fleece jacket) and a shell layer (waterproof jacket and trousers). In the rainy season an umbrella can also be useful. A hat is essential, a cotton one being more practical than a straw one. It's very refreshing to fill the hat with water, then plonk it on your head!

Shirts and trousers should be mostly cotton; jeans are not suitable as they're heavy, hot, hard to wash, and take ages to dry. (However, pure cotton doesn't dry well and can rot surprisingly quickly in tropical climates.) Nor is army-surplus wear appropriate in Central America, with its enduring civil conflicts; khaki or camouflage patterns are out. You're safest in brightly coloured clothes, remembering that mosquitoes are attracted to dark clothing. It's always been inadvisable to dress outlandishly in Latin America: officials generally treat travellers who look dirty and penniless with suspicion and hostility, and if you look (to them) like a drug user you may have drugs planted on you. So short hair and trimmed beards for men, and reasonably conventional clothing for women are sensible.

The Central American countries are Roman Catholic and it is offensive to the local people to wear shorts in most areas, or for women to be conspicuously bra-less. In addition, the latter invites attention from all those macho men. If you prefer to go without a bra because it's cooler, you'll find that a man's shirt with breast (sic!) pockets handily hides your feminity. Bear in mind the problems of getting to your money-belt if you're wearing a dress.

Few of these hikes require heavy boots, although good ankle support and shock absorption are essential. If hiking on volcanoes, 'Vibram' soles or the like are the only ones that won't be cut up by the lava. Canvas jungle boots are ideal for jungle hiking, as they drain and dry out quickly; you may need to look for these in army surplus stores rather than hiking shops. Basketball boots are recommended for fording rivers, and these or trainers are handy to change into at the end of the day. Rubber thongs, flip-flops or — better — sports sandals are also good to have, but be careful and never go barefoot. Take a spare pair of bootlaces, and use them as a laundry line. You'll also need to waterproof your boots from time to time.

To carry all this you need a backpack or rucksack — above all make sure it has a padded hipbelt, and preferably a so-called internal frame (meaning only that it's better hidden away than the old-fashioned external frame!). This is less likely to be caught on jungle creepers, and is handier for travelling on trucks and buses. At airports wrap the hipbelt backwards around the pack, do it up in reverse and tuck away or tie up any strap ends, both to stop them getting caught in conveyor belts and to delay anyone wanting to sneak a look inside; a small padlock is also useful, although more as a deterrent than as a real barrier. No rucksack is ever totally waterproof, so you should keep clothes and the like in plastic bags. Ideally you should carry 50% of your load on the hips — any more and you slip out of your shoulder straps, even with a chest strap. Nowadays there are also likely to be straps to adjust the balance of the load for uphill or downhill work, away from the body going uphill, and closer to the body downhill.

You're also likely to need a tent, and don't wait till you get there to buy one. It'll need to be bugproof and waterproof, and as light as possible — no more than 2.5kg for a two-person tent. Ventilation is important; if your tent is inadequate in this respect, you might wish to cut windows in the front and rear and face them with mosquito netting. In fact it's easy enough to make a basic tropical tent entirely out of mosquito netting, using a tarpaulin as a fly.

Many people prefer a hammock to a tent. They are very comfortable, and often it's easier to find two trees suitably spaced, or hammock hooks in a jungle hut, than to clear an area for your tent. However, remember that two hammocks can weigh more than a light two-man tent, and you must be able to rig up netting so that no insects can get inside. Excellent cotton hammocks can be bought in El Salvador, while some army-surplus stores stock jungle hammocks which are a combination of hammock, mosquito netting and a waterproof roof. We haven't put them to the test but they seem ideal.

While on the subject, did you know that there's a right way and a wrong way to lie in a hammock? If you lie diagonally across it, your body and legs are more or less horizontal, not sagged into a 'U' position which is uncomfortable for a whole night. If you're particularly tall or heavy you'll probably resort to sleeping on the ground in any case after a night or two in a hammock.

You won't need a particularly warm sleeping bag, and the tropics are too damp and humid for down to be ideal as a filler. A very light artificial filler is preferable (as light as possible), as a 'bivi-sac' cover will add a lot of warmth at high altitudes and can be left behind for hiking in warmer areas.

Some sort of insulation and protection from the cold hard ground is essential; closed-cell 'ensolite' foam mats are the most efficient, providing good insulation and tolerable comfort even when less than a centimetre thick. The most comfortable mat of all, though, is the combination of air-mattress and foam-pad made by Thermarest, available in three-quarters or full length.

Rather than a conventional flashlight, use a headtorch, which frees your hands and is ideal for cave exploration and for putting up your tent after dark. Remember a spare bulb; alternatives are a candle-holder or a Camping Gaz-fuelled lantern.

See *Health and Safety* for the contents of the definitive first-aid kit. Other useful items include a sewing kit (with heavy thread and needles for tent repairs), safety pins, pencils or ball-point pens, a notebook and paper for writing home, travel alarm clock, penknife (preferably Swiss Army type), plastic bags (preferably the 'zip-loc' type), a universal bath plug (or punctured squash-ball), clothes-pegs, scrubbing brush, dental floss (excellent for running repairs, as well as teeth), toilet paper, and a Spanish dictionary or phrasebook.

It's very useful to pack an extra bag (a lightweight nylon one with a lockable zip is ideal) to leave things in a hotel while you're backpacking; in any case you invariably end up coming home with more luggage than you started with.

A camera should be as robust as possible (I have destroyed several in the past by travelling on rough roads; remember not to sit behind the rear axle of a bus). Simple work-horses are the best in tropical climates, above all mechanical Nikons and Leicas, if you can afford them. It may be worth taping over flash and motordrive sockets, when not in use. It's also worth remembering that sun shining directly into the lens can warp delicate camera innards — keep that cap on... Nature-lovers will probably want a macro lens for close-ups of all those wonderful flowers and insects, and also a telephoto lens for shots of birds and animals (the latter can replace binoculars or a telescope), but otherwise a 35mm compact camera is most practical; even those incorporating a small zoom lens are now pretty affordable. You will need a spare battery for a long trip, and plenty of film; it's very expensive in Central America and there is a limited range except in Panamá, which is also the only country where you can safely risk having film developed (even black and white!). Slide film is hard to find, as is film of ASA 400 and faster, which you'll need in the jungle, as there's little light there. Humidity may also be a problem in the jungle, so keep your camera in a plastic bag, together with a small sachet of silica gel.

Insurance

Baggage insurance is well worth having. With all the care in the world you can lose something, and it does ease the grief somewhat if it's insured. Read the small print carefully. If something is stolen you must report the theft to the police and get a copy of their report. Often a time-consuming and expensive process, since some police won't help without a bribe.

Documents

Check current visa requirements in guidebooks, with embassies or with the Foreign Office, State Department or your equivalent. Be sure to work out when planning your trip which countries require you to have a visa (as opposed to a tourist card, obtained at the border), and get them either before leaving or in the first capital city you visit. Consulates tend to be situated in the suburbs and to keep strange hours (often something like 10.00-12.00 a couple of days a week). If you are planning to pass through a country twice (ie returning the way you came) ask for a multiple-entry visa, which should cost less than two single-entry visas. This may require a passport photo, so carry some of these with you.

It's a good idea to keep a strong rubber band around your passport to hold all those papers that countries require you to keep during your stay. Another idea you might try is to stick a coloured dot of paper (such as you can buy in stationery shops), or even a gold star, onto the front of your passport. That way you'll recognize it the many times it has to be taken from you and given back by calling out an unintelligible version of your name. Your passport, air ticket, most of your travellers cheques and so on should then be kept in a money belt.

Many countries have requirements for an onward ticket or a minimum level of funds; I've never been asked a single question at any Central American border, but if you are of student age or have a nose-ring or half your head shaved, you can expect some tough questions and maybe higher fees at borders (the norm is about US$2 to enter or exit). Don't change all your money until you've completed the emigration procedure; there are always money-changers around (those at the borders are much safer than those in cities, although you should still be aware of possible problems), and you can always spend what's left on a few oranges or a drink. Likewise change some money before immigration, or else you'll have to pay in dollars at a bad rate. In a way it's more straightforward than in Europe, where you rarely stop at borders, can never find a money-changer, and have to contend with varying exchange and commission rates when you do.

Border officials often ask the name of the hotel you'll be staying at in the capital. Simply say, "Hotel Centro America" with confidence. There's always at least one.

Chapter Four

Health and Safety

GENERAL HEALTH

It's advisable to be vaccinated against typhoid, tetanus, TB, poliomyelitis and yellow fever before travelling. It is essential to start a course of prophylactic pills against malaria. For up-to-date details on the most effective, phone the Malaria Reference Laboratory in the UK (tel: 0891 600 350) and in America the Center for Disease Control in Atlanta, tel: (404) 332 4559. (See *Mosquitoes*, further on in the chapter for more information.) It's also wise to have your teeth checked before leaving. Your best protection is to be fit and well before you set out on a hiking trip. Carry your prescription if you wear glasses and, finally, be sure to take out medical insurance. The gamma globulin injection against hepatitis A has now been superseded by a vaccine (known in Britain and Canada as Havrix) which offers full protection and is well worth having. Cholera vaccination is largely ineffective, but given that the major outbreak of 1990-91, which started in Peru, has now spread as far as Mexico you may wish to have some protection.

Virtually any medicine can be bought over the counter in Central America, but you would be best advised to bring all your normal medication (and contraceptives) and a first-aid kit from home: anything bought in a *farmacia* may be well past its expiry date or may not have been refrigerated properly.

If you become ill, head for a hospital or clinic, or failing that, see a private doctor. Although the experience may be somewhat alarming, remember that these local doctors have a more intimate acquaintance with tropical diseases than does your GP back home. There is a reasonable supply of English-speaking doctors, and in the capital cities your embassy can recommend a good doctor.

It's also worth knowing about the *análisis clínico* laboratories found all over Central America. If you are pretty sure of your diagnosis but want it confirmed you can take a sample of urine or faeces to the lab and they'll give you the results of the analysis a few hours later: useful for women who fear they may be pregnant!

There are some excellent books on the market which supplement the necessarily skimpy health information we have space for. Some are listed at Appendix Two.

COMMON MEDICAL PROBLEMS

Many of the ailments that beset travellers are caused by poor toilet practice, eating contaminated food and drinking unclean water, so you can do much to avoid illness by taking a few simple precautions: wash your hands after using the toilet (to remove other people's germs, not your own), don't eat raw vegetables, salads or fruit you haven't peeled yourself; boil water or purify it with chlorine (Sterotabs, Puritabs or Halazone) or better still with iodine (which kills amoebae). Compact water purifiers are now available which filter out and kill amoebae, viruses and bacteria. Tea and coffee are usually made with hot rather than boiling water, and ice is also unsafe. But don't spoil your trip by never eating in wayside restaurants or from street stalls. Just be cautious at first, while your system adjusts, and don't eat food that's been sitting around cooling. If it's any consolation, in two decades of travel in Latin America Hilary has had serious stomach upsets only after eating in expensive restaurants!

Diarrhoea

Montezuma's Revenge is caused by the bacterium *Escherischia coli* which everyone has naturally in his or her intestines. The trouble is that each geographical area has its own strain of *E. coli*, and alien strains may cause inflammation of the intestine, resulting in diarrhoea. On a long trip you'll acquire a nice collection of the local *E. coli* in your gut and will be troubled no more. The first few weeks can be tough, though. Everyone has a favourite remedy but most people agree that it's best to let nature take its course rather than bunging yourself up with strong medication. Drink lots of liquid but don't eat any greasy or fatty food for 24 hours, then for a few days stick to a bland diet with plenty of mashed potatoes or rice, papaya and bananas. Avoid alcohol, fatty and spicy foods and milk products and take plenty of fluids, and you should be OK. Replace the lost salts and minerals by sipping a solution of half a teaspoon of salt and four teaspoons of sugar or honey in a litre of water; if possible add baking soda (½ teaspoon) and potassium chloride (¼ teaspoon) as well, or a little lemon or orange juice. You can buy or make up some of this rehydration or 'electrolyte replacement' formula before leaving home.

There will be times when you'll want to block the symptoms of diarrhoea: before setting off on a long bus journey, for instance, or when you're camping in heavy rain. Probably the best 'chemical cork' is loperamide (Diocalm or Imodium), but Paracetamol/Tylenol is an effective codeine-based bum-blocker and pain-killer. The antibiotic ciprofloxacin has been successful in halting attacks of travellers' diarrhoea with one 500mg pill, but antibiotics should be used with caution; apart from possible side effects, overuse will soon lead to a resistant strain of the bug.

Dysentery

If you have diarrhoea with a fever, bad gut cramps and blood in your stool you may have bacterial (bacillary) dysentery. Amoebic dysentery is similar but starts more gradually, and the diarrhoea is persistent but not dramatic. Get your stool analysed and take the result to a doctor, who will probably prescribe a week's course of Flagyl (metronidazole or tinidazole) for amoebae, or an antibiotic such as ciprofloxacin for the bacterial variety.

Fever

If you develop a fever for any reason you should rest and take aspirin or Paracetamol/Tylenol (acetaminophene). You should also bring with you a supply of antibiotics, such as ciprofloxacin or tetracycline, in case you are struck by some more serious infection in a hopelessly remote place. If this happens, take antibiotics as instructed on the packet and see a doctor within four days. For gut infections taking ciprofloxacin for three days should suffice, but otherwise you should finish the course (usually seven days).

Injury

Be prepared. If you're not familiar with first-aid carry a booklet on the subject, and pack an appropriate medical kit (see below). Wash and treat even minor cuts and sores since they easily become infected in the tropics.

When there are only two of you and one has an accident, the other should stay with the injured one and wait for help to arrive. The temptation is to rush for help, but being injured, worried and alone could have a disastrous effect on the patient. So, except for the rare cases when you know the trails are little used, wait for someone to come along, and keep the injured person warm and comfortable.

On some of these hikes serious injury would be one hell of a problem, so be careful. Don't hike when you're tired, and don't take risks.

Suggested medical kit

- Elastoplast (Band-aids)
- butterfly closures
- micropore tape
- bandages
- tubular bandages
- Melolin dressings
- vaseline (for cracked heels and tick removal)
- 'moleskin' (for blisters)
- antifungal foot powder
- scissors
- safety pins
- tweezers
- earplugs
- sterile hypodermic needles
- drugs:
  malarial pills
  aspirin or Paracetamol/Tylenol (for fever and toothache)
  a more powerful pain-killer/anti-inflammatory such as ibuprofen (Nurofen)
  diarrhoea medicine (Diocalm, Imodium)
  antihistamine tablets such as terfenadine (Seldane)
  antibiotics (ciprofloxacin, tetracycline, ampicillin)
  antiseptic and wipes
  travel sickness pills.

Heat-related problems

The very humid conditions that prevail in Central America cause problems because not enough perspiration can evaporate for the body to be able to cool itself sufficiently. After a week or two your body becomes acclimatized and begins to sweat more freely while losing less salt in the process.

You can help your body by drinking lots of water, avoiding alcohol and taking extra salt in your diet. Avoid hiking during the hottest part of the day and don't wear or carry too much. A sun-hat is far more important than sunglasses, as sunburn can occur remarkably quickly in the tropics, especially at altitude. However you should have sunglasses with 100% UV protection, as well as lipsalve and sunscreen or sunblock.

Heat exhaustion

This is caused by over-exertion when the body cannot dissipate its heat quickly enough: blood rushes to the skin, depriving the brain and other vital organs of oxygen and producing symptoms of nausea, florid complexion, stumbling, lack of alertness, cramp and eventual collapse. It tends to affect those unaccustomed to being outdoors in extreme weather, the old, the unwell and convalescents; it's not life-threatening but is a clear warning to rest in the shade, sip cool, salty drinks and munch a high-energy trail snack.

Heat stroke

This is far more serious and is the result of a complete breakdown of the body's cooling mechanisms; if untreated this results in brain damage or even death. The symptoms are feeling generally ill, a very high body temperature and (usually) flushed hot, dry skin where sweating has ceased. This may be followed by splitting headaches, loss of coordination, confusion or even aggression, and ultimately delirium. Resting in the shade is not enough: the victim's body temperature must be brought down by any means possible. If there's a river handy, that's dandy, but heat stroke is more likely to hit in waterless areas. Remove the victim's clothing and sponge him or her with water from your bottle or canteen, then fan vigorously. Massage arms and legs to divert blood to the extremities, and keep it up until temperature is normal. Then abandon the hike and look for a doctor; if you press on, a recurrence is likely.

Fungal infections

Fungi, flourishing in the humid heat of the rainforest, are a common problem, especially for your feet. To avoid infection, wear loose clothes of natural fibres, wash them and yourself frequently and dry well. If infected, wash and dry the affected area regularly, and sprinkle it with an anti-fungal powder, such as Tinaderm (easily found). If you have a persistent and itchy rash, this could be a type of fungus that can only be killed by antifungal drugs.

Another type of fungus lives in tropical rivers and can infect bathers' ears: it's best not to submerge your head.

NATURAL MEDICINE

The indigenous people, of course, have always used medicinal plants (and animals), and their knowledge has benefitted modern medicine in many instances. If you become ill while you are among Indians (or *mestizos*) you are well advised to try any remedy they offer. Don't be too enthusiastic, however, as dosage is hard to measure and even natural medicines have side-effects. You can also try the following products of nature if you're stuck without medicine while off the beaten track.

Papaya

The fruit of the papaya speeds up the healing of cuts or sores, soothes diarrhoea and stomach upsets — and tastes good. It has been reported that the seeds (which are strongly alkaline and taste disgusting) kill intestinal parasites; chew them thoroughly on an empty stomach.

Honey

This excellent cure for persistent sores is now used (externally) in some hospitals.

Urine

Yes, it really is good for you, and it's certainly always available! Burns, cuts and sores all seem to clear up more quickly if covered with a urine-soaked dressing; it's said to be a particularly good treatment for jellyfish stings. It's said to be a beneficial drink, too, but we don't expect anyone to rush behind the bushes with their little cup.

Ginger

This has found a modern use as an antidote to travel sickness: it can be taken in capsule form as well as in food.

Charcoal

This is the traditional treatment for diarrhoea, and it still works. If you habitually make a camp-fire you'll have medicine galore; take it mixed with water several times daily.

Other plants that the locals may unleash on you include the bark of *Spondias sp.* trees (*cimarron*) for wounds, *Giniicida maculata* (*madero negro*) for skin irritations, *Veronica patens* (*tuete*) for parasites, and *Bixa orellana* (*achiote*) against dysentery and scarring, as well as a mosquito repellent body paint and food colouring. Do let us hear of any other interesting ones.

Prickly heat (Miliara)

This is an irritating rash caused by the blocking of sweat glands, particularly when acclimatizing to the tropical climate. Loose-fitting cotton clothes will help prevent it, and washing with cold water and a solution of soda bicarbonate will help to clear it up. Don't use creams which will further clog the pores.

Mountain health

Altitude sickness

Quite a few hikes in this book take you into mountainous country and to heights of over 3,000m, where you may fall victim to altitude sickness, or *soroche*.

Most people will need to do little more than rest for an hour or two on arrival at this sort of altitude for the usual symptoms of thumping heart and gasping breath to pass; however, some will experience hangover-like symptoms including headaches, fatigue, dizziness, loss of appetite and nausea. If this fails to clear up overnight, consider descending at least 500m and then returning in shorter stages. If there is no time for this, you may choose to take acetazolamide (Diamox) for five days, starting two or three days before the ascent, to counter the symptoms. Take lots of fluids and carbohydrates (up to 70% of your diet).

If you intend to spend much time at high altitudes read up on the two potentially lethal problems, pulmonary oedema and cerebral oedema.

Hypothermia

In the jungle you will long for a touch of hypothermia, but you should take it seriously on some of the high exposed walks. The danger is that since most of the trips are tropical, you may be tempted to skimp on warm clothing. If you're going above 2,000m or so, bring a good sleeping bag, a light sweater or fleece jacket and, most important, a thoroughly waterproof jacket. It is the combination of wet and cold that kills, with fatigue often a contributory factor; temperatures can easily drop below freezing, and the unimpeded wind of the high mountains can make it far colder. As soon as it gets dark the temperature plummets; be sure to camp in good time.

The symptoms of hypothermia are lethargy, shivering (initially only), numbness (especially of fingers and toes), staggering, slurred speech and irrational perceptions and behaviour. Above all get the victim out of the wind and into dry warm clothing, or even a sleeping bag, and give high-energy food and warm, non-alcoholic drinks.

FANGS AND STINGS

By Hilary Bradt with additions by Tim Burford

Certain members of the animal kingdom are definitely hazardous to the health. Not the ones you may be thinking of, such as jaguars and snakes, so much as disease carriers like vampire bats and a multitude of insects. Knowing the life cycle and habits of these creatures will help you to avoid them, or to understand, forgive and even like them!

Pumas and jaguars

Pumas (mountain lions or cougars) are still found in the mountains of Central America, and in some low-lying areas. The only time one might pose any danger to a hiker would be if it were injured and/or cornered. Like the jaguar, pumas do prey on livestock, however, and are the scourge of some villages.

Snakes

It will surprise many readers to learn that far from being snake-infested, jungles harbour relatively few of these reptiles. The reason is simple: snakes, being cold-blooded, need sunlight to raise their body temperature, and there's precious little sunlight in a tropical rainforest (other than in the canopy, where some snake species spend their whole lives). But there's no denying that snakes are a danger, especially in cleared areas, and for the backpacker venturing into these places, our best advice is not to get bitten. Most of you probably know that snakes attack only when provoked or cornered, so don't give them that excuse. If you keep to the trail, watch your feet, and never put your hands where you can't see them, nothing will happen to you. You may see snakes, but they will be in a hurry to get out of your way. Wearing good boots and thick socks is an extra precaution. Most snakes hunt at night, so you should move cautiously after dark and make sure your tent or hammock is snake-proof. It's also a good idea to shake out your boots in the morning in case a snake thinks it's found a marvellous new hidey-hole.

Snakebite is certainly an alarming prospect, but if you or your companion are bitten, take comfort in the fact that more than half the victims of snake bite receive minimal or no poisoning, even from venomous species, since snakes tend not to use their full amount of poison (if any) in self-defence. The most venomous snake in Central America is the coral snake (*corál/Micrurus nigrocinctus*), a small land snake striped in red, black and yellow, but this is nocturnal, very timid and often too small to bite a human; the false coral is similar but harmless. Others to watch out for are rattlesnakes (*cascabel/Crotalus durissus*), eyelash vipers (*bocaracá/Bothrops schlegelii*) and the *fer de lance* (*terciopelo* or *barba amarilla/Bothrops asper*), identifiable by a diamond pattern on its back; this can be found in undergrowth and often lies on warm roads at night. It's up to 2m long and is less timid than other species. Boas (*boa/Boa constrictor*) can bite, although of course they kill by constriction; they may be up to 6m in length and can kill ocelots and young deer.

One of the first symptoms of poisoning may be tingling in the mouth, and a metallic taste, followed by swelling, pain and numbness at the site of the bite. Sweating, nausea and fainting may be a symptom of shock rather than of poisoning.

Views vary on how to treat snake bite in remote areas, but doctors agree that you should *not* make razor cuts around the fang marks or try to suck the poison out. You should merely gently wash the surface of the wound to get rid of any sprayed venom which could subsequently enter the wound. A crepe bandage (rather than a tourniquet) should be applied to the whole limb (assuming the bite is on a limb) to slow the blood flow, and released for one minute in every ten; the limb should be kept below the level of the heart. The victim should be kept quiet and calm.

And if you're days away from medical help, that's all you can do. Hospitals hold stocks of serum; these are specific to the exact species of snake, so do what you can to help accurate identification.

Vampire bats

These rather endearing little creatures (we'll tell you why in a minute) are definitely dangerous, because of all the animals listed here they are the only ones to actively seek you as a prey, and because they're carriers of rabies. However, the dangers of vampire bats have been exaggerated, as studies show that only one in 200 carries the rabies virus. But with a disease that is invariably fatal once established, you don't want to take any risks, so always sleep under a mosquito net; completely under — we met a rather sheepish looking Indian in the Darién Gap with a bandaged foot: he'd found the night too hot for his liking so had stuck his foot out under the netting to cool off. A nice treat for a passing bat.

Now a little about the habits of vampire bats (*vampiro/Desmodus rotundus*), which are different in many ways from those of other bats. Vampires can stalk their prey 'on foot'. They have specially elongated legs and arms that enable them to walk on the ground, and they usually attack the feet or legs of their warm-blooded victims. Domestic animals such as horses, donkeys and cows are frequently attacked, but chickens are often victims of the smaller *Diaemus youngii*. The animal feels no pain from an attack: if the vampire strikes while flying it lulls the animal with its rapidly beating wings, and its saliva may contain an anaesthetic which makes the bite painless. Certainly it does contain an anticoagulant. Contrary to popular opinion these bats don't suck blood, nor do they have hollow teeth. They make a slashing cut with their razor-sharp canine teeth, and lap up the blood with the help of a groove on their lower lip. They drink their own weight in blood, so that they can barely fly away, and then don't feed for several days. Because of the anticoagulant the victim continues to bleed copiously after the bat has left, and several vampires may feed successively from the same wound, so that many animals eventually die from blood loss.

So why does Hilary find them so endearing? Well, apart from their nasty feeding habits, vampire bats are social animals leading impeccable family lives. The gestation period is a remarkable seven months, and the infants are suckled for nine months. While the mother is out feeding, the young are left in the care of 'foster parents' which may also suckle them. On her return, the mother and baby recognize each other's calls. Vampire bats keep themselves and each other immaculately clean, and this can lead to their downfall. One method of destroying a colony is to catch one and paint it with a sticky mixture containing strychnine before releasing it to return to its cave. The other bats crowd around to clean it and are poisoned.

Rabies

Rabies may also be carried by almost any mammal that bites — most obviously dogs. As ever, prevention is the key, so you should avoid dogs that seem to be behaving erratically and consider carrying a stick or hiking pole. Most dogs will keep clear if you throw stones, or even pretend to pick up stones. If bitten, or even scratched, scrub the bite at once under running water for five minutes with soap and then with iodine or a 40-70% alcohol solution; it's been shown that this alone reduces the risk of contracting rabies by 90%. Then head for a doctor: the traditional advice about catching the beast and hanging on to it for ten days to see if it develops symptoms is a waste of precious time if you're in the back of beyond. Ideally you should start a two-week course of jabs within a week of being bitten, but if the wound is on an extremity (bats often bite on the toes, so wear socks in bed!) you may have a couple of months before the virus reaches the brain, from which point death is certain within 20 days.

An alternative to the expensive course of injections after being bitten is the only slightly less expensive three-jab course of vaccinations before travel; this should be enough to keep you safe, but if bitten you should still have a booster.

Bugs

Understanding the habits of man-loving mites and insects can help you to outwit them. And if that fails, we have suggestions below on how to deal with the misery they inflict.

Prevention is always better than cure, and a good insect repellent is the best preventative. The two main active ingredients are Deet (diethyl-metatoluamide), on your skin, and Permethrin, on your clothing. Deet is present in concentrations from 30% up to 95% in the leading brands of repellent. The higher the concentration, the longer protection lasts, but it's neurotoxic and 95% concentrations may cause rashes or seizures in children. Some people find that 100mg of vitamin B1 (thiamine) taken daily will stop mosquitoes and other insects from biting, although there's no scientific evidence for this. You can also sleep under a mosquito net; the ones with their own frame that you can set up on top of a bed (or anywhere else) are best, as few budget hotels provide hooks for tying up the conventional nets. It should also be impregnated with permethrin; if not, you can get a DIY kit from MASTA. Permethrin is available in the USA as Duranon or Permanone, but not in Canada; it should stay active through four or five washings. In a tent you'll certainly need ventilation, but make sure that any opening is covered with fine-gauge netting. Sprays containing pyrethrum can zap any beasties inside your tent or ones that have just attached themselves to your body, and mosquito coils (which give out an insect repellent odour as they burn) last all night and are very effective in a closed room.

Experience shows us that, although in theory you can do a lot to deter insects by wearing long-sleeved shirts, long trousers tucked into long socks and so on, in practice it's difficult to do so in hot humid jungle, at least during the sweltering days. You're lulled into a sense of false security by the fact that you're not usually aware of the mites and insects that are busy feasting. Probably the best advice is to spray like crazy during the day, and wear bite-proof clothing at night when the *Anopheles* (malarial) mosquito is doing her rounds. Bite-proof means closely woven material; a nylon 'shell' jacket does the trick but is sweaty. You should still spray your clothes, of course, but not the nylon, which will disintegrate. Don't forget that washing whenever you cross a stream will dislodge some bugs before they've settled in.

Once you are bitten, calamine lotion or an analgesic cream or spray containing mepyramine (antihistamine) or benzocaine can help soothe the itching, while hydrocortisone (tablets or cream) reduces the swelling. Aspirin or paracetamol may help (after all, an itch is just a specialized form of pain). Toothpaste (applied externally) is said to have a soothing effect, as may anaesthetic cream. Scratching may not help but it feels awfully good. Let's be honest, it's one of life's supreme physical pleasures, isn't it?! But be careful and keep your nails short; if you break the skin apply antiseptic, as the bite can easily become infected.

Mosquitoes (zancudos)

Above all, these carry malaria; symptoms of this potentially fatal condition include flu-like fever, headaches, shivering, sweating and chills. It is on the increase throughout the world as the malaria parasite becomes resistant to drugs such as chloroquine, and mosquitoes to pesticides. Most areas in Central America below 2,500m are affected, and Panamá has the killer strain, *Plasmodium falciparum* or cerebral malaria. In low-lying areas of Central America mosquitoes also carry Dengue fever: this virus produces fever, headaches and musculo-skeletal aches, followed by a rash, and should pass within a week, although in very rare cases it can kill. In Darién province, Panamá, mosquitoes also carry yellow fever; they can also carry bot fly eggs. Thus the emphasis should be on avoiding mosquito bites rather than on medication.

Before we discuss this, however, you should recognize your enemy. Of at least 2,600 species of mosquito, and 400 species of *Anopheles* mosquito, only about 60 can carry a malarial parasite, and of the 100 or so species of malarial parasite only four commonly affect man. In Central America the main risk is from *Anopheles albimanus*, which feeds at night; however *Aedes aegypti*, which carries Dengue fever, prefers daylight, so you can never relax altogether. As with other types of mosquito, it's only the female who sucks blood, which she needs for egg production, and she has a definite preference for women in dark clothes. The *Anopheles* is under 1cm long, rests with her tail end in the air and lacks that high-pitched hum so characteristic of most mosquitoes. In towns and hotels you'll usually be confronted with the (relatively) harmless *Culex quinquefasciatus*.

In addition to the preventative measures above, you should take antimalarial drugs. These do not prevent the disease, but kill the parasites in your system. You must take the medication regularly, starting a week before arrival in a malarial region, throughout your stay there, and for six weeks after leaving it. Chloroquine (sold as Avloclor, Malarivon, Nivaquine, Aralen or Resochin, and taken weekly) is still the best in most cases. However in the San Blas and Darién areas of southeastern Panamá chloroquine-resitant mosquitoes should be countered by also taking Paludrine (Proguanil), which is taken daily (easier to remember). Mosquitoes in this region carry the *Falciparum* malaria, which must be treated with a single dose of three Fansidar tablets or two Halfan tablets followed by two more after six hours and another two after six hours more. If you contract another type of malaria, you can treat it in the short term by taking four chloroquine tablets (600mg) followed by two more six hours later and then two daily.

Assassin bugs (vinchuca/Triatoma dimidiata)

These carry Chagas' Disease, a nasty complaint which kills 50,000 persons a year throughout Latin America, but is, fortunately, seldom contracted by travellers. Also known as the reduviid, cone-nosed, kissing or barber bug, it is an oval brown insect with a long thin head which lurks in crevices and between palm fronds, notably in thatched roofs, at up to 1,500m (South American species go up to 3,600m). It emerges at night to feed on the blood of vertebrates, including humans: it is likely to bite on the face, feeding for at least 20 minutes, and leaving faeces containing *Trypanosoma* parasites. These enter through the bite and reproduce inside fat cells which burst and release them. In some victims a hard violet swelling appears at the site of infection after about a week, and soon the parasites invade organs such as the heart, brain and liver. Symptoms are fever, vomiting, shortness of breath and a stiff neck. An acute form of the illness can kill you within three months, but it's more usual for victims to show no symptoms after a month or two, but then to die of a weakened heart up to 20 years later. It has been speculated that Charles Darwin died of Chagas' disease.

If bitten on the face, see a doctor; a blood test after six weeks will show if the disease is present. Benznidazole and nifurtimox are effective against most strains of the parasite in the first six months of infection, but it is better by far to avoid being bitten. Avoid sleeping under palm trees or palm roofs, use insect repellents and a mosquito net, and check for hidden insects. It should be stressed that this is a disease of poor villagers and extremely rare among travellers.

Wasps, bees and hornets

Some people are allergic to the sting of *Hymenoptera* or thin-waisted flies, as this group is called. If you already know you're allergic, you'll presumably carry a sting kit with you.

Generally these stinging insects are not a problem in the jungle, but Hilary once inadvertently shook a branch which was the nesting site for some small blue wasps. Furious at this apparent assault, they pursued her, tangled in her hair, and she ended up with her head in the river trying to get rid of them. No fun, so be careful not to disturb nests in any way and don't even go near them if you see any activity. If attacked, stay calm and don't flail about.

Scorpions (escorpiones)

These chaps can do a fair amount of damage, but they become aggressive only when disturbed. Don't move stones, timber, or mess around in leaf litter unless you can see what you're doing. If you need to clear a site, use your boots and a knife rather than your hands. If your boots really must spend the night outside the tent, be sure to shake them out before putting them on in the morning. In cheap hotels, check around the bed and under the toilet seat.

If stung, treat the place with a topical anaesthetic cream, and take pain killers and plenty of fluids.

Bocones
I don't know the English name for these tiny blood-sucking beetles, but their bite itches a lot for a few minutes, then eases off. They only bite during the day.

Ticks (*garrapatas*)
These are plentiful and persistent in jungle areas and savannah grasslands. You may finish a walk with hundreds of these crawlies. If removed before they dig in and start sucking your blood, they're harmless, but there are few things less conducive to a peaceful night than to feel hundreds of ticks crawling around on you. And once established they cause an itch lasting several days. They may also carry typhus, a fever which requires medical attention; in this case there's usually a large painful swelling around the bite and nearby lymph nodes will be inflamed.

Keep ticks off your skin by tucking trousers into socks and tops into trousers, and spraying them (but not bare skin) with a repellent such as Permanone. Inspect your body periodically for ticks (some are so small as to be practically invisible) and remove them with masking tape, by far the best way of trapping the creatures. At the end of the day wash thoroughly (Neko soap, available in tick countries, is very effective) and change your clothing. Before going to bed inspect yourself carefully, sharing the job with a friend if possible, and be sure to check those warm clammy areas so dear to a tick's heart. Yes, that's when you learn who your friends are!

Once established, ticks must be removed by firmly pinching them as close to your skin as possible and steadily pulling at right angles to the skin; tweezers and kerosene, alcohol or vaseline may help.

Chiggers (*chigos, coloradillas* or *coloraditos*)
The secret life of chiggers (*Eutrombicula sp*) was revealed in an article by E F Rivinus in the *Smithsonian* magazine of July 1981, and it's so fascinating we can't resist going into some detail. Apparently these creatures have long been misunderstood. No, it's not that they're nicer than we thought, it's that they're even nastier, and all the traditional cures such as killing the beastie by painting nail varnish over the spot are quite futile. It's going to itch like hell for about ten days and there's nothing you can do about it.

But to begin at the beginning. First, the chigger is not an insect, but the larval stage of a mite. Second, it doesn't suck blood, and third, it doesn't burrow under your skin. What happens when you pick up a chigger (more likely a hundred chiggers) in long grass is that it bites into your skin and liquifies the tissue with its saliva. In reaction to this your tissue creates a hard tube called a stylostome, which makes a handy drinking straw for the chigger. After about four days the fat and happy chigger leaves, but the stylostome remains, and you will go on itching for a week or more, because your skin goes on reacting against the stylostome.

Mr Rivinus has a sensible and scientific explanation for this behaviour:

"First there's no love in a chigger's life (no sex, I'm sorry to say, and no parent/child relationship) ... so it's obviously inappropriate to expect them to show a mite of compassion towards their hosts ... secondly, the adult has a blind gut and is consequently unable to defecate. Anything that spends its entire adult life in a constipated state is bound to develop a pretty nasty nature, and that may be reflected in its offspring."

So, once the stylostome has begun to form there's not much you can do. As usual, prevention is better than cure, so use lots of repellent (sulphur powder may help) and keep away from long grass, especially if there are cows there. Or don't lounge around in it, anyway. The itch can be somewhat relieved with analgesic ointment, and of course if you scratch hard enough you may rip the stylostome out. If so, use antiseptic to prevent infection.

Jiggers

Not to be confused with a chigger, a jigger is a flea (*chigoe/Tunga penetrans*) which burrows imperceptibly into your toes and remains there to enjoy its pregnancy. It can grow to the size of a pea, but you should use a sterile needle to hook it out before it gets to this stage. Treat the resulting hole with antiseptic. Don't go barefoot — that's also the way to pick up hookworm.

Bot fly larva

This creature deserves a proper description and I'm grateful to Linda Rosa of the South American Explorers Club for this information. The adult bot fly (*Dermatobia hominis*) is a harmless insect which doesn't even have mouth parts, but its larva is parasitic on humans and other warm-blooded animals. The bot fly attaches its eggs to the abdomen of a blood-sucking arthropod, such as a mosquito, which conveys them to the host. As the mosquito has its meal, the bot fly eggs hatch and the larvae burrow into the skin through the mosquito bite or a hair follicle. Here they prosper and stay, maturing in 40 to 60 days, by which time they may measure up to 2cm in length. The grub is all body, with no head or legs, but has an effective mouth and strong oral hooks which, with the spines which encircle its body, keep it firmly anchored. It breathes in a most undignified way through its backside, and its unfortunate human hosts, who can't tell a face from an arse, mistakenly talk of the creature 'poking its head out'.

A cyst or hard mass forms around the grub and this often becomes infected, so you should deal with the creature as soon as it makes its presence felt. In a follow-up to Linda's article in the *South American Explorer* magazine, Barb McLeod writes:

"Graced with the dubious distinction of having extracted more than forty of the beasties from myself and other people over some ten years in Belize, I thought I should pass on a tried and true remedy: Cover the breathing hole generously with Elmer's Glue, or better (unless skin is sensitive) Duco cement or other non-water base glue. Place over this (it need not dry) a circular patch of adhesive tape, 1-2 cm in diameter, depending on size and location of cyst. Along the edge of tape, apply a second seal of glue. Allow this to dry well, being on the lookout for lymph leakage around the edge — that is the larva's devious means of forcing a new breathing channel. Leave on overnight; the next day the suffocated beast can be easily squeezed and tweezed out.

"Before I arrived at this method I'd tried: glue alone, peanut butter, toothpaste, nail polish, lard, Sno-Seal and nicotine extract. None but the last killed the larva — they only induced (at best) the critter to poke its rear end out. Grabbing it alive is inadvisable; not only will it dig in painfully with its spines, but accidental rupture could also cause a serious allergic reaction as well as infection. Nicotine extract will send the beast into convulsions for fifteen minutes — most distracting to the host. The recommended method is painless and 100% effective *if* the second seal is carefully applied.

"I've noted, in myself and others, lymphatic complications (swelling of face, tenderness of nodes) whenever the larvae locate in the neck or head. Normally they hook directly into the lymphatic system and feed from it.

"Considerable lore has accumulated around this exotic affliction — even stories of hosts lonely or curious enough to keep their worm as a pet until nocturnal twinges begin to keep them awake at night."

Sandflies (*Phlebotomus sp*)

These feed only at night, and the females carry the parasite *Leishmaniasis* which, if left untreated, can lead to disfigurement or even death. Again, you can avoid them by sleeping under a permethrin-impregnated mosquito net. Here's a cautionary tale sent to us by Barbara Clark of New Hampshire:

"Staying in a cheap hotel in Guatemala City, I awoke with my hands covered with hard bites. These went away, but after we'd been home about a month, a sore appeared on my arm and one on my back. These gradually got bigger and uglier. My doctor sent me to a surgeon, who removed the smaller one on my back. It reappeared. Finally I went to a dermatologist, and here I was in luck, because he happened to have studied and treated a form of the disease. I was approaching the time when the disease could appear in the nose and throat area, which it would start eating away. The doctor treated the disease with antimony injections, and the sores went away like magic and without any side effects."

Don't let a doctor excise these sores, which serve as a useful 'barometer' of treatment.

For some reason as yet unknown to science, Avon 'Skin-So-Soft' works wonders in repelling sandflies; it also repels mosquitoes, but only for short periods.

Sandfleas

You'll meet swarms of these creatures biting your ankles on some tropical beaches. They are very unpleasant at the time, but the effects are short-lived.

Blackflies

Clouds of viciously biting blackflies (*mosca negra/Simulium sp*) can make hiking a misery, as anyone who's hiked in the eastern USA or Canada knows. Fortunately, they are less common in Central America and the irritation of their bites doesn't last long. In central Guatemala they may carry river blindness (*Onchocerciasis*, known locally as Robles' Disease) — brought from Africa by the slave trade. 40,000 to 90,000 Guatemalans are infected, but it is hoped to eliminate the disease by 2007.

Crabs and lice (*piojos*)

Travellers sleeping in cheap hotels are liable to catch these. If in your hair, you can deal with them by using a shampoo containing *gammabenzene hexachloride*.

Finally some happy news. There are no leeches or bears in Central America. Few insects will bother you above 2,000m (and in this area there's no malaria above 1500m), so if you're thoroughly put off by this section, keep high and you'll be alright. In any case, the dry season is far healthier than the wet; avoid the dampest parts of the Caribbean coast and you'll have few problems.

CRIME

Theft

Robberies always figure prominently in travellers' tales, and certainly Central America has its share of skilful thieves. Fortunately violent robbery is very rare (though a real danger in Panamá City and Colón, and on some overnight buses), and theft is almost unknown in rural parts. Travellers are most likely to be parted from their possessions unawares, particularly in towns or areas frequented by tourists. The *Tropical Traveller* has an excellent section on safety (see Appendix Two), but here are a few do's and don'ts:

- Do keep your valuables in a money belt, neck pouch or secret pocket. John Hatt, in his book *The Tropical Traveller*, has the idea of using a tubular bandage (such as Tubigrip) to secure his valuables to his leg. This comes in various sizes so you can choose the most comfortable and practical place to wear it. Bear in mind that it can be embarrassing to be seen with your hand deep inside your trousers.

- Don't carry a handbag or any type of shoulder bag into known danger spots. That means markets, fiestas and crowded buses. A leather bag is easily snatched or slit.

- Do be wary of performing chivalrous acts. A standard trick is for some poor old lady on a bus to ask a gringo to lift her bag on to the luggage rack. Meanwhile his own bag disappears. If you agree to help, make sure your own luggage is safe. Equally, don't let yourself be distracted by someone telling you about dirt on your back or sitting in your reserved seat.

- Do select a hotel room which has bars on the window or one that can't be entered from a neighbouring room. Lock your valuables in your luggage when leaving your room.

- Do bring a combination lock (harder to pick than an ordinary padlock) to secure your hotel door or luggage. A chain is a useful and versatile addition.

- Don't leave your money in your clothes when you go swimming.

- Don't camp in an urban area unless well guarded.

- Don't become paranoid. As a backpacker in rural areas you will experience incredible honesty and generosity in the face of grinding poverty. It's a humbling experience. In any case, the more alert, open and friendly you seem, the less likely you are to be a target.

There's always the problem of whether to carry your passport with you at all times or to leave it in the hotel strong box. It's often better to leave it behind but to carry some other form of identification. Something impressive-looking with a photo and a number (we use our Hostelling International cards) will usually serve just as well as a passport. Carry a photocopy of the key pages of your passport plus any other appropriate identification. Keep a note of your passport details and the numbers of your travellers cheques, plastic cards and air ticket separate from your valuables, so that if they are lost you can more easily replace them. Divide your money and travellers cheques between at least two different places, in your baggage and on your body.

Officials

You will be up against petty bureaucracy time and again, and it's great training in the art of public relations. However frustrating the situation, however corrupt the official, you must remain calm and pleasant. This is particularly important if you are arrested. Providing you keep cool you'll almost certainly be released within a few hours (assuming you haven't actually committed a crime). Try to assume an air of authority and quiet confidence, but don't do anything to threaten the ego of the official in question. Often a potentially awkward situation can be defused with jokes and a friendly gesture such as the offer of a cigarette or some chocolate. Don't resort to money bribery unless you know what you are doing; it's best to wait for the suggestion to come from the other side.

Revolutions and civil wars

Always a topical subject in Central America. Although you obviously don't want to be caught in the middle when soldiers and guerrillas are trading shots, you are pretty safe as a tourist. However, you should never wear military-surplus gear in this part of the world. If you find yourself in a country where fighting has suddenly broken out, keep calm and wait. Don't rush to the airport — everyone else will have got there before you, and anyway the border will be closed. Stay in your hotel, fill your water flask and be prepared to live off your backpacking food for a while. When the situation is calmer you can go outside, but move slowly and obey any curfew which may have been imposed. In this situation you should carry your passport at all times.

ON BEING A *GRINGA*

Wendy Dison

There is an ambiguity about the status of women in Central America: on the one hand they are seen as sex objects and on the other is the revered mother figure of the Catholic church. The Virgin Mary is displayed alongside a pin-up over the bus driver's seat and no-one thinks it odd. These attitudes are reflected in the way you will find yourself treated in Central America — one moment with lack of respect, the next with old-fashioned chivalry.

Being a foreign woman makes the situation even more confusing. Stereotypes exist about Western women and a woman travelling alone is often assumed to be "available". Dressing modestly helps to avoid unwanted attention, but as a *gringa* you will never escape it entirely. Not frequenting bars and other male-dominated places is also a good idea, yet often there is no choice when you want a meal or a drink. I have at times been made so uncomfortable by stares and comments that I've wished to disappear into my bowl of beans. Restaurants where families are eating are likely to have a more pleasant atmosphere.

Harassment usually takes the form of whistles and hisses. This is the *ladino's* way of paying you a compliment and many local women seem to expect and even welcome it. But, while being whistled to like a dog can make your blood boil, it generally isn't threatening and the best thing to do is to ignore it.

However, meeting people is one of the reasons for travelling and you need to distinguish between unwanted advances and friendly approaches. Use your intuition, but also use your discretion. Making friends isn't difficult as there is a lot of curiosity about foreigners, but it is harder to meet other women, particularly indigenous women, who are very shy. Long bus journeys are a good place to meet and talk and I enjoyed getting to know women who run guesthouses. Questions about husbands and children always came first and, instead of pitying me for having neither (which is a common reaction in many other countries), I found that generally women were envious of my freedom.

Women travellers have some advantages, too: we pose less of a threat than men do and I'm sure I'm invited into people's homes more often than men are because of this. There still exists in Central America a chivalrous attitude to women and should you need help, or even appear to need it, men are ready to pitch in.

The world is an increasingly dangerous place, but the mountains are safer than the cities. The further off the beaten track I go, the safer I feel. In the mountains of Central America the friendliness and hospitality I have met have been humbling. Once, I lost my way in the Todos Santos area of Guatemala and had to beg shelter for the night. An elderly couple, poor farmers, welcomed me and shared their food; when I left in the morning they refused my offer of payment. This was in a remote area. Other places are not so safe, especially where there are many tourists, and I would strongly advise women walking alone to seek local advice. Robbery, assault and even rape are not unknown. Local people will have information that is more up to date than that in guidebooks. In some places walking with a friend may be safer.

I have given a lot of warnings, but it is important to keep things in perspective. Don't ruin your trip by being paranoid; be aware — but don't let it stop you from travelling. The world is full of wonderful people and you won't meet them if you stay at home.

Chapter Five

On the Road

TRANSPORT

The PanAmerican Highway (equally known as the InterAmerican Highway) is now paved from the US border to beyond Panamá City, enabling you to travel fast and in comfort by long-distance bus. Just because all of Central America would fit into California or Spain doesn't mean that border formalities are dispensed with. In a day's bus journey you may pass through six border posts (leaving and entering three countries) and the process may take hours: passports are scrutinized, forms filled in, questions asked, and luggage may be searched. You'll have to pay a couple of US dollars at each border, so you should have a supply of single bills for this purpose; if you're passing through a country without stopping, vendors will accept dollars for drinks and snacks, but be sure to have a vague idea of prices and exchange rates: one dollar should buy quite a lot.

The PanAmerican is the domain of the famous Tica Bus and newer competitors, linking all the capitals of Central America. These are pretty speedy, but a lot more expensive than travel by local buses, particularly if you have to backtrack to the capital to take the Tica Bus. They're usually fully booked for days in advance, which may further increase your costs if you have to wait. The much touted air conditioning usually doesn't work and the windows don't open — the metal window frame on our bus was dented by the efforts of heat-crazed passengers. Balanced against this is the ease with which you pass through frontiers, the (relative) comfort, and the fact that you stop each night in a capital city and push on next morning.

Hitchhiking is easy along the Highway, particularly if you don't mind hounding people as they pass through frontiers. No, let's re-phrase that: politely ask if they have room for an extra passenger. It's normal to pay for rides, although this is often waived for foreigners.

On occasion you may use planes, boats and the very few remaining trains, but otherwise transport is likely to be by local bus (*autobús* or *camioneta*), almost all retired North American school buses. These are such an institution that even new Freightliner/Mercedes buses are designed to look like school buses! Many are still painted bright yellow, but all are decorated with religious stickers and the names of mythical women (*Janeth, Lensley* et al). It's always a colourful and entertaining experience, and even long-legged gringos don't find it *too* agonizing. As a rule you just pile on board and your money will be taken in their own good time; your luggage will normally be put up onto the roofrack for you, at no cost. In Panamá and Costa Rica long-distance buses, often retired Greyhounds, may have advance booking and external luggage lockers.

Car rental prices are extortionate, but four-wheel-drives are widely available (especially in Costa Rica) and may be worthwhile if you don't have time to get to the remote places otherwise. If you do have time it's possible to take a pickup or a taxi to just about anywhere you want to go, or at least to within hiking distance. Fuel costs less than in Europe, but also seems extortionate to North Americans. Don't drive at night (cattle, bicycles without lights, bandits, you name it), don't leave valuables inside and take care generally. However, you no longer have to worry about army (or guerrilla) checkpoints.

ACCOMMODATION

There are, of course, all classes of hotels and restaurants throughout Central America. If you're not on a tight budget you'll find the *posadas, quintas* and *hosterías*, often converted colonial mansions, charming, good value and much more enjoyable than international chain hotels. At the lower end are the *hospedajes* and *pensiónes* which range from a couple of dollars a night (in Honduras and Guatemala) to maybe ten (in Panamá). These rock-bottom places are extremely basic: no hot water, no hygiene, lumpy beds, a wide variety of the local fauna scurrying about the floor and up the walls — but with loads of atmosphere. In high crime cities such as Panamá you are advised to pay more for an hotel, however, due to the location of most cheap lodgings in the 'bad' part of town.

Most hotels will look after baggage while you're away hiking; this is usually free, although of course there's an expectation you'll want to stay the night when you return. Remember that no matter how good an hotel you're staying in, the local sewage system will not be too good: always put your used toilet paper in the basket provided, or risk blocking the whole system.

FOOD

Generally speaking, you'll get better food in an independent restaurant than in your hotel. In any event, Central American food is far less exciting than Mexican cuisine. Fish is usually fresh and good, as it should be with two oceans so close to every town. Helpings tend to be large, so if you are economizing it's sensible to ask for one meal and two plates. Few restaurants object to this. It's also sensible to see what other people are eating, and if you like the look of it, point it out to the waiter who takes your order. Safer than ordering from a list of strange names, and the locals know what's good in a particular place.

Markets often serve the best food. Each market has a *comedor*, or eating area, where hot food is prepared. You see what's cooking and pay the lowest prices. Always ask the cost of a dish before ordering it, however. If in doubt just ask for the *comida corriente* or *comida tipica*.

While on the subject of markets, with all that wonderful fresh food for sale it would be a pity not to cater for yourself at times. It's fun to get together with other gringos and make a large fruit salad, or a green salad, providing you wash it well in sterilized water. Vegetarianism is no great problem, but your diet is likely to become rather boring; rice, beans and eggs will be the staple, with green vegetables making relatively rare appearances.

There's plenty of food and drink available at bus stops and along the way; drinks are often poured from bottles into plastic bags for bus passengers — make sure ice (*hielo*) isn't added. The same applies to *licuados*, the local version of milkshakes, made with all the wonderful local fruits and, all too often, with ice.

COMMUNICATIONS

The regular appearance of capital cities throughout Central America makes receiving mail much less of a problem than in South America. You can ask your friends to send mail c/o the Post Office, American Express, or in some cases your country's embassy. The first, *Lista de Correos* (*Entrega General* in Panamá) is the equivalent of General Delivery or *Poste Restante*, and tends to be unreliable. Letters may be filed under your first name, last name, Mr, Ms or Esq depending on how the letter is addressed. However the central post office in San José, Costa Rica, now has a computerised system which will find your mail, as long as the correct names have been logged, of course. Your chances of receiving a letter are improved if you instruct your nearest and dearest to write your last name in capitals or underline it. Aerogrammes tend to arrive much faster and more reliably than regular mail, which is often tampered with to see if it contains money.

American Express offices will hold clients' mail and are much more reliable than post offices. To use this service you must have either AmEx travellers cheques or an AmEx credit card. However, the hours during which you can collect mail are often restricted. American Express can send you a list of their offices in Latin America.

Embassies provide the safest service of all, but many will not accept travellers' mail. As a rule you must write to each embassy in advance and request that they hold mail for you. No US embassy will do this.

There are more high-tech ways of keeping in touch nowadays: faxes are common and some fax agencies, notably in Costa Rica and Guatemala, will hold faxes for you. Some Guatemalan agencies provide the same service for e-mail. Phoning home is also a lot simpler nowadays with the arrival of services such as USA Direct, BT Direct and so on, which put you straight through to an operator in your home country and bill your home number or the person you're calling. It's wise to enquire before departure, as there are many variables regarding the types of phone you can use, whether you have to deposit a coin or wait for a second tone and so on.

As for the local addresses given in this book, in most cases we give both the street location and the postal address, usually a PO Box and post code, thus: *Apdo 1234, 56789 San José*. If writing from abroad it's preferable to add 'Central America' after the country name.

Almost all Central American cities are laid out on a grid plan, with numbered *Avenidas* running one way and *Calles* at right angles to them. However this logical scheme is confused by many variations; sometimes all streets on one side of a central axis (which may or may not be Avenida/Calle 0) have odd numbers and all those on the other side are even; or they may be North and South, East and West. Some cities, such as San Pedro Sula (Honduras), are divided into quadrants, so that '3a Avda, 3a Calle' could be in any of four locations if the address isn't given precisely. Panamá City has its own system, using letters as well as numbers. In Guatemala '1 Avda 1-2' means Avenida 1, number 2 between Calle 1 and 2 (or 1 and 3); in other countries, where building numbers are less common, Avda 1, C1/2 might just mean Avenida 1, between Calles 1 and 2. Avda 1/Calle 2 means a location on or near the junction of the two streets. *Un cuadra* and *cien metros* both translate as 'one block'; in Nicaragua in particular addresses are often given from some local landmark such as a cinema or hotel.

ECOTOURISM

In case you hadn't noticed, you are a consumer in the world's largest industry — tourism. Worldwide this now accounts for 6% of GNP and 7% of jobs, and is predicted to grow by 50% between 1990 and 2000 (from 400m to 600m tourist arrivals). In fact in 1994 they'd already reached 528m, bringing revenues of US$321bn. This affects Central America as much as anywhere: Guatemalan tourist entries tripled between 1984 and 1992, and tourism is Costa Rica's principal source of foreign exchange, increasing 18% in the first quarter of 1995. It's worth around US$200m annually to each of Guatemala, Costa Rica and Panamá. Mass tourism has brought many problems, such as environmental, social and cultural degradation, unequal distribution of the profits and the spread of disease. Many tourists come, of course, to lie on beaches, but in addition there's the Unique Selling Proposition of Central American tourism, which is 'ecotourism', or more accurately nature tourism. This tends to involve groups in air-conditioned buses visiting nature reserves, raft rides and hot springs, and hotels with satellite television, and is little more than a variant on tourism anywhere else. It brings money in to the local economy, and some of that may end up helping to protect wildlife and habitats. It also helps convince governments and tour companies of the value of the reserves.

This is relatively unproblematical (if you accept the waste of fossil fuel inherent in any kind of travel) as long as a few basic rules are observed: leave no garbage (especially plastic and other non-biodegradable materials) in a reserve, buy no products of endangered species of plant or animal, including coral jewellery and woodware, keep nothing you catch from the sea (unless you plan to eat it), don't leave TVs, lights or showers on when not needed. In addition you can choose hotels (and ships) that don't dump their waste and that use solar heating, automatic light switches and recycled water for watering lawns and golf courses. Don't eat agouti, iguana or turtle, and suggest that the restaurant ceases to serve it and indeed advertises the fact that it *doesn't* serve it. Avoid over-crowded resorts and seasons, and choose operators that only take small groups, that support community projects, and that use local goods and staff.

So far, so good. However this is essentially inward-looking tourism, in which the vacationers are concerned purely with resting and having fun. True ecotourism is *not* just to make the tourist feel good, but should also be about education, consciousness-raising (for both the tourist and the local populace) and actually making a difference somehow. Basically, things get complicated once you're dealing not only with animals but with indigenous peoples too. They are not to know that ecotourism is their best hope for avoiding the destruction of their habitat and the survival of their traditional lifestyle — to them ecotourism is something that just arrived unasked, something that's happening *to* them. In the Río Platanó, for example, it's provided money that enables the Pesch to buy supplies and thus spare the forest somewhat, but at the same time working as guides has given them time for more hunting, so that tourists could find themselves being fed the guans, currassows and tapirs that they had come to see alive. This, at least, is something that can be solved. However 'ecotourists' also bring whisky and marijuana, and the injection of cash into a largely cash-free economy has led to resentment and quarrels. There is also danger in an unhealthy economic dependency on tourism, which could collapse in response to many outside factors. Western ideas tend to separate man from his environment, ie they tend to focus on species preservation at the expense of indigenous peoples; it's more important to see both as part of the same ecosystem — equally entitled to respect and to a sustainable and secure future.

Local participation is vital, not just in profits but also in planning and decision-making. In Costa Rica, ATEC (the Talamanca Association for Eco-tourism & Conservation) defines ecotourism well as 'a cooperative relationship between the non-wealthy host community and those sincere, open-minded tourists who want to enjoy themselves in a Third World setting and, at the same time, enrich their consciousness by means of a significant educational and cultural experience. Real eco-tourism is a phenomenom that produces tangible political and economic results: educated and motivated tourists who return home ready to do something about our common crisis on Spaceship Earth, and educated and economically viable Third World communities whose residents have the commitment and the resources to exercise an ongoing, ecologically sound stewardship of the rainforests, beaches and wetlands.'

This can be summed up in three key criteria: is it sustainable (environmentally, socially, economically)? Is it educational? Is it participatory and beneficial locally?

For hikers there are more specific requirements: keep quiet, stay on the trail (in single file) even if it's muddy, never take shortcuts, don't cut live trees, if possible don't make fires from dead wood either, and erase signs of fires afterwards. Camp and wash (with biodegradable soap) at least 50m from water, wear lightweight shoes in camp. Burn toilet paper, bury your waste and remove all litter. Take something for park staff, even it's just a pack of biscuits or a newspaper from the city.

Deforestation

Most species become extinct because they lose their habitats and cease to breed rather than through being actively killed. Although all natural habitats are at risk, the rainforests of the tropics contain a far higher variety of species than any other habitat in the world. One aspect of its high biodiversity is that distinct species can develop in remarkably small areas, and thus can be rendered extinct very easily, often without ever having been identified. Only West Africa is currently being deforested more quickly than Central America, and contrary to the usual perception, one of the worst offenders is Costa Rica, which is losing 2.9% of its forest area each year and now has only 28% of its forest left. By contrast Brazil, usually seen as the demonic deforester, is only losing 0.6% per year and still has 66% of its forest cover. In the Americas only a few Caribbean islands have higher rates than Costa Rica, notably Jamaica (7.2% per year) and Haiti (4.8%), which has just 1% of its forest left.

Haiti is an extreme example of the most intractable type of deforestation, caused not by commercial logging or by clearing for cattle or coffee, but by the undeniable need of poor people for fuelwood. Around most towns in the poorer Central American states you'll see a ring of devastation where every tree has been either savaged or cut down, and women and children (above all) carrying bundles of wood on their backs to sell or for their own homes. In the last decade, as populations have grown and environmental degradation has advanced, the distances that people have had to go to find *leña* have increased, so that it now takes several hours a day for many people. In Honduras 75% of homes use fuelwood, accounting for 60% of total energy use, a total of five million cubic metres a year, equivalent to 22,500ha of forest lost each year. Forest cover fell from 35.7% in 1980 to 27.6% in 1990. In El Salvador fuelwood is also used in three quarters of homes, with an average consumption of 3.1kg/capita/day, against a Central American average of 2.5kg; this is due to the traditional design of stove with a heat loss of 90% — they're very good at heating the wall, but not the food. Fortunately coffee plantations provide 6.5m³ of wood per hectare/year, a quarter of total needs.

Of course, this produces many problems in addition to habitat and species loss; erosion for example, now affecting 77% of El Salvador and 90% of Panamá, causing silting, floods, loss of fertile topsoil, and reduced rainfall.

ON GETTING LOST

By Hilary Bradt

It looked like a perfectly simple bit of bushwhacking; our trail had suddenly ended and the pine forests dropped away sharply. One the other side of the valley we saw patches of cultivation indicating a village nearby, and decided to descend through the trees to the road or trail that we expected to find on the valley floor. What we hadn't taken into consideration was the effect of altitude on vegetation. After about 300 metres our nice pines became a subtropical rainforest and our nightmare began. Everything was damp, furry-green and rotten. The ground gave way beneath our feet, branches we grabbed for support broke off in our hands, and many friendly looking shrubs turned out to prick or sting. It was also incredibly steep. Our descent was faster than we'd intended, with plants or branches that we grabbed to break our slide simply accompanying us down. "Be careful, that's a long drop!" called George helpfully as I glissaded past him hugging a loose tree. "I'm not doing this on purpose!" I said through my teeth, landing with a thump on my backpack.

The lower we dropped the denser the vegetation became until we finally reached the bottom. Relief? No, it was a river. The patches of cultivation that had tempted us down from the top were no longer in sight. All we could see was trees, trees, and more trees. And the river, which we decided to follow downstream.

We made our way down the river for several hours before camping for the night. The next morning George persuaded me that we must climb up the almost vertical canyon side since he was pretty sure he had located those cultivated milpas. We climbed. It was a repeat of the previous day, except this time we were sliding backwards. We had to grab any handhold available, relying on luck and balance when there wasn't one. As we got higher the vegetation turned into dense scrubby thorn bushes. We had to force our way through. Just as I'd reached the stage when I thought that death was preferable, we entered a clearing. A milpa!! An old one, but a definite sign of civilization. We soon found a weak trail, then an abandoned house, and finally an inhabited house with a clear trail leading up over the mountain.

Our ordeal had come to an end; it has lasted for about eight hours which was quite long enough. Looking back on the experience we realized how stupid we'd been to make the initial decision to bushwhack. When you think of the basic rules of jungle hiking, like never putting your hands or feet in places you can't see, like not taking undue risks in remote areas, we were extremely lucky. Had we been bitten by a snake, or fallen and injured ourselves, the chances of survival would have been small.

We hope our readers will profit from our experience. It takes more courage to turn back than to continue on, blindly.

BACKPACKING

An aspect of hiking in Central America which surprises many North Americans, accustomed to vast protected wilderness areas, is that the hand of man is conspicuous in all but the most strictly protected national parks. This sounds like bad news, but in fact provides many delights. You will walk through pastures full of cows, pass under trees heavy with avocados or papayas, brush by coffee bushes, or stroll past a beach hut where the fisherman is setting out his day's catch to dry. You are never far from people: women run shyly past you on their way to market, men straighten from their stooping position to greet you before continuing to work their *milpas* (corn fields), gangs of children shout questions as they trudge to school, and old grannies mumble. Domestic animals are everywhere: pigs snuffle and root in the undergrowth, brahmin calves flick their lop-ears at your passing, and hysterical dogs burst from their huts at your arrival.

Here is a perfect balance to the national parks with their holiday-makers from the towns, gringo-naturalists, and all the wild nature that you came to see.

Hiking in the rainy season
By Rob Rachowiecki

Many people have vacations during the northern summer and so are obliged to hike during the wet season. Don't despair! You can go backpacking at this time and still enjoy yourself; once you're accustomed to the rain you'll find many advantages: few other hikers, friendlier villagers and green countryside. Your senses are heightened. The damp forest scenes are unforgettable. The huge, heavy tropical clouds make for spectacular sunsets and sunrises which you can almost touch and smell. And the turtle egg-laying season peaks in September, the wettest month in many areas. Here are some hints.

For day hikes you can start early in the morning, hike all day and return to a dry room at night. Carry your rain gear and if it rains, enjoy the fresh smell, the peeps of sun between the showers, and the rainbows.

On longer trips be patient. Only on the Caribbean side does it rain for days on end. The Central and Pacific areas often have dry days in the rainy season. Look in the newspapers for weather forecasts, or just sit it out. Study the weather patterns: in Costa Rica's Chirripó National Park, for instance, the rain falls only in the afternoon. During 13 days spent in the park it started to rain between 11.00 and 15.00, and then continued for the rest of the day; so getting up at dawn gives you six to ten hours of dry hiking.

A big problem when backpacking in the wet season is the extremely muddy state of the trails. Bring rubber boots, jungle boots, or even baseball boots — but not your best hiking boots. A little mud on your legs won't spoil your trip.

You don't want to tramp through humid wet jungles or up rainy mountains sweating profusely in waterproof clothing. There are several solutions. You can use breathable rain gear (Gore-Tex remains the best type) which allows most of your perspiration to escape. You can wear a rain poncho which is loose-fitting enough for you not to perspire greatly. Or you can wear your rain gear over underwear, or swimsuit, while your clothes stay nice and dry in a bag inside your pack. If you're sure you won't be exposed to high winds and cold temperatures, you could dispense with rain gear and have one set of 'wet' clothes and one set of 'dry' clothes. Remember that wool keeps its warmth even when wet, but cotton doesn't. The same distinction applies between down (useless when wet) and synthetics such as Polartec or dacron (warm when wet). The best clothing for cold, wet weather is artificial pile or fleece. Bring a wool or fleece hat and if you get chilly, wear it (70% of heat loss is from the head, although this includes the breath). Finally, if you don't want to be scrambling in and out of rain gear every time it showers, bring a collapsible umbrella! The combination of an umbrella over your upper body and waterproof trousers over your lower body works well in all but the most severe rain.

In the heat of the tropics wet clothes mildew very fast, so at the end of a hike, wash and dry your clothes thoroughly. Your tent must be completely waterproof. Some new tents are sold without sealed seams, so you may have to buy some seam sealant (from any good camping store) and do it yourself, or else it'll leak like a sieve in the first storm. The same applies to much raingear. Allow plenty of time for this before leaving on your trip. Alternatively you can try to spend each night in a village or mountain hut and not use the tent.

In damp weather using a stove is far preferable to trying to light a fire, but if you must have a fire, bring fire-starting ribbon, which is available in tubes such as toothpaste comes in. Remember those waterproof matches, or keep ordinary ones safe in a film canister.

Insects can be a problem during the wet season, so bring plenty of repellent and apply frequently and thoroughly.

Finding your way

In all the countries covered in this guide there's a National Geographical Institute from which you can buy maps, generally at a scale of 1:50,000, which are usually slightly out-of-date but adequate for most hikes. None of them mark national parks, forest reserves, or tourist sights, so you have to work out their location yourself. Guidebooks may still tell you that there are various bureaucratic hurdles such as obtaining permission from the head of the army, but in every case these are no longer valid.

Bear in mind that these maps do not compare in quality with those you're used to at home. It is hard to follow a particular trail since there's such a plethora of trails to choose from, so a compass and a reasonable command of Spanish are also useful. You'll find topographic features reliable, however, though many roads and dams will be missing. A map will tell you the direction in which to walk, the physical features you'll see along the way, and give you some idea of the distance between points. But you must still choose between a path made by a farmer on his way to his fields, or the long-distance routes for the transport of cargo, usually linking villages with a market town. The latter are the ones you want; droppings from pack animals are a good indication that you are on one of these trails, and many are now being converted into four-wheel-drive roads.

In the dry season you'll also need your topographical map for finding water. Generally speaking a blue line (often a broken line) marked *Quebrada* is a watercourse that is likely to be dry by the end of the dry season, while a *Río* is a river flowing all year round.

One of the best maps of the whole of Central America (at 1:1,800,000) is produced by International Travel Map Productions, of Vancouver BC, Canada. They also publish maps of Costa Rica and Guatemala & El Salvador (both at 1:500,000). In the UK these are distributed by Bradt and are available at Stanfords (Tel: 0171 836 1321) among other places. Locally produced maps are mostly at a scale of 1:50,000 (2cm:1km).

ACTIVITIES

Rafting

Rafting is an immensely popular feature of ecotourism in Central America: punters who wouldn't go near the nasty cold rivers of temperate climes will happily spend a day being soaked in warm water and tropical scenery. It's best established in **Costa Rica**, as you might expect, but other countries can also offer good runs. Rafting is possible somewhere in Costa Rica at any season, but the most popular area is around Turrialba, where most of the commercial operators have their bases. Almost every tour company in San José offers day trips here (subcontracted to these operators), but some excellent multi-day camping trips are also on offer.

The most popular river is the 145km Reventazón, and the most popular run the 20km from the Cachí dam Power House (*Casa Maquinas)* to Angostura (by Turrialba), which is graded as Class IV (lots of long difficult rapids) to Tucurrique and then Class III (plenty of world-class rapids, but suitable for beginners as if you go overboard you'll be washed into calmer deeper water between them). The next 24km to Peralta and Pascua are Class IV-V ('extremely difficult — long and very violent rapids', only possible in the low water season, from December to May). From there to the town of Siquirres (where the old and new Atlantic highways meet) is 23km of Class III-IV, and from there to the sea (although few people bother) is pretty tame. The 180km Río Pacuare runs through wilder scenery and is popular for camping trips: the upper part (from the Moravia road) is 15km of Class IV-V, and the lower (below Tres Equis/San Martin) is 25km of Class III-IV. The most exciting river in this area is the Guayabo, 15km of Class V white water; others here include the Pejivalle (or Pejibaye), Tucurrique and Orosí.

In the north of the country the rivers are less precipitous and ideal for leisurely floating and watching wildlife. The most popular are the Class I-II Río Corobici and the Río Sarapiquí (12km of Class III from La Virgen to Chilamate, then 12km of Class I-II to Puerto Viejo). There's also plenty of scope for kayaking in the tributaries of the Sarapiquí: Kayak Jungle Tours (Rancho Leona, La Virgen de Sarapiquí, Heredia; tel: 761 1019/710 6312) are the people to contact in this area. In the southwest, one of the world's best long-distance runs is the three-day trip down the Ríos Chirripó Pacifico and General from above San Isidro to Brujo, which is 75km of Class III-IV rapids — a hundred of them in the first 60km, ending with *Chacalaca*, a 6m standing wave. A far less well-known river in the same area is the Class II-III Río Savegre, flowing from the Cerro de la Muerte to the Pacific.

The best-established rafting company is Costa Rica White Water, owned by Costa Rica Expeditions; proprietor Michael Kaye pioneered most of the standard runs. Ríos Tropicales is at Calle 32, Avda 2, San José, just south of Paseo Colón/Apdo 471-1200 Pavas; tel: 233 6455, fax: 255 4354/Interlink #124, PO Box 526770, Miami, FL 33152, USA. Others to check out are River Treks (Calle 7, Avda 9, Apdo 3827-1000 San José; tel: 221 7940, fax: 222 8063), Costa Sol Rafting (Centro Cars Building, opposite the Hotel Corobici, Sabana Norte, Apdo 8-4390, 1000 San José; tel: 233 6664, fax: 233 6881) and Costaricaraft (Avda Central, Calles 33/35 no 51N/Apdo 10736-1000 San José; tel: 225 3939, fax: 253 6934), which is affiliated to Aventuras Naturales and EuroRaft.

Sea kayaking is another possibility: try High Tide Ocean Kayak Tours (tel: 777 0403), Iguana Tours (Centro Si Como No, Quepos; tel/fax: 777 1262/0574) or Costa Sol Rafting. The Golfo de Nicoya offers ideal sheltered conditions. There's an expats' Canoeing/Kayaking Group in San José — contact Jay Morrison (tel: 282 6697/6053). See also *The Rivers of Costa Rica: a Canoeing, Kayaking and Rafting Guide* by Michael Mayfield & Rafael Gallo (Menasha Ridge Press, Alabama 1988).

In **Panamá** companies in the capital run trips on the Río Chagres (class II, with a few class III rapids). The Collins family of the Hotel Panamonte in Boquete are planning rafting on the rivers of Chiriqui, flowing to the Pacific. In **Honduras** there's rafting near the main resorts on the north coast: the leading company is Ríos Honduras (Apdo 137, La Ceiba; tel/fax: 43 0780/in the USA 800 255 5784, or at the Caribbean Travel Agency, Edif Hermanos Kawas, Avda San Isidro) who offer day trips on the Río Cangrejal and in the Cuero y Salado Reserve, as well as a four-day trip down the Río Sico.

In **Guatemala** rafting is the best way to visit many of the Mayan ruins in the Petén and into Mexico along the Río Usumacinta (Class I-II). There's more exciting rafting on the Cahabón and Lanquín rivers, which are Class III-IV, with breaks at the unrunnable Chulac cataract and the hot springs of El Paraiso. In this same area is one of the more unusual options: rafting on the Río Candelaria right through the wonderful Candelaria caves and on down to the Río Chixoy. The easiest day trip is on the upper Río Motagua (Class II-III), just north of the capital, usually combined with a visit to the ruins of Mixco Viejo. Rafting is possible all year, but it's best from June to October. The leading operators are Maya Expeditions, but many smaller companies offer trips from Antigua.

Yachting
Yachting seems to be a bigger business in Guatemala than in Costa Rica, with

outfits like Aventuras Vacacionales (1 Avda Sur 11b Antigua; tel/fax: 320 563), Lago Grande Adventures (RR1 Union, Ontario N0L 2L0, Canada) and Timeless Tours (2304 Mass Ave, Cambridge, MA 02140, USA; tel: 800 370 0142) all offering trips on Lake Izabal and out to the Belize cays. In Costa Rica try Veleros del Sur (Apdo 13-5400, Puntarenas; tel: 661 1320, fax: 661 1119). Game-fishing is more popular in Costa Rica, especially out of ports such as Quepos and Tortuguero.

Diving and surfing
Diving (*submarinismo*) is also popular with big-budget visitors to Costa Rica: try Ecotreks (tel: 289 8191) or Diving Safaris (Hotel El Ocotal, Playa Ocotal, Guanacaste; tel: 670 0012). Budget travellers can generally only afford to dive in the Bay Islands of Honduras.

Windsurfing is big in a few specific areas, such as Lake Arenal, Costa Rica (Hotel Tilawa, Apdo 92, Tilarán, Guanacaste; tel: 695 5050, fax: 695 5766, among others), and Lakes Atitlán, Amatitlán and Izabal in Guatemala.

Surfing is also popular along the Pacific coasts of Costa Rica and El Salvador. In Panamá it's possible at Playa Venado, at the southern end of the Peninsula de Azuero.

Cycling
Cycling is, as anywhere, a great way to get around; the region is not huge, so it's possible to tour right through it and then put the bike on a plane home, and bikes have even been taken through the Darién Gap. There are millions of cycles in use through the region, both Chinese single-gear bikes and newer pseudo-mountain bikes, but they are only used locally; touring is almost unknown. The most up-to-date information is available in the South American Explorers Club's *Central and South American Bicycling Packet* (US$18 to members) — they also have a *Driving Packet* which includes motorcycling. See also Walter Sienko's *Latin America by Bike* (The Mountaineers, Seattle WA, 1993); and JP Panet's *Central America On Bicycle* (Passport, Champlain NY, 1987). In Panamá and Costa Rica roads are excellent and drivers relatively civilized; in Costa Rica there are plenty of Sunday cyclists, and the roads from San José to Cartago and up the Cerro de la Muerte can be pretty busy with bikes. Nicaragua is a bit rougher, and very hot, but buses have roof-racks, so you can always stop and get a ride. In Honduras the main highways have broad shoulders, and if the hills get too much you can put your bike on top of a bus, as also in Guatemala. The dirt roads of Costa Rica's Nicoya peninsula and Guatemala's Cuchumatane highlands offer particularly fine opportunities for mountain biking.

There are also, of course, plenty of companies hiring out mountain bikes and offering day rides, above all in Costa Rica and Guatemala. You can take a van to the top of Volcán Irazú and then roll down to Turrialba, which makes a good base for visiting Guayabo, CATIE and the Orosí valley as well. In Guatemala the main centre is Antigua, with a few bikes also available in Panajachel. One of the best is Mayan Mountain Bike Tours (6 Avda Sur 12b,

Antigua 03001; tel: 322 768, fax: 320 602), who offer everything from local trips around Antigua (US$15/half day, US$29/day), through tours of the Lake Atitlán area (US$80-100/day, with first-class accommodation) and of Tikal and into Belize, to rugged tours of the Cuchumatanes (US$50/day).

Others

Central America also offers fantastic **caving**: Honduras and Guatemala have huge areas of limestone where even the best-known caves have not been fully explored. In the west of the Sierra de Agalta are inaccessible sinkholes perhaps 100m deep by 500m wide, which have only been seen from the air. In Guatemala in particular huge portions of the maps are clearly marked 'karst', with all kinds of caves and sinks shown. Rick Finch (Box 5062 Tennessee Technical University, Cookeville, TN 38505, USA) is perhaps the leading authority on the caves of the region.

Horse riding is most easily available in Costa Rica, particularly in the posher suburbs of San José, such as Escazú, and at lodges on the lower slopes of the nearby volcanoes. Other possibilities are in the Monteverde and Lake Arenal areas; just ask around locally. In Panamá City ecotourism companies offer riding in the Chagres National Park; in Nicaragua, head for Selva Negra. In Honduras lots of kids around Copán offer horse-riding, although this is all far more informal and disorganised, and in Guatemala there's riding around Antigua: look on the noticeboard in Doña Luisa's.

What else? **Bungee jumping** is catching on in Costa Rica (Tropical Bungee, tel: 233 6455) and Guatemala (Maya Expeditions, tel: 562 551).

Paca

Part Two

THE GUIDE

64

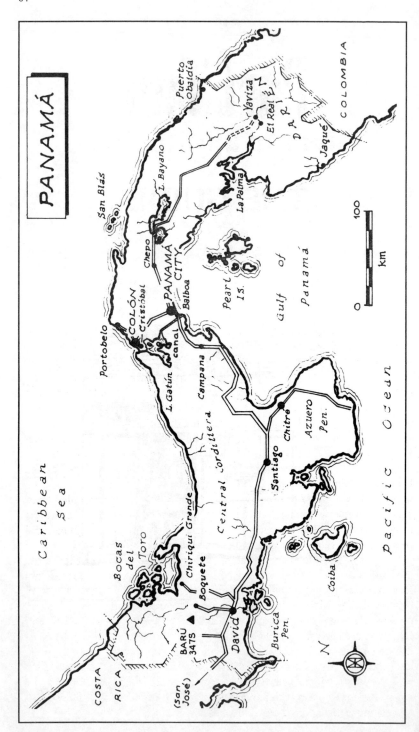

Chapter Six

Panamá
General Information

Panamá is the youngest country in Central America, both geologically and politically, most of it rising from the sea a mere three to five million years ago, and gaining independence (from Colombia) only in 1903. Its history is above all the history of its transport routes — first as the land bridge bearing humans and other mammals from North America to South America, and back again, and then as the route between Atlantic and Pacific oceans: and much of the best hiking in Panamá reflects this fact.

The route through the Darién Gap is the same as that taken by early man to South America, more recently by Kuna and Waunan Indians moving back northwards from Colombia, and nowadays by cocaine smugglers and would-be illegal immigrants to the USA. To the Spaniards, the Panamanian isthmus was the key to the silver and gold traffic from Peru to Spain: in 1519 they settled to the east of the present city, in the area now known as Panamá Viejo. Mule trains set out from here across the Puente del Rey (still to be seen) on the Camino Real (Royal Road), heading for the Atlantic coast, first to Nombre de Dios and then, when this proved indefensible, to Portobelo. The Atlantic ends of both of these routes can still be followed, although the growth of Panamá City and Lake Alajuela, which feeds the Canal, have smothered much of the rest of it. Later, in the early 17th century, the Spaniards used the Camino las Cruces, taking their bullion from Panamá to the Chagres River, and then on by boat to Fort San Lorenzo on the Atlantic. Part of this cobbled track survives in the Soberanía National Park and can be hiked. Then came the railway, and then the canal: much of their route now runs through national parkland, and we give an outline of a fine touristic route here.

Nowadays Panamá is one of the most ethnically diverse countries in the area and also one of the most prosperous, deriving most of its income not from agriculture and tourism like the others, but from the Canal and from banking: Canal tolls bring in US$369m a year (the record being US$141,088.61 paid by the *Regal Princess* in 1992), and US$100m is invested each year, largely in dredging. Seven of Central America's ten largest banks (and 23 of the 30 largest) are based in Panamá, and the secret of their success can be deduced from the fact that around US$1bn of dirty money is laundered each year. New laws against laundering have been passed, but in April 1995 a plot to kill Panamá's police chief and the national co-ordinator of the campaign against money laundering was discovered.

Money

The currency of Panamá is the US dollar. Yes, they're your actual greenbacks. But to show a little independence they call them balboas, and the small change is mostly in Panamanian centavos. Prices in the interior are sometimes quoted in *reales* (one *real* is five centavos). It's the most expensive country in Central America, though still cheaper than most South American countries.

Transport

Trains are more or less useless as a means of passenger transport: the Panamá Railroad was badly damaged in the 1989 US invasion and now only operates on Sundays between Panamá City and Summit. Buses go everywhere, with minibuses and pickups on the back roads; pensioned-off Greyhounds run every hour from the capital to David. In the capital itself there are plenty of buses on the main radial routes; the system is cheap but chaotic, and there's no way to get from one suburb to another without going into the centre and out again. Taxis are omnipresent in the city and carry a map showing the fare zones. The fastest way to reach the far ends of the country is by air, from the Paitilla airport in the east of the city; there are two internal airlines, Alas (tel: 23 9079) and Aeroperlas (tel: 69 4555/fax: 23 0606), both using mainly British aircraft. Their main routes are to David, Bocas del Toro and Changuinola, while Aeroperlas also flies to La Palma, El Real and Jaqué in Darién. AeroTaxi (tel: 64 8644) and Transpasa (tel: 26 0932) fly to the San Blas islands, and Parsa (tel: 26 3803) to Yaviza.

Maps

Good maps are available from the Instituto Geografico Nacional "Tommy Guardia", on Calle Tommy Guardia, just off Via Simon Bolivar immediately north of the university (open Mon-Fri 09.00-16.00).

Food

The national dishes are *sancocho*, a stew of chicken, yuca, corn, potatoes, plantain and onions with coriander, and *ropa vieja*, shredded beef with fried onions, garlic, tomato and green pepper. Another speciality is *carimañola*, a roll of ground boiled yuca filled with mince and boiled eggs, and fried. In cafés and snack bars you'll eat rice, eggs, *platanos* (plantains) and corn (perhaps in the form of *empanada*, like a Cornish pasty, or *tamale*, like a tortilla, with chicken or pork rolled inside, and boiled in a banana leaf). Pizza and Chinese food are widely available in towns.

Hotels

Hotels rarely cost less than US$6, but you get a few amenities for your money, such as soap, a towel and toilet paper.

Naturalists' Panamá

Much is heard about the wildlife riches of Costa Rica, currently one of the world's most popular destinations for ecotourism, but in fact Panamá has even more to offer, due to the country's position at the meeting point of North and South America. There are, perhaps, 15,000 species of flora of all types (including 1,200 orchids and 1,500 trees), 933 bird species (of which about 750 breed here), 225 mammals, 214 reptiles, 143 amphibians and 207 freshwater fish — a truly mind-boggling diversity.

However I have to admit that many of the South American species are found only in Darién. For example, in addition to the howler monkeys, spider monkeys and capuchins found throughout the region, there are South American types such as the tiny red-naped tamarin monkey (*mono titi/ Saguinus geoffroyi*) and the night monkey (*miriguoina/Aotus trivirgatus*), a nocturnal species with huge eyes, as well as squirrel monkeys (*mono ardilla/ Saimirii oerstedii*), which are found as far north as the Pacific lowlands of southern Costa Rica. Huge numbers of birds are only here for a day or two, passing through on their migrations, and they're much more visible here than further north, due to the funnelling effect of the isthmus.

The Mother Earth Party (*Movimiento Papá Egoró*) is the third largest party in Panamá (with 6 of 72 seats, enough to hold the balance of power); sadly, its success may come more from its leader Rubén Blades being the world's greatest *salsa* star than from its environmental policies.

Climate
The rainy season comes earlier to Panamá than to the rest of Central America, in mid-April. In fact it rains for most of the year on the Atlantic coast, which can receive up to 3,300mm a year — almost double the rainfall on the Pacific coast. In an intermediate zone, Lake Gatún is known for fog.

National parks
To visit Panamá's national parks, other than the Metropolitan Park in the heart of Panamá City and, de facto, the Sendero Charco and the Camino Las Cruces/Plantation Loop in the Soberanía Park, you should have a permit. This requires you to take (or send) a letter to the Director of Protected Areas Division (*Director Nacional Areas Protegidas*) of INRENARE (Apdo 2016, Paraíso, Panamá, Republica de Panamá), stating, in English or Spanish, which parks you want to visit, why and when. After two days you can return to collect your permits — take the Paraisó bus from Plaza Cinco de Mayo and get off when it turns right after the Paraisó Civic Center. The Protected Areas Division is upstairs in the old building, on the left. They can give you leaflets describing some parks: the library, in the first new block, can at least show you others (in Spanish). To head north to the Soberanía Park, the nearest *real* jungle to the city, walk back past the Civic Center and turn left down the dead end by the sports ground to reach the bus stop across the main road.

Ecotourism companies
Are also useful for information on the wilder parts of the country, such as Darién: contact EcoTours de Panamá, Calle Ricardo Arias 7, Apdo 465, Panamá 9 (tel: 63 3077/8, fax: 63 3089); Aventuras Panamá, Apdo 9869,

Panamá 4 (tel: 60 0044, fax: 60 7535); or Centro de Aventuras, Avda 5 Sur, Bella Vista, Apdo 6-4197, El Dorado, Panamá (tel: 27 6476, fax: 27 6477); in Boquete talk to Río Monte Tours at the Hotel Panamonte.

Ecological organisations

The leading conservation body in Panamá is ANCON, the *Asociación Nacional para la Conservación de la Naturaleza*, found on Calle 53, Bella Vista, Panamá City (Apdo 1387; tel: 64 8100; fax: 64 1836). It's involved in agroforestry and environmental education, and 3,000 volunteers work with Inrenare in the National Parks; more use to you, perhaps, is the library or *Centro de Documentación*, open from 0900 to 1630 Mondays to Fridays and to 1130 on Saturdays. The Smithsonian Institute (see below, under Barro Colorado) also has an excellent library. The Panamá Audubon Society (tel/fax: 24 4740, or tel: 52 1908) is not only a birdwatching club but is active in conservation generally. The *Fundación de Parques Nacionales y Medio Ambiente* (Apdo 6-6623 El Dorado, Panamá City; tel: 27 5370) is an umbrella for 25 environmental groups: it's known as *Fundación PANAMA*, naturally.

White-face capuchin

Chapter Seven

Central Panamá

PANAMÁ CITY

Generally known just as Panamá, this is the most diverse and lively city in the whole of Central America and one of the oldest, with a unique blend of races that has produced an impressive level of cultural tolerance, even if not every race has the same economic success. Its most historic areas, Panamá Viejo and Casco Viejo (San Felipe) lie near the extremities of the present city's 10km sweep along the coast. Its main axis starts as Avenida Central in Casco Viejo or the Old Compound, the Spaniards' second walled city, and follows a logical progression to Avenida Central España and then Via España as it heads east, heading eventually for Tocumen airport and Darién. Soon after leaving Casco Viejo a recently pedestrianised stretch forms the city's main shopping strip, and shortly after this it reaches Plaza Cinco de Mayo (5th May). East of here you'll find avenues with numbers (and names) roughly parallel to España, and numbered *calles* or streets running at right angles; to the west avenidas and calles have letters instead of numbers. The main banking area, with the best hotels and much of the tourist industry, is around España and Calle 50. Many of the city's more useful bus routes, including that to the airport, follow España, although in fact it is one-way for a while east of Plaza Cinco de Mayo, and you'll have to catch eastbound buses on Perú (Avenida 1a Sur or 1st Ave South).

Museums

The Natural Sciences Museum (Avda 2 Sur, Calle 29/30; Tues-Sat 09.00-16.00, Sun 13.30-16.30) is the usual collection of stuffed animals, although there's also a library of environmental information. The Anthropological Museum, in the old train station on Plaza Cinco de Mayo, is perhaps the best in town (Tues-Sun 09.30-16.15).

Tourist information

IPAT, the Panamanian Institute of Tourism, is hidden in the Atlapa Convention Centre on Vía Israel, opposite the Marriott Hotel — enter by an unmarked door on the north side. Once you find them they're very helpful and will give you a free booklet *Focus on Panamá*. The Panamá phone directory is also surprisingly useful.

Gear shops

There's a military surplus store, Army Force, at the east end of the pedestrianised section of Avda Central; also try the Central Market near the Presidential Palace, and the Supermercado El Rey on Via España.

NEAR THE CANAL

Panamá boasts some of the world's best and most easily accessible rainforest, largely thanks to the Canal, and many sites of outstanding interest to naturalists and bird watchers can easily be visited as day-trips from the city. In the early years of this century the Canal authorities evicted settlers because it was thought that 'jungle' provided the perfect defensive barrier; later it was realized that in fact it's very easy to move through the forest and so banana plantations and cattle grazing were encouraged. Nowadays however, the priority is to protect the watershed of the Canal and its main reservoir, Lago Alajuela (Madden Dam), by preventing erosion and deforestation, and much of it is preserved as national park.

You should of course start by taking one of the orange buses from the Canal Area terminal at Plaza Cinco de Mayo to Miraflores Locks, where the main Canal Visitor Centre is situated; after learning all about this amazing phenomenom, you can continue north to Paraíso for your National Park permits (see *Chapter Six* above), or take either a Chilibre bus (one of the gaudy city buses) to the Camino Las Cruces, or an orange Gamboa bus to the Summit Botanical Gardens, the Plantation Loop, the Sendero El Charco, or the Pipeline Road.

The **Summit Gardens** were founded in 1923 as an experimental station and now contain 15,000 species of plants from all the tropical regions of the world, as well as a small zoo of Latin American animals. There are plenty of wild birds as well, making it a lovely place to stroll for a day; however it can be crowded at weekends. In early 1995 the Panamá Railroad, damaged in the 1989 invasion, reopened with a Sundays-only service from Panamá City to Summit (via Miraflores and Paraíso); its name in fact derives from its position at the point where the railway crosses the Continental Divide.

Soberanía National Park

The most accessible National Park is Soberanía, along the east side of the Canal beyond the Summit Gardens. It is currently being developed, with a new Environmental Education Centre at Gamboa, and new trails being created. This is moist tropical forest with an average of 3,000mm of precipitation per year, and at least 3,000 species of plant and 561 animals; in addition to rainforest standards such as giant figs, guayacan and ceiba, you'll also see trees more commonly found in dry forest, such as *indio desnudo, guanacaste* and *capulín blanco*.

In theory you need a permit from Paraíso or from the park headquarters in Gamboa to visit this park, but in practice the route described here along the **Las Cruces Trail** and the **Plantation Loop** is open without formalities. Buses to Chilibre will drop you at the start of the Las Cruces Trail, marked by an ancient Spanish cannon (just beyond a layby and dirt road to the left). It takes about three hours to reach the Gamboa Highway from here.

The cobbled colonial road from Panamá City emerges from impenetrable jungle on the right/south and continues past a picnic shelter and bad toilets to the north. It starts as a good trail cleared by leaf-cutter ants and echoing with the constant chainsaw screech of millions of other insects, but soon passes below a power line and gets narrower; it climbs for 20 minutes, latterly in a narrow twisting cutting. Here it's easy to imagine the feelings of the Spanish guards, sweltering in their armour in the humid and alien jungle and constantly fearing an attack by English buccaneers; being seadogs, these were mostly likely to attack on the Río Chagres, but there was always a chance of their doing the unexpected and ambushing the mule train. In both 1671 and 1681 Henry Morgan came this way to sack Panamá Viejo, just as Drake had come along the Camino Real in 1573. Columbus himself sailed up the Chagres in 1502 on his last voyage, but didn't know that a bit of hiking would have brought him to the Pacific. On a lighter note, the trail is now lined by mango trees, a species introduced by the Spanish, showing exactly where they bared their bottoms.

Two minutes after the top of the hill turn left over a bridge, and after 15 minutes ignore a cobbled path to the left, which leads only to a watering point. The trail continues parallel to the stream for a couple of minutes and then crosses it; take the left-hand path, which climbs to the west. After 20 minutes swing left from a stream bed, and climb for five minutes. After another five or so minutes duck under some bamboos (marked with a red ribbon) and turn left onto a gravel track; this is the Sendero del Pisbae, which runs southwest from the Transisthmica highway. You can continue on the Camino Las Cruces, dropping down to the Río Chagres, but unless you arrange for a boat to pick you up you'll have to return to this point.

The track climbs steadily to cross an overgrown meadow and continues in fine forest; eventually it drops down a valley with a stream (the Río Chico Masambi) below to the right. This is the Plantation Road, now blocked by fallen trees but well walked; after about an hour and three-quarters you'll reach asphalt about 100m from the Gamboa Highway. Less than 2km left/south are the Summit Gardens, and about 1km to the right/north is the **Sendero El Charco** (the Pond Path), an easy nature trail.

If you take the bus all the way to Gamboa, you can take a much longer and wilder hike into the Soberanía Park on the **Pipeline Road** (*Camino del Oleoducto* or *Tuberia*). This is a disused 18km dirt road passing through humid forest with plenty of streams and several camping spots. It's known for its superb birding: the Panamá Audubon Society has recorded 380 species in one weekend here, a world record. It's best to camp overnight, as relatively few birds are active after 09.00. You should get permission at Building 4 in Gamboa (tel: 32 4325; Mon-Fri 08.00-15.00).

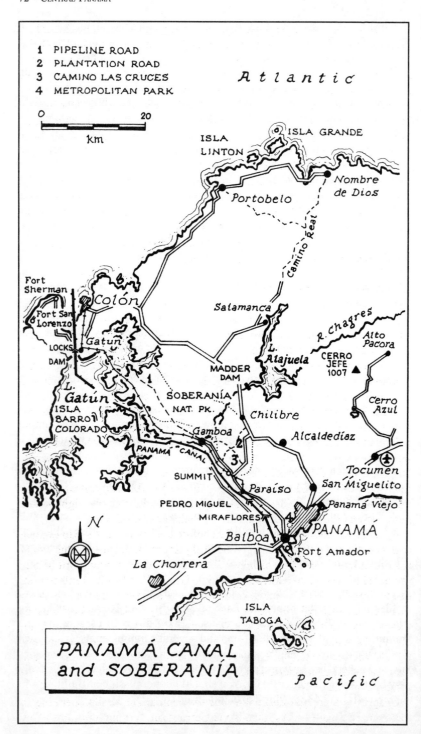

1 PIPELINE ROAD
2 PLANTATION ROAD
3 CAMINO LAS CRUCES
4 METROPOLITAN PARK

0   20
km

Atlantic

ISLA GRANDE
ISLA LINTON
Nombre de Dios
Portobelo
Camino Real
Fort Sherman
Colón
Fort San Lorenzo
Salamanca
R. Chagres
Alto Pacora
Gatún
L. *Alajuela*
CERRO JEFE 1007
LOCKS
DAM
L. *Gatún*
MADDER DAM
ISLA BARRO COLORADO
SOBERANÍA NAT. PK.
Chilibre
Cerro Azul
Gamboa
PANAMÁ CANAL
Alcaldediaz
SUMMIT
Tocumen
San Miguelito
Paraíso
PEDRO MIGUEL
MIRAFLORES
Panamá Viejo
Balboa
PANAMÁ
N
Fort Amador
La Chorrera
ISLA TABOGA

PANAMÁ CANAL
and SOBERANÍA

Pacific

To get here, get off the bus where it turns right onto Morrow Boulevard (if the train is running to Gamboa again, turn left out of the station and walk for five minutes to reach this point); continue along the Canal for ten minutes, then swing right onto a dirt road beyond a pond (where muscovy ducks and tiger herons may be seen at dusk). After seven minutes take the first right, and you'll soon reach a barrier where the Pipeline Road heads into the jungle. In the first couple of kilometres you'll see two forks: take a right at each. You'll be constantly crossing streams on wooden bridges — there's one about every kilometre. After the fifth one, over the Río Limbo, a trail leads 100m to the right to an excellent camping spot.

Shortly beyond this the road passes from secondary into old-growth forest and begins to rise and fall more. There's little traffic as the road is in a bad state with plenty of fallen trees, and so the wildlife is plentiful. The road continues without any other special features for another dozen kilometres to Lake Gatún, where you can camp. The insects aren't terribly bad, but there are always a few around, so bring repellent.

Chagres National Park

The **Camino Real** was and is a much more ambitious undertaking than the Camino Las Cruces, running due north from Panamá Viejo all the way to the Atlantic. Much of the southern half has been lost, but to the north of Lago Alajuela some is protected in the Chagres National Park, considerably wilder and wetter than Soberanía. There's very moist tropical forest, very moist premontane forest, and premontane rainforest here. To hike it you should take a Colón bus to the Salamanca turning and then a local bus or pickup towards Salamanca. You need to get out where the bus turns right about one and a half kilometres before Salamanca, and continue across the Río Salamanca to the Río Boquerón; a dirt road follows this to an old manganese mine, from where the trail continues upstream and up to the the Continental Divide, which it crosses at little more than 300m. Almost at once you pick up the Río Nombre de Dios, which leads you down to the road just west of the village of Nombre de Dios. You'll have to camp for at least one night on this hike, which used to be done annually by Panamá's Boy Scouts.

A harder variant would be to fork left before the Divide, up the Río Longue and then down the Río Cascajal to the road just east of Portobelo; this would require at least two nights camping. The coastal forest around Portobelo is protected by a national park; this is also on UNESCO's World Heritage List, due to Portobelo's 18th century fortifications. However since the late 1970s this area has suffered from severe deforestation by settlers from the west of the country; now there is some reforestation and environmental education taking place, and at Puerto Lindo, between Portobelo and Nombre de Dios, there's a centre for rehabilitating birds and animals seized from smugglers. You can visit, but do phone 41 5233 in advance; they also have a refuge just offshore on Isla Linton.

Chagres is a popular destination for the ecotourism outfits operating in Panamá. The main access route is via Cerro Azul, turning left/north a few kilometres east of the Tocumen airport; the 4WD road climbs past Cerro Jefe (1,007m, with a microwave tower on top) to the Alto Pacora coffee plantation. Here you can hike on nature trails, go horse-riding, or even (with Aventuras de Panamá) ride to the Río Piedras and then take a raft down this river and the Río Chagres to Lago Alajuela. There's good bird-watching on Cerro Jefe, in dwarf forest with some endemic palm species. It's also possible to go by boat to Choco-Embera villages to see their culture and buy handicrafts — a bit touristy, but the lack of road access keeps them relatively untainted. These people are not actually native to this area, having moved here from Darién.

OTHER POSSIBILITIES NEAR PANAMÁ CITY

The **Parque Nacional Metropolitano** is widely visited as a rare example of tropical forest within a a major city. It is composed largely of lowland semi-deciduous forest, a habitat which has largely vanished along the Pacific coast. The dominant species is *Cavanillesia platanifolia* (*cuipo*), a tall straight deciduous tree reaching 30-40m in height; others include *Tabebuia rosea* (an oak), cedar, *guanacaste* (known here as *corotú*), indio desnudo and palms such as *Acrocomia panamensis*. Fauna includes the Titi monkey (*mono titi/ Saguineus geoffroyi*; found mainly in South America), both types of sloth, anteaters and iguanas, which can easily be seen sunbathing on branches if you get there early in the morning. The park is officially open from 09.00 to 15.00 except on Mondays, but there's nothing to stop you going in as early as you like. In fact from January to March there are guided tours at 08.30 on Saturdays and Sundays.

Access is by the Curundu bus; get off where it turns left off Calle de la Amistad and walk a few hundred metres northeast along Avenida Juan Pablo II to reach the visitor centre. You have to continue along the road to reach the trails; the interpretative trail (which in fact offers no information at all) goes to the left and loops back to join the Mono Titi Road just below a hilltop lookout.

The island of **Barro Colorado** is probably the most intensely scrutinised 1,560 hectares anywhere in the world. It's a biological reserve run by the Smithsonian Institution, and at least 1,500 dissertations have been based on studies here! The island was formed as Lago Gatún filled during the building of the canal, and was left with a very rich population of fauna that fled there as the surrounding area was flooded. However, a gradual process of species loss is now under way, illustrating what happens whenever an area of forest is isolated.

A visit here is excellent preparation for hiking the Darién Gap, as well as being a fascinating experience in itself. A day of wandering around the island's back trails, picking ticks off yourself, tripping over roots, sliding down hills and sweating profusely would be an ideal way of deciding whether you're really ready for the Gap.

Animal and bird viewing is better here than in most other protected areas in Central America; there are several completely tame creatures that roam at large, such as the tapir which crashes through the undergrowth like a small tank. The vegetation is splendid, semi-evergreen tropical moist forest with an amazing variety of species, at least 365 trees and 171 lianas. The eastern third of the island and some of the northern promontories were deforested before 1905 and still appear to be evolving towards their climax stage. We found the rainforest so engrossing we missed the boat back, thus giving ourselves a view of the dusk activities of various animals, and hearing a chorus of howler monkeys.

The staff had warned us about ticks, even told us about their life cycle, but nothing could have prepared us for the reality. We would suggest that you bring a complete change of clothes and a towel, as well as insect repellent. When you return from your explorations, you'll have to spend some time de-ticking, showering and changing into tick-free clothes. It's perfectly acceptable behaviour to check your body for ticks while discussing esoteric scientific matters with the residents.

Visits must be arranged with the Smithsonian Tropical Research Institute in the Tapper Building in Ancón, opposite the Legislative Assembly (tel: 27 6022, fax: 62 6084); they are allowed on Tuesdays and Saturdays only and cost around US$20. You'll need to catch the 0600 bus to Gamboa, where a boat meets you. Visits can also be arranged through Eco-Tours de Panamá. When you reach the island and climb the long steps from Laboratory Cove up to the central lodge you'll be given a welcome, a map and an invitation to lunch. There's a complex 37km network of paths, mostly radiating out from the Laboratory Clearing and Tower Clearing (the island's highest point, 140m above the lake) and running down to the shores. These all have markers every 100m, so that scientists can pinpoint their position in a way that's impossible in wilder settings.

The Smithsonian also has a Marine Biology Research Station on the Amador causeway, south of Balboa at the entrance to the Canal, and a useful library in the Tapper Building (Mon-Fri 08.00-16.00).

Chapter Eight

Western Panamá

Panamá's first national park was founded in 1966 in the **Altos de Campana**, just north of the PanAmerican Highway, 60km west of Panamá City. For many years it existed on paper only, with no rangers or funding; nowadays it is in a better state, but there is still much to be done to protect it from squatter farmers who now occupy 500 of its 4,816 hectares. The surviving parts of the park are moist tropical forest, moist premontane forest and tropical montane forest, with an average of 2,700mm of rain per year, a variety of conifers and 176 species of birds, including tanagers, pygmy-tyrants, the orange-bellied trogon and the yellow-eared toucanet. There are few large mammals remaining (nothing bigger than collared peccaries and red brocket deer), but you may see some opossums or bats.

The park can be reached by a 10km road from the PanAmerican Highway (turning right opposite some ornamental gates at about km59, as the road goes over a crest); this passes the ranger station, where you can get information and may be able to sleep. At Las Uvas (km97) another road turns north to the pleasant hill resort of El Valle de Anton, and I chose to hike to the Altos de Campana from here; this is a two-day hike through attractive settled countryside, crossing a few steepish ridges but staying south of the main mountain ridge.

El Valle is a scattered resort set in an extinct volcanic caldera at 600m altitude; it's known particularly for its superb oranges (so plentiful in season that you can just pick them up from the ground) and its Sunday morning market, which attracts day-trippers from the capital. There are also hot springs, impressive petroglyphs, and a 35m waterfall. More bizarrely, it boasts square-trunked trees and an endemic species of orange and black frogs (*Atelopus varius*), also supposedly found in the Altos de Campana park. There are buses more or less hourly from the capital and various places to stay, from the *Pension Niña Dalia* at US$8 upwards.

From the southern rim of the caldera (get off at the 'Canada Dry' bus shelter at about km16) you can walk west to the radio towers and beyond to a cross on Cerro Guacamayo (807m); this is an open grassy ridge with great views south to the Pacific and north to the Continental Divide. The northern side is forested, but there's said to be a path from the waterfall (El Chorro Macho or the Strong Spout) east to the Cerro Gaital, the highest peak on this side. To the west you can see La India Dormida (the Sleeping Indian Girl), so called because of its silhouette. To get here, walk along Avenida Central to the Casa el Valle shop, turn left past the Cabañas Potosí to follow the Río Anton to the point where it leaves the caldera, and then climb to the right to a chapel and follow the ridge back north.

In Chiguri Arriba, to the north (bus or pickup from Penonomé), the Posada del Cerro Viejo (tel: 23 4553, fax: 69 2328) is said to offer hiking trips through the hills to El Valle, or hiking and canoe trips to the Caribbean coast.

El Valle to Altos de Campana

The hike from El Valle to Altos de Campana starts at the Hotel Campestre, El Valle's best (15 minutes walk north of the Hotel El Greco on Avenida Central). There are a few square trees in its grounds, and some captive golden frogs just outside the gate. Turn left at the hotel entrance and then go right and right again around the hotel grounds; this is an asphalt road that climbs for 20 minutes, then drops for ten minutes to the village of Mata Ahogado. A track continues north up the valley of the Río Mata Ahogado, getting rougher and

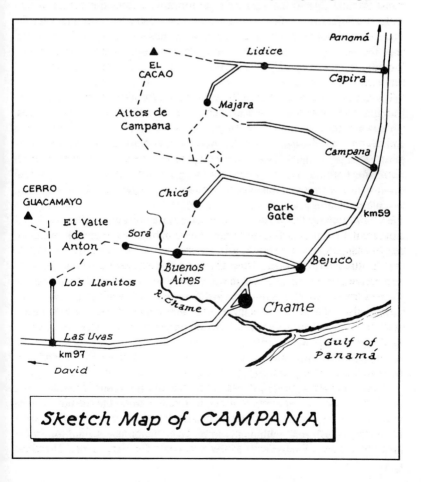

Sketch Map of CAMPANA

swinging to the east; after almost 20 minutes it passes the last kiosk and ends at a stream. A good path continues on the other side through well-irrigated tomato fields; after five minutes climb fork right and climb much harder for another five minutes to reach the watershed, at just over 800m.

Just beyond the ridge you should fork left and drop down to the northeast and then to the east, into the Río de Jesús valley. Fork right after about seven minutes, to drop into the woods and cross a good stream; the path climbs to pass a house and then continues down the valley, passing through an impressive gorge, which might be a bit tricky in the wet season, after 30 minutes. The path heads south, crossing and recrossing the river, but the main route is always clear enough; after ten minutes it climbs to the right and becomes a jeep track. After another ten minutes turn left to drop down to cross the Río de Jesús; to the right at this junction it's only about 2km south to Los Llanitos on the main road to El Valle.

After climbing for about five minutes the route forks left and climbs east for another ten minutes to cross another watershed (at just over 700m) into the Río Teta valley. An excellent smooth path continues along the ridge, and then drops to cross a stream after ten minutes. Heading east, after another ten minutes you pass through a gate (just before a useful shortcut down to the left) and then follow a fence to the left; beyond this are some interesting-looking hills, but there's a way to go yet. Keep left for 15 minutes; after this I turned right, but I think the other route would also lead to La Laguna, the next village. I climbed to the north for five minutes, crossed a stream, and after 15 minutes turned left to cross another stream and then climbed steadily for ten minutes.

Here you turn left onto a dirt road which leads north into Laguna Grande: turn right and right again past the kiosk and follow the road for ten minutes across a valley to the foot of a steep cliff. The road continues north to a small reservoir, but your route follows a zigzagging path up to the right, which climbs steeply for ten minutes and then more easily onto an open ridge with horses and cattle grazing; you're at about 900m here, just south of Cerro Picacho (1,049m). On the far side of the ridge there's a great view south and east, with Sorá, the next major village east, visible above the wide valley of the Río Maria that lies below you.

From the viewpoint you can either drop straight down an obvious shortcut or head south to the next ridge and curve down to join the shortcut just before a spring. Turn right after ten minutes to follow a good path down to the southeast through the village of El Picacho and then straight on across a blasted heath; after 20 minutes without a single junction turn right through a fence towards Sorá, and drop down to reach the river in 15 minutes. There's a suspension bridge and plenty of flat sandy ground; if you can get here (about eight hours from El Valle) it's a great place to camp, with no-one around.

Continuing, the path up to Sorá climbs steeply for about 25 minutes and then more easily for another 20 minutes, looping around to the north of the village before at last turning right on to a track and entering Sorá. From here there's an asphalt road with plenty of pickups, which you should follow for about 8km to a point just west of Buenos Aires. The path north up to Chicá and the national park begins at just over 200m on a hairpin bend about 50m west of the Finca Los 30 Hermanas. After about 20 minutes there's an interesting small petroglyph in the middle of the path; after another half-hour of steady climbing you reach a couple of streams, and it takes another 20 minutes to reach the village, at almost 600m.

Turn right/east here up the road and keep climbing: the road curves left through dry scrubby land past some radio masts, and after 30 minutes reaches a junction. A track turns left and the road curves right, but you should go straight ahead up a path towards the main Intel radio masts, about 15 minutes away. A path passes to the left of the masts to join a dirt road that leads into the trees and the park.

There are some nice houses around here, mostly weekend homes for Canal staff, but there were once many more: a resort for the wealthy of Panamá was built here in (introduced) Honduran pines in 1948. When this closed, the Smithsonian Institute managed to persuade General Torrijos to create a national park, and since then the forest has reclaimed its territory, although you'll still come across the resort's water tanks and pipes.

To the right beyond the first two houses is an interpretative path, which loops around to join the road; from *estación 2* there's a path up to Cerro Campana (947m) and on to a viewpoint marked by a cross, from where you can see both Lake Gatún to the east and the Pacific to the south. However, I spent another day hiking northwest through the park, out to the north and around to the town of Campana to the east: this is a long way to go for little more than an hour in the real forest, and you may well prefer to go in and come out the same way.

The route into the heart of the Park starts very inconspicuously about 50m before the last house on the 4WD road, perhaps ten minutes after entering the forest. Take a tiny path up to the right by some boulders and a dry stream; in five minutes you'll reach a yellow National Park sign on a ridge, where you should turn left/north. This is a narrow, little-used path through good jungle which climbs up and down steeply, although you have a general sense of following a ridge (the Cordillera de Lloron). After ten minutes you reach a peak with a bit of a view to the northwest, and after a steep slippery descent turn right at a big tree. In about quarter of an hour you'll swing more to the west and begin to drop into more open forest (on a rather better path); another quarter of an hour brings you to a junction with another yellow National Park sign. From here it should be possible to continue westwards into the western half of the Park, but I couldn't find a trail which kept going — every one seemed to be a poacher's path which died out before long. In theory it shouldn't take too long to get beyond Cerro los Monos (Monkey Peak, 893m) to the headwaters of the Río Trinidad, which you can follow north to Trinidad Abajo and El Cacao, from where you can get a pickup west to Lidice and the PanAmerican. There's also a more intrepid two- or three-day hike from El Cacao north through largely unsettled rainforest to Ciri and Boca Río Indio on the Atlantic coast, from where you can take a bus east to Colón.

The other route takes you down to the northeast (across a large ants' nest) and after just five minutes out of the forest and into scrub; at least you finally get a good view to the northeast. You'll drop down through long grass and after ten minutes turn left onto the path from a squatter's hut. This follows a ridge and then drops to reach the Río Capira after 15 minutes; there's a good patch of forest here, with monkeys and plenty of colourful butterflies. The path follows the valley for ten minutes but then climbs up to the left into a field, across a stream, past a solitary machete-scarred tree and through a gate after about 15 minutes. The path continues up and to the left and into the next valley, mostly cleared for cattle-grazing. It crosses two streams and then heads down the left bank of the second before crossing it and then zigzagging down into a big boulder-strewn field, 20 minutes from the gate. From here you could continue north to the village of Majara, just below, and then hike on to Lidice, where you should be able to find a pickup to Capira and the PanAmerican. However, I chose to climb over the hill to the right/southeast (the Loma Nuñeco), to regain the Capira valley and the shorter route out to Campana; eventually no doubt a path will develop all the way down this valley, but it certainly didn't exist in early 1995. Lidice, incidentally, is named after the Czech village obliterated by the Nazis in World War II: across the world towns and villages changed their names so that the memory of Lidice would live on.

To climb the hill, take the main path across the stream and turn right at a gate to climb up through a field. There are plenty of cattle paths that gradually coalesce into one, rising to a shoulder and then to its right to reach a gate in a barbed-wire fence, just below the ridge, in 20-25 minutes. There's another gate on the other side, leading into some squatted fields. Heading downhill, pass through a gate between two machete-scarred trees: when I was here the next field was *very* overgrown and required serious scrub-bashing for maybe ten minutes to reach its bottom left-hand corner. From here head slightly to the right to reach a gate below a large low spreading tree: with any luck this will all be clear and straightforward when you pass through. At any rate, from here on there is an excellent path down the valley to the left. After 15 minutes the path climbs to the left, then swings back to the right, passing a large abandoned house after ten to 15 more minutes and reaching a T-junction below a model farm in another 25 minutes. Two minutes to the left you'll reach the asphalt and enter Campana; it's 15 minutes more to the PanAmerican Highway, where you can catch a bus in either direction.

Volcán Barú

The chain of volcanoes that runs through Central America comes to an end in western Panamá, where there is only one substantial volcano, Barú. At 3,475m this is by far the highest peak in the country and offers great views from ocean to ocean. It can be pretty wild, with between 2m and 4m of rain per year and winds of up to 170km/h; it's largely covered with various types of moist montane forest and rainforest, and marks the southern limit of the ranges of both the resplendent quetzal and (at the summit) the volcano junco. It's a particularly attractive destination because the base is the very friendly and relaxing little town of Boquete; at 1,060m this has a cool, damp climate and very fertile volcanic soil. It's reached by taking the express bus from Panamá to David and then a local bus (every half-hour) up to Boquete, an hour north. The most expensive hotel is the **Panamonte**, which has been in the ecotourism business for many years, but for many budget travellers the **Pensión Marilós** is the best place to stay in all Panamá. There are good restaurants and a laundry as well. Most visitors simply hike up the 4WD road to the radio masts at the top and back again, but it's possible to descend to the west and either pick up a bus south or, as described here, hike back to Boquete from Cerro Punta around the north side of the volcano. An early start is essential if you want to go down the far side, and you'll need to camp. The route from Cerro Punta is not always obvious and you shouldn't take this route if you're not used to getting lost and having to backtrack. **Río Monte Tours** (at the Panamonte, tel: 70 1327) can provide a guide for this hike.

It's possible to get to the top of Barú by 4WD vehicle, either hitching a ride early in the morning with Intel staff, or by booking a trip (for about US$120) with Río Monte Tours; Frank at the Marilós (who speaks perfect English) may help you find a cheaper ride. Certainly you'll be able to get to the end of the asphalt in one of the *Zona Urbana* minibuses that cruise around the plantation roads; make sure the driver knows where you're going, and he should let you off where he turns right to the Finca Lerida. The finca is worth a visit in itself: it's owned by the Collins family of the Hotel Panamonte and is well known to bird watchers in pursuit of quetzals and other montane species. There are also shared pickup taxis that have been known to give hikers a free ride if they happen to be going up the hill anyway.

If you choose or are forced to walk all the way, you should leave town by heading north up the main street and turning west on Calle 2a Norte, the second left after the Roman Catholic church. After one block you'll pass a National Park sign and start to climb through coffee plantations, worked by Guaymí Indians, the women in maternity-style dresses with appliqué decorations. The asphalt ends about five minutes beyond the right turn to Finca Lerida, about 8km from Boquete (with about 13km to go); it's just a couple of minutes more to the Park gate, where you're asked to sign in and perhaps show your permit.

From here on you're in the forest, on a steep, rough road with a surface that offers very little traction for mountain bikes. There are increasing quantities of creepers, bromeliads and ferns; there are also a few side tracks leading to huts so there's probably water around, though not along the road. Cloud and haze permitting, there are also great views. After almost an hour we passed a gate, from where it's at least 80 minutes to a sign marking (for some unknown reason) *Curva Ratón* (Mouse Curve). After another 25 minutes you reach a path left to a viewpoint over the *Potrero Muleto* (Mule Pasture); from here on both trees and breath get shorter. Fortunately (or not) there's a dip, and then you climb on; after 25 minutes or more you'll pass a sign to the right to *La Nevera* (The Icebox) and soon after see the radio masts at last! There's another, bigger, drop and again you climb on, now through dwarf forest; birds here include timberline wrens, silky flycatchers and large-footed finches. After

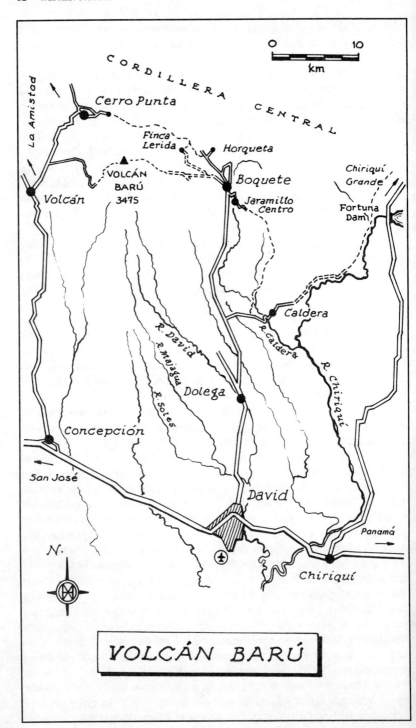

VOLCÁN BARÚ

almost another hour there's a sign left to the campsite (no water), and after another 25 minutes you'll finally crawl up to the masts. Alas, it takes another ten minutes (on a path along the crater edge) to reach the highest point, marked by a cross and a geodesic point. We took four and a half hours from the Park gate, but you should allow at least six from there, eight or nine from Boquete; remember that you have to gain over 2,400m, although from the town the mountain looks remarkably squat.

The main crater (of seven) is to the right; a steep and tricky little path that drops left into the dwarf trees *just* on the summit side of the Intel compound leads down to the south crater, although you could cut across from the crater to the route down to the Cerro Punta road. The direct path starts just before the final graffiti-painted scramble to the summit; if you're feeling tired it may be a bit tricky at first but soon gets easier. The craggy outlet from the south crater is also steep and fiddly; there's a cable to help in places, but in any case it's impossible not to kick loose a few chunks of the mountain. After an hour and ten minutes I entered short trees and the shade of a low escarpment, and progress got a bit easier and faster. After 20 minutes there's a camping area, but in the dry season there was no water.

The path climbs up to a low ridge and along to its end; it drops steeply to the left, but is increasingly obstructed with fallen trees. An hour after passing the campsite I emerged from the trees, crossing a broad but dry stream and turning left to follow it downstream. In five minutes I reached a spring, with a pipe feeding a cattle trough; you can camp here or further on down the valley, depending on progress, but if it's windy you're better off here. A track continues, curving left and then climbing back up to a plateau; you can take a short-cut to the right. It crosses another track 25 minutes from the spring and continues as a gravel road; in the right (or rather wrong) weather this was at first reminiscent of the walk-out along a Scottish stalking track, but it then passed through the local tip, before reaching the road after 40 minutes at a sign reading *Parque Nacional Volcán Barú*.

Buses run every half-hour between David and Cerro Punta; 4km to the left/ south of this junction they pass through the small town of Volcán, with a couple of reasonably affordable hotels. Heading north, the road is soon climbing up the steep attractive valley of the Río Chiriquí Viejo into an area known as 'Little Switzerland' due to the influence of settlers from Switzerland and the then Yugoslavia. The luxury **Hotel Bambito** is opposite a trout hatchery in the middle of nowhere; in Nuevo Suiza, just south of Cerro Punta, there are some cheap cabins for rent (as well as one owned by the Panamá Audubon Society), and in Cerro Punta there's a small hotel.

To begin the hike back to **Boquete**, stay on the bus and get off just north of the town, immediately after a small bridge (just below the 2,000m contour), at the turning to the village of Bajo Grande. Follow this road up to the right/east, passing through the village in ten to 15 minutes; the asphalt swings right and ends 25 minutes from the junction. A 4WD track continues, often lined with sacks of potatoes and carrots: the combination of the misty weather and fertile volcanic soil makes this one of the most productive areas of Panamá. The track climbs, seems to be running into some cliffs but zigs on up to reach a pass at about 2,460m after 50 minutes more. The track ends here, with a couple of houses up to the right, and a path leads on under a fallen tree, past a National Park sign and into the cloud forest. This soon becomes remarkably small and overgrown; after 30 minutes you should not go up above a large tree which has fallen down the slope, but below it and then east of south down a ridge, through more mature open forest. You'll pass through a logged area and down to pasture in a valley bottom, where you'll find a hut and a stream, about 45 minutes from the pass.

From here you essentially have to follow the valley to Boquete; there's a path up to the left at the end of the pasture, which leads through forest to cross a stream and reach a hut in a clearing (signposted as the *Ruta Alianza* picnic area) after 50 to 60 minutes. You have to cross back across the stream, just below its confluence with the Río Caldera, and then cross it again, by a log bridge this time, after 20 minutes. The path becomes a track and climbs to pass through small-holdings and reach the Park's Alto Chirico station after 30 minutes; from here it drops way down into the Caldera valley and follows it downstream. After 35 minutes turn left onto the asphalt road (if doing this hike in reverse, turn right on a left bend; the second building on the right should have bright orange gates). Continuing down the valley, the road crosses a bridge to the left bank after about 12 minutes, with some good cliffs on the right bank. You'll pass a side bridge from the right bank after 20 minutes, and then meet a road from Horqueta, to the left/east, after 15 more. Here both road and river swing right through a small narrow gorge; the road soon crosses to the right side, meets a road from Alto Quiel (to the west) and then another from Lino (to the east), and continues south to Boquete, about 5km or almost an hour's walk from the Horqueta junction.

From Cerro Punta you can also reach PILA, the **Parque Internacional La Amistad** or International Friendship Park. Extending along the Cordillera de Talamanca well into Costa Rica, this preserves perhaps the largest surviving area of primary forest in Central America, and one of the areas of greatest biodiversity in the region. Facilities are better on the Costa Rican side, but here they are distinctly unsophisticated, which is all for the best. From Cerro Punta a 4WD road is signposted to the Panamanian Park headquarters about 7km away at Los Nubes, where you'll find a couple of interpretative trails, after which you're on your own. There's good bird-watching here too, with resplendent quetzals, black guans, hummingbirds and many other cloudforest species.

El Camino Tres de Noviembre
by Peter Sterling
This is a rugged three-day hike across the *Cordillera Central* of northwestern Panamá, from Chiriquí province to the Caribbean coast of Bocas del Toro province. You'd be best off hiring a guide, in Boquete or Caldera, although

you should manage alright with detailed maps. The Fortuna Dam now lies just east of this route, together with a road and parallel oil pipeline from Chiriquí (on the PanAmerican Highway) across the Divide to Chiriquí Grande on the Caribbean; these are not marked on my IGN maps.

We started from the village of Caldera, southeast of Boquete; there are some hot springs here, also owned by the Collins family, where you can camp on condition you leave the place tidy. There are buses here from David, as well as pickups from the Boquete road, 14km away. You can also walk from Boquete in four or five hours: cross the suspension bridge and take the road uphill to the right to the Jaramillo Centro crossroads 40 minutes away. Carrying straight on, in five minutes you have a good view down the Caldera valley all the way to the Pacific, and then in about 20 minutes more cross a ridge to the upper valley of the Río Agua Blanca. The track runs down its left/east side for about 13km, meeting the road to Caldera about 2km after the confluence with the Río Caldera. To reach the springs, go through the village, fork left after the bridge and turn left in 100m or so.

The trail onwards is a rough dirt road, negotiable for a few kilometres by 4WD vehicles. It begins at just below 400m, crosses the Río Los Valles, and then follows the right bank of the Río Chiriquí, a large, rapidly flowing river full of white water. The views of the river below as the trail ascends are magnificent, and I kept stopping to take photos, only to find that the view at the next bend was even more spectacular. On the first day the trail crossed the Quebrada Mariposa, Quebrada Cupe and the Quebrada Algarrobos. At this point the 'road' ends and the trail becomes narrow and rocky, ascending (with many sharp ups and downs) to the Río Zarsiadero at 1,000m, where we stopped for the night.

Here we had just left the dry, windy region and entered true cloudforest, full of mists which become indistinguishable from rain. With the sun out, there are many brilliant rainbows that descend into valleys below, leaving no doubt as to where the pot of gold must be. The trees are gigantic, covered with moss, spectacular bromeliads, lianas, and full of chattering birds and, if you stop to look, monkeys. Our guide Juanito killed a snake (1.5m long) on the trail and claimed it was the feared *boca racá* (fer-de-lance): "*Muy venenoso! Mata la gente!*". I am doubtful, however, as I was unable to see the characteristic 'pit' between the eyes and the nostrils.

We stopped for the night at the finca of Perfecto Samudio, a gentle man then about 45 with ten children, six of them under the age of ten. His house, a three-room shack with a cooking shed, at first seemed incredibly poor. It was of rough, hand-sawn boards with great spaces between them where the cold wind blows through. Chicks were feeding on the 'living room' floor, piles of yuca root lay on the dirty floor and sacks of coffee, rice and maize were strewn around. A kerosene lantern, rifle, machete, hammer and saw were about the only items that distinguished the household (at first appearance) from the Stone Age. Though raggedly dressed, the children were healthy-looking, shy, and well-behaved. Perfecto chatted with Juanito, then reached up into the rafters and brought out a dog-eared Spanish-English dictionary. He explained that he was taking a correspondence course in English, but couldn't get the correct pronunciation from the book, and asked for my help. I worked with him for almost an hour, after which his daughter served the best coffee I've ever tasted: grown, roasted and ground right there. Perfecto then took a crude guitar, of which he was very proud, and began to play and sing sweet, melancholy tunes while the wind howled and mist-rain poured off the rattling galvanised metal roof. All the while the late sun illuminated the poinsettias and roses that surrounded this house of unutterable squalor. I asked jokingly if he had also learned guitar by correspondence, and was astonished to be answered affirmatively. His nine year old daughter cooked dinner over the fire in the shed — our dried soup, mixed with their rice and vegetables, and shrimps, which I'd guess they catch in the river. I was given a bed (a board with two grain sacks for a pillow), while Juanito slept on the floor, and the family, all eight of them, slept in the main bedroom on one big bed. After breakfast the next day I gave him a *regalo* of US$2, which he tried to refuse until I made it clear that it was a present and not payment. He gave us a package of home-grown sugar, fresh ground coffee and grapefruits, and we were off.

We left at 08.00 in the sun-rain. I tried wearing my poncho, but we had to cross many extremely swift rivers, where the poncho caught the wind like a sail, almost sweeping me downstream. Besides, when you're up to the thighs in cold water, keeping your shoulders dry at a considerable cost in energy makes little sense. We crossed the Río Zarsiadero and climbed sharply all morning, reaching Pinola (Cerro Pinola on the map) at 10.00. Here there is another small finca, an alternative stopping place. Just before Pinola, Juanito pointed out the place where one of their horses had died from exhaustion on the last trip over the mountains; that gives some idea of the kind of walk it is. As it turned out, we moved more quickly without pack animals. We stopped at noon in a small shed to cram food into our mouths, but could not pause for long because the wind was howling through our wet clothes and we were bitterly cold when not on the move. At 13.00 we reached the Continental Divide (at almost 2,000m), and began our descent into the province of Bocas del Toro. Although it was still raining, the afternoon was warmer because there was no wind on the Caribbean side and the trail leads through dense forest. There are no fincas here, and we didn't see a soul for the next 24 hours. We did see giant plants of the kind that grow in dark Boston living rooms, 'elephant ear' leaves as big as I am, great buttressed trees covered with moss and bright red and yellow fungi. At two places along the trail, Juanito stopped to point out the tracks of *el tigre* in the mud, and there could be no doubt that he was right.

By 16.00 I was tiring and beginning to stumble, though trying to be careful because the trail is rocky and rooty, and a broken leg here would be a disaster. At 18.00 we reached a meadow of waist-high grass, the greenest, lushest meadow I've ever seen, shrouded in clouds, with coconut palms and flowers, flocks of parrots and parakeets. This area (altitude 500m) is called "Buena Vista" and when it cleared in the morning we could see the Caribbean on the horizon. After drinking the sweet milk of green coconuts (*pipas*) we cooked dinner. At Buena Vista we slept in the larger of two small huts with floors of split cane and thatched palm roofs. At dusk, fireflies glowed throughout the valley and frogs croaked loudly outside the hut. We all passed out by 19.30; it had been ten hours of strenuous walking. I was wakened at 03.00 by a sharp bite on my eyelid, then on my arm, followed by repeated bites virtually everywhere on my body — I was writhing in a swarm of *carniceros*, or butcher ants. My torch revealed a virtual carpet of them on the cane floor, and in a minute my companions were up slapping themselves and stamping the floor to drive the ants back up into the thatch overhead. Unconvinced of the efficacy of the stamping, I moved to the other hut, where I finished the night in peace.

Dawn at Buena Vista began with grey mists drifting across the valley and shrouding the huge trees of the surrounding hills. By 08.00 the weather had cleared, as we started our descent through lush jungle, knee-deep in mud at times, crossing several waist-deep rivers that were cool and rapid with rocky bottoms and gravel beaches. In one of these river beds a friend had found a stone carving, obviously a phallus (circumcised), an artefact of the Guaymí civilization. My own search for such a prize was unsuccessful.

We stopped for lunch at 13.00 after crossing the last large river, the Río Pasa Coñasa. By 14.00 we were in Punta Peña, a small *pueblo* with a 'boarding school'. Almost no one was in the village when we arrived, but we were fed more lunch by the three men who were working on the school. Again, as throughout the trip, no one waited for us to ask for food or lodging — it was supplied as a matter of course, with great generosity and obvious pleasure.

It may still be possible to travel the last 10km from Punta Peña to Chiriquí Grande by *mesilla*, a small flatcar pulled on ramshackle railroad tracks by a horse. Unfortunately for us, the *mesilla* and the villagers were attending a festival at the other end of the line, so we walked the track to Chiriquí Grande. It was a hot, painful three-hour walk, as the sleepers (ties) are irregularly spaced, making it impossible to establish a stride. Nowadays you should be able to get to the new road, which follows the Ríos Guabo and Guarumo almost to Punta Peña and then swings northeast to Chiriquí Grande. In any case the countryside is beautiful: stands of rice and *plátano* and dark groves of cacao trees, the fruit of which is attached by a tough stem to rather stout branches — almost as if they had been glued on. The cacao trees are covered with moss and bromeliads and thick with birds: parrots and several large colonies of oropendolas, with their magnificent scrotal nests.

After seven hours walking, encountering the Caribbean shore was like entering paradise. Discounting Juanito's warning of "*muchos lagartos*" (many crocodiles) in the water, I stripped and dived in. It was great to rinse off three days of sweat and change into clean clothes. From a distance Chiriquí Grande looks like a town out of a Club Med advertisement: one street right along the beach with green hills rising sharply just behind it, no more than 10m from the water. Coconut palms grow right up to the water's edge, shading the houses, and there's hibiscus everywhere. The only jarring elements are the black vultures that soar in large numbers overhead, stalk the beaches and wharves, and perch in the palms over the water. They are to Chiriquí Grande what seagulls are to Cape Cod. Pelicans and frigate birds cruise overhead and, as dusk falls, the sounds of fireflies and frogs dominate the town.

From here you can take a bus (several daily) back to David; at the Continental Divide (north of the Fortuna Dam) there's a restaurant and checkpoint, and Ridgely describes a trail just beyond this to the right/west that runs along the Divide with great bird-watching (black guan, barbets, wren-thrushes, ant-thrushes, toucanets, bellbirds and tanagers). Equally you can leave by ferry (at 1330 daily) to Bocas del Toro, a backpackers' favourite (especially the *Pension Peck*) and the start of the Caribbean route into Costa Rica. The **Bastimentos National Park** protects much of the Bocas del Toro archipelago, an area of mangroves, coral reefs and white beaches, with manatees, marine turtles and over 200 species of tropical fish.

Other national parks

There's a group of relatively little-visited National Parks in the Azuero Peninsula; these include **Cerro Hoya** (at the southern end of the peninsula, protecting at least 30 endemic plant species and the endemic carato parakeet, in various types of moist forest and rainforest), and **Sarigua**, just north of Chitré. This is primarily a pre-Hispanic archaeological site, but also protects dry premontane forest in one of the country's most arid areas, with an endemic gallnut tree, as well as mangroves. The Humboldt Ecological Station, at Playa Agallito, at the park's southern end, studies migratory birds; staff are helpful and informative. Off the peninsula's southeastern corner is the **Isla Iguana Wildlife Refuge**, protecting not only iguanas but also marine birds. **Isla Coiba** (west of the peninsula) is far larger, with a permanent population, and can be reached by plane; it boasts a variety of largely unspoilt marine and coastal ecosystems, including Panamá's only scarlet macaws.

The **El Cope** (or Omar Torrijos) **Park**, founded in 1986, is the country's newest, and is still pretty well inaccessible; it lies in rainforest on the north side of the Continental Divide, to the north of Gatún, 60km north from a junction on the PanAmerican 6km east of Divisa (the junction south to Chitré).

Taboga Island, south of the southern entrance to the Canal, is a popular excursion (ferries from Pier 17/18 in Balboa); it was settled by the Spaniards in 1515 (before Panamá City) and the town is quaint and largely traffic-free. It's known for its flowers and much of the island is a Wildlife Refuge, protecting a pelican rookery. The hill at its eastern end is an interesting savanna-like habitat, with stunted *nance* and sandpaper trees.

Chapter Nine

Eastern Panamá and Darién

"When you go to Darién
Entrust yourself to the Virgin Mary
Because your arrival is in your hands
But your departure is in God's."

Conquistador rhyme

Darién province covers a quarter of Panamá's area and is a true frontier territory, where forest is being cleared rapidly and replaced largely by cattle pasture. The PanAmerican Highway, which reached Yaviza on the Río Chico in 1975, was inevitably followed by a swathe of deforestation; fortunately, the swampy nature of the terrain and the numerous rivers have so far prevented its completion through the so-called Darién Gap betwen Panamá and Colombia. Now the environmental value of this area (and the rights of its indigenous inhabitants) are increasingly recognised, which, coupled with Panamanian fears of foot-and-mouth disease (*fiebre aftosa*, present in Colombia, together with 23 human viruses not found in Panamá) makes it likely that there'll be a hell of a fight if governments push ahead with the highway. However, internal migration and agricultural colonization continue to be a danger, with pressure greatest along the Río Tuira from El Real to Pinogana and along the Río Sambú, in western Darién.

This roadless forest provides a wonderful experience for backpackers, with huge trees and gaudy birds, and the colourful Kuna and Choco people. Yet it's received some of the worst publicity of any wilderness in the world. It has the reputation of being a swampy wasteland, crawling with venomous creatures and ready to suck unsuspecting explorers without warning into its oozing depths. This reputation has been fostered by expeditions such as that of the British Army in 1972, which insisted on seeing it as a combat experience and forcing their way through in vehicles. In fact the Darién, done properly on foot and by canoe, presents no special challenges. Yes, it is hot and full of bugs, and there are human dangers, but these are easily outweighed by the sheer joy of being away from civilization for the ten or so days it takes to cross the Darién Gap.

Most of the southern part of the province (excluding an enclave around Jaqué) was created a National Park in 1980; UNESCO placed it on its World Heritage List in 1981 and declared it a Biosphere Reserve in 1983. It's Panamá's largest National Park (579,000ha), and was said to be the second largest in Central America before Costa Rica began to group its parks into mega-parks. The Park's headquarters are in El Real, where you'll be able to get some help and advice. In addition there are two forest reserves at Canglón (between the PanAmerican Highway and the Tuira estuary) and Chepigana (on the Tuira estuary south of La Palma).

The rocks of the area are of Upper Cretaceous volcanic origin with more recent middle-Miocene sediments; its highest peaks, such as Cerro Tacarunca (1,875m), have been more or less isolated since the Pleistocene, allowing species not found elsewhere to evolve. A 1977 botanical expedition found three new species here, in a unique ecosystem; 25% of the species collected in the oak forest between 1,400m and 1,800m had not been described until then. At this meeting point between North and South America, most of the flora represents Northern taxa, but the endemics are mostly Andean (especially fast-evolving epiphytes and palms). This evergreen forest (premontane rainforest covering most of the hills, and low montane rainforest on the highest peaks) covers 30% of the park; 40% (largely along the Colombian border) is very moist tropical forest and the rest, apart from patches of mangrove along the coast, is moist tropical forest and very moist premontane forest. The former covers just 9% of the park's area, but is the natural covering of much of the rest of the province as well. There certainly is plenty of rainfall: over 4m a year on the Atlantic coast, 2-3m in the Tuira valley, 3-4m in the Balsas valley, and over 5m near Jaqué.

In all there are over 2,000 species of flora in the PND, and about 550 bird species (of which 19 are endemic and at least 33 are seen only here in Panamá). There are 132 of the 214 Panamanian species of mammals, 38 of which are seen only in Darién or east of the Canal; these include an estimated seven jaguars, 870 of the more tolerant ocelot, 2,200 tapir and 24,000 black-handed spider monkeys, as well as about 40 harpy eagles.

The Indians of Darién
Kuna
The Kuna have lived around the Gulf of Urabá since the 16th century, later migrating to the Panamanian side of the Darién Gap to occupy territory abandoned by a group known as the Cueva. Although small groups still live by rivers in those areas, the majority were displaced by the Chocós in the mid-19th century and now live (about 24,000 of them) in the San Blas Territory, enjoying political autonomy and sending a representative to the National Assembly.

Kuna dress is very distinctive, especially for women. Gold nose rings are worn, and elaborate earrings. A rich Kuna will display his wealth by the gold ornaments worn by his wife — up to a thousand dollars' worth. Women and girls wear the distinctive 'reverse appliqué' blouses known as *molas*. The geometric and animal designs so popular on molas may have their origins in body painting: when missionaries decreed that the Indians should cover up, they transferred their favourite patterns to their clothing.

Kuna traditions and tribal customs are still intact in many areas. Puberty rites play an important part in the social life of each village. There is much feasting and *chicha* drinking, and a variety of musical instruments are played. Finally the girl is led out of her 'seclusion hut', her hair is cut short, and she is given a ceremonial name. She is now available for marriage. (Darién Kunas seem to have abandoned puberty rites; all women wear their hair long.)

We found the Kuna women in Paya very self-assertive and certainly the equals of their male counterparts. They often went to the plantations to pick fruit and poled their *piraguas* up and down the river, carrying cargo and passengers.

The Kuna call themselves 'The Golden People', and certainly gold plays an important part in their lives and legends. Like all Indians, they have a strong belief in the after-life, although details vary. The Kuna believe in an eight-tiered system of the universe, with the Supreme Being living on the top floor, and the underworld occupying the lower areas. Only Kuna *kantules* (curers) can move up and down these levels at will during their lifetimes. One version of what happens after death was told to us in Paya. After being transported to the Land of the Dead, helped by the Chant of Death performed by the villagers, the Kuna enters a sort of drawer, which is then pulled through on the other side. If he's been a good Kuna he will emerge gold-painted and be sent to one of the upper tiers of the universe, where the quality of his life is dictated by how many white-faced monkeys he killed during this lifetime. These monkeys are the bankers of heaven, so as many as possible are sent up there in advance to have time to pick many flowers which form the heavenly currency. This belief probably accounts for the necklaces of monkey teeth worn by Kuna males.

Chocós

The Chocó Indians live in the Darién and the Chocó department of Colombia. Many of them moved about two or three hundred years ago from the Río San Juan region of Colombia, and are now the dominant group in the Darién National Park; some have now moved on as far as the Chagres National Park. They have strong cultural ties to the Indians of South America, with their blowpipes, loinclothes and housing materials. Two dialects of their language are spoken, *waunana*, mainly in Colombia, and *embera* in Panamá. Chocó huts are built on stilts high off the ground, with access by a long, notched-pole ladder, and have open sides. Traditionally the women weave baskets and the men work in wood, particularly constructing dug-out canoes and carving animals and the *bastone* sticks used in curing rituals.

Traditional Chocó dress, or lack of it, is striking, although nowadays shorts and T-shirts are widespread. The women wear only a simple wrap-around skirt called a *paruma* and heavy necklaces, and the men a loin cloth. On fiesta days men wear elaborate necklaces of coins, and beaded loin cloths. Scanty clothing is made up for by the copious use of body paint. *Jagua* (from the plant *Genipa americana*) is daubed on the face and body of both sexes. This is light grey when first applied, but dries to a darker shade, and exposure to the sun finally turns it black. It won't wash off, but wears off gradually over a period of eight to ten days. Chocós claim that *jagua* keeps insects away, although it doesn't seem to work for gringos!

Traditional medicine plays an important part in the lives of the Chocó. They believe that illnesses are caused by evil spirits and only a *jaibaná* (shaman) can get rid of them. Songs, stories and prayers to the spirits are used, as well as herbal cures. The *jaibaná* has a collection of *bastones*, sticks in the shapes of humans and animals, each representing a disease, and these are used to drive out the evil spirits.

It's hard to be sure of population numbers of jungle-dwelling *indigenos*, but there seem to be about 2,000 Kuna, 8,550 Embera and 2,600 Waunana in Darién; perhaps 400 Kuna and 1,670 Chocó live within the National Park's boundaries. There are also perhaps 16,000 *Darienitas* or Afro-Hispanics, a blend of the Spanish settlers and their African slaves, and at least 9,000 (and rising) *colonos* from elsewhere in Panamá, mostly still outside the Park.

Hiking routes

The first edition of this book more or less created the hiking route through the Darién Gap, where the PanAmerican Highway gives up. Now the trail is well established. In early editions of this book we said, 'the biggest danger in making the trip is your effect on the local people, and we implore you to avoid doing anything that will affect their way of life or their attitude to gringos in any way'. In vain, alas. In the last few years the prices for boats in particular have risen steeply, and there have been increasing numbers of robberies, some involving murder. Your embassy will advise you not to go this way, but most people (100 to 200 a year) get through without incident; problems seem to arise more if you get off the beaten track or appear unduly curious. There are illegal immigrants, drug-runners and other shady individuals passing through the Gap, and certainly Colombian guerrillas, who nowadays spend most of their time guarding coca plantations high in the hills. However the classic route simply follows the rivers, climbing no higher than 155m. On the Panamanian side at least, the Tuira valley is pretty well populated and the inhabitants are to a certain extent accustomed to outsiders. In any case you should not travel alone, and should consider taking a guide, either through Inrenare in Paraíso, through a company such as Eco-Tours, or locally, perhaps with the help of police in Yaviza or El Real. Avoid the rainy season if you can.

Although the Tuira valley offers the most obvious route into Colombia, there are other possibilities: after all, the Gap is by definition an absence of roads, and (as with the Silk Route of Central Asia) it's more a loose skein of trading links rather than a single route. We shall of course describe the main Tuira valley route, but given the increasing dangers of this hike you should also consider other possibilities. Firstly if you are trying to get to Colombia, remember that there's a new (December 1994) car-ferry service from Colón to Cartagena, which is usually cheaper than walking it, at about US$100 plus taxes. Even if you hike every possible bit of trail the very least you can expect to pay for boats is about US$60, and most people will spend at least US$120 in all.

Next consider the route along the east (Atlantic) coast, starting from **Puerto Obaldía**, the last town in Panamá, which can be reached either by ship (a very scenic but very slow route from Colón through the San Blas islands, for about US$25) or by plane (US$40, with Ansa or Transpasa from Paitilla). Get your exit stamp here and walk across the border to Capurgana; this takes about four hours, via the last Panamanian village, La Miel, over the ridge of Cabo Tiburón (Shark Cape), and down through the first Colombian village, Sapzurro. From Capurgana (a resort with good diving) you can fly to Medellín or continue along the coast to Acandí for the daily (weather permitting) boat to Turbo, where you hit the Colombian road system. There are boats to Acandí but you can equally well hike in about five hours. Follow the coast through the hamlets of Aguacate and Rufino, then head inland to follow a river (with several crossings) to Acandí. There's no point walking onwards as the swamps of the Gulf of Urabá block your way. Turbo is an uninteresting but dangerous port which you have to pass through to get an entry (or exit) stamp in your passport; you can change cash but not, it seems, travellers cheques here.

Alternatively you can go along the Pacific coast; as a rule this involves no walking, although according to the *Mexico and Central American Handbook* the route has been hiked. You need to fly or take a boat from the capital to Jaqué, and then a boat to Jurado in Colombia, four to five hours away. From Jurado you can take a plane, or continue by boat (for two days) to the resort of Bahía Solano. There's also a Trans-Isthmus route, involving four or five days of hiking and boating on the Río Truando, from Jurado to Riosucio and Travesía (see the *South American Handbook*). Jaqué is the only town in the southwestern corner of Darién and a base for expeditions up the Río Pavarandó. There's one hospedaje, but the town's mostly visited by tourists heading for the game-fishing resort of Puerto Piña, just to the north.

There are other land routes, such as that from Yaviza up the Río Chico to Acandí, or via the Ríos Balsas (in Panamá) and Salaquí (in northwestern Colombia). But why give in to this fixation with reaching Colombia? There are plenty of other ways to explore the jungle without crossing the frontier, notably the ocean-to-ocean routes pioneered by Panamanian ecotourism outfits such as Eco-Tours and Centro de Aventuras. These roughly follow the route taken by Balboa in 1513 when he (not stout Cortés) 'discovered' the Pacific Ocean. He started at Punta Carreto, north of Puerto Obaldía, while today's expeditions start at the village of Pito, just south of the point, and follow the Río Pita to the watershed and then the Río Membrillo. Balboa took a tough cross-country route to the coast well north of Yaviza, but the present-day expeditions take boats down the Río Chucunaque to Yaviza and La Palma. An alternative route runs parallel just to the south, from Puerto Obaldía along the Río Tuquesa to the Chucunaque just north of Canglón, from where you can walk to the PanAmerican or take a boat out. These trips involve six days travel and six days exploring the jungle and visiting Indian villages; shorter trips visit Indian villages on the Mogue, Pihuila, Balsas and Pirre rivers, to the west of Yaviza, and the Chucunaque. You could also hike from Yaviza to Puerto Obaldía, following either the Río Tupisa (the more direct) or the Tuquesa to the north: both are lined with small villages, but you'd certainly need a guide to get over the watershed. However, a group of Belgians paid just US$10 each per day (for four days) for the guides and all their food (which the guides carried); the guides normally bring through illegal immigrants and are happy to do legal work for a change, but should be watched carefully on the last day.

In the last few years the Darién National Park has begun to open a few of its research stations for tourism, and this may well be the best way to get to grips with and learn about the ecosystems of the area. The best is **Cruce de Mono** (Monkey's Cross), five hours walk from Boca de Cupé on the Río Tuira; the last hour is hilly as you ascend the slopes of the Serranía de Pirre. There's plenty of wildlife to be seen, including cats, motmots and puffbirds. From here, you can continue for five hours to the former mine of **Cana**, where Ridgely describes the birding as superb; there are Darién endemics such as the golden-headed quetzal, the grey-and-gold tanager, the Pirre warbler, and the Pirre bush-tanager, as well as four types of macaw, the black-tipped cotinga, and the red-throated caracara (a sort of falcon). The Spaniards took US$30m worth of gold from the *Espirito Santo* mine here, all through the labour of local and African slaves. It was rediscovered in 1853 during the preliminary surveys for the Panamá Canal and worked by an Anglo-American company between 1900 and 1907.

On the other side of the Serranía de Pirre is the **Rancho Frio** (or Cerro Pirre) station, reached by three hours walk west from El Real (or in the wet season by taking a boat to Piji Baisal and then walking for an hour). Here there are interpretative paths where you can see lowland species such as tanagers and woodpeckers, and camping sites at 500m, 800m and 1,000m altitude. The third station is **Balsas**, at the confluence of the Balsas and Tucutí rivers, at least four hours by boat from El Real; this is the most recent, even boasting electric power, but the forest is pretty degraded in this area. You should obtain all necessary permits from Inrenare in Paraíso before coming to Darién. Obviously, if entering from Colombia you won't be expected to have a national park permit, and there doesn't seem to be much need southbound either.

Warning Northwest Colombia (and therefore the southern end of the Darién Gap) is dangerous. Guerrilla activity is increasing and the region has one of the world's highest murder rates.

Practicalities
When to go
The season for crossing the Gap is short. Only between December and March can you be sure of reasonably dry weather. In the rainy season the rivers are roaring torrents full of broken trees and other debris, the trails become squelchy quagmires, and the bugs eat you alive. You *can* cross the Gap then, but it's very difficult and unpleasant. Towards the end of the dry season the

rivers are very low and it's often dificult to get a canoe up them. Given a choice, you should plan your trip for January. I'd say that up to 100 gringos make the trip in a period of about three months.

What to bring
One of the biggest problems in crossing the Gap is luggage. You need to cut down on weight as much as possible for any jungle hike, and you need at least a week's supplies for this one. However, chances are you're continuing towards the Andes, where you'll need plenty of warm clothing. If you can find some way of sending this gear ahead, do so. If you can persuade a friend to take it by plane or ferry, that's ideal; air freight is usually more trouble than it's worth as it takes a lot of time and money to collect it at the other end. Here are a few specific ideas:

Boots
Your regular boots will suffice, but undoubtedly army surplus jungle boots are the best for jungle hiking. These have holes to allow water to drain out, and the canvas uppers dry quickly. Basketball boots also dry rapidly, but be warned that they do shrink: get half a size larger than you need. Remember that there are rivers to ford and they have stony bottoms. Hiking sandals are ideal as you can slip them on for the river crossings and then hook them on the back of your pack to dry.

Tent or hammock
A hammock with a *very* well-fitting mosquito net is ideal. If you use a tent, make sure it is totally insect-proof, yet also properly ventilated.

Bugs
There's no escaping the fact that the Darién rainforests are a haven for many biting insects; read the *Health and Safety* chapter carefully. At the end of their crossing Hilary and George had a competition for the most bites: 368 on one leg was the winner — but then he had insisted on wearing shorts!

Clothing
Pure cotton is the coolest, but it is liable to suddenly burst into holes and fall apart as a result of jungle rot. Mixed cotton and synthetics are unaffected, but it's too hot for underwear!

However light you travel bring at least one change of clothing. In the evening your clothes will be soggy with sweat and they won't dry out in the humidity.

Maps
The IGN sells a map of the Darién; the topography may be correct but most villages are misplaced or missing. The South American Explorers Club (126 Indian Creek Rd, Ithaca, NY 14850, USA; tel: 607 277 0488), which you should almost certainly join if continuing through South America, has lots of trip reports on the Darién Gap and all points south.

Miscellaneous
Ziploc plastic bags are needed to keep your luggage dry in leaky canoes.

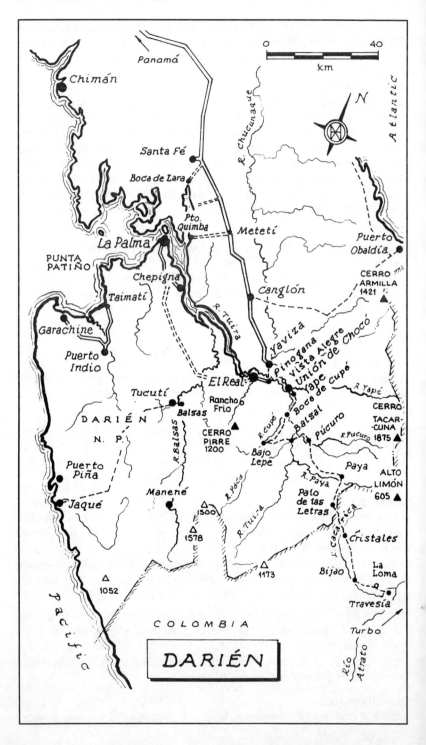

You'll need plenty of water purification, and may also wish to add salt to your drinking water, just below the taste threshold. Take a compass, and perhaps a machete, though this isn't essential. Be sure to have lots of single dollar bills.

THE ROUTE

Coming from Panamá along the PanAmerican Highway, the asphalt ends at Chepo, 37km beyond Tocumen airport. Another 18km east at El Llano the only road into the San Blas *comarca* heads north to reach the coast at Cartí Suitupo; just beyond the Continental Divide (at about 450m) is the Nusagandi Lodge in the **Pemasky Nature Park**, which has an interesting history. The road was built in 1970 and at once the Kuna found that their land was being colonized by squatters; although the Kuna are supposed to have autonomy in San Blas, Panamanian law said that 'unused' land could be squatted. Eventually the Kuna had the bright idea of declaring an area of 3,200km² a nature reserve, which was sufficient to persuade the courts that the land was being used. Now the local ecotourism companies run overnight trips here from the capital. There's simple dormitory accommodation, and you can hike to waterfalls or to watch parrots, manakins, kites and hummingbirds; at night you can listen to owls, nightjars and frogs. The name actually stands for the *Proyecto de Estudio para el Manejo de Areas Protegidas Silvestres de Kuna Yala*, which can be contacted at Apdo 2012, Paraíso, Ancón (tel: 25 3409).

The road passes over a bridge between the two halves of the Bayano reservoir and on across open savanna. There's a checkpoint at Cañazas, about six hours from Panamá, and half an hour later, at Agua Fría, you enter Darién province. It's another two and a half hours to Metetí, where the midday bus from Panamá may terminate. There are two reasonable *hospedajes* here. The road gets worse from here on, and is likely to be impassable in the rainy season.

The roadhead, another two and a half hours on or 12-plus hours from Panamá, is **Yaviza**, a pleasant little town with a population of 1,000 Darienitas and one hospedaje almost opposite the ruins of a tiny Spanish fort; you should register with the police here, at the far end of the town. You can fly into Yaviza or the larger town of **El Real** (one hospedaje), just down the estuary, which can also be reached by boat from Yaviza, Panamá City or **La Palma**. The last, at the mouth of the Tuira estuary, is the capital of Darién province, with a population of all of 5,000 people; however it's not a place you're likely to need to visit. If necessary, there are one or two places to stay there, and you can get there by plane or boat from Panamá; from the PanAmerican Highway you need to take a boat from either Puerta Lara (south of Santa Fé) or Puerto Quimba (west of Metetí). Indeed, if heading for Yaviza in the rainy season, when the highway is often impassable beyond Metetí, you may be obliged to go either by this route or down the Río Chucunaque, about 10km east of Metetí.

Starting from Yaviza it's possible, with a guide, to hike to Unión de Chocó in four hours (see below). To go it alone, you need to cross the river Chico and hike to Pinogana to hike or catch a boat up the Río Tuira. Coming from La Palma or El Real, you should be able to find a boat upstream from El Real, although there is also a dirt road from the port of El Real through the town (4km south) and on to Pinogana. There are dug-outs across the Río Chico from where the buses drop you in Yaviza, costing about US$0.25. To the left is the hospital; to reach Pinogana turn right and follow the path into the forest. If in doubt keep left (except once after about 35 minutes, when the path left leads only to an abandoned hut); after about one and a half hours you reach the Tuira and follow it upstream to reach the crossing point to **Pinogana** (US$1). There's not much to this Darienita village, although it does have a kiosk. It's very expensive to hire a boat here; what you want is to flag down a banana boat returning from El Real. These go downstream early in the morning and return in the late morning and afternoon, although Sundays are pretty quiet. These boats are basically dug-outs, but all now have large outboard motors which move them along fairly rapidly, shoals and sunken logs permitting.

Equally you can hike upstream; from Pinogana follow a track along the left bank for perhaps three hours and ford the river at the Waunan village of Vista Alegre (or Aruza), from where it's half an hour on to **Unión de Chocó**. This is a largish village, with 95 houses and perhaps 400 people, both Embera and Waunan. They don't like photos but are very friendly and welcoming; I stayed in the thatched meeting hall in the centre of the village; a new concrete one was being built beside the school, which will be less atmospheric but won't have any *vinchucas* lurking in the roof. It's just a kilometre further to **Yape**, but this is a Darienita village, and it's more interesting and enjoyable to sleep in Unión de Chocó.

If you only have time for an overnight trip, you can head north from here to reach the Río Chico in at most three hours and take a boat back to Yaviza: leave Unión de Chocó across the soccer ground to the north-northwest, on a good path through banana plantations. After 30 minutes this reaches Vista Alegre, where you should turn right along the right bank of the Tuira. Ignoring a left turn after about 15 minutes, you'll find yourself on a good 3m-wide trail that goes over a small hill to a house by the river; turn right here to leave the river and head into the forest. After about 45 minutes you should fork right to climb quite steeply for ten minutes, drop for five and climb steeply for ten more. You soon descend and reach the Chico in half an hour; here you need to wait for a boat, as there's no trail along the river, only short paths that get swamped in abandoned and overgrown banana plantations. With a guide, it is possible to hike from Unión de Chocó to Yaviza in four hours, although this involves 'thick mud, several nerve-wracking river crossings in leaky piraguas and negotiating a few smaller gullies by balancing on bouncy log bridges'.

Continuing towards Colombia, at Yape you have to ford the river of the same name and continue up the right bank of the Tuira through Capetí to reach **Boca de Cupé**, about five hours from Unión de Chocó. Another

Darienita village, this is the last outpost of 'civilization' and you need to get your entry or exit stamp here (although there may also be a check at Púcuro). There's a blue house near the landing place which will give you food and a bed (US$2-3). Villages are more scattered from here on and paths are less well-used, therefore virtually everyone travels on by boat at least as far as Púcuro. You might have to wait a couple of days for a boat, unless you want to hire a boat just for yourselves. However, Rob hiked from Boca de Cupé to Púcuro in two days, and this is his account (note that it hasn't been updated recently):

"This is a rugged trip and the ability to follow a faint trail and use a compass is necessary, but the hike provides a good challenge and is often very beautiful. You leave Boca de Cupé by a very wide trail behind and to the right of the football field (where you can camp). In about a kilometre you pass the cemetery and the trail narrows, passing several houses. Some two or three kilometres beyond the cemetery you'll reach the Río Cupé which the trail will cross and recross several times. If you meet anyone, ask for the village of **Bajo Lepe** three or four kilometres up the river, which is inhabited by Chocos and blacks. So far the countryside has been cultivated all the way, mainly with bananas, and the trail has been easy to follow. The next section is rather more difficult; however you can console yourself with the knowledge that the Lepe area is home to the endangered yellow pine (*Centrolobium yavizanum*) and the harpy eagle.

"The name of the next village is Balsal, and it's about a day's hike from Bajo Lepe. The trail starts easily enough following the Cupé upstream and crossing it a few times until after three or four kilometres it passes a couple of disused houses and soon after crosses the river and leads inland. The trail becomes very thin and overgrown, but you can distinguish it from the surrounding jungle. If in doubt, remember you are heading roughly southeast, and also that however overgrown it appears the trail is passable and has been used, though not often. After two or three kilometres you'll come to another trail, also very overgrown but much wider, being the route taken by an expedition of five jeeps that passed through in about 1977. Follow this wider trail as best you can, roughly southeast for two or three hours, until you come to a river. After fording this, look for an abandoned banana plantation to your left and a weed-covered hut. The trail passes the hut and skirts the plantation, and is very difficult to follow. On the far side of the plantation, cast around for that jeep trail again. Follow it for a further three hours or so to another river which also has to be forded. The trail continues a little to your left on the far side of the river. It's still very rough and overgrown, but if you persevere you'll reach a cultivated area in two or three hours. This marks the outskirts of **Balsal**, and you can ask a field worker to show you the way through the maze of field trails to this mixed Kuna and Chocó village."

You can sleep in the communal hut here and the locals are generous with their main crop, *plátanos*. Balsal is not a usual place for Darién Gappers to stop in so you'll be the centre of attention, with children vying with each other for choice positions close to the gringos.

Here you have to cross the Tuira and hike for about 3½ hours to Púcuro, up and down through lush forest, again pretty overgrown. A guide would be sensible, certainly for the first kilometre or so through the fields. If you don't take a guide, keep left by and large for the first kilometre, after which there are no junctions until the last hilltop before Púcuro, where you need to fork right. The forest abounds with birds and flowers, all sizes, shapes and colours of butterflies and whirring hummingbirds, and lovely red cactus flowers like splotches of red paint in the thick, leathery green of the undergrowth.

Púcuro is the first wholly Kuna village you'll come to, but it's not really typical. Missionary influence has been strong here, and the houses are raised off the ground in the Chocó style, in the interests of hygiene. The people have also been converted to long-drop latrines! The sight of a camera is still enough to send the locals scattering for cover, but they are friendly and hospitable. You can ask the chief (*corregidor*) for permission to sleep in the communal hall, although you may be invited to sleep elsewhere; there's a kiosk here as well. If the river is high enough you can continue to Paya by boat, but in the dry season it's usually necessary to hike from here; therefore the trail is clear and well used, although after rain it can be a mess of steep-sided gullies.

Paya is 18km away and can be reached in 4½ hours, although other guidebooks give a minimum of six hours. After finding your way out through fields again, the trail follows the river for the first 2½ hours and then cuts inland. You have to make several river crossings; at the first, after 3km, the crossing is less slippery about 100m to your left. You then have to return and go about 20m up a tributary before branching left. In about 4km there's another crossing, where you have to head diagonally to the right to cross both the main river and a tributary, landing on the left bank (facing downstream, of course) of the tributary. There are some good camping spots by the river, with excellent fishing if you have a line and hook.

Paya is slightly smaller than Púcuro and in older accounts is generally reckoned to have a more relaxed and friendly population; however, the feeling now is that it's seen rather too many gringos, and you may be better off camping or staying with one of the families living outside the village. People try to charge US$5 per photo and gear can go missing in the night. Three American missionaries of the New Tribes Mission, who were working on a Kuna dictionary, were kidnapped in January 1993 and are now presumed dead; they had air-conditioning and PCs and other expensive toys, and were assumed (wrongly) to be CIA or DEA agents.

You have to go 2km east to a police post for an immigration check. If entering Panamá, any gear that looks like leather will be dipped in chemicals to kill off the foot-and-mouth disease — rinse this off as soon as possible. You can sleep either at the police post or in the communal hall. Although it's hard to believe now, until the end of the 19th century Paya was the seat of the Kuna 'university', to which Kunas came from all over to learn the arts of medicine, history, leadership and magic, until the white man's diseases brought about the decline of their culture about 100 years ago.

You may need a guide once again to get you out of the village and across the river; alternatively you can get a dug-out to bring you to this point in about ten minutes. In any case, it may be wise to take a guide (more usually a pair) for this stretch to give added security; always hire them through the *corregidor*. From here the trail up to the border is clear enough, but it's steep up and down all the way and there's no water. The highest point, at the border, is supposedly only 155m, but you climb far more than that in total. It's worth it, though: at last you leave behind all signs of deforestation and plunge into the jungle (tropical wet forest, technically). There's wildlife everywhere, including tapir, peccary and howler monkey. It takes a minimum of three hours to hike the 12km to the border marker at **Palo de las Letras**; this means Tree of the Letters, as there was once a huge tree in which passers-by carved their initials. The tree is no more, so the energetic and omnipresent government of Colombia has placed a small concrete marker here instead. This achievement is rather undermined by their spelling: the sign reads "Carretera Darién, Colmbia". Ludicrously, Inrenare has a plan to open a visitor centre here!

Entering **Colombia** and the Los Katios National Park, it's an hour (not three, as in the *Handbook*) to reach water at the Río Tule, which you should follow downstream; you have to cross it seven times and it's not always easy to find the continuation of the trail. After two hours the Tule flows into the larger Río Cacarica (politely put 'rich in excrement'), which you should follow downstream for about two or three hours to the park station at Cristales. Guides are often reluctant to cross the border and hikers routinely get lost in overgrown plantations and so on here, so it may end up being easier to walk in the riverbed itself, especially if the water level is low. There are some lovely deep pools which are perfect for cooling off in. But beware, they contain toothy fish which apparently devour soap and also nibble bare flesh — but don't worry, they're not piranhas! Cristales is on the left bank; the rangers are friendly and usually let hikers sleep on their floor or porch, and will help to find a boat onwards.

From here on you're largely dependent on boats to get through the swamps and across the Gulf of Urabá, and the locals know it. It can be very frustrating trying to find a boat at a less than astronomic price, and you may be stuck in some mosquito-infested hamlet for several days. Yes, swamps of course mean insects, and this is the section of the trip where you have to take great care not to end up with yellow fever or cerebral malaria; the ticks are bad, too. The ideal, naturally, is to get a ride all the way from Cristales to Turbo when the park staff go for supplies, but this requires lots of luck. Otherwise you'll have to get a canoe down to the run-down and rather expensive village of **Bijao** (or Vijado), two hours downstream at the confluence with another river. As Hilary wrote:

'this is the most spectacularly beautiful boat ride of the whole trip, through a seemingly impenetrable carpet of mauve-flowered water hyacinths. The river was seldom more than four metres wide, and sometimes so shallow that we had to jump out and haul the canoe over boulders or submerged logs. Huge double-crested basilisks, looking like mini-dragons, basked on the banks and plopped into the water at our approach, while their young, nicknamed 'Jesus Christ Lizards', scurried across the surface of the water on their hind legs. I can't remember how long the trip took, but it certainly wasn't long enough.'

It's also possible, but hard work, to hike down the right bank of the Cacarica to Bijao. From here there are more frequent boats, taking two to three hours to **Travesía** (or Puerto América), on the Río Atrato. This is an unfriendly place, best avoided if possible; you should be able to find a passing boat for Turbo fairly soon, but if not they drive a mean bargain, and prices rise 50% if you're ill. Watch your belongings closely at all times. Having said this, there's a communal hall to sleep in for free, a hospedaje and a shop. Alternatively it's now possible to reach a new branch of the PanAmerican Highway at Cuarenta, about 20km east of Travesía through dense swamps; you may have to take a boat north beyond Sautatá and then down the Río Tumaradó to Cuarenta. As you do need to pass through Turbo for entry/exit stamps, this may be more use if heading towards Panamá — turn off the PanAmerican at Guapá.

The Río Atrato is great for bird-watching, with lots of herons, kingfishers and screamers, as well as howler monkeys. If you want to spend time here you should stop at the headquarters of **Los Katios National Park**, Sautatá, downriver from Travesía. Otherwise take a boat through the Atrato swamps and across the Gulf of Urabá to Turbo.

Well done! You've crossed the Darién Gap; welcome to South America.

LOS KATIOS NATIONAL PARK

The Parque Natural Nacional Los Katios was established in 1974 and covers an area of 52,000 hectares. The tropical moist forest receives between 2m and 4m of rain a year and harbours an abundance of flora and fauna. Mammals include tapir, capybara and three-toed sloth, and among the 300 bird species are such beauties as the red-and-green and military macaws, keel-billed toucan, great curassow and sooty-capped puffbird. The park exists partly as a barrier to foot-and-mouth disease, and so far tourism has barely been considered, making the place most attractive to the independent traveller. There are three main ranger stations: Sautatá (the headquarters), La Loma (near Travesía) and Cristales. The first two have primitive accommodation for visitors, at a very reasonable cost. You may, of course, camp and cook your own food for free.

Chapter Ten

Costa Rica
General Information

Costa Rica has far and away the best developed and the best publicized tourist industry in Central America, and tourism is now its leading source of foreign exchange; in particular, ecotourism is the key to the marketing of Costa Rica. No doubt it did begin as the sort of small-scale operation that has the minimum impact on the environment and a reasonable benefit for the locals, but nowadays ecotourism is indistinguishable from other types of international tourism. Groups of tourists are carried around in buses to gawp at whatever they're told to gawp at, they stay in air-conditioned hotels, and the profits go to big companies, mostly abroad. Some of the older companies retain their principles while there are some idealistic new outfits starting up, but overall the situation is depressing. However, you can do it yourself, and there's certainly plenty of forest and wildlife to see.

Successive governments have rightly earned kudos for preserving large areas of forest as national parks, and there's been plenty of foreign aid and scientific cooperation. Currently over 11% of Costa Rica's area is preserved as national parkland and 14% protected by forestry reserves and two dozen private reserves; in 1995 plans were announced to increase this to a total of 31%. Costa Rica accounts for 0.03% of the earth's area but 5% of all its species, though many of these are threatened by ever advancing deforestation.

Costa Rica sees itself as the most civilized of the Central American states (putting up plaques whenever a public toilet is built), and it does have many of the comforts of Western life. There are over 20,000 North Americans living here permanently, often retirees, and there's also a big business in 'mail-order wives' from Costa Rica. The population is the whitest in Central America, due to the decimation of the indigenous population by European diseases, and the Ticos (as Costa Ricans are known) see themselves as honorary gringos. Less than 1% of the three million population is indigenous. At the end of the day, the country can seem rather tame and safe compared to the rest of Central America. Yet the tourist industry suffered in 1995 due to a perceived rise in crime, brought about in part by its own over-rapid expansion. Although hire cars do get held up sometimes, there are muggings in San José, and there are specific problems of crime in places like Cahuita, overall the country remains pretty safe for visitors. Nor are corruption and ecocrime comparable with that in the countries to the north, although the quick bucks to be made in tourism have led to some shady deals. With its democracy and

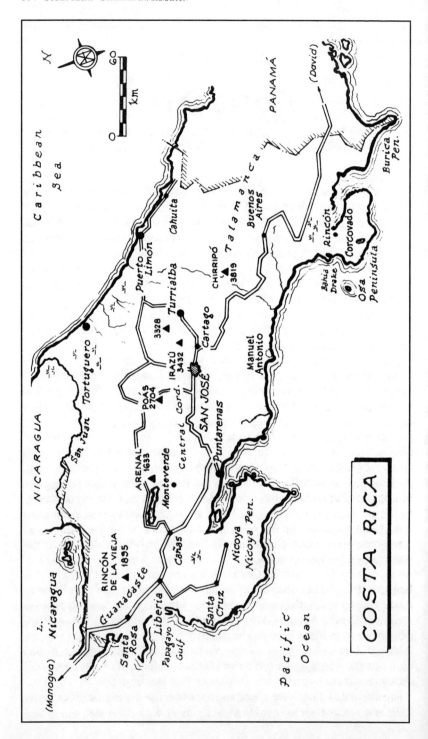

stability (the last two presidents have been the sons of former presidents) it's all a bit safe, a bit Swiss perhaps? But Switzerland is also a great place to take a hike.

Money

Costa Rica's currency is the *colón* (plural *colones*), often referred to as a *peso*. In theory it's divided into 100 centimos, but you're unlikely to come across these. VISA ATM cash machines are becoming more popular, especially at main branches of the *Banco Popular*.

Transport

Costa Rica's railways were closed down in mid-1995; it's not clear whether the 'tourist train' from Limón to Siquirres will continue to run. Inter-urban bus services are good, with lots of modern machines, particularly from San José to San Isidro, Limón and Puntarenas. All Costa Rican buses have fares clearly posted above the driver's head.

Around the capital, buses are frequent and cheap, although they follow circuitous routes and you often end up a long way from your destination. However San José is not very large and it's less frustrating just to walk a kilometre or so; you soon get to know the city and keep fit for hiking in those national parks! Each bus line has a set fare, usually displayed on the windscreen — easily confused with the route number.

There are two internal airlines, both serving tourist destinations such as Golfito, Palmar Sur, Quepos, Liberia, Tortuguero, and Barra del Colorado. Travelair (tel: 232 7883; fax: 220 0413) flies from Pavas in the western suburbs of San José; SANSA (Calle 24, Avda Central/1; tel: 221 9414) uses the international airport at Alajuela, further west on the PanAmerican.

Maps

Decent maps are available from the *Instituto Nacional Geográfico* just inside the north gate of the Ministry of Public Works at Avda 20, C 9-11; open only from 07.30 to 12.00 Monday to Friday. You can also find most at Lehmann's Bookshop and the Universal department store, although they cost more.

As usual, there are hiking maps at 1:50,000 and more general ones at 1:200,000; the 1:200,000 map of San José gives a good overview of the whole area from Arenal to Tapantí.

Food

Costa Rica is the southern limit of the *boca* tradition. *Bocas* are small dishes of savoury goodies which inspire you to drink more beer. Not every bar has them, but *Chelle's Bar* at Avenida Central and Calle 9 in San José (open 24 hours) is well known for its selection. You can also buy snacks from bakeries such as *Muswanni* (open 05.00-21.00), where you serve yourself with tongs — very hygienic!

Not altogether surprisingly, rice and beans are the staple foods, but Costa Rica makes them interesting by sautéing them with coriander, onion and pepper and spices to make *gallo pinto* — as *pinto huevo*, with an egg, it makes a great breakfast. *Sopa negra* (black bean soup) is popular too. There are plenty of *sodas* or snack bars which serve *casados*, good cheap lunches of meat or fish, rice, beans and vegetable or salad. Again, they're remarkably hygiene-conscious, with cutlery coming airline-style in a plastic sleeve.

San José's Central Market, at Avenida Central and Calles 6-8, is not to be missed. It's open daily from 06.00 to 18.00 and is packed with leather goods, fruit and vegetables, medicinal plants, souvenirs, curios and cheap restaurants, many of which do excellent *ceviche* (raw fish or shrimp marinated in lime juice, vinegar and spices). An educational and delicious experience!

Hotels

Despite Costa Rica's tourist-friendly reputation, cheap hotels are not great. Not only are the rooms coffin-sized wooden boxes, but there'll be no toilet paper, no toilet seat, no soap, no towel and no smile on the face of the management. In many hotels, it seems, a guest is seen as akin to a domestic animal, a source of income but of no interest otherwise.

In San José, most of the cheap hotels are in the area of the Central Market and the so-called Coca-Cola bus terminal, west of the centre; this area isn't totally safe at night. There is a genuine youth hostel on the Cartago road, Avenida Central, between Calles 29 and 31, 15 blocks east of Calle Central (Apdo 1355-1002; tel: 253 6588, fax: 224 4085); it's worth paying US$9 for bed, breakfast and genuine hot showers. This is a quiet area close to the National Parks HQ and the National and Railway Museums and it's a good place to stay if you've just flown in and are feeling a bit timid; it's a pleasant place for single women as well. Other so-called hostels are in fact commercial operations offering discounts for HI (Hostelling International) members, but they're still not cheap.

There's been a rash of hotel building in the last few years, especially in the Nicoya peninsula where 30 are due to open in 1995; growth in tourism has not kept pace with this, so that 3- and 4-star hotels are only 50% full and may be willing to give you a good deal.

Naturalists' Costa Rica

The general layout of Costa Rica is fairly standard for Central America, with broad plains on the Atlantic coast with high rainfall producing swamps and thick rainforest, a largely volcanic ridge down the western side of the country, and drier land, now mostly pasture, on the Pacific slope. The highest peak, at 3,819m, is Chirripó, in the non-volcanic Cordillera de Talamanca, which runs from Cartago to the Panamanian border. San José and other major towns are set at about 1,000m on a plain known as the Meseta Central or Central Tableland. To the north of this runs a line of four volcanoes, from west to east Poás, Barva, Irazú and Turrialba, all frequently and easily visited.

The dry season or *verano* runs from late December to April, but there are dry periods known as *veranillos* in July and August. On the Atlantic coast it is always more humid than on the Pacific coast and tends to rain throughout the year; the sunniest season is in fact in September/October when the Pacific side is at its wettest. In San José the average temperature is a spring-like 20°C with 1,950mm of rain a year; in the Cordillera de Talamanca the average temperature is 16°C.

The biodiversity of Costa Rica is pretty amazing: 35,000 species of insect, 205 mammals, 200-plus reptiles (almost half of them snakes), 150 amphibians, 848 birds (including 57 hummingbirds, 16 parrots, 6 toucans, 75 flycatchers, 45 tanagers, 29 antbirds, and 19 cotingas), and between 9,000 and 12,000 vascular plants (including 1,200 orchids, 88% of them epiphytic).

National parks

The *Servicio de Parques Nacionales* is not far from the centre of San José in the MIRENEM (Ministry of Natural Resources, Energy and Mines) tower at Calle 25, Avda 8-10 (Apdo 10104-1000; tel: 233 4118/4246, fax: 223 6963). Permits, valid for 90 days, can be bought very quickly and easily here (Mon-Fri 08.00-16.00), except for Corcovado and Chirripó, which require reservations and take a little longer.

Forest protection in Costa Rica dates from 1863, when land on either side of the Northern Highway was protected from logging; as you'll see, this hasn't had much effect; in 1913 the same was done for the areas around the summits of the higher volcanoes, with more effect. The first nature reserve was created in 1963 at Cabo Blanca, and the main national parks came into being in the 1970s. Costa Rica led the way in Central America, and indeed in much of the developing world, in recognizing the value of these areas, both in themselves and for tourism. Now they are being grouped into regional units or conservation areas, combining national parks, nature refuges and indigenous reserves. On paper, 28% of the country's area is now protected, and there are plans to further increase this. However, Costa Rica's deforestation rate is one of the highest in Latin America, a seemingly inevitable product of economic growth, and soon there'll be little forest left outside the park system.

In September 1994, with just a month's warning, fees for visiting national parks were increased from a flat rate of US$1.25 per day to US$15 for foreigners on entry. If bought in advance, however, they vary from US$5 to US$10 (depending on the park) and a five-park pass can be purchased for US$29. Fees remain unchanged for Ticos and local residents. This caused quite a shock; suddenly private parks such as Monteverde which had seemed expensive before became the cheaper option. The number of foreign visitors to national parks from September to December 1994 was just 63,298, against 107,886 for the same period in 1993; however, the number of Costa Rican visitors also fell 12%, and visitor numbers had begun to fall before the fee increase, making it possible to argue that over-crowding was to blame. The debate rages on, but at the end of the day parks' income was US$5m higher in the last third of 1994 than in 1993, so it's clear that they have benefitted, with more funds and less disturbance. Government policy is for parks to become self-supporting, and Poás has already been able to build a US$330,000 extension to its visitor centre.

The Wildlife Directorate (tel: 221 9533), managing wildlife refuges, and the Forestry Directorate (tel: 221 9535), managing forestry reserves, are both in the Bolivar Zoo, north of the centre of San José.

Ecotourism companies:

Costa Rica Expeditions, Calle Central & Avda 3, San José, Apdo 6941-1000 (tel: 257 0766, fax: 257 1665) or Dept 235, PO Box 025216, Miami FL 33102-5216. Established in 1978, CRE is the grand-daddy of ecotourism in Costa Rica and is easily the highest quality operator in the area. They don't do much hiking, but their guided trips to national parks are excellent. They now own the Monteverde, Corcovado and Tortuga Lodges and Costa Rica White Water, but haven't altogether lost their soul to big business, frequently taking the lead in campaigning against unsuitable development.

Adventure Land, Avda 1, Calle 1/3 San José (tel: 222 3866, fax: 222 3724); mountain biking and hiking in La Amistad.

Expediciones Tropicales, Calle 3 bis, Avda 11-13, San José (Apdo 6793-1000; tel: 257 4171, fax: 257 4124); standard day trips to Poás and Irazú, Tortuguero, Carara, Arenal etc, and rafting.

Braun Eco Tourismo, Hotel Ritz, Calle Central, Avda 8/10, San José (tel: 233 1731, fax: 222 849); almost identical to above.

Dos Montañas (c/o Ríos Tropicales/tel: 233 6455); hiking in Chirripó and Corcovado.

TAM, Calle 1, Avda 0/1, San José (Apdo 1864-1000, tel: 22 2642, fax: 21 6465); since 1964, day tours for the AmEx market, though prices no worse than the others.

Eco Treks, Flamingo Marina Hotel, San Rafael de Escazú (tel: 228 4029); mountain biking and diving trips.

Ecological organizations

Most of the groups working in conservation in Central America are based here.

Amigos de los Aves, Apdo 32-4001 Río Segundo (tel: 441 2658).

APREFLOFAS (Association for the Preservation of Wild Flora and Fauna), Apdo 917-2150 San José (tel: 240 6087).

APROCA (Aquatic Conservation Association) Apdo 1863-1002 San José (tel: 255 3365).

Arbofila, Apdo 52 or 512-1100 Tibás, San José (tel: 236 7145); reforestation.

ASCONA (Association for the Conservation of Nature), Apdo 8-3790-1000 San José (tel: 222 2296); a pressure group, lobbying government and educating the public.

Asociación para la Conservació del Medio y Recursos Naturales, Puntarenas (tel: 661 1221).

Asociación para la Defensa de los Recursos Naturales, Apdo 1080-1250 Escazú (tel: 228 1092, fax: 228 9999).

Asociación Tsuli Tsuli, Audubon Society of Costa Rica, Apdo 4910-1000 San

José (tel: 273 4219); and San José Audubon, Apdo 300-1002 San José (tel: 224 8910). I don't know what the relationship is between these two. Most Central American Audubon Societies are concerned with general habitat conservation rather than specifically with birds.

ASVO (Association of Volunteers for Service in Protected Areas) (tel: 222 5085).

CODESCOS (Centre for Conservation and Sustainable Development of Coastal Ecosystems) (tel/fax: 273 3022).

Costa Rican Association for the Protection of the Rivers, Apdo 4600-1000 San José (tel: 223 1925).

Fundación Neotrópica, Paseo de los Estudiantes, Apdo 236-1002 San José (tel: 233 0003); well established, with a variety of projects and shops at some national parks.

Organisation for Tropical Studies, Apdo 676-2050 San Pedro (tel: 240 6696; fax: 240 6783) or PO Box DM, Duke Station, Durham, North Carolina 27706, USA. The OTS, or OET in Spanish, is a consortium of 53 North and Central American universities, founded in 1963, that runs three research stations, at La Selva, Palo Verde, and the Wilson Botanical Gardens (QV); to book accommodation you can visit their offices 50m west of the Plaza Los Colegios Commercial Centre in Moravia, reached by the *Florida por El Cruce* minibus (21A) from Calle 2 north of Avda 5 in San José.

Conservation Media Center, Apdo 138-2150 Moravia, San José (tel: 236 3073, fax: 240 2543); an offshoot of the Rainforest Alliance (65 Bleecker St, New York, NY 10012-2420, USA; tel: 212 677 1900, fax: 212 677 2187), distributes environmental news through its Tropical Conservation Newsbureau and helps train local journalists.

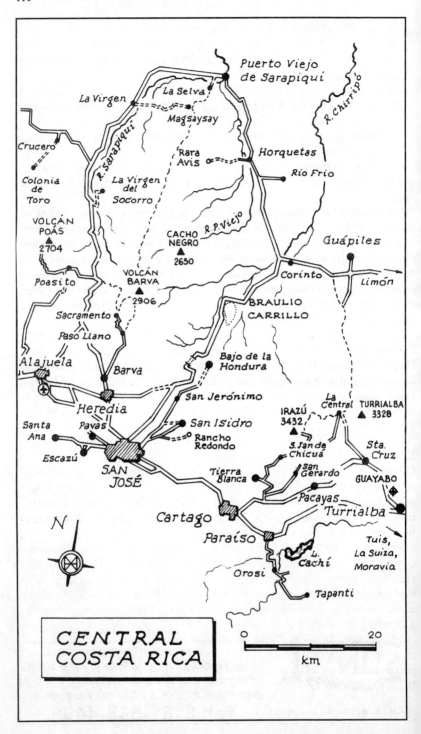

CENTRAL
COSTA RICA

Chapter Eleven

Central Costa Rica

SAN JOSÉ

San José seems very much like home, which may be good or bad depending on how travel-worn you are. It can seem strange to see white people eating in American-style burger-bars, and the rather uninspiring commercialism can be depressing, but San José has much to offer the tourist, including probably the best museums in Central America.

There's a large expat community, with such features of North American life as realtors, Hash House Harriers, a synagogue and an English-language newspaper.

Tourist Information
Below the Plaza de la Cultura, Calle 5, Avda Central/2 (tel: 223 4481, fax: 223 4476), open Mon-Fri 09.00-17.00 and Saturday to 13.00. Pretty helpful, for the usual sort of hotel information and so on. The annual *Tourist Orientation Guide* is an information-packed free booklet. You should also be sure to see the weekly English-language *Tico Times*.

Museums
Our favourite is the Jade Museum, up on the 11th floor of the *Instituto Nacional de Seguros* (Avda 7, Calle 7/9; Mon-Fri 09.00-15.00); they have a large collection of jade and other archaeological finds, impressively laid out and of uniformly high standard. And it's free: if you only have time for one museum here, make it this one.

The Natural History Museum, in the LaSalle College at the southwestern corner of the Sabana (Mon-Fri 08.00-16.00, Sat 08.00-12.00, Sun 09.00-16.00) is a long trip to see some of the most macabre, ghoulish and comical taxidermy ever visited on poor dumb animals. There's a more academic Insect Museum at the university, in the basement of the *Artes Musicales* building (Mon-Fri 13.00-16.45).

The National Museum (Calle 17, Avda 0/2; Tues-Sun 08.30-16.30) houses a well laid-out archaeological display, some fine gold work and informatively presented exhibits on recent Costa Rican history. You may have to ask to see the natural history collection.

Gear shops

Easily the best is at the offices of *Ríos Tropicales* (Calle 32 and Avda 2; shop open Mon-Fri 09.00-18.00, Sat 09.00-13.00); they have new and second-hand cycling/climbing/ kayaking gear, also books and a noticeboard. Costa Rica Expeditions' Travellers' Store (Mon-Sat 09.00-18.00) is really just a souvenir shop; oddly the Camping Shop (*La Tienda del Camping*) on Avda 8 east of Calle 11 sells picnic-type gear, while the Sports Palace (*El Palacio del Deporte*) at Calle 2, Avda 2/4, sells camping gear. There are plenty of decent supermarkets, notably at Avda 3 and Calle 3 in the centre of San José, or just beyond the youth hostel on Avenida Central.

THE CORDILLERA VOLCANICA CENTRAL

In 1913 an area of 2km radius around the crater of Volcán Poás was declared a protected zone; in 1955 and again in 1963 a zone of 2km radius around each of the country's volcanoes was declared protected for tourism, eventually developing into the national parks that now protect, among others, Poás, Barva, Irazú and Turrialba, the four volcanoes forming the northern and eastern boundary of the Meseta Central. Now they, with the Juan Castro Blanco National Park and adjoining forestry reserves, have been amalgamated into the Cordillera Volcanica Central Conservation Area, one of the first of Costa Rica's new generation of super-parks.

Volcán Poás

Volcán Poás (2,704m) remains the most developed of Costa Rica's parks and is the most visited because coaches can drive right to the top on an asphalt road. It's not of much interest as a hiking spot, but you might wish to take a trip up to see the immense crater, 1.5km across and 314m deep, one of the deepest active craters in the world. Records of eruptions date back to 1828, with three major periods of activity during the years 1888-95, 1903-12 and 1952-55. There was more activity in 1974, 1978, 1989 and 1994, and steam still vents from fumaroles near the main crater. Water from a hot lake in the main crater was once sold as a cure for toothache, but it's now forbidden to enter this crater due to the poisonous fumes. To the north is the von Frantzius cone, the volcano's oldest eruptive centre; 20 minutes to the southwest is a beautiful lake of rainwater in the Botos crater, inactive for 7,500 years. This is reached by a trail through Costa Rica's only true dwarf cloudforest, dominated by *mamey* (*Clusia odorata*) and blueberries (*Vaccinium sp*), starting just before the viewpoint and returning to the Visitor Centre. Another short path runs for 1km through cloudforest, mostly oak with local species such as Poás magnolia (*Magnolia poasana*) and escallonia (*Escallonia poasiana*). It can get chilly quickly, and a low of -6°C has been recorded. There are only a few fairly small mammals (cats, coyotes, rabbits, squirrels, skunks and weasels), but about 80 species of birds, notably the *Simoni* subspecies of the volcano hummingbird *Selasphorus flammula*, which was until recently thought to be a distinct species. There are also fiery-throated hummingbirds, black-billed nightingale-thrushes, clay-coloured and sooty robins and lots of finches; lower down in the cloudforest are emerald toucanets and black guans.

Plenty of companies in San José offer trips to Poás for about US$30, often combined with a visit to the touristy craft centre of Sarchí. This is the easiest way to get to the top except on Sundays, when a bus leaves at 08.30 from Calle 12 Avda 2/4 in San José, returning at 14.30. There's also a bus from Alajuela's Central Park at 08.00 on Sundays, and others that run daily (at 05.00, 12.00 and perhaps other times) from Alajuela to Poasito, 7km below the summit. As with all of these volcanoes, visibility is best early in the morning, and you should certainly aim to be on top by 10.00; to be sure of this you might have to hire a car or stay in one of the expensive guesthouses around Poasito.

An area of 14,258ha immediately to the northwest of Poás is protected by the **Juan Castro Blanco National Park**, hilly and thickly forested terrain that is little visited due to its position on the 'wrong' side of the mountains from San José and due to its lack of facilities. At least half of the park is covered by tropical premontane wet forest and montane cloudforest (mostly oak, with lancewood or *quizarrá*); much of the higher forest is stunted due to cold and wind. The highest point is Volcán Porvenir (2,267m), and just north of this is the active Volcán Platanar. Birds to be seen include quetzal, black guan, chacalaca and curassow. Mammals include two species of monkey, jaguar, margay and other cats, tapir, red brocket deer, agouti and armadillo.

Hiking is permitted, but apart from minor paths on the park's fringes the only access is along the Río Toro, on 4WD roads built for a controversial hydro-electric scheme completed in 1995. Several waterfalls have dried up as a result (although the Río Claro Falls, possibly Costa Rica's highest, will be allowed to flow at weekends) — but no-one's really complaining, as there's never been any access to them anyway. The upper part of the scheme is reached from the village of Bajos del Toro, north of Sarchí, while the lower part is reached through Colonia de Toro, south of Crucero and Marsella, both just south of Highway 140, to the north of the park. There have also been attempts to mine sulphur in the park, but these were cancelled after protests.

Volcán Barva and Braulio-Carrillo

To the east of Poás, Highway 126 continues north to the Sarapiquí valley, where there are several private reserves and research stations. To the east of this is **Volcán Barva** (or Barba; 2,906m), which is visible immediately to the north of San José. Although it's the closest to the capital it's less visited than Poás or Irazú because the road doesn't go all the way to the top; this makes it interesting as a hike, but there are regular incidents of cars being broken into at the roadhead. Buses run from Heredia, a pleasant town 10km north of San José, at 06.00, 12.00 and 16.00, with the last back at 17.00; the road ends at Sacramento, at about 2,300m, but most buses make you walk from Paso Llano (also known as Porrosatí), 6km below at about 1,950m. From Sacramento it's about a 3km walk on a good trail to the top, where you'll see several craters, including one that contains a lake 70m across. Barva is known for its orchids; birds include the quetzal, black guan, red-tailed sparrow-hawk and solitaire;

there's also an endemic species of toad, *Bufo holdridgei*.

Maps may show a route from Paso Llano to the summit; if you had advanced bush-bashing skills you could make it this way, but essentially the path is badly overgrown and lost. It is partly marked with plastic tags, but these are, I think, only for the use of researchers going a little way into the forest. It's a nice walk into great forest and well worth a look if you have time. From the road junction at the Chagos Bar, asphalt heads up to the right for ten minutes to the Finca Los Bambinos; a decent dirt road carries on climbing steeply, following the Río Ciruelas past fields of cows for half an hour. Here it turns left through a gate to a farm, but you should continue ahead on a level track; in three minutes this reaches a water tank on a ridge and turns left into the woods to the northeast. At first this is well used by horses and cows, with a waterpipe running along it as well. If you don't see the orange markers heading off to the left you can climb up the rockfall above the second stream to get into clearer dwarf cloudforest. Take great care; in 1989 three German hikers were lost in this area for eleven days!

Volcán Barva is part of the **Braulio-Carrillo National Park**, and again, looking at the map you might think you might be able to hike east to the rest of the park — but no, don't even think of trying it. The park was created in 1978 to protect a large tract of unspoilt rainforest from development arising from what is still called the 'new' highway from San José to Limón via Guápiles, and it's best reached from this road. It's one of the country's bigger parks, at 45,899ha, and is important because it has a large altitudinal range, allowing plenty of biodiversity. Its lowest point is below 500m altitude, with 4,500mm of rain per year, and the highest point is Barva at 2,906m. There are five types of moist tropical and premontane forest, containing 6,000 species of plant, half of all those found in Costa Rica. There are at least 347 species of birds (or 515, depending on whom you believe), including the king-vulture, black-chested hawk, bare-necked umbrella birds, lattice-tailed trogon, yellow-eared toucanet, white-crowned manakin, sooty-faced finch, ant-vireo, scarlet-chested cacique and many more. Mammals include three species of monkey, jaguar, puma, ocelot, margay, porcupine, tapir, coati, kinkajou, peccary, paca, sloth, raccoon and coyote.

There are various short paths off the highway, well known to bird-watchers who come by car, but no decent long hikes; nevertheless it's a good place to look at the forest without bothering with a permit. Buses to Guápiles, Siquirres and Limón will set you down and (usually) pick you up along the road, so it's easy enough to visit without a car. The park headquarters are at about km17, just after the tolls if coming from San José; there's a dormitory here and a 2.5km loop trail to a lookout above the road tunnel, where you may be able to see quetzals. From the tunnel at km19 the road drops down towards the Atlantic, with great views and a few fairly poor lay-bys and miradors. At km35 the Waterfall Trail (to the right/east at the bottom of a broad straight with crash barriers on both sides) is popular with birders, but is now marked 'At your own risk', with parking forbidden.

At km36.7 (where there's a cable slung over the road, for some reason) there's an unmarked turning to the left to a picnic area and the start of the Ridge Trail, one of the most interesting in the park. There are concrete steps up to the right, to meteorological instruments with a great view to Volcán Irazú. Naturally enough, the Ridge Trail follows the ridge east, leading to the Sendero Botella (Bottle Path), which drops down towards the Río Patria; there are collared anteaters and white-faced monkeys here, and lots of chestnut-headed oropendolas and tanagers. Cars left here have been broken into, and there have even been armed robberies; arriving by bus or on foot is far more discreet.

At km39.5 the road crosses a high modern bridge, where the Río Hondura flows into the well-named Río Sucio (Dirty River — silt, not pollution). Just beyond it a track drops down to the right to the shingle banks along the river, where you can camp; here you may see white-collared swifts and torrent tyranulets. Almost 2km further along the road is the Quebrada Gonzaléz Park Station, with the best-maintained trails in the park. Behind the buildings to the east is the Las Palmas Trail (1.6km), the only one in the park you actually need a permit for. Across the road is the El Ceibo Trail, a nice 1km loop through lowland rainforest, with guans, woodpeckers and long-tailed tyrannulets.

In the early days of coffee-growing in the Meseta Central, before the railway was built to the Atlantic coast via Turrialba, coffee was carried to the coastal plain by ox-cart along the Río Hondura valley. There's no sign of it now at the Río Sucio bridge, but you can follow the cobbled trail for some way from the terminus of the San Jerónimo de Moravia bus (from Avda 3 Calle 3/5 in San José) to the Bajo de la Hondura Historic Site. After about 15km you reach the Braulio-Carrillo Park's southern boundary, beyond which there's no access.

Just beyond the park boundary, on the Limón road, are some private reserves, operated on a fairly commercial basis for the benefit of coach parties; for US$40-50 you can sample some high-tech methods of seeing the forest canopy, with either the Rainforest Aerial Tram or the Automated Web for Canopy Exploration. At km49 there's a turning left to Horquetas, 15km north; 11km to the west, on the fringes of the Braullio-Carrillo Park, is the Rara Avis Reserve, notable for being reached by a 2.5km ride by tractor and trailer, and for the fact that you sleep in an former prison, the *El Plastico* Lodge. It's expensive even with youth hostel discount, but it's for a good cause; they have 607ha in which they're experimenting with sustainable use of the rainforest. Book through Apdo 8105-1000 San José (tel/fax: 253 0844). There's also access to the Braulio-Carrillo Park through another prison, to the north at Magsaysay, 10km east of La Virgen de Sarapiquí. From here it's about 8km north to La Selva, and in time a 30km trail may also be developed south to Barva.

Between Horquetas and La Virgen lies Puerto Viejo de Sarapiquí, immediately south of which is the **La Selva** research station of the OTS. This is a continuation of the Braulio-Carrillo Park and marks the northern end of the Cordillera Volcanica Central Conservation Area, but the very wet lowland forest is often seen as an alternative to Tortuguero, more accessible and with no national park fees. At one time, in fact, access to Barra del Colorado was usually by boat from Puerto Viejo down the Río Sarapiquí and Río San Juan, but new roads mean that you're now less likely to find a boat taking this route. The most striking feature of the forest is the very dense understorey of shrubs and dwarf palms growing on the rich basaltic soils. In it you can see herons, kingfishers, tanagers, oropendolas, hummingbirds, howler monkeys, kinkajous, crocodiles, iguanas and poison dart frogs. The research station (tel: 710 1515) is heaving with researchers and field trips, but for US$20 you can get a day permit (and map) for their excellent network of trails (though I gather permits are rarely checked). There's accommodation, also at prices that subsidize scientific research; there are plenty of 'ecolodges' and the like in this area, some very cheap, others pretty luxurious. Most have excellent birding and can also arrange riding and fishing. Kayaking is provided by Kayak Jungle Tours, at Rancha Leona in La Virgen (tel: 761 1019) — a great way to creep up on the wildlife.

Volcán Irazú

Further to the southeast, the Río Sucio rises on the slopes of **Volcán Irazú**, Costa Rica's highest volcano at 3,432m; the Irazú National Park covers all the land over 3,000m on both Irazú and Volcán Turrialba, just east. Irazú was particularly active between 1962 and 1965, with an eruption in March 1963 that scattered several centimetres of ash over San José; it's been more or less dormant since, although there are active fumaroles and occasional earth tremors. In all there are five craters, of which the main one is 1,052m across and 305m deep, with a weird green-yellow lake at the bottom. Prior to the 1963 eruption Costa Rica's only tropical montane wet forest was found here, dominated by oaks and bamboos, but plant life is still struggling to re-establish itself in what is now a lunar landscape. Above about 3,300m there are only blueberries growing. Mammals are also scarce, with little other than rabbits, squirrels, weasels and coyotes; birds are more interesting, with the volcano junco, solitaire, ruddy treecreeper, sparrow hawk, pygmy-owls, hummingbirds and woodpeckers.

The path to the north of the car park is closed after a short stretch and is dangerous; a better bet is to go to the south towards the highest point, and to keep going beyond the crowds. Other than the craters themselves, Irazú's main attraction is the chance of seeing both oceans, most likely on a clear day early in the morning. As a consequence, the park has been developed more for motorists than for nature lovers. If driving from San José, turn left at the Ferreteria San Nicolas as you enter Cartago to bypass the town, after about 7km take two lefts and then turn right at the sanatorium about 1km before Tierra Blanco. If you don't drive or cycle up (it's a climb of exactly 2,000m in 21km from Cartago, an average incline of almost 10%), you may get a ride with technicians going to work on the radio masts. A bus runs to the top on Saturdays, Sundays and holidays, leaving from the Grand Hotel Costa Rica (Avda 2, Calle 3, San José) at 08.00, picking up at the *ruinas* in Cartago at 08.30 (but you don't want to spend the night in Cartago), and returning at

12.15. On other days hourly local buses from Cartago (Calle 4, Avda 6) to Tierra Blanca will drop you at the sanatorium, from where you have a 14km walk to the summit through misty fertile farmland. On Mondays and perhaps Thursdays buses run at 06.30 as far as San Juan de Chicuá (where there are a couple of affordable places to stay), at almost 2,800m, just 8km from the end of the road. There are also plenty of tour buses from San José, which usually combine Irazú with visits to the Lankester Gardens (the University of Costa Rica's botanical gardens, with about 800 species of orchid, at their best around April) and the Orosi valley (where you'll see Costa Rica's oldest church and the artificial Lake Cachí); prices range from US$27 for Irazú alone to US$56 for the full works. The visitor centre is open from 09.00 to 16.00; there's no gate so you can camp at the top but there are no facilities.

Volcán Turrialba

Traditionally Poás and Irazú were the most visited of the volcanoes lining the north of the Meseta Central, as these were the ones with asphalt roads all the way to the top. **Volcán Turrialba**, the furthest from San José, was the preserve of the backpacker and a remote and lonely place. This may be about to change, as the asphalt was due to arrive in February 1995, but it is still unlikely to be visited by coach parties. There's no national park gate, and thus no need for a permit, and you can easily combine it with Irazú (coming down from Irazú, turn left after about 3km to reach San Rafael de Irazú, above San Gerardo). As so often, it's at the edge of four 1:50,000 maps, and two 1:200,000 maps.

Most people start by taking a bus from Turrialba to Santa Cruz, but in fact it's easier to take a bus from Cartago (Calle 4, Avda 6) to San Gerardo de Oreamuno — it's a longer walk, but the bus takes you so much higher that it's well worth it. Buses leave at 06.15, 14.30 and 17.30 daily (possibly marked Santa Rosa) and crawl uphill, almost entirely in first or second gear, for an hour, finally stopping in San Pablo, ten minutes beyond San Gerardo at about 2,400m. From here you just have to take the dirt road to the left, passing occasional signs to the Turrialba Lodge (tel: 273 4335), which offers horseback trips to the volcanoes; you'll cross the Río Birrís, and pass the church of San Rafael de Irazú after 40 minutes. It's marvellous soft green country, all mist and potatoes and cows being milked by hand beside the road. After climbing easily for another 30 minutes, you just walk around the east side of Irazú, more or less on the level, and then drop gently into forest. After an hour you'll reach a farm with red barns at a turning left to another San Gerardo, on the northern slopes of Irazú. Just beyond here you'll find plenty of flat grassy areas for camping in the fields to the left: never have I sunk a peg into softer, more receptive turf, and the setting is great, too. Almost 20 minutes from the farm there's the left turn to the Turrialba Lodge; after eight minutes more you should turn right to enter La Central, the last community on the road (just below 2,700m). The road left goes down through some pretty wild country to eventually emerge at Guápiles, on the coastal highway.

The route to the top of Turrialba turns left in La Central by a disused chapel (now a store) and climbs to a ridge in 12 minutes; then it continues around the mountain to the right, passing through some forest and more fields. After 20 minutes a shortcut to the Turrialba road heads down through a gate on the right, where the main route turns sharply left at a small farm and climbs more steeply. Again it traverses around to the right, reaching the last farm after 30 minutes. From here the track zigzags steeply up the hill, through shorter trees and bamboo with lots of views to Chirripó and beyond. After about 30 minutes you'll reach the summit, with picnic benches set below a radio mast; a path runs along the rim to the right to the highest point, while the track continues another 4km to the farm of Bajos Bonilla. You could easily spend the best part of a day walking around the summit and inside the three huge craters on well-worn footpaths; this volcano is impressive and atmospheric, but the walk up is easily as beautiful.

Coming from Turrialba, there's an 07.00 departure to Santa Cruz on Mondays, Wednesdays and Fridays, but otherwise you should catch the noon bus, which will take you an extra 3km to the bar La Cañada and Soda Glenda, at about 1,600m, just below the village of La Pastora. One bus a day runs from Cartago (Avda 4, Calle 8) to Santa Cruz via La Pastora, arriving at about 15.00. Turn north at La Cañada and you'll see the sign 'Volcán Turrialba 18km' — the road goes left, but you can take a more direct route by going straight ahead and taking the first left, before the school. After a few hundred metres you'll pass the Hacienda Palmira; where the road bends left you can take a direct path up through the fields ahead. After a few more bends (3km by road from La Cañada) you pass a hut on the right with a sign 'Stress-Free Zone'. Here you'll find Iris, who lived in California and speaks good English. She welcomes campers, and may have built some *cabanas* by the time you get there. The road climbs on; every few kilometres you pass a turning to a small farm but the main route is always clear, usually the higher option. Once the whole area above La Pastora was one estate, the Hacienda Volcán, but it has now been divided — even so, most of the people, and their dogs, are clearly closely related. La Central lies 12km from La Cañada, and 1,100m above.

An alternative is to turn right at the Finca La Fuente, the last farm before La Central (at 2,590m), cross the stream and then turn left to follow a more direct (and non-asphalted) path to join the track to the summit. This makes a particularly easy and pleasant descent.

Turrialba and Guayabo

The town of **Turrialba** is not an especially attractive place, but it does have some interesting features. It's Costa Rica's rafting capital, with all the companies based here and operating out of Angostura, a few kilometres southeast of town, where the main road crosses the Río Reventazón. Groups come from San José for day trips, but if you corner a rafting guide in one of the bars around the main square you might be able to get the same trip for less.

Halfway to Angostura lies the campus of CATIE, the Centre for Research and Teaching in Tropical Agronomy, the leading centre of expertise in this area. It has an excellent (British-built) library where you can read-up on deforestation or integrated pest management and, more realistically, beautiful grounds in which you can see waterbirds and a huge variety of fine trees.

Continuing east, ten buses a day turn right off the Siquirres road just beyond the Angostura bridge, to reach La Suiza and Tuis. Set in the premontane rainforest here is the very expensive *Rancho Naturalista* (Apdo 364-1002 San José, tel: 267 7138), where wealthy bird-watchers can see up to 345 species including the snowcap hummingbird, the mountain gem (also a hummingbird), the dullmantled antbird and the lanceolated monkbird, as well as morphos and many other butterflies. Beyond this lies the Río Pacuare, a wild and beautiful river that offers more exciting rafting than the Reventazón; however, there are plans to dam it, which are causing protests by rafting operators, environmentalists and local people.

Turrialba is also the base for Costa Rica's most important archaeological site, **Guayabo**; this was occupied from 1,000BC at the latest to AD1,400 by a largely unknown people, perhaps 10,000 of them at its peak. About 10,000 tombs have been found, but the acidic soil, coupled with 3,500mm of rain a year, have left little trace of what was buried there. There are also aqueducts, water-tanks and bridges, in remarkably good condition. The enveloping forest is home to plenty of chestnut-headed oropendolas, as well as scarlet-rumped caciques, rainbow-billed toucans, agoutis and anteaters. Camping is allowed here, but there are only limited facilities; buses leave Turrialba at 11.00 (returning 12.50) and 17.00 (returning 17.50).

Railway walks from Turrialba

Turrialba is set on both the old highway to Limón (incredibly slow and twisty compared to the new one) and the railway: the latter was renowned for its spectacular route down the Reventazón valley east of Turrialba, but it was exactly this stretch of line that was blocked by landslides and then earthquakes in 1990 and 1991. The railway is now totally abandoned except (perhaps) for a tourist train in the Atlantic plains — the San José to Cartago service was closed down in June 1994. This means, of course, that you are at liberty to hike this route as far as you can; the railway has always been used as a footpath anyway, and some of the houses along the line just west of Turrialba can't be reached any other way. Walking west, about 1km from the level crossing in the centre of Turrialba, the permanent way has been covered and converted to a dirt road; this ends after less than 2km but a well-used path continues. It's not particularly scenic in this direction but there are plenty of small birds.

Heading east, the route is more interesting. Starting from the level crossing, you pass the cheap hotels and the station at km102 and cross a bridge to leave the town. For a while after this you should follow a path to the left, as the track is overgrown, but then you can continue along the tracks. You'll cross a dramatic high bridge and then (30 minutes from the start) another, in a less dramatic setting but with plenty of sleepers (ties) missing. It's easy enough to cross, using the longitudinal girders below the rails, but it wouldn't be so simple with a heavy pack or a mountain bike. After another ten minutes walking through a coffee plantation you come to Finca Azul; you can use a parallel track, but after five minutes this drops away to the right while the railway curves to the left and drops towards the Reventazón Gorge. The trackbed is attempting to revert to jungle but it's still well used. It would be very interesting to continue to see if it's possible to get past the landslides, and if all the bridges are still intact; however, most people will prefer to loop back to town after an hour or so, and I therefore turned north to take a track through the finca to the parallel road. This takes a long route back to Turrialba, but there are buses (from Azul and El Mor), and you could cut back left to get back to the bridge to the station.

Anhinga

Chapter Twelve

Southern Costa Rica

The backbone of southern Costa Rica is the Cordillera de Talamanca, beginning south of Cartago and extending into Panamá. These are highly faulted and folded metamorphic rocks with intrusive igneous formations. The highest peaks were glaciated 25,000 years ago in the Pleistocene, producing moraines, cirque lakes and other postglacial formations found nowhere else in Central America. Here you'll find *paramó*, a subalpine scrub habitat ('tropical tundra') found mainly in the Andes, as well as high-altitude bogs. Slopes are steep (45° or more), with poor soils; on the Atlantic slope these can receive up to 7,000mm of rain, and would clearly be washed clean instantly were they not bound in place by the forests. This is largely oak cloud forest, with some winter's bark (*Drimys*), sweet cedar, cypress, elm and Poás magnolia, and a largely bamboo understorey. It's home to over 3,000 species of butterfly and moth, 215 species of mammal, many of them endangered, including large numbers of tapir, all six Central American species of wild cat, and the giant anteater, no less than 263 species of reptiles and amphibians, and to 400 species of birds, including the resplendent quetzal, harpy eagle, and at least 50 endemics. This is the southern limit of the range of many North American bird species.

These are the largest, most diverse wildlands left in southern Central America, notably in the Tapantí National Park and the La Amistad International Park (shared with Panamá), as well as the Chirripó National Park, which protects the highest peaks. All these are now part of the Amistad Conservation Area, a UNESCO Biosphere Reserve, almost half a million hectares of protected land of various categories stretching from an altitude of 1,000m on the Pacific side to sea-level on the Atlantic coast, and adding up to 10% of Costa Rica's area. It's home to almost all of Costa Rica's remaining indigenous peoples (the Boruca, Bri-Bri, Guaymi, Cabecars and others), and indigenous reserves form a large part of the conservation area. There are countless archaeological sites — petroglyphs, burial sites and so on, very different both to those of the Mayas, Toltecs and Aztecs to the north and to those of the Incas to the south. Despite all this, there are still regular proposals to exploit the area's oil, copper and hydro-electric reserves or to build a trans-Talamanca highway.

Tapantí
The Tapantí National Park protects the northern end of the Talamanca range, but is reached from Cartago and the Orosi valley, with tours usually combined

with Volcán Irazu. There's a very wild broken topography, draped in primary evergreen forest and rising to 2,560m; with at least 6,500mm of precipitation every year, there's no doubt that this is low montane rainforest. It's not all been explored properly as yet; there are trails but they don't penetrate too far. The forest is mostly oak, with magnolias and tree hibiscus, and plenty of *Gunnera* (poor man's umbrella), orchids, bromeliads, ferns and mosses. There are at least 211 bird species, including quetzals (supposedly nesting within sight of the ranger hut), hawks, falcons, guans, solitaires, collared trogons, three-wattled bellbirds, golden-bellied flycatchers, hummingbirds, parakeets, Chiriqui quail-doves, tinamous and tanagers, and 45 mammals, including cats such as jaguar, ocelot, jaguaroundi, margay and manigordo, tapirs, agouti, red brocket deer, mountain rabbit, coati, kinkajou, raccoon and white-faced monkey. In addition there are 28 amphibians and *Thysania agripina*, the largest moth in the Americas.

The hourly San José-Turrialba buses will drop you in Paraíso, 19km from the park gates; local buses to Cachí run from Cartago (one block east and three south from the Ruinas) via Paraíso and Orosi every 1½ hours and can take you on to Río Macho, 9km from the gates, and a few go as far as Purisil, 5km from the gates. There are one or two lodges before you get to the gates, there's camping inside, and possibly accommodation in the rangers' hut if you don't annoy them. About 1.5km beyond the gate you'll find toilets and water, with the *Sendero Arboles Caídos* (Fallen Trees Path), a simple loop of 2.5km, to the left and the *Sendero Oropendola* to the right; this soon leads to a loop with another loop, the *Sendero Pantanoso* (Marshy Path) running off it and down towards the Río Orosi. These trails can be busy, and you'll probably prefer to push on 2.5km along the main track into the cloudforest to the *Sendero Pava* (Turkey, ie: Guan, Path) and a viewpoint to a waterfall.

The Cerro de la Muerte

The PanAmerican Highway runs south from Cartago and climbs almost 2,000m on to the ridge of the Talamanca range; the highway reaches its highest point anywhere, at about 3,300m, in a *paramó* zone known as the *Cerro de la Muerte* or Peak of Death. The area is credited with 'the best highland bird-watching in Costa Rica', with 400-odd species present, and there are now plenty of lodges and so on set up to welcome birders in particular, many with forest trails on their own property. Some streams have been stocked with rainbow trout to attract angling types. In addition, Braun Ecoturismo runs daytrips from San José for US$75.

As well as quetzals, there are local endemics such as the silky flycatcher, the coppery-headed emerald hummingbird, and the peg-billed finch, as well as the timberline wren, silvery-throated jay, black-billed nightingale-thrush, volcano junco, and long-tailed silky flycatcher. At km51 a road turns west to Santa María de Dota and San Gerardo de Dota, two small villages at about 2,100m which are developing quite a nice line in ecotourism. There are affordable hospedajes, and more expensive lodges (tel: 771 1732 for the *Cabañas Chacón*, or 223 2421 for the more expensive *Trogon Lodge*, which allows outsiders onto its trails for US$5 for 2 hours). At Cañón church (km58) there's a turning 4km east to *Genesis II* (Apdo 10303-1000 San José, tel: 225 0271), a private reserve at 2,360m with a mere 175 species of birds, including all the usual cloudforest suspects.

There are three places to stay right on the highway: at km62 the *Albergue de Montaña Tapantí* (tel: 233 0133), at km70 the *Albergue Mirador de Quetzales* and at km95 my favourite, the *Hotel Georgina*. Before this the road enters *paramó* at km88.5 and passes the Restaurant Las Torres and the radio masts on the summit (3,491m) a kilometre further on. Although the true *paramó* of Chirripó is quite open, allowing reasonably easy hiking, here it is very different, a man-made secondary habitat, largely due to burning for charcoal, I gather. It's dominated by clumps of dwarf bamboo (*Swallenochloa subtessellata*) like big shaving brushes, and by *Hypericum* shrubs up to 1.5m tall, and is more or less impenetrable. Even so it's possible to see volcano hummingbirds, volcano juncos, slaty flowerpiercers, wrenthrushes and timberline wrens from the road; there's also a large population of *Bolitoglossa subpalmata* salamanders.

Beyond the *paramó* (in Villa Mills, at just below 3,000m), the Georgina is a small wooden hotel, built in 1947, the year after this road was built, and serving as a food stop for southbound buses. It's cheap and friendly and, as you might expect, known to cheapskate British birders. I found it a handy place to acclimatize before tackling Chirripó; it's very easy to drop down into the marvellous oak woods (dominated by the endemic *Quercus costaricensis*) and not so easy at this altitude to climb back. There are more level paths across the road and underneath the powerlines (through a different dwarf bamboo, *Chusquea tonduzii*), as well as another track down into the forest at about km96.7. These woods are managed by the Río Macho Forestry Reserve, Costa Rica's oldest (set up in 1964), which stretches north to Tapantí. Quetzals and barred parakeets have been seen right outside the hotel, and even an idiot such as I can see hummingbirds, large-footed finches and ruddy treerunners. From La Division (km107), where there's a checkpoint and the 'Road Warriors' (*Guerreros de los Caminos*) cafe, the road descends steeply, with fantastic views over the clouds to Chirripó, to San Isidro (de El General) at 702m, capital of southwestern Costa Rica and jumping-off point for Chirripó.

CHIRRIPÓ

Chirripó National Park offers a type of hiking almost unique in Central America, with high peaks and open ridges that offer you big views; we've always loved this kind of wild country where you can walk all day and see no-one, and much as we'd enjoyed the months of walking along beaches, up volcanoes, through jungles and into Indian villages, this was a real treat, away from heat, humidity and people. This is in fact best achieved in the wet season, as all hikers have to sleep in huts at the Crestones Base Camp, which can get pretty busy in February, March and April. It's really no problem to come here in the

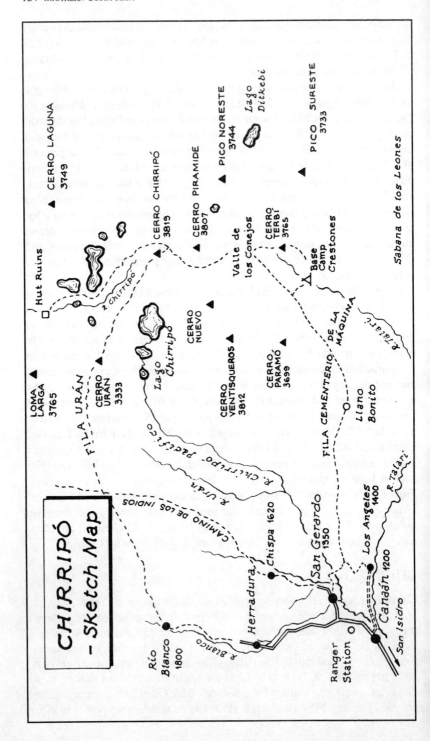

CHIRRIPÓ
– Sketch Map

wet season; fortunately the area has a very predictable climate, raining nearly every day but almost always in the afternoons. Armed with this knowledge you can just alter your normal schedule and stay dry. Setting out at first light (about 04.45), it's wonderful to watch the sunrise and be high in the mountains early enough to have a crystal clear view of both oceans! The earliest it rained during the 13 days Rob was there in the wet season was 10.30, but it usually stayed dry until 13.00 or later. So you can hike for seven or eight hours before returning to the huts for the afternoon, to yarn and yawn, write or read, and cook an early dinner, heading to bed soon after dark. You don't need a tent because the huts keep you dry, but warm clothes and a good sleeping bag are necessary (at any time of year) as the temperature often drops to near freezing, and sometimes below. You can get by with a very light tropical bag by sleeping in all your clothes; an umbrella is handy for quick trips to the outhouse during rainstorms.

You need to book your trip at the National Parks Service in San José; the park is supposedly always booked weeks ahead, but space can usually be found for one or two people if you're flexible. You should book a minimum of two nights — one day up, one to explore, and one down. When your time comes, take a bus to San Isidro (hourly from Calle 16, Avda 1/3 in San José), and another to San Gerardo de Rivas. These leave at 05.00 (from the plaza, though it may soon move to the new bus station) and 14.00 (from the bus station); the asphalt ends at Rivas (also served by buses to La Piedra, Buena Vista and Pueblo Nuevo), from where it crawls up the Chirripó Pacifico valley on a dirt road, reaching San Gerardo (1,350m) after an hour and a half. This is the only bus in Costa Rica that charges for rucksacks, but it's justifiable enough.

Traditionally the trail to Chirripó started at Canaán, 2km before San Gerardo, but nowadays everyone takes the bus on to San Gerardo; it terminates immediately above the park ranger station, where you must check in; if you don't, they'll give your place to someone who's turned up without a permit. There are plenty of places to stay: the *Cabanas Marín* (with camping) are just below the ranger station, and there are others in the village, up the hill for 200m and across the bridge to the right. The *Roca Dura*, by the football ground, is good value, but the best is the first one you pass, the *El Descanso*, where you can eat a good meal, rent stoves and waterproofs, arrange for a horse, and get good information on conditions on the mountain. The owner, Francisco Elizondo, is a champion fell-runner and a lovely man. Every year on the weekend closest to February 24 (when you will not be allowed into the park) there's a race, the *Campo Traviesa*, from San Gerardo to the Base Camp and back — in 1995 the winner got up and back in 3 hours 18 minutes! It's going to take you all day, though: no matter how well acclimatised, almost everyone finds they've bitten off more than they bargained for on this climb of 15km with an altitude gain of 2,100m to Base Camp.

Actually, there's an easy way out — horses. These can be hired to take your gear, and even your feeble body, up to the huts. There's an association of about 30 *arrieros*, whom you can generally meet in the pool hall. Prices are fixed (about US$24 one way, for up to three packs) and posted at the ranger station, which is the easiest place to book a horse.

The route up

Breakfast is available from 05.30 or 06.00, but there's no need to panic; a good night's sleep is just as important as an early start. The trail starts five minutes beyond the church, turning right off the road to Chispa and crossing a stream. After five minutes you'll cross a covered bridge over the Chirripó Pacifico and head up its left bank past the scattered houses that make up the Finca Santa Clara. After 12 minutes turn right through a gate and climb the *Cuesta el Termómetro*, so called presumably because it's rising as fast as your temperature. In fact, it's not very steep or very long, and you soon reach the ridge and turn left, after 15 minutes, onto the path from Canaán. Here you enter intermittent woodland and in 20 minutes reach a sign 2km from the park boundary and 12km from Base Camp. The path continues along the forest edge, climbing steadily above the Talari valley, before finally entering the forest, and reaching the park boundary (about 2,000m) in just over 30 minutes. The path continues, relatively easily but with steeper sections, along a ridge marked on maps as the *Fila Cementerio de la Máquina*. After an hour you reach the halfway point at Llano Bonito, at around 2,600m; the sign reading '2km to Llano Bonito' should clearly be lower down the path. There's a water tap here, and a shelter with four part-walls and a sleeping platform; some people aim to spend the night here, but there's really no need to break the journey. This is great montane forest, with epiphytes galore, bamboo and tree ferns, and plenty of birds — I've seen toucanets, woodpeckers, tinamou and lots of hummingbirds, tanagers, finches and flycatchers, as well as monkeys, squirrels, bright blue and green frogs and hairy stinging caterpillars. Experts may spot quetzals, flame-throated warblers and buffy tufted-cheeks. The call of the bellbird, a single, pure, resonant note, is unmissable, though it's hard to see the bird itself. The *arrieros*, heading up before dawn, often see manigordo, ocelot and deer on the trail.

From here you climb steeply up the *Cuesta del Agua*, hard work but there are enough insects to keep you moving, although the wonderful wildlife conspires to slow you down. After about 45 minutes things get easier, and after 20 minutes more you enter a burnt area, due to fires in 1979 (reportedly caused by disgruntled settlers evicted when the park was formed) and 1992. It's a pretty bleak area, but it's interesting to see how nature recovers its territory. After almost half an hour you reach the top of the *Monte Sin Fe* (Faithless Mountain) at 3,200m, but there's still a way to go, although you'll be feeling pretty tired by now. After about 20 minutes there's a sign reading '1.5km to Base Camp'; there's a spring here, and a path to the left to a cave in which you can sleep. Many people have enjoyed sleeping here, but it's now surrounded by burnt wasteland and not particularly attractive. On the other hand, there's plenty of dead wood to make fires with, although as it was probably a camper's fire or cigarette that caused the 1992 fire you should take great care. It can be pretty cold, although it's slightly less likely to freeze here than at the Base Camp.

It's a steep climb back to the ridge, and then you continue to the left up the *Cuesta de los Arrepentidos* (Hill of the Repentents), reaching a sign reading

Valle de los Leones after half an hour. The Valley of the Lions is not here, but where the sign points to, just east of south, a high marshy meadow also known as the Sabana de Chirripó, which you can hike to from the Base Camp. A disused trail continues past Cerro Lohmann and Cerro Palmital to the village of Cedral, south of the park; at one time the park authorities were talking of opening this up for hikers, but now everything is centralized on San Gerardo. The main path continues easily above the Talari valley and drops down to the Base Camp (somewhere around 3,300m) in ten minutes; check in with the rangers in the first hut and then find somewhere to sleep in one of the two blue huts. There's solar lighting and cold tap water, but little else; you need to bring your own food and a stove, unless you can face cold food and drinks. It took me seven hours in all to get here including rests (the timings above are net, without any allowance for rests), but many people take twice as long.

Hiking within the park

More or less everyone does the logical thing and hikes on up the valley towards the summit of Cerro Chirripó itself; there are other peaks around the Base Camp, but it's easier to take those in on the way back, if you feel like it, as you'll be starting the climb from higher up the valley. Returning to the main trail and turning right, it takes almost 20 minutes to reach a turning left to the peak of Ventisqueros (3,812m) and another 20 minutes to a sign reading *Valle de los Conejos*, although in fact the rabbits were all killed off by a fire. Just two minutes beyond this, turn 90° left (there used to be another hut near here, but it's totally vanished now), and climb for 35 minutes up over a rock shelf and on to the saddle between Cerro Nuevo and Cerro Piramide. The latter is the peak that dominates the head of the Talari valley, hiding Cerro Chirripó, which only comes into sight now. The path drops slightly for five minutes, passing above Lago Chirripó, which lies at 3,500m, to a junction below Cerro Chirripó itself. One path goes to the right, to the Valle de los Morenos, while the other leads straight up to the summit (3,819m). The air is thin here, and although it doesn't seem far you may need 20 minutes to get there, with some use of your hands.

Here, on the highest point in southern Central America, you'll find a visitors' book in a tin box, full of impassioned Spanish comments on the beauty of nature and the grace of God, and a few matter-of-fact notations in English. Add your own, in either style (or your own). The first 'white man' to reach the summit was a missionary, in 1904, and until the 1940s scientific expeditions were almost the only visitors; it's got a little busier since then. Views are great, with both oceans visible early in the morning, as well as to Volcán Barú and further into Panamá. Nearer at hand there are sweeping views of apparently endless virgin forests, like old Costa Rica used to be before the days of cows, bananas, sugar and coffee.

Northwest of Cerro Chirripó is the Fila Urán, a very rugged ridge, where rough vegetation, large loose boulders and steep scree slow progress to a crawl. This is now being opened up as an alternative route into the park from San Gerardo, although you are only allowed to do it with a guide (at about

US$18 per day, for two days). Starting from Herradura, 3km up the road to the left from the San Gerardo bridge, follow the Río Blanco for at least three hours before crossing the river, entering the national park and climbing steeply to a ridge known as the Fila Palmito Morado. This is also used by the *Camino de los Indios* (the Indians' Path), a route from San Gerardo via Chispa over the watershed to Chirripó Abajo, which is closed to hikers. The night is spent at the Paso de los Indios, the only place in the park where camping is permitted; it's well set up, with an outhouse, drinking water and a cooking area. I'm told it's 'brutal going' along the Fila Urán for about two hours to Cerro Urán (3,333m), where there's another visitors' book with aged Instamatic photos, but then it 'mellows out', reaching Cerro Chirripó in about 3½ hours.

Only eight bird species are found this high up, including the volcano junco, sooty robin, and red-tailed hawk. The area is alive with lizards (especially *Gerrhontus monticola*) and covered with a spiny shrub, in fact a dwarf bamboo (*cañuela batamba/Swallenochloa subtesselata*), which thrives in the dry soil of the *paramó*. It may seem very tough, but in fact it's a delicate ecosystem, which is why camping is prohibited, with everyone having to sleep in the Base Camp. Also, the remains of another hut survive at the outlet from the glaciated Valle de los Lagos (Valley of the Lakes), immediately north of Cerro Chirripó. Reaching this from the Fila Urán requires finding (or forcing) a way through thick scrub, and it's preferable to go both up and down on the one clear path, which starts along the Valle de los Morenos path, to the north of Cerro Chirripó, circles around the east side of the peak, and drops down past some beautiful lakes. It takes about forty minutes to reach the hut, which is doorless and partly roofless, but is clearly still used a bit; the trail is marked with both mini-cairns and plastic tags. Heading east from Cerro Chirripó, you'll find it a fairly easy scramble to Cerro Truncado (3,685m) and can then continue north along a sprawling ridge to Cerro Laguna (3,749m), some two or three hours from Chirripó, above the disused hut. The going is a little rough but not too bad, and from Cerro Laguna there are good views of the wild and largely unexplored Fila Norte and the northern stretches of the park.

Returning towards the Base Camp, you can either take the path up to Ventisqueros — continuing via Cerro Paramó (3,699m) and dropping down to the San Gerardo trail above the cave — or continue straight across the Valle de los Conejos and across the stream. There's a clear path, marked with yellow plastic tags, which leads up through a gully between two large outcrops to a viewpoint over the valley. It gets steeper, climbing up another gully to reach the ridge in just over half an hour. It's pretty bare sub-alpine terrain here, well above the *paramó*, and it's easy going. The summit of Cerro Terbí (3,765m) is just five minutes to the right, and a good path continues to the dramatic outcrops of the Crestones, overlooking the Base Camp, in under ten minutes. There's scope for some scrambling and bouldering here, and then it takes just 25 minutes to drop down to the huts, although the path (marked with mini-cairns) isn't always easy to follow across the bare rock.

You could go up to the Crestones first thing in the morning (from the uphill corner of the third hut), but it would be much harder work. You'll need to get away from the Base Camp by about 09.00 to be sure of catching the bus to San Isidro at 16.00, unless you want to get up for the 07.00 departure. If you leave earlier you'll have time to clean up in the hot springs just 50m up the Herradura road from the San Gerardo bridge (behind the obvious stone dam across the stream from telegraph pole 34). There are other hot springs further up the road, but you have to hike up the hillside and then pay.

Maps
The park is split between four of the 1:50,000 maps, so you may prefer to rely on the leaflet produced by the National Parks Service (try to get it in San José, as they may run out in San Gerardo), or the 1:200,000 map (sheet CR2CM-8 Talamanca). Trying to hold four maps together in the wind on a cold peak is a pain, so if you do take the 1:50,000 maps it's worth cutting the borders off and taping them together (with the masking tape in your first aid kit!) before the hike.

A small outfit called Chirripó Trekking Adventures (tel: 252 1559, fax: 254 6072) operates trips to Chirripó, hiking from Canaán and spending two nights at the Base Camp. This would be useful only if you were on a flying visit and needed to get your trip booked before arriving in the country. 'Above the Clouds' also include Chirripó in their trips.

LA AMISTAD

From Chirripó to the Panamanian border the Talamanca range is protected by **La Amistad International Park**, a huge expanse of primary forest with very little public access. What facilities there are are right down by the border, reached through the Italian-settled town of San Vito (served by Tracopa buses from Avda 18 Calle 4 in San José and from the PanAmerican at Avenida Central in San Isidro). The Amistad Conservation Area has an office in San Isidro itself, but the Amistad Park Visitor Centre is in Progreso, north of La Lucha. Just east of here, near the Las Mellizas ranger station, is the *La Amistad Lodge* (tel: 773 3193; book through Tropical Rainbow Tours), where for US$360 for two nights you can stay on an organic coffee farm with 23km of trails in their 780ha of untouched forest (from 1,400m to 1,900m). It's an interesting place, with hydro-electric and solar power and ambitious plans for sustainable development in the region. From San Vito it's also possible to take a bus north to Santa Elena and then hike 17km through Agua Caliente to the Sector La Escuadra ranger station below Cerro Pittier (2,844m).

While in San Vito you should also see the **Wilson Botanical Gardens** at Las Cruces, almost 6km south of town (tel: 773 3278); owned by the Organisation for Tropical Studies, this is part of the Amistad Biosphere Reserve, although physically detached from the bulk of it. There are 10ha of gardens, with about 2,000 species of native plants, and 145ha of mid-elevation (or premontane) tropical rainforest, mostly of oak and Lauraceae; the gardens have beautifully designed trails laid out thematically and designed so that you can look across from a hillside into the canopy of the trees below. The River

Trail runs for 1.5km down to the Río Jaba, through secondary forest with plenty of birds. A fire recently destroyed the library, a terrible loss, but the rest of the facilities are unaffected.

There are also a couple of places to stay near Buenos Aires, halfway between San Isidro and San Vito (reached by Tracopa buses from San José, and 11 buses a day from San Isidro). About 20km north the *Finca Anael* (Apdo 6, Buenos Aires; tel: 240 2320, fax: 223 0341) is a commune of Ticos practising yoga and organic farming; they rent out cabins for US$40-plus, including transport from the town. From here you can take a camping trip to reach Cerro Dúrika (3,280m) and the Sabana Dúrika, a highland swamp at around 2,150m with many *paramó* species of birds and plants. There's plenty of wildlife throughout this area, including quetzals and other trogons, black hawk-eagles, crimson-fronted parakeets, monkeys, jaguars, peccaries, agouti and raccoons. Turning off the PanAmerican Highway 24km south of Buenos Aires via the Paso Real ferry and Potrero Grande, you can get to the Helechales ranger station or Monte Amou Lodge near Cerro Mosca; AdventureLand operates two-night hiking and birding trips here.

Looking at the 1:200,000 map, you might think that there's an easy and straightforward 65km hike along a track across the watershed from Buenos Aires to Bribrí; in fact it's very easy to get lost, and you should only hike this route with an indigeno guide, best found on the Atlantic side. It's worth talking to Allan Foley of Jaguar Tours at the *Hotel Jaguar Cahuita* (tel: 758 1515 ext 238). There are three buses a day from Bribrí to Shiroles, from where you have to walk up the Río Coén to Sepeque and Kichuguecha before crossing the Continental Divide.

Not far northwest of Shiroles lies the **Hitoy Cerere Biological Reserve**, only 9,154ha in area and without any facilities, but packed with wildlife. It's named after two rivers, the Hitoy (meaning 'woolly' in the Bri-Brí language, referring to the mossy rocks) and the Cerere ('clear waters'), and the park is full of streams, rapids and waterfalls. The steep wet slopes are covered in trees, up to 50m tall, including Spanish cedar, ceiba, indio desnudo, *maría*, and *guayabón*, plastered with orchids and other epiphytes. Animals and birds are remarkably untimid; mammals include three-toed sloths, silky anteaters, four-eyed and woolly opossums, otters, tapir, jaguar, ocelot, tiger cat, brocket deer, collared peccaries, howler and white-faced monkeys. There are at least 115 species of birds, including vultures, parrots, toucans, the slatey-tailed trogon, Montezuma oropendola and green kingfisher. Camping is not allowed, and the only trails are unmarked and rough; indeed you generally end up hiking up the watercourses. But if you can get there it should be well worth while; take the bus from Limón to Fortuna in the valley of the Río Estrella, and then a taxi or pickup 24km south (through a maze of banana plantation roads) to the reserve entrance.

On this stretch of the Caribbean coast there are two other reserves that are managed by the Amistad Conservation Area, though separate from the bulk of it. On the Panamanian border is the **Gandoca-Manzanillo National Wildlife Refuge**, which protects a coral reef and oyster beds in the only

Camprosperma panamensis mangrove swamps in Costa Rica, as well as primary tropical rainforest. Wildlife includes toucans, caimans, crocodiles and manatees. It's reached by a daily bus from Puerto Viejo to Manzanillo, north of the refuge, or more frequent buses from San José, Limó and Bribrí to Sixaola, to the south, from where you can take a boat to the mangroves.

To the north of Bribrí is the **Cahuita National Park**, the country's second smallest national park (after Manuel Antonio) and its second most visited (after Poás). It protects one of only three living coral reefs on the Caribbean coast, and some rainforest, with howler and white-faced monkeys, sloths, coatis, raccoons, basilisks, trogons, toucans, kingfishers, parrots, pelicans, yellow-crowned night-herons and Northern boat-billed herons. There's the best snorkelling in Costa Rica, with 240ha of coral (don't touch) and an old Spanish shipwreck. There are at least 34 different species of coral, over 100 of seaweed, 140 of molluscs, a great variety of sea fans, starfish, sea cucumbers, sponges, sea urchins, anemones, lobsters and crabs, and hundreds of types of fish, including flying fish. The park is to the east of the village; take a bus or walk 5km down the road and then 2km north to the Puerto Vargas ranger station, where you can camp in reasonable safety. You can take a far more direct route back to the village, or hike about 6km around Punta Cahuita, off which is the reef.

However, something has gone very wrong at Cahuita, with the place turning into a resort for travellers to hang out and tune out. The largely Afro-Caribbean local population has permitted the development of a distinct drug culture, and also of clear racial resentment and tension; so young people come here, relax, but may then find themselves being mugged or worse. There are frequent cases of tourists' cars being robbed or held up, and there have been rapes and at least one murder. The locals are clearly more interested in the tourist business than in nature conservation; when the national park fees were raised in 1994, they ran the rangers out of town to allow free access. There are now police supervising the collection of the fees. The beaches are stunningly beautiful, but take care. There are also problems with pesticide run-off and silt from the Río Estrella affecting the corals, already damaged by the 1991 earthquake.

THE OSA PENINSULA

In the far southwest of the country is the Osa Peninsula, which boasts some of the richest and wettest — and buggiest — tropical rainforest in Central America. Most of it is now protected by the Osa Conservation Area, one of Costa Rica's new 'super-parks', but far and away the best known of its components is **Corcovado National Park**. This is very important for scientific research (one visitor in five is a researcher), but it is also not easy to get to, entailing a stay of several days; therefore reservations are required, which may be hard to arrange, especially in the dry season (January to March only), which is far and away the best time to visit.

You should be prepared to be wholly self-sufficient, bringing in all your food. In other respects you can travel light, as the area is very, very warm and

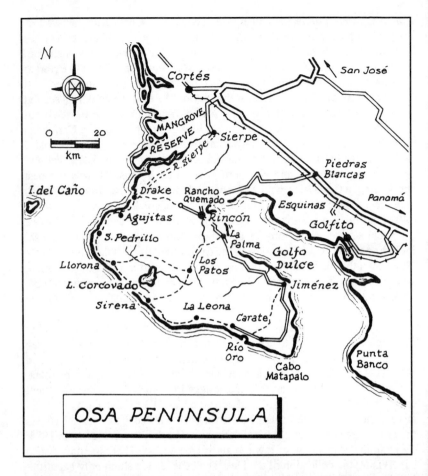

OSA PENINSULA

you'll need little in the way of clothing and sleeping equipment. There are enough shelters for a tent not to be totally necessary, but one is certainly advisable. A mosquito net is in any case indispensable, as is insect repellent. Don't bother with rain gear — it's too hot and humid to wear it, but an umbrella is useful. Your footwear will be thoroughly soaked, so maybe trainers or hiking sandals are the best bet. A machete is useful (for opening coconuts, not trails).

Alternatively you can take a trip with Costa Rica Expeditions (high quality), Dos Montañas (part of Ríos Tropicales) or Braun Ecoturismo.

There's up to 6,000mm of rain a year here, which is a great deal, especially on the usually drier Pacific coast. This has produced the most exuberant forest in Central America, with a huge diversity of trees, with some ceibas and espavés over 70m tall, and innumerable vines, creepers and epiphytes. More than half of the park is very wet tropical forest, with cloudforest (mainly oaks and tree ferns) in the higher parts (up to 745m), and also mangrove and raffia palm swamps. There are 500 species of tree, about a quarter of all those found in Costa Rica (up to 100 in an area of two acres, about 0.8ha), and many are

South American genera which meet their northern limit here. There are 104 species of mammal (with large herds of white-lipped peccary, and spider, howler, white-faced and squirrel monkeys, tapir, jaguar, puma, ocelot, manigordo, giant anteater, agouti, coatis and *tayra* or *Eira barbara*, a kind of weasel), and over 300 species of bird, including scarlet macaws, parrots and parrotlets, king vultures, white hawks, crested guans, bronze-tailed sicklebills, scarlet-rumped tanagers, Baird's or vermilion-breasted trogons, manakins, hermit hummingbirds, and water birds such as pelicans, herons, spoonbills and moorhen. There are 117 amphibians (including poison dart frogs) and reptiles (including lots of snakes), 40 freshwater fish, and at least 6,000 insects.

WARNING: the bugs here are terrible. There are chiggers galore, and ferocious horseflies, but it's the sandfleas that will drive you berserk. Try any precaution you can think of, including long socks, gloves, and a bee-keeper's hat! Watch out for snakes as well. The sun on an unsheltered tropical beach can be mercilessly hot. There are illicit gold-miners in the forests, who may not be pleased to see you. Still interested? Read on.

Access to Corcovado

Most hikers will take a bus to Puerto Jiménez, on the north coast of the peninsula; it can also be reached by ferry or plane across the Golfo Dulce from Golfito. SANSA and Travelair operate regular flights from San José to Golfito, but as a rule only charter flights to Puerto Jiménez; Carate and Sirena, in the heart of the park, are also served by charters, which can be pretty frequent in the dry season. You may be able to cadge a seat, if not from San José then perhaps for the hop from Puerto Jiménez. Failing that, your easiest option is to take the pick-up that leaves from outside Carolina's restaurant in Puerto Jiménez at about 07.00 on Mondays, Thursdays and Saturdays. This takes two and a half hours to get to **Carate**, a gold mining settlement with an airstrip. The Corcovado National Park was enlarged in 1980 but they were unable to remove the gold panners until 1986, when they were bought out for US$5,000 each; the money was all spent within two years and the panners returned — kick them out and buy them out had both failed. Known as *coligalleros* ('league members'), they're now allowed to work on the Río Carate, so there's no tension and you can join them about an hour upstream. There's also the Río Oro (Gold River) further east, where there's a settlement with a shop, and a lagoon with plenty of water birds.

From here a trail follows the coast westwards, reaching the Corcovado Lodge tent camp (owned by Costa Rica Expeditions) in half an hour, and La Leona (the park entry point) in another ten minutes. You can camp or sleep in the ranger station, and there's a network of trails in the largely secondary forest behind La Leona and the Lodge. It's another 18km along the beach to Sirena, the hub of the park, which can take up to seven hours on a path named the Paraíso (Paradise) Trail. You have to ford the Río Madrigal and other streams, walk the length of Playa Madrigal (partly sandy, partly rocky), and then cut inland into the forest for a while. Returning to the beach, you reach Punta

Salsipuedes (a discouraging name, meaning 'Leave If You Can' Point!), where there are caves and legends of buried treasure, and the Río Claro, just before Sirena, which can only be crossed at low tide. Sirena boasts the finest tropical lowland rainforest in Central America, and you'll find all the facilities necessary to keep groups of North American scientists happy for weeks at a time. You can also hire horses.

Another way in (or out) of the park is to the west, via Sierpe, which is reached by bus from Palmar Sur, on the PanAmerican Highway. A road has been under construction for many years from Sierpe down the coast to Bahía Drake (pronounced the Spanish way, though named after the British navigator, who passed through in 1579) and Agujitas, but until it's completed you'll have to take a boat down the Río Sierpe, which is very expensive if you hire one for yourself, but affordable enough if you can wait for the shoppers' special. The Río Sierpe itself ('the Amazon of Costa Rica') is known for its water birds, as well as otters, iguanas, basiliscs, crocodiles and caimans. Bahía Drake is developing quickly, even without the road, as a resort for diving, boating and game fishing. Agujitas (about 90 minutes walk south, if the boat only takes you to Bahía Drake) has more affordable accommodation; immediately south, adjoining the Corcovado Park, is the private Marenco reserve, originally 700ha but now expanded through further land purchases. There are cabins (tel: 221 1594, fax: 255 1340, Apdo 4025-1000 San José), and 20km of trails.

Another possibility is to hike from Rincón, on the main road in to Puerto Jiménez, to Bahía Drake or Agujitas; it's an interesting walk, although much of the forest has been cleared, despite being within the Golfo Dulce Forestry Reserve. Fork right 8km out of Rincón on a dirt road to Rancho Quemado, and then ask for the trail to the Río Drake. Be aware that all the dirt roads in the Osa become impassable after heavy rain, due to the ubiquitous orange clay of the region. Even light rain can turn them into awkward slides, hard for hikers and vehicles alike. Local vehicles (all four-wheel drive, of course) often use snow chains, and we seriously considered bringing crampons next time! The trail onwards is used by horses and can be an horrendous clayslide after rain; tough going, if not impossible. It climbs up a ridge through cleared fields and then goes mostly downhill, reaching the river, a good place to bathe and relax, after about three hours. After about half an hour walking downstream the path disappears into a river bed (since most of the traffic is on horseback this isn't seen as a problem). After reaching some banana plantations (you *never* find any ripe bananas; it's a fact) the path starts to fork regularly, but it's not hard to find your way to Drake.

It's about 20km or 3½ hours walk from Agujitas to San Pedrillo, the park entry point, but it's possible to go by boat, as most of the park staff are from Agujitas — however they've learnt that tourists will pay not to walk. Indeed you can rent their boat to go further along the coast, if need be. You can camp or sleep in the ranger station here too; the rangers are starved of company, though not as badly as those on **Caño Island**, a biological reserve 15km offshore. This has been isolated since the Pleistocene and has gradually lost species so that now only eight to ten birds and five butterflies remain; it's of importance largely for its marine fauna (five coral reefs, with starfish, sea urchins, lobsters and giant conch, as well as regular fish), and for its preHispanic remains. It seems that it was almost covered with graves (marked with almost perfect stone spheres, like those outside the Natural History Museum and the Merced church in San José) and may also have been used to grow cowtrees (*Brosimum utile*) where animals and parrots would not take its fruit. You need permission to visit, but there are camping facilities and marked trails.

If you choose to hang out at San Pedrillo while your clothes dry out after the boat ride, you could wade up the San Pedrillo river, with some difficulty (the bottom is first boggy and then rocky) to a 30m waterfall — virgin forest all around you, and the tracks of large felines in the sand, too.

Entering the park, the next small settlement is **Llorona**, about 2½ hours leisurely walking, first along the beach, then some way inland along a well-kept and little-used trail, and finally through an abandoned banana plantation. This is mostly level and leaf-covered, but there are stretches where the famous orange clay would make for awkward rainy season walking. Llorona consists of a few houses by the river of the same name, a rather damp, mouldy place. There are untold numbers of hermit crabs around, and sometimes a crab researcher. It should also be possible to hike directly south from Agujitas to the smallest of the park's entry points, at Los Planes, and on to emerge at Llorona. There are two trails heading inland from Llorona, a short one to a waterfall where you can bathe, and a longer one leading in two or three hours to a shelter near Laguna Corcovado, which is said to be bug-ridden, and on to the Los Patos route.

From Llorona you can walk southeast along the beach to Sirena in about four hours, but there are some catches. Firstly, three rivers that can't be waded at high tide. At San Pedrillo you asked when low tide was and planned your departure accordingly, right? If not, you'll probably be stuck at one of the rivers waiting for the tide. You have to check the depth of the water before crossing, which is when you discover another catch: hordes of sandfleas make wading naked into the water a thoroughly unpleasant experience. In fact, even standing by fully clothed is pretty painful. Another problem is also easily noticed: as the sun climbs you'll start cooking until, at about 13.00, the whole world feels like a giant frying pan. Yep, there's nothing like a tropical beach with no shelter anywhere. Another little catch: the Pacific tides have a huge range, and can totally cover the broad beach, forcing you into the coconuts, where the undergrowth is too tangled to walk. Luckily, you brought your machete, so you can entertain yourself eating coconuts. Drinking them too, as there is no fresh water at the rivers' mouths. And need we mention that there are small sharks at the river crossings? By now you'll certainly be thinking of chartering a plane. Be of good cheer; the hike is uncomfortable but perfectly possible, and even getting to Sirena after dark won't kill you. And there are funny moments; what could be less dignified than crossing a river stark naked with a pack on your head, possibly with sharks snapping at your heels?

Back to the rivers: two hours after the Río Llorona you'll get to the Río Corcovado (not the Río Corcovado that flows into the Laguna Corcovado;

this one just drains a smaller lagoon right by the coast). There are said to be crocodiles here. Two more hours take you to the Río Sirena. If you have an IGN map, note that the river's mouth has apparently moved a fair bit east since the map was made. The beach is coarse gravel, which makes for uncomfortable walking. Put up with it for 20 minutes and then turn inland, to reach the park headquarters across the grassy airstrip. The grass at Sirena is said to be covered with chiggers, though we never got any. Take due care, nevertheless. You may also see the world's largest cockroaches: they are very slow-moving and actually quite cute.

Walks from Sirena

A surprising amount of land around Sirena is secondary growth, which in the Osa apparently means *bananillas* galore. But there is some primary forest close by, and an excellent short trail takes you through it. It's an hour of walking, ending up at the Río Claro, which you can follow upstream or down to the beach. You're sure to see monkeys and plenty of birds, notably three species of kingfisher. You can return along the beach and then by any of several paths to Sirena. The vegetation is striking and well worth attention; one trail has tags on many trees giving common and scientific names. If you cross the river, make sure you don't get trapped by the high tide. From the headquarters the *Sendero Olla* runs north for 2½km into the hills, covered in thick and highly diverse forest; it should be possible to loop back to the left on the *Sendero Danta*, but this may be overgrown.

The Laguna Corcovado, populated by caimans and alligators, lies at the centre of the park. You can only get there by boat, as no trail can penetrate the thick swamps ringing the lake, but one path approaches it, branching off the trail we describe below as our exit from the park. It starts as a road beyond the airstrip, passing mostly through secondary growth, with plenty of guavas (*Inga vera*) which may help to diversify your diet. After an hour you pass a shelter and ten minutes later cross the Río Pavo. Entering virgin forest, you turn left at a flagged junction; this may not be too well marked, so keep an eye open. The path towards the lake is well tagged, but there are a few false trails made by clearing vegetation to set up bird nets (for study purposes), as well as a few weird detours around treefalls. A few river gullies may also cause trouble during the wet season. A compass would also help; the trail goes generally north.

There are some truly outstanding individual trees on this trail: a mangrove on aerial roots reaching 10m into the air, and some giant trees with twisty, dinosaur-like *gambas* (buttress roots) like a rocket's tail. The raffia palms (*Raphia taedigera*) are the main attraction, however, with leaves up to 18m long; these are found at the end of the trail, some 45 minutes from the fork.

Leaving Sirena

When the time comes to return to civilization, there are various possibilities. You can fly, or continue along the coast whichever way you didn't come in, or head north to the road west of Puerto Jiménez. This starts across the airstrip and crosses the Río Pavo, as described immediately above, and continues through primary forest. You pass an abandoned farm with a shelter, and then, roughly two hours from the Río Pato, another shelter in an overgrown clearing. Here the trail takes a right-angle turn to the left, crossing the nearly dry sandy bed of the Río Sirena and veering sharply to the right after 20 minutes; if you miss the turn you'll reach the riverbed anyway — turn left to find the trail, but it's easy to miss. You'll cross a low watershed, cross one more river, and two hours after the last shelter leave the park at Los Patos ('The Ducks', for some strange reason), which is a bit of a dump.

Half an hour beyond this you'll reach the Río Rincón and turn left to cross and recross it for an hour. After passing three farm buildings the path is better used, sticking to the right bank, crossing a last river (keep left at a fork) and reaching the road to La Palma after two and a half to three hours. It's a short walk to La Palma, where there are a couple of *pulperías*, and buses and pickups from Puerto Jiménez to Piedras Blancas on the PanAmerican Highway.

Around Golfito

Much of the rest of the Osa Peninsula is protected by the Golfo Dulce Forestry Reserve; on the far side of the Gulf there's a relatively small Wildlife Refuge behind Golfito (the **Refugio Nacional de Fauna Silvestre Golfito**), with a dirt road climbing for 7km through forest to radio masts on a 486m-high hill. The refuge office is to the west of this turning, towards the airstrip. The area to the west of this is Costa Rica's newest national park, **Piedras Blancas** (also known as Esquinas). This was proclaimed in 1991, but remained a 'paper park' because the government couldn't afford to compensate the landowners, giving them the right after a certain period to resume logging. The situation was saved in 1995 by *Regenwald der Österreicher*, a charity formed in Austria to save the rainforest, and by a carbon-sequestering deal by which a US company saves trees in Costa Rica in return for the right to pump out excess amounts of carbon dioxide at home. The University of Vienna has a field station here (in which you can stay for US$5/day), and claims that these 12,000ha contain a higher biodiversity than Corcovado. There's also the *Esquinas Rainforest Lodge*, at La Gamba 20 minutes drive west of the Golfito airstrip (tel: 775 0131, tel/fax: 775 0849). Trails were due to open here late in 1994, and you can hire a guide.

MANUEL ANTONIO AND CARARA

To the southwest of San José are two coastal parks that are both immensely popular, though for different reasons.

The **Manuel Antonio National Park** has some similarities to Cahuita, in that it is now very popular as a beach resort for young backpackers. It doesn't have the same crime problems, but instead it's suffering from over-development, so that many of the better tour companies no longer come here. However, it is bearable in the rainy season, and visitor numbers actually fell by 54,000 in 1994. The 7km road south from the town of Quepos to the park

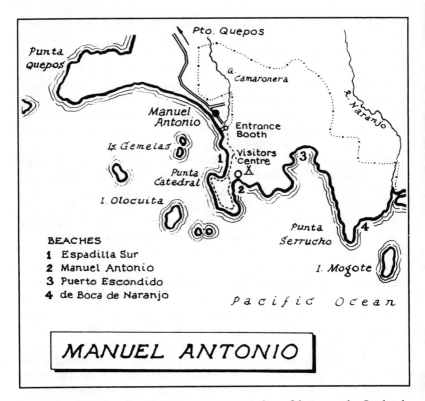

MANUEL ANTONIO

Pto. Quepos

Punta Quepos

a. Camaronera

r. Naranjo

Manuel Antonio

Entrance Booth

Visitors Centre

Is. Gemelas

Punta Catedral

3

I. Olocuita

Punta Serrucho

4

BEACHES
1 Espadilla Sur
2 Manuel Antonio
3 Puerto Escondido
4 de Boca de Naranjo

I. Mogote

Pacific Ocean

gate is lined with hotels and restaurants; once you're safely across the Quebrada Camaronera (best at low tide) and into the park there's no commercial activity, but it can still be pretty busy, especially at weekends in the dry season. In fact numbers entering may be limited, and the park may be closed on Mondays to allow it to recover from the weekend. Camping is no longer allowed in the park; it's open from 07.00 to 16.00, after which the rangers check that there's no-one lurking inside.

You walk in along Playa Espadilla Sur (the north beach is outside the park), which has strong waves and interestingly gnarled mangroves at the high tide mark. Then you can either walk around Punta Catedral (45 minutes through primary forest) or straight across the neck of the point to the beautifully sheltered Playa Manuel Antonio, where there's an information centre, toilets, drinking water and a coral reef off the beach. For geologists, the narrow neck of land to Punta Catedral is composed of sedimentary material known as *tombolo* which is inexorably being washed away by the sea — an island in the making. Archaeologists will be interested by the row of rocks found in the western corner of Playa Manuel Antonio, which appear to form a turtle trap at low tide, probably built many centuries before the arrival of Europeans. A trail continues (for 50 minutes) over another headland to Playa Puerto Escondido (Hidden Harbour Beach), where there's a blowhole and lookout. Then you can push on past Punta Serrucho on a vague trail through dense forest to the almost deserted Playita de Boca de Naranjo, at the mouth of the Río Naranjo.

The main wildlife interest is on the dozen offshore islands where brown boobies and many other seabirds nest; the mainland section of the park (just 682ha) shelters 109 mammal species, including the red-backed squirrel monkey (*Saimirii oerstedii*), as well as howler and white-faced monkeys, two-toed sloths, coatis and at least 60 bat species. Iguanas in particular will come begging for food — far too tame for their own good. You can also see passing whales and dolphins.

The **Carara Biological Reserve** is the nearest rainforest on the Pacific coast to San José, linked to the city by a good road soon to be replaced by a better one; therefore every tour company runs day-trips here, for around US$70. The 7,700ha reserve is in a transition zone between the dry forests of the northern Pacific coast and the humid southern forests, and protects some of the last forest of this type. It's mostly moist tropical forest with tall evergreens and plenty of vines and epiphytes. There are also marshes and a lagoon, and a high degree of biodiversity. Despite (or perhaps because of) the fact that this is more or less an isolated island of protected forest, the wildlife is abundant. In the past there was a lot of hunting here, and today there are still problems with poachers taking exotic species such as macaws (worth US$1,500) for the pet trade. When the reserve was set up in 1978 it was a textbook example of how not to do things; the forest guards were initially very aggressive, and no attempt was made to involve local people — it was illegal to engage in commercial activities within the reserve, such as guiding or selling drinks. Only in the mid-1980s did the US Peace Corps begin a programme of environmental education, to explain the purpose and benefits of conservation to the population, and in 1983 3,000ha were released for settlements. There are still only about seven guards, when 30 are needed to cope with poaching and the large numbers of visitors.

In fact the most popular sight is just outside the reserve itself, when large numbers of scarlet macaws come at sunset to roost in the mangroves by the road bridge over the Río Tárcoles. The river is pretty polluted, but in the daytime you can also see plenty of crocodiles here, up to 3m in length. There's a 4km trail along the river, starting about 500m south of the bridge, and others forming a figure of eight just inside the reserve entrance, 3km south of the bridge. With permission, you can also hike the 6km Vigilancia trail, which offers particularly good birding. There are 106 species of bird in the various ecosystems, including waterfowl such as roseate spoonbills, anhingas, jacanas, pied-bellied grebes, tiger-bitterns, and toucans, trogons, the collared araçari, collared plover, American egret, spectacled owls, turkey vulture, red-crowned woodpecker and great tinamou. Mammals include four species of monkey, two-toed sloth, kinkajou, agouti, four-eyed opossum, jaguar, ocelot, margay, white-tailed deer, armadillo, collared peccary, *tayra* and paca. There are lots of fer-de-lance snakes — don't leave the trails or walk after dark.

The reserve is open daily from 08.00 to 16.00; camping is permitted, but there are no facilities other than toilets at the entrance.

Just south of Carara (turn right through Coopebarre village) is the Iguana Park (08.00-16.00 daily, US$10 entry), home of a captive breeding programme, for meat and for release into the wild; there's also a 3½ hour Canopy Tour, partly on trails and partly dangling from pulleys between tree-top platforms.

Divers and snorkellers will also be interested in the **Ballena National Marine Park**, the longest coral reef on the Pacific coast of Costa Rica; its terrestrial area is only 110ha and it still has plenty of human residents, so entry fees have not yet been imposed here. The reef itself is made up of five coral species (mostly of the genus *Pocillopora*), and is 50% empty space, so it has lots of residents, of the fishy and molluscular sort. From December to March migrating humpback whales can be seen; olive ridley and hawksbill turtles come here to breed in the autumn. There's a camping site, with water and showers; rooms are available in Playa Hermosa, Uvita and Playa Ballena. The coast road has recently been improved, with the occasional bus south from Dominical.

Chapter Thirteen

Northern Costa Rica

The northwest of Costa Rica is dominated by the ridge of the Cordillera de Tilarán and the Cordillera de Guanacaste, separated by Lake Arenal; the Tilarán range is a non-volcanic extension of the Cordillera Central, while the younger Guanacaste range consists of a line of volcanoes, of which only two, Rincón de la Vieja and Arenal, are active. The Tilarán range and Volcán Arenal are protected by the Arenal Conservation Area, and Rincón de la Vieja and the important dry tropical forests between it and the coast by the Guanacaste Conservation Area; some small parks dotted around the Nicoya peninsula are grouped together, largely for administrative convenience, in the Tempisque Conservation Area. And finally, at the northern end of Costa Rica's Caribbean coast, there are the immensely wet swamps and lagoons of the Tortuguero Conservation Area.

MONTEVERDE

Monteverde began as a settlement of Quakers who came from the USA in 1951 and started a dairy and cheese-making business, buying 328ha of forest to preserve their watershed. Now it has developed into one of the most remarkable complexes of environmental projects and reserves in the world, and one of Costa Rica's most popular destinations among those who are prepared to head beyond the asphalt.

Monteverde lies on the ridge of the Cordillera de Tilarán, with the village and the best birding on the Pacific slope; it's known above all as cloudforest, but in fact contains six habitats, and most of the cloudforest is on the Atlantic slope. Its best-known residents are the quetzal and a great variety of gorgeous hummingbirds, as well as the three-wattled bellbird and bare-necked umbrella bird; there are also black guans, white hawks, tinamou, emerald toucanets, blue-crowned motmots, orange-bellied trogons, azure-hooded jays, wren-thrushes and house wrens — somewhere between 315 and 400 species of birds. There are around 100 species of mammal, including all six cat species, tapir, collared peccary, brocket deer, both species of sloth and white-faced and howler monkeys. One notable amphibian is the golden toad (*Bufo periglenes*), found only in Monteverde, and only between 1,500 and 1,600m; this was discovered in the 1960s, and last seen in 1990. The abundance and diversity of epiphytes is amazing, with some growing on top of each other and

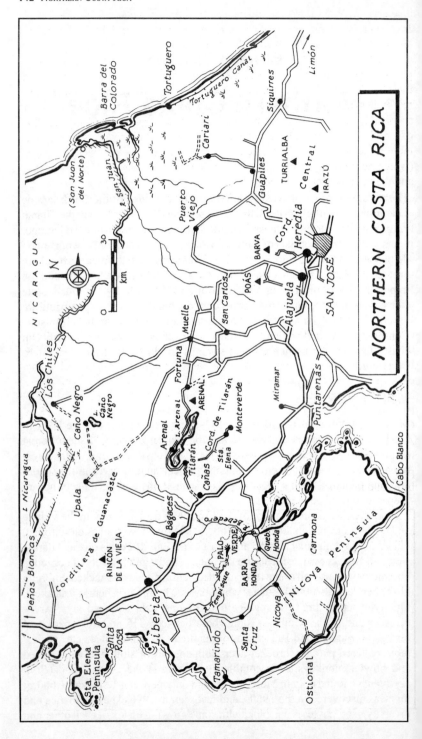

through a bed of moss 10cm deep. The best time to visit is from the end of July to early August, when there is no wind and the air is clear. There are almost daily thunderstorms from May to October.

Most backpackers stay in the village of Santa Elena, where there are cheap pensions and eateries, as well as a bank, a laundromat and a health centre; there's a lively, engaged feel to the place, due to the many volunteers and researchers passing through. On the other hand, it has grown recently, so much so that it has a lawyer, an accountant, and even suburbs! Strung along the 5km of road from Santa Elena up to the Monteverde Cloud Forest Reserve are the more expensive hotels, the original Quaker settlement and cheese factory (which now produces up to 20,000kg of cheese per week; free visits daily), and the main conservation bodies.

The **Monteverde Conservation League** is based about a third of the way along the road by the service station; it owns the *Bosque Eterno de los Niños* (known as BEN, or the Children's Rainforest), which dates from a collection in 1987 by Swedish children alarmed by the destruction of the rainforests. The thing snowballed, so that MCL now owns 17,000ha of rainforest (but it only costs US$250 per hectare); they've also planted half a million trees in five years. It's almost all closed to visitors, but there are 3km of trails in a detached portion known as *Bajo del Tigre*, just beyond the wonderful Stella's Bakery. This is tropical moist forest (cool transition), as distinct from the cloudforest further up the mountain; it costs US$4 and is open daily from 08.00 to 16.00. It's expected that there will be access to the rest of BEN before too long, though this will be from the San Ramón-Fortuna road, to the east, where there's already a small visitor centre in San José de la Tigra. There are also two research stations in BEN, at Poco Sol, at 900m, 12km by 4WD track from the La Tigra road (near a beautiful lake and waterfall), and at San Gerardo, at 1,220m, 14km northeast of Monteverde (with great views of Volcán Arenal). Like the other conservation bodies here, MCL is now moving more into activities outside its own property, tackling environmental education, and planting tree corridors as windbreaks and to allow altitudinal migration of birds and maintain biodiversity by linking islands of forest.

CONSERVATION GROUPS IN MONTEVERDE

Monteverde Conservation League, Apdo 10581-1000 San José (Monteverde tel: 645 6065, fax: 645 5104).
Tropical Science Center (originally a consultancy, and since 1971 managers of the MCFR), Apdo 8-3870-1000 San José (tel: 225 2649, fax: 253 4963).
Friends of the Monteverde Cloud Forest, 1601 W 5th Ave, Suite 108, Columbus Ohio 43212-2302, USA.
Monteverde Institute, Apdo 10165-1000 San José; in the USA, Alliance for the Monteverde Institute, PO Box 1477-1, RR#1, Marshfield, Vermont 05658.
Fundación Centro Ecológico Bosque Nuboso de Monteverde (Santa Elena Forest Reserve), Apdo 57-5666 Sta Elena-Monteverde, Puntarenas (tel/fax: 645 5238).
Centro de Educación Creativa, Apdo 23-5655 Monteverde, Puntarenas (tel/fax: 645 5161).
Any donation or offer of help is invaluable!

EL TRIANGULO

Just beyond the cheese factory is the Monteverde Institute, like MCL founded in 1986, which deals mainly with education, both in local schools and for visitors, as well as with co-ordinating volunteers to the other conservation bodies. The Institute is planning an Education Centre next to the cheese factory that will include the first visitor centre for Monteverde as a whole.

The road ends at 1,530m at the entrance to the Monteverde Cloud Forest Reserve (MCFR), the flagship reserve and all that the majority of visitors see, although there are many other trails and reserves in the area. Few of these visitors realize that they are only allowed into a miniscule part of the 10,500ha reserve, known as *El Triangulo*. Most follow the *Sendero Bosque Nuboso*, with a self-guiding leaflet, which climbs 65m in 1.9km, and return by the parallel *El Camino*; if the notional limit of 250 visitors is reached, you'll simply be told not to take this route. A more interesting loop would be the *Sendero Río* from the car park and along the Quebrada Cuecha and over the Continental Divide (quetzals often feed near the start of the trail, and there's a waterfall 700m out), then down the *Sendero Pantanoso* (Swamp Path), onto *El Camino* for 400m and then back via the *Senderso Roble* and *Chomogo* —

5.2km in all.

Entry costs US$8 and the reserve is open from 06.00 to 17.00, with a night tour at 19.30. More than half the 30,000 visitors per year take a US$12 guided walk, preceded by a slide show, which is warmly recommended unless you think you know everything about neotropical ecology already. While here, you shouldn't miss the hummingbird feeders outside the Hummingbird Gallery, where seven of Costa Rica's 51 species come to feed, including the endemic copper-headed emerald, and also tanagers, which have learnt how to feed without hovering. You can get a very close view and identify them with the pictures on the wall. The shop opens at 09.30, so it's best to be here by 09.00.

With permission (not hard to obtain), it is possible to go on into the main part of the reserve: from the end of the *Sendero Río* it's about two hours to the El Valle shelter, and the Sendero Brillante runs south from the La Ventana viewpoint at the end of the *Sendero Bosque Nuboso*, with no particular destination. The main route through the reserve is the *Camino Río Peñas Blancas*, which is a continuation of *El Camino*, leading in another couple of hours to the La Leona shelter; this is a very basic two-room hut, quite well used, which is frequented by a pestilential coati. A rather worse trail continues down the right bank of the Río Peñas Blancas (White Cliffs River) for about 8km to the Portland Audubon Centre, also known as Eladio's, at 820m. Switching to the left bank, the trail continues in another half day or so to Poco Sol and out to San Miguel, over a dramatic suspension bridge. The premontane rainforest around Poco Sol is owned by MCL, but there are proposals to hand it over to the MCFR.

The highest reserve in the Monteverde area is at 1,700m at Santa Elena, 5km northeast of Santa Elena village; take the main road north from the bank (see below) and follow the signs. This is dense cloudforest (17% secondary growth), with 8km of trails, much quieter than those in the MCFR. It's open from 07.00 to 16.00 and costs US$5. Other trails are the Sendero Tranquilo (ask at the Hotel Sapo Dorado), the Bosque Mariano Arguedes (2km southwest of Santa Elena) and the Monteverde Cloud Forest Lodge (5km of paths in 30ha); there's a free path from the service station up to Cerro Amigos, on the northern boundary of the MCFR and, at 1,842m, its highest point, with good views of Volcán Arenal. At the Monteverde Cloud Forest Lodge (north of the Sapo Dorado — not the Monteverde Lodge) you can also take a Canopy Tour for US$40, traversing with fixed ropes and pulleys from treetop platforms; book at their Base Camp opposite the Pension Tucán in Santa Elena (tel: 645 5243).

There's more! In addition to the Hummingbird Gallery, you can visit the Butterfly Garden (*Jardin de los Mariposas*), which breeds 40 of the total 545 species found in the area (open 09.30-16.00, US$5), or the Serpentarium (09.00-16.00; US$3). Horse riding is big here, too; the best-known stables are Meg's, just before Stella's Bakery. Community-based ecotourism projects are being developed in villages such as Los Olivos, Cañitas (tel: 661 2757) and San Gerardo Abajo (c/o MCL), all just north, and San Luis (tel/fax: 645 5277), just south; these involve homestays, horse riding, and farm visits.

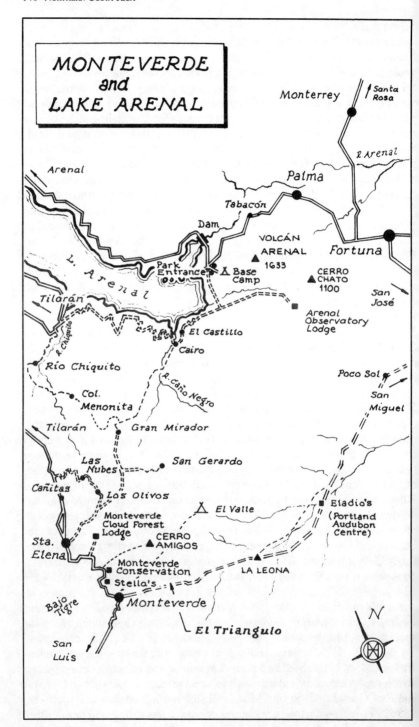

From Monteverde to Lake Arenal

Volcán Arenal is almost as popular a tourist sight as Monteverde. Costa Rica's most active volcano, it is usually rumbling and banging away and, weather permitting, produces some pretty spectacular night-time fireworks. Although not far from Monteverde, getting there by road involves a roundabout journey via Tilarán (bus at 07.00); however there's no reason why you shouldn't hike directly over the Continental Divide and down to Lake Arenal and the volcano, from where you can hitch or take a bus on to the resort of Fortuna. You'll probably have to camp by the lake. This is well established as a pony-trekking route out of Monteverde, but it hasn't yet caught on for hiking. The Arenal Conservation Area (which includes Monteverde) is very diverse, at altitudes from 40m to 2,000m and with average temperatures ranging from 13-18°C and precipitation from 3,500mm to 6,000mm. However, this route takes you mostly through tropical montane rainforest, premontane rainforest and tropical moist forest, until you reach the drier zone beneath the volcano itself.

The route starts from the Banco Nacional, where the buses terminate at the north end of Santa Elena, past the ICE building and tower. Ignore a road which turns left to the school and then rejoins the direct road; turn right after ten minutes, following the sign to the Santa Elena reserve, and likewise after 12-plus minutes, mostly uphill. The road is more undulating now, passing the Hacienda Hira Rosa, and after about 40 minutes (just beyond a bridge) you should take the turning left, just 800m short of the Santa Elena reserve. After about 40 minutes more, following this muddy 4WD track along a forested ridge, you'll reach the Gran Mirador de San Gerardo; this area receives an average 6,000mm of rain each year, but I believe there is, as the name implies, a big view of Arenal, Tenorio and Miravalles volcanoes from time to time. There's a lodge here (tel: 645 5087 in Monteverde), with dormitory beds for US$7, as well as cabins, and trails in the forest; I can't believe it's ever full.

Carry on past the lodge, on a path which you'll immediately notice is used by horses; this drops northwards through cow pasture, turning right through a gate after 20 minutes. After almost ten minutes ignore a path to the right, pass through a gate and past a pond and climb steeply, before dropping eastwards through a quagmire. In 20 minutes you'll climb briefly to another gate, and soon pass above a finca to the left. After this it's very easy to go wrong, plunging downhill in long grass; you need to swing to the left, beyond a locked hut with a corral and an orange tree, to follow a path along a ridge past a palm tree and three other trees and through the remains of a gate. After about half an hour, just beyond an Arenal Conservation Area sign, you need to take a small path down to the right and into the forest. It takes about 15 minutes to cross a side stream and reach the right bank of the Quebrada Malanga, which you follow to Lake Arenal. After a minute you have to cross to the left bank, and you cross eight more times in just under an hour (generally it's about knee-deep), before emerging into the meadows of the Caño Negro valley and swinging sharp left. After five minutes you have to cross this bigger and stronger river: it's thigh-deep, but there are staves provided to help you.

In five minutes you reach a hut where you can sleep, and in 15 more, at a point marked on the map as Cairo, the track along the lakeshore will come in over a ford from the left. The track swings right above the shore, and in about 20 minutes you see Volcán Arenal ahead. From here on the hike can be pretty dull unless the volcano is putting on a show or there are some especially interesting birds about, but there are a couple of places to stay, with boating facilities. The small natural Lake Arenal was hugely enlarged in the 1970s when the river was dammed, and it now provides much of the country's electricity which is, of course, one reason why the government has been keen to protect the forests on its watershed. A road passes along its northern shore, which is more developed for tourism: in particular, the lake offers ideal conditions for windsurfing, as well as fishing for *guapote* (rainbow bass). Anyway, five minutes after first seeing the volcano you'll pass the *Arenal Vista Lodge* (tel: 220 1712), after 20 minutes the village of El Castillo, where you have to ford a stream, and after five minutes more the *Linda Vista del Norte* cabins, just before another ford. There's another shallow ford after 20 minutes, and after ten more (about 80 minutes from Cairo) a bridge and the junction right to the *Arenal Observatory Lodge* (tel: 695 5033). The river just beyond the junction was being bridged in 1995, which will please the many tour groups that come here; there's also a research station and dormitory. From the lodge you can follow trails onto the 1992 lava flow and to the extinct Cerro Chato, with a lake on which the lodge keeps a boat.

You're now walking right below the volcano itself, a perfect cone 1,633m high, covered with lava flows and no greenery. After 45 minutes, crossing the scrubby secondary vegetation that has re-established itself here since the big eruption of 1968, you'll reach the entrance to the **Arenal National Park**. There's not much here, certainly nothing that justifies paying US$15, unless you have an interest in seeing how mosses, lichens and other pioneer plants colonize the lava and gradually break it down into soils that are usable by other species. There's a trail just 2km long towards the foot of the volcano, and toilets. It's not a good idea to go further; some do, but not all return. The volcano has been in varying states of activity since the 1968 eruption that destroyed a village on this site and killed 78, but it's never quiet for long. Rob went some of the way up and was given a nasty fright by flying rocks. Wildlife here includes tapir, jaguar, sloths, coati, white-tailed deer, quetzals, parrots, parakeets, Montezuma oropendolas, keel-billed toucans, scarlet-rumped tanagers, parrot snakes, fer-de-lances, and boas.

It's about 3km to the road from Tilarán and Arenal town (occasional buses) and about 3km more to the Río Tabacón, where you can view Arenal's evening activity from the comfort of a thermal pool. Most tour companies run day trips from San José (just 2½ hours away) for about US$75, so the pools can be unpleasantly crowded. There are free pools just across the way, which may be more congenial. It's 10km east to Fortuna, a small town full of tourists with little to do but wait for the evening fireworks. I didn't like it much. Nevertheless, there are things to do, including horse riding, cycling and trips to the caves at Venado.

Heading east from Fortuna to Muelle San Carlos or Ciudad Quesada (San

Carlos) and then heading north, you'll come to Los Chiles, right up by the Nicaraguan border. From here you can go by road or by boat on the Río Frío to the **Caño Negro Wildlife Refuge**, some of Costa Rica's most important wetlands, frequented by large numbers of both native and migratory birds. During the northern winter up to 300 species can be seen, including jabiru, northern jacana, roseate spoonbill, white ibis, American anhinga, neotropical cormorant and black-bellied tree-duck. There are few mammals, but you can see crocodiles, caimans, turtles and basilisks; garfish are found here at their southern limit. It's a low marshy area, mostly flooded in the wet season; the higher ground is covered by palm forest. You can camp and hire a canoe at the refuge headquarters.

RINCÓN DE LA VIEJA

At the northwestern end of Lake Arenal rises the little-known **Volcán Tenorio** (1,916m), the southern extremity of the Guanacaste range, apart from the isolated Volcán Arenal. It's not much visited and has few facilities; access is generally from the lake road to the south or from the hamlet of Quebradón de Guatuso to the east. It's covered with tropical moist and wet forest and cloudforest, with familiar montane wildlife such as hummingbirds, black guan, and quetzal.

A bit further to the northwest lies **Volcán Miravalles** (2,026m), the highest peak in the Guanacaste range, like Tenorio protected by a forestry reserve. This one covers 10,850ha of lush cloudforest, with mudpots and geysers at Las Hornillas on the south slope. Access is via Guayabo, 30km north of Bagaces. It's the southern limit of species such as the rock wren (*Salpinctes obsoletus*) and the northern limit of the wren-thrush (*Zeledonia coronata*).

Immediately beyond Guayabo lies the **Rincón de la Vieja National Park**, one of Hilary's favourite parks. For one thing, any long term traveller appreciates a hot bath, and this is one delight the park has to offer — hot springs! In addition there are fumaroles and mudpots, and an impressive and quietly active volcano, Rincón de la Vieja (1,895m). There's also the plentiful wildlife we've come to expect in Costa Rica, with a distinct flavour of the dry tropical forests of the Pacific coast rather than the cloudforests of the country's other mountains. We saw monkeys, coatis, anteaters, armadillos, and even a smartly dressed little skunk caught in the beam of our torch.

The climb to the crater *can* be done in one long hot day, but you'd miss most of the park's more interesting features, so why rush it? It's not easy to get to the park, but once there you can camp or stay in haciendas outside the gates, only paying for permits for the couple of days you spend actually inside the park. Take a compass if you're going above the tree line, and remember it can be cold and damp on the summit.

If you don't have your own wheels, it's not easy to reach the park, and particularly so if you want to do the traverse from the Santa María sector to the Pailas sector of the park described here. It's a long hot road to the Santa María entrance (to the south) with very little traffic, although a few vehicles go to the village of San Jorge; the *Hotel Guanacaste* in Liberia (which has

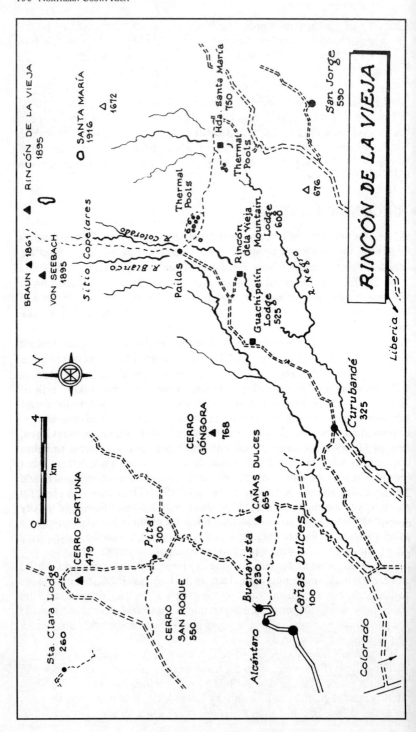

'youth hostel' beds for US$7, if you ask firmly enough) will take you out to the Pailas entrance for US$6, with a minimum of four passengers. There are two haciendas here, which may also provide transport: these are the *Guachipelín Lodge* (Apdo 636 Alajuela, tel: 442 2848, fax: 442 1910), and the *Rincón de la Vieja Mountain Lodge* (Apdo 191-1007 San José, tel: San José 225 1073, fax: 234 1676, Rincón de la Vieja tel/fax: 695 5553). Buses do go to Curubandé, about halfway along the 20km dirt road from km240.1 on the PanAmerican north of Liberia. In season, on either road, you'll normally get a ride with other tourists, if you're patient. Note that it costs US$2 per person to cross the property of the Guachipelín Lodge (inwards only).

The lower slopes are covered with dry forest, with trees such as *indio desnudo, guanacaste*, false laurel and bitter cedar; from around 1,200m there are mangabey, manwood and calabash trees, and from 1,400m it's mainly cupey (*Clusia rosea*, with thick round waxy leaves), mangabey and crespon, much shorter trees covered in mosses and epiphytes. Above the tree line there's little greenery on the ash and lava slopes, other than poor man's umbrella and more cupey. You'll find all the usual forest wildlife — several cats, tapir, brocket deer, howler, white-faced and spider monkeys, collared peccary, tamandua, coati, agouti, armadillo and two-toed sloths. There are 257 species of bird, including numerous black guan, and three-wattled bellbirds, great curassow, emerald toucanet, elegant trogon, spectacled owl, Montezuma oropendola, bank swallow, white-fronted parrot, orioles and solitaires.

Hiking directions

The road to the Santa María entrance of the park starts with a left turn immediately south of the Calle 7 bridge in the Barrio La Victoria area of Liberia. This leads out past the garbage tip and soon deteriorates into a very rough road on very white rock (a Pleistocene rhyolitic tuff that gives Liberia the name of 'the white city'); after 18km you pass the right turn to San Jorge (where you can stay in the *Miravieja Lodge*, tel: 666 2004). From here it's 2.5km further to the left turn in to the park, and it's another 2.5km to *La Casona*, a farmhouse until 1973 and now the park headquarters and visitor centre. It's a pleasantly tatty old building with a one-room museum and a room next to it with a few old bunks in which you can sleep. You can camp on the picnic site just west of this building; the grass is notoriously crawling with ticks, and there's a troublesome coati as well. There's also a 450m path up to a viewpoint, but there's no public access to Volcán Santa María, which at 1,916m is the highest peak in the park.

The trail west runs through the picnic area, as a good red clay path through very English-seeming woods. After ten minutes there's a turn to the right to some mudpots and fumaroles, and three minutes further on is a left turn to the *Bosque Encantado* or Enchanted Wood, where there are some attractive cascades, orchids and trees with great root systems. Returning to the main path, it's just a minute to the Quebrada Zopilote (Vulture Creek) and eight more to the Río Negro, just after which you should fork left to the thermal pools on the Quebrada Azufrales, ten minutes away. It's an attractive spot, and at 40°C the pools are just right for lazing in. You might be tempted to take the faint path up the left bank of the stream to return to the main path, but it soon fades away. Back on the path, it's 6.2km to Pailas, and at this point you leave the relatively well trodden paths of the Santa María sector and strike out into largely untrodden territory. The path climbs steadily for ten minutes and then continues more up than down for 15 minutes more, before dropping gently, crossing four dry valleys. The armadillos and anteaters, in particular, in this area are not particularly bothered by passing humans, and keep on snuffling around in the leaf litter. After about 50 minutes you'll reach a path from the right and cross a stream marked as not drinkable.

Here you enter the Pailas sector, and you can probably hear the first mudpot bubbling away beyond the stream. At once you leave the forest and enter open savanna with scattered cacti; the best mudpots, the Pailas de Barro, are just a couple of hundred metres down a path to the left. They're now fenced off, but otherwise as Hilary described them: 'There are two pits of boiling mud surrounded by ghostly mud-spattered trees. The mud is a beautiful smooth, creamy grey; some 'blups' throw it 3m into the air, while others have only enough energy to push up a soccer ball-like protuberence which then bursts and collapses into petals. Each 'blup' has its own personality and watching through binoculars you can admire the various shapes and patterns. Your own kinetic art display.'

Returning to the path and turning left, there's a right turn almost at once to some fumaroles, just a minute away — more steam, less mud, less fun. Once more on the main path, you'll enter dry forest again after five minutes (woodpeckers, armadillos, squirrels, white-faced monkeys) and in five more minutes reach the start of a loop trail to the right. This is fully signposted, with a map at the start, so suffice to say that the waterfall is dry in the dry season, that there are some truly massive trees and amazing root systems to be seen, and that it brings you back after 1.5km to the undrinkable stream. Otherwise, it's just a minute from the map to the Río Colorado and a campsite, and five more to the Las Pailas (or Las Espuelas) ranger station and car park, where you should fill up your water bottle at the tap. This is right by the park boundary, so you can camp nearby, and it's under 3km to the *Rincón de la Vieja Lodge*, the original 'Old Woman's Corner' hacienda.

If you're ready to head for the summit, follow the path up the field to the right and into the forest after five minutes; soon there's a left turn to Pozo Río Blanco, some cascades and a pool just a couple of minutes away. Just above this junction there's another, also to the left, to two waterfalls 4km west. The main path continues more easily up the hill, with no special features, for 70 minutes to a sign marking the *Sitio Copelares*, where you enter dwarf forest, with copey trees and dwarf palms. In just ten more minutes you're at the tree line; there are a few sheltered camping spots just below, and if the weather is unsettled you might plan to camp here to make the most of the clear morning weather. The second path to the right, two minutes further, brings you down into a deep narrow gorge where you can get water in an attractive pool near the head of the Río Colorado. This continues as a short cut towards the summit, but the standard route continues ahead up the steep grassy hill. As you arrive puffing at the top, the grass gives way to volcanic scree. You plod on, skirting precipices, following a reasonably distinct path marked by cairns. From the ridge, roughly an hour from the tree line, the route continues east to the crater of Rincón de la Vieja, where the views should make the trip well worth while. To the west are the Braun (1,861m) and von Seebach (1,895m) peaks, which are also easy to reach.

Keep an eye on the weather, which as all along the Continental Divide, is unstable. It should take you only two hours to get down to Las Pailas, and then one and a half hours to that lovely hot bath. You can lie in it all night and no-one will bang on the door!

SEMI-WARNING: We've been taken to task for recommending that people soak for hours in hot baths. Apparently it does something terrible to your internal organs. So, farewell then internal organs!

SANTA ROSA

In the far northwest of the country it's not hard to find the Santa Rosa and Guanacaste National Parks, facing each other across the PanAmerican Highway; above all they protect the rare tropical dry forest now found almost nowhere outside the Guanacaste region. They form the core of the Guanacaste Conservation Area, Costa Rica's first megapark, created in 1989, together with the Area Recreativa Bahía de Junquillal (north of Santa Rosa), the Isla Bolaños (a nesting site of brown pelicans, magnificent frigatebirds and American oystercatchers) right up by the Nicaraguan frontier, and Rincón de la Vieja. It protects a total of 120,000ha, with 40 different habitats, including all of those found in Costa Rica between 400 and 2,000m. It boasts the best scientific research facilities in Costa Rica's national parks, now cooperating in the world's first All Taxa Biodiversity Inventory (INBITTA), an attempt to record all of the estimated 300,000 species in the GCA.

The **Santa Rosa National Park** was established in 1971 as the site of the historically important battle of Santa Rosa of 1856, when the American filibuster William Walker was beaten off by Costa Rican patriots; it's a popular destination for Ticos and so has been well funded over the years. To get there, take the PanAmerican to the well marked Cruz de Piedra junction at about km272, and turn west; it's 7km to the *casa historica*, just before the park headquarters and campsite — a hot exposed walk if you don't have wheels. This is a fine old hacienda built by early settlers well over two centuries ago, which has been restored to more or less its original state, with colonial furniture, cookware, weapons, farm tools and the like. There's a good exhibit explaining its historical importance, and a natural history display, including over 200 moths and butterflies.

The best time to visit is during the dry season (December to April), when the profusion of wildlife is concentrated near the water-holes and in shady

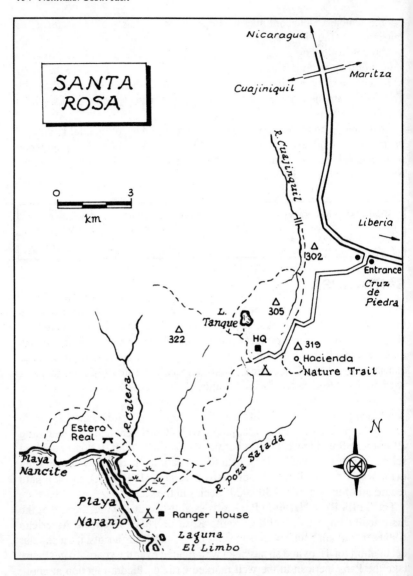

parts of the forest. The trees are a beautiful sight as many of them bloom in the dry season, although they remain leafless until the rains come. To avoid the crowds you should visit midweek during this season, although this is also school holiday season. A visit in the wet season is by no means out of the question; in June we had the park well nigh to ourselves. Admittedly there is no concentration of wildlife around the waterholes at this time of year as there is water everywhere, but we still managed to see several troops of white-faced monkeys as well as howlers, coatis, white-tailed deer and peccary. The spiny pocket mouse (*ratón semiespinosa/Liomys salvini*) is the most common animal of all, and there are also spider monkeys, armadillo, anteater, tapir, puma, jaguar, coyote, porcupine, tayra and raccoon. Of the 155 species of mammals, half are bats. There are plenty of birds — 253 species, including the magpie-jay, orange-fronted parakeet, elegant trogon, common black hawk, crested caracara, great curassow, rufous-naped wren and long-tailed manakin. There are at least 10,000 species of insects, including 3,140 butterflies and moths. If you visit around September you're likely to see olive ridley and leatherback turtles laying their eggs, which makes it a memorable visit even though this is the wettest month of the year. If you really want to stay out of the mud you can hire a mule or horse from the rangers; often a ranger will accompany you if you wish. The main problem in the rainy season is that you may be stuck in your tent.

The dry tropical forests which thrive on the Pleistocene volcanic soils of the Guanacaste area contain 240 species, though not at the density found in cloudforests: these include oak, guanacaste, indio desnudo, madroño, tempisque, jobo (*Spondias mombin*), pochote (*Bombax quinatum*), guácimo (*Guazuma ulmifolia*), and níspero (*Manilkara achras*). There's also savanna, mainly oak (*Quercus oleoides*), acacia, nance (*Byrsonima crassifolia*) and jícaro, and mangrove and beach habitats.

The camping facilities are excellent, with a large wash-house and cold showers, and during a heavy storm you could always cook there if your tent's too cramped. There is also a small *comedor* where you can eat simple meals if you ask in advance. Huge fig trees provide welcome shade from the heat during the dry season, when you could manage without a tent, as there's no rain or mosquitoes.

Hiking in Santa Rosa

Several trails have been cut which provide the hiker with choices between short strolls and hikes in excess of 20km. The **Nature Trail** is a fine introduction to the ecology of the area; it begins right across the road from the hacienda and is best seen before 08.00 and after 16.00. It's called the *Indio desnudo* trail, which translates as 'the naked Indian', but before you start getting excited remember that this is the colloquial name for *Bursera simaruba* or *gumbo-limbo*, a very important tree in the dry tropical forest community. Its name comes from its habit of constantly shedding its bark to reveal new green bark underneath, thus resisting invasion by parasites which burrow under tree bark. Some scientists also believe the green bark can take the place of leaves. The old bark is digested by wasps and hornets to make their nests, and many animals, such as the white-faced monkey, eat its fruit.

When you reach the natural bridge (under which live three species of bats), look behind you to find three rocks with ancient pictographs. There's also a water-hole 50m away, where'll you see plenty of wildlife in the dry season. Climb down the rocks following the right bank of the river, and you'll see a good rock to sit on beyond the water-hole. Here you'll have a good view of the animals without getting in their way. You don't want to be between water and lots of thirsty peccaries!

The rivers are home to many animals, fish, frogs, aquatic insects, land crabs and turtles. They are dependent on the forest, whose vegetation forms a sponge, preventing sudden flooding, retarding evaporation and providing a year-round flow, as well as filtering the water and providing shelter. Some species are inactive during the dry season, reviving when the rains bring life and activity.

The **Beach Trail** is an 11km jeep track, leaving from the middle of the administrative area and passing through open grassland and then increasingly wooded country (with turnings signed to a couple of miradors) before dropping steeply for 2.5km past a viewpoint called *Cañon del Tigre*. At the bottom, at an altitude of 20m, you can fork right along the *Estero* (estuary) trail, to reach a picnic site about 4km away, where you could camp, although the only water source is about a kilometre back at the Río Calera. The left fork leads to **Playa Naranjo**, passing through flat, marshy country with huge buttressed trees, prolific birdlife and, during the rainy season, literally hundreds of red crabs scuttling into their holes. At times the forest floor looks almost like a moving carpet of crabs; there's a fetid but not altogether unpleasant smell of over-ripe onions. After about a kilometre you enter a *salina* or salt marsh, and if you move slowly and carefully you'll be able to observe the marsh's amazing birdlife. We saw herons, egrets, toucans, kingfishers, sandpipers and storks, to name only a few, and we didn't even have binoculars. The trail crosses the marsh on a causeway, occasionally underwater in places but easy enough to follow. After about 3km you come to a ranger station, with water and toilets, a few hundred metres short of the beach. You can camp here; mosquitoes and sandflies are not a major problem, but mosquito netting and repellent would be advisable.

The trail emerges near the south end of Playa Naranjo, nearly 6km of beautiful sand, which is ideal for cooling off after the hike down; it's also known for good surfing, with strong winds from December to March. If you continue south you soon come to Laguna el Limbo, another area of prolific birdlife, beyond which the beach tapers off into rocky headlands which continue about 3km to the park boundary and beyond. Northwards the beach stretches in an unbroken line for about 4km to the estuary of the Calera and Poza Salada rivers, where you'll find different species of coastal flora and fauna. You have to wade across, but it's not deep — in fact at low tide it's almost dry. To the left is a rocky headland beyond which lies **Playa Nancite**, but you should head to the right to join the *Estero* trail; beyond the picnic site a small path continues over the headland to this small sandy beach. This is famous for the large numbers of olive ridley turtles nesting here between August and October; access is restricted, and you should get permission before coming here.

To see the park's freshwater birds you should walk north from the administrative area to the **Laguna Tanque** (or *Escondida*). Take the first road right from the beach track and after something over a kilometre fork right at a Y-junction to the lake about 300-400m away. The left-hand fork continues through fairly open country for about 5km to the former park boundary. This is a pleasant walk, and in the wet season we saw deer, peccary, and various birds, including crested guans.

At the lake you'll see plenty of wildlife in the dry season, especially early and late in the day when many birds and animals congregate here for water. During the rainy season it's different however — we only saw a solitary grebe. Returning to the Y-junction, continue north for 500m and fork right again; this leads north, through a variety of habitats, to a bulldozed road, on which you should turn right/east to the Río Cuajiniquil. Cross this and either follow a dirt road left/north for 4km to some lovely high waterfalls (not in the dry season), or turn right to hit the park entrance road in one and a half hours, 20 minutes from the campsite. You may see tapirs, or at least their tracks, but you will see plenty of other birds and mammals. In the dry season you should take plenty of water as the river will be just stagnant pools. It's about a five-hour round trip, excluding the time spent at the Laguna.

To the north (turn off the PanAmerican at km280 and go west through the village of Cuajiniquil), the Hacienda Murciélago is an annexe of the Santa Rosa National Park, an old farm now being reforested; you can camp wild on the beaches and hike along the coast or across country. Beyond this to the west is the Finca Santa Elena, a farm expropriated from a wealthy US citizen in 1978 to form part of the park, and the subject of litigation ever since. The Murciélago Islands are popular for diving.

Across the highway is the **Guanacaste National Park**, which protects more dry tropical forest, as well as tropical wet forest, rainforest and even cloudforest (with maybe 3,000 species of epiphytes) on the slopes of the extinct volcanoes Orosí (1,487m) and Cacao (1,659m), providing a vital migrational link betwen Santa Rosa and the mountains. In the higher parts the average annual precipitation is 2,000-3,500mm, pretty high for the Pacific coast. There are around 300 bird species (including guans, solitaires, toucanets, bellbirds, the king vulture, the Montezuma oropendola and the magpie-jay); the Guanacaste Cordillera is the southern limit of the range of the rock wren and Botteri's sparrow, found on lava flows on the Pacific side. There's the usual cast of forest mammals (agouti, white-tailed deer, jaguar, puma, tapir, coati, collared peccary, armadillo, two-toed sloth, white-faced monkey and so on), and there are 5,000 species of butterflies and moths.

The park information centre is on the PanAmerican, just north of the Cruz de Piedra entrance to the Santa Rosa park; access is further north, at km280, from where a dirt road leads 17km east to the Maritza research station on the Río Tempis Quito. There is a dormitory here, but you should book in advance by phoning 695 5598. From here you can hike to petroglyphs on the slopes of Volcán Orosí, to the Cacao and Pitilla research stations, and on up Volcán Cacao.

TEMPISQUE CONSERVATION AREA

The Nicoya peninsula has suffered badly in recent years from uncontrolled development on its beaches, which now resemble Spain in the 1960s. A few beaches are now protected, but most of the ecological interest in this area is inland, in the valley of the Río Tempisque. These reserves are loosely grouped together as the Tempisque Conservation Area, totalling 21,378ha. The northernmost is the **Lomas de Barbudal Biological Reserve**, known as the 'insect park' due to its innumerable insects — at least 250 species of bee (many solitary rather than colonial), 60-odd moths, and so on; consequently there are also many insectivorous birds. The main habitat is dry tropical forest, with trees such as *indio desnudo* and spiny cedar (*Bombacopsis quinatum*) that shed their leaves in the dry season. The gallery woods along the permanent streams also contain evergreens such as chicle and tempisque; there is also open grassland savanna. In all there are 130 bird species, including the keel-billed toucan, scarlet macaw, white-capped parrot, elegant trogon, and turkey vulture; mammals include howler and white-faced monkeys, armadillo, coati and raccoon.

Alas, at least 70%, perhaps as much as 85%, of the park was destroyed by a disastrous fire in 1994, and it'll be a considerable time before it recovers.

The offices of the Tempisque Conservation Area and of Lomas de Barbudal and the Palo Verde National Park are all in Bagaces, by the filling station on the PanAmerican Highway (tel: 671 1062); call in here for information, and if it's worth continuing, head north on the PanAmerican for 12km to Pijije and take a signposted road left for 7km to the entrance at the northern end of the reserve. Here you'll find the information centre of the *Projecto Ecoturistico Local*, run by the nearby community of San Rafael. Camping is allowed, but there are no facilities.

Just south of Lomas de Barbudal, at the mouth of the Río Tempisque, is the **Palo Verde National Park**, one of the best places for seeing waterbirds (mostly migratory) in Central America. The area is a seasonal floodplain below a limestone ridge, and comprises at least a dozen different habitats, including salt and freshwater lakes and swamps, mangrove swamps, grassland and wooded savannas and evergreen forests. The park takes its name from the *palo verde* or horse bean (*Parkinsonia aculeata*), a leafy bush with green branches. In the hills are an endemic cactus, *Lemaireocerus aragonii*, and the seriously endangered *lignum vitae* (*guayacán real/Guiacum sanctum*), the densest timber in the world at 1,250kg per cubic metre, and thus very valuable.

Up to 300 species of birds may be seen here, including deciduous forest species such as scarlet macaws, streak-backed orioles, rufous-naped wrens and yellow-olive flycatchers, as well as water birds such as herons, grebes, ibis, duck, jacana, and jabiru. Most of these are present from September to March, the northern winter, but the dry season here, which causes them to mass where there is water; there can be 50,000 at a time on the main lake. Mammals include howler and white-faced monkeys, felines, coati, paca, agouti, peccary, white-tailed deer, squirrel, porcupine and coyote; there are also crocodiles up to 5m in length in the Río Tempisque.

Access is by a 28km road which starts in the centre of Bagaces opposite the park office; you can camp at the Hacienda Palo Verde ranger station in the centre of the park, where there are showers and toilets. The Organisation for Tropical Studies has a research station here (tel: 284 6105); you can stay there for US$50 a night, including three meals, if you can convince them of your deep and sincere scientific interest (not too hard, if there's space). Book at their San José office. Apparently there's another ranger station to the southeast at Catalina, reached via Cañas and Bebedero. There's a good network of paths in this park.

Most of the rafting companies offer trips down the Ríos Corobici and Bebedero, emerging into the Tempisque estuary just south of Palo Verde; this is known as floating rather than rafting because instead of white water you have a very tranquil ride, with the focus on the wildlife. The base for this is La Pacifica, where the PanAmerican crosses the Corobici 5km north of Cañas; there's a hotel here (with 1,000ha of forest), a restaurant, free camping and *Safaris Corobici* (tel/fax: 669 1091), who run the rafting trips.

Barra Honda

The Barra Honda National Park exists above all to protect a score of caves in a limestone reef (formed as coral around 60 million years ago), although its 2,295ha are also covered in deciduous forest of *ron-rón, indio desnudo, guanacaste, madroño* and the like. There was, however a lot of logging before the creation of the park. Residents include howler and white-faced monkeys, coyotes, nine-banded armadillos, white-tailed deer, peccaries, raccoons, coati, opossums, orange-fronted parakeets and turkey vultures. The caves, several of them over 100m deep, shelter a variety of interesting fauna: bats, rats, birds, snails and beetles. Some species of fish and salamander have the blind vestigial eyes found in permanent cave dwellers.

The caves have been largely protected from vandals and souvenir hunters because most can only be entered by a vertical shaft. The deepest is the Caverna Santa Ana (240m), and the La Trampa cave (108m deep) boasts a 52m vertical drop; the Terciopelo cave (55m) has the best formations, such as stalactites, stalagmites, cave pearls and flowers and sharks' teeth, and the Pozo Hendiondo (66m) is known for its bats. Human remains and preHispanic artefacts have been found in the Nicoya cave. The only tours here that I've come across are run by *Viajes Turinsa*, on Avda 3 just north of Parque Morazán in San José (tel: 221 9185). The park headquarters are in Santa Ana, reached either by the main road from the Río Tempisque ferry or by bus via Nicoya (twice daily); the ranger station at the entrance is 7km north by dirt road from the east end of Santa Ana, and you'll find limited camping facilities about 300m further on. Outside the gates there's the community-owned *Las Delicias* ecotourism project, with a restaurant, cabins, campsite, and guides with caving gear.

The park is essentially two ridges joined in a U-shape; one ridge is a flat-topped mesa, on the edges of which are the caves. The lower paths are muddied by cows, so you may need to ask a ranger to show the way at first, but the higher paths are clearly marked. Once you pass a large concrete water tank, go up a fairly steep path, disregard all left turns, and you'll end up at Terciopelo cave, near the edge of the mesa. If you'd taken the left path, the *Sendero Ceiba*, at the last bifurcation, you would have crossed to the north side of the mesa; this trail then goes down to the plain and by country lanes to Quebrada Honda. It's less steep, and therefore more suitable if you have a lot of gear.

This access was originally a road, built when the park was created, but the friable hillside quickly eroded into huge gullies, making it impassable to vehicles. There is, by the way, no water on the mesa itself, so you may not want to camp there.

The TCA includes a few more small coastal sites and islands, most of which are breeding grounds for turtles or marine birds. On the west coast of the Nicoya, the **Las Baulas Wildlife Refuge** surrounds the beach resort of Tamarindo (flights and direct buses from San José); leatherback turtles lay their eggs here from October to March but are threatened by the development of tourism. Further south, the **Ostional Wildlife Refuge** is a thin strip of beach, including the village of Ostional itself, one of the six nesting sites of the olive ridley turtle; tens of thousands of them appear over a couple of nights (from August to November) in a mass nesting frenzy known as an *arribada*, after which it goes quiet for a while. The flora is typical of sandy beaches, with coconut and royal palms and tea mangroves; there are seabirds and a few crocodiles. This has always been a quiet, simple place, but is now at risk from development — Costa Rican law forbids building less than 200m from the coastline, but that's exactly what may happen here. Artificial light confuses turtles and may cause them to about-turn and head out to sea without laying their eggs.

At the southern tip of the Nicoya peninsula, the **Cabo Blanco Strict Nature Reserve** was Costa Rica's first reserve, set up in 1963 after relentless lobbying by Olof Wessberg, who had immigrated in the 1950s and raised US$30,000 to save the area. Its importance is as a marine bird sanctuary, with terns, gulls, brown pelicans, brown boobies and magnificent frigate birds nesting on the guano-stained cliffs that give it its name. It receives only 2,000mm of precipitation per year and is covered with largely evergreen dry tropical forest (119 tree species, notably oak, spiny and bastard cedar, indio desnudo, dogwood and frangipani) and intermittent grasslands. Animals include howler, spider and white-faced monkeys, kinkajou, anteaters, armadillos, white-tailed and red brocket deer, collared peccaries, porcupines, coyotes, margay cats, agouti and pacas.

It's reached by 11km of dirt road south from Montezuma, a very laid-back resort frequented by young travellers; there are 4WD taxis. There's a pension with camping outside the gates, and more rooms in Cabuya, 2km away. Unmarked trails lead to the cape and to attractive beaches.

In the Gulf of Nicoya the **Guayabo, Negritos and Pajaros Islands** are likewise reserves protecting the nesting sites of seabirds such as the brown pelican, magnificent frigate bird, laughing gull and brown booby; peregrine falcons winter here. More or less the only fauna consists of crabs. The islands are largely covered with thorny deciduous scrub and palms. Access is by permit only, and camping is not allowed.

TORTUGUERO

The northern end of Costa Rica's Caribbean coast is immensely wet, with an average of 5,080mm of rain a year; it's also immensely popular with tourists, possibly because seeing the wildlife is done not by walking but by boat, using canals built in 1974 to link natural lagoons just behind the beach. There's just one 2km nature trail south of Tortuguero village, or you can walk along the beach for about 20km. Its chief importance is as the main nesting site in the western Caribbean for the green turtle (*Chelonia mydas*); these come ashore to lay their eggs between June and October. September is the best month, but stragglers may be seen at any time of year. Leatherbacks (*Dermochelys coricea*) and hawksbills (*Eretmochelys imbricata*) may also be seen here. They have been protected since 1963, and the area has been a national park since 1975. Tortuguero also protects crocodiles, caymans, river turtles and manatees. The manatee (*Trichecus manatus*) is a seriously endangered mammal that spends all its time underwater, only sticking its nose out to breathe every five minutes or so; however it does suffer from flatulence, so rising bubbles are the best way of tracing one. One of the rarest and most interesting fish in the world is the gar or lungfish (*Lepidosiren paradoxa*), a relict form, often called 'a living fossil', from the Mesozoic era, about two million years ago. It's a voracious eel-like fish which inhabits swamps and marshes and receives about 90% of its oxygen through lungs, its gills playing a minor role. During the dry season it sometimes burrows into the drying mud, relying solely on its lungs to breathe. Tarpon (*Megalops atlantica*) and snook (*Centromus parallelus*) are so-called game fish found in low-salinity waters such as river mouths, mangroves and the Tortuguero canals.

On dry(ish) land there are eleven different habitats, with over 100 species of large trees and palms alone. Spider, howler and white-faced monkeys, ocelot and three-toed sloth are all common in the forest, as are otters in the rivers. There are 320 species of birds, including eight types of parrot, three types of toucan, boat-billed and three-coloured herons, the slaty-tailed trogon, Swainson's hawk, roseate spoonbill, white-collared manakin, purple-throated fruitcrow, and white-fronted nunbird, as well as a variety of hummingbirds, finches, kingfishers, woodpeckers and the like. Reptiles and amphibians include iguanas and basilisks, seven species of land turtle, parrot snakes and poison dart frogs. Offshore there are enough sharks to make swimming unsafe.

The better tour companies usually fly in their groups (and most of their food), at least in one direction; Travelair fly daily, and there are charters. Traditionally the only alternative was to take a barge (for about four to eight hours) from Moín, just north of Limón, which became increasingly problematic for independent backpackers as tourism grew and boat owners concentrated on groups. Now roads are creeping closer to Tortuguero and there's a variety of ways in; this means that it has become possible to take a day-trip from San José, including a coach ride through Braulio Carrillo. These start at around US$60, but are really too rapid to be worthwhile; three-day trips cost from US$190. At the same time it's become much harder to direct independent travellers to any specific place to find a boat to Tortuguero; Freeman (San Rafael), at the mouth of the Río Pacuare, is perhaps the best bet, but boats may also go from Siquirres (further up the Pacuare), or Cariari, Millón or Agua Fría on the Río Tortuguero. It's also possible to enter via Barro Colorado to the north.

In Tortuguero village you'll find luxury lodges (for the game-fishing market as much as for jungle-viewing) and the odd cheap hospedaje; the park headquarters is here, with some information available, as well as the new visitor centre of the Caribbean Conservation Corporation. There are scientific stations, including the Casa Verde and Caño Palma (6km north, 2km beyond the airstrip), which may have cabins or dormitory space; you can camp in most places.

Barra del Colorado

The 92,000ha of swamps between Tortuguero and Nicaragua are now the **Barra del Colorado National Wildlife Refuge**, known chiefly for game fishing, mosquitoes, turtles and crocodiles. There are also 240 species of bird, spider monkeys, sloths and poison-dart frogs. The town of Barra del Colorado is big enough to have regular flights with Travelair, and it's possible to take a slow, rough bus trip from Cariari, north of Guápiles, to Puerto Lindo, from where it's 25km by boat to Barra del Colorado. Likewise it's a 25km boat ride from Tortuguero. The mouth of the Río Colorado (one of the main branches of the Río San Juan) is one of the breeding grounds of the bull sharks found in Lake Nicaragua, and hammerhead and nurse sharks and at least eight other species can be found here.

The best bits of the refuge are pretty wet and boats are the best way to get around. At the southern end of the refuge, by the canal to Tortuguero, is the research station of the Canadian Organization for Tropical Education and Research, where you can camp (and perhaps stay in their dormitory) and walk into some untouched forest.

When the reserve was created in 1985, it became the classic example of how not to do it. It was implemented without the knowledge of the local populace, who were understandably peeved at being told out of the blue that their traditional hunting and tree cutting were now illegal, and resisted strongly.

TURTLE ETIQUETTE

Any serious ecotourist will, of course, wish to stay well clear of the nesting turtles and not use a torch or camera flash, at least until she has reached the point at which nothing can distract her from laying her eggs. Artificial light disorients and confuses turtles, so that they may return to the sea without laying. However, when there's a scrum of tourists with cameras and videos clustered around a turtle's rear end, it can be hard to maintain that respectful distance. Of course the better companies use guides who keep things within acceptable bounds.

You can, in fact, do one useful thing: turtle eggs are still regarded as a delicacy, and it may be that if you hang around on the beach when the tour groups have adjourned to the bar you can deter the odd thief.

Implementation was delayed until 1988, and then carried out more diplomatically. Even so, the western, drier part of the refuge has been largely logged and settled.

COCO ISLAND

In 1993 just 400 visitors (paying over US$1,000 each) made it the 500km out into the Pacific to the **Isla del Coco National Park**, and a largely undisturbed natural paradise with a very high degree of endemicity (the presence of species found nowhere else). It's a volcanic summit on the 1,500km Cocos Ridge, and it catches about 7m of rain a year, as much as anywhere in Central America. Therefore it's covered in dense evergreen forest, with about 200 spectacular waterfalls; of the 235 plant species, mainly of South American taxa, 70 are endemics, including the palms *Euterpe macrospadix* and *Rooseveltia frankliniana*. Of 315 species of insect, 65 are endemic, and of 85 birds three are endemic, the Coco Island finch, flycatcher and cuckoo. There are two endemic lizards, the Coco Island gecko and anole, and one endemic freshwater fish, and how their ancestors got here is anyone's guess. However, there are flies in the ointment, or rather pigs and cats, left here by pirates and now disrupting the natural systems.

Marine life is rich, with a 30m reef and fantastically clear turquoise water; there are 118 species of mollusc and 57 crustacea. With about 200 species of fish, including parrotfish, manta, tuna, white-tipped sharks and hammerhead sharks (up to 4m in length), it's not surprising that people (wealthy white males, mostly) pay large sums to dive here. If you're that rich and foolish, you could also come to seek pirate treasure, although 500-odd expeditions have failed so far.

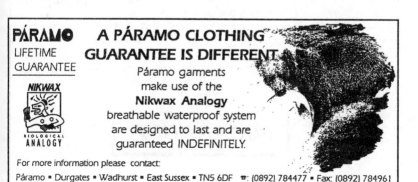

164

NICARAGUA

Chapter Fourteen

Nicaragua
General Information

Nicaragua is the largest Central American state but has the lowest population density — a seventh of that in El Salvador. It has the highest population growth in Central America, at 3.4% per year, and 60% of the population is under 17. Urban growth is around 5% per year. It's also the poorest country in Central America, with average GNP per capita at US$750, 69% of the population rated poor or very poor, and unemployment/underemployment at 60%. Since 1991 a readjustment programme has reduced inflation from 13,000% to 12%. During the Contra period there were about 350,000 refugees (both internally and in Costa Rica and Honduras); these have now returned, but now perhaps 500,000 are working illegally in Costa Rica. They're needed there, but they're also blamed for much of the increase in crime.

Nine years of war under the Sandinistas killed 30,000 people, and cost over US$1,100m; the US trade embargo cost nearly US$600m; and to cap it all, in 1988 Hurricane Joan destroyed 10,000km² of trees and did almost US$800m damage. During the Sandinista period Nicaragua received aid from Scandinavia and the Soviet Union, and plenty of volunteer (*sandalista*) help. Much of this has dried up, but the USA, despite having done so much damage and got what it wanted, has not come through with the aid needed. Of US$300m promised for 1990, only half had been paid by mid-1991. International charities are still involved, but the country is out of the spotlight now and it's harder to raise funds.

The country is slowly recovering from the economic effects of the war and of Sandinista mismanagement, with the same sort of readjustment programme as in other Central American states. One of the key problems was, with luck, solved in mid-1995 when Jimmy Carter brokered a compromise deal to compensate the victims of Sandinista land reform with some of the proceeds of privatising *Telcor*, the state telecommunications company. Both the FSLN (Sandinista) opposition and the UNO government coalition are splitting up, with Sergio Ramírez creating a social-democratic alternative to the hard-line FSLN establishment, and Antonio Lacayo (President Chamorro's son-in-law and probably her most influential minister) creating a new alliance (the *Proyecto Nacional*) to context the presidential elections of early 1996. However, to Chamorro's and Lacayo's fury, in mid-1995 the legislative assembly forced through constitutional amendments that give it more power and prohibit relatives of the president from running for the presidency.

Panamá and Costa Rica are the developed countries of Central America, and crossing into Nicaragua seems like entering the Third World, but without a very noticeable reduction in prices. Therefore it's not surprising that while many visit Costa Rica to the south and Honduras to the north, not so many actually pass through Nicaragua, so if you do pass through you'll find good hiking with no-one else on the trails, and a good variety of volcanoes, cloudforest, rainforest and so on.

Transport
All of Nicaragua's railways have been closed and torn up. Buses are much the same as elsewhere in Central America, although they're generally older, with some wonderful air-smoothed 1950s models still at work. There are fewer private cars and pickups, so buses carry lots of baggage, with well-loaded roof-racks. The Sandinista heritage lives on in a few female conductors, although they only take fares and don't do the macho business of hustling for custom and loading the roof-rack.

Managua has a fairly chaotic bus system; you'll generally have to check where each bus is going. Drivers are as keen as those in Panamá City to hang about hustling for passengers, but to much less effect, though they're still well enough used, especially in the rush hour when pick-pockets are active. In Managua you should be ready to pay the driver one Cordoba (currently) on entry; elsewhere fares are taken once you're on the move.

If renting a car, note that some *contras* have refused to give up their guns and have become bandits, known as *recontras*. In the far north and east of the country you are at risk if you drive after dark.

Maps
1:50,000 maps can be bought from *Ineter,* the *Instituto Nicaraguense de Estudios Territoriales*. It's not easy to find — in the second building from the east in the Civic Centre, on the north side of Pista de la Municipalidad (east of the Lewites/Boer bus terminal and the Pochocuape road), there's a small sign *Servicios Graficos* on the easternmost door up the external stairs. It's to the west of *Inatec*, and opposite the *Banca Nacional de Desarrollo*; bus 118 passes along Pista de la Municipalidad. It's open Monday to Friday; there's no bureaucracy, no need for permission; and no 1:200,000 maps.

Food
The staple is rice and beans, perhaps with egg, chicken, beef or *maduro* (fried plantain), and in the *campo* you'll find little else. One speciality is *vigorón*, boiled yuca with pork rinds, which you might in theory find as part of a *caballo bayo* or buffet.

Most stores have both Coca-Cola and Pepsi, although rarely the far more refreshing products of the same companies such as 7-Up or Sprite. Another triumph for marketing overkill. Nicaragua produces (probably) the world's best rum, *Flor de Caña*, drunk with cola as a *Nica Libre*. *Leche agria* (drinking yoghurt) is nice when you can find it. The water is definitely not for drinking.

Hotels

These are basic but without the pretensions of those in Costa Rica.

Naturalists' Nicaragua

Nicaragua is rather off-balance to look at, with a large flat empty area to the east, some mountains well to the west and to the north, and a line of volcanoes right by the Pacific coast. The Continental Divide runs west of Lake Nicaragua, barely inshore from the Pacific. The volcanoes, being relatively low and close to one coast, do not seem to suffer from cloud and sudden changes of weather in the way that the Costa Rican volcanoes do.

The valley of the Río Grande de Matagalpa, flowing east across the centre of Nicaragua, marks two important divides across Central America. In the first place it marks the end of 'nuclear Central America', the peninsula that existed before the emergence of the land bridge to South America; so the rocks to the north are very ancient (early Permian or Pre-Cambrian granitic and metamorphic rocks) while those to the south are a Pliocene-Pleistocene volcanic system. The Segovia mountains to the north are more rugged, while the Cordillera Chontaleña to the south is a rolling plateau.

In the second place, the Río Grande de Matagalpa marks the southern limit of pine trees in the Americas, although as mentioned below they can be found along the coast as far south as Bluefields (and also as plantations even in the Panamanian mountains). They are now found mainly in a man-made association, dating back to preHispanic times, due to the clearing of the original broadleaf forest and then regular burning. Only pine is able to compete with fast-growing tropical plants where burning every few years allows pine to regenerate and grow to a height beyond the reach of most fires, while other saplings are killed. In the mountains north of the Río Grande de Matagalpa maybe 90% of pines between 600m and 1,500m are *Pinus oocarpa (ocote)*, the species adapted for less rain (1,500-2,000mm pa) and a longer dry season than any other Central American pine. This is associated with broadleaf trees, mostly thorny and fire- and drought-resistant, dominated by *Bursera simarouba* (here known as *jiñocuabo*) and *escobillo (Phyllostylon brasiliensis)*; others include false laurel, acacia, gourd tree, caoba, tempisque, maría, avocado, *guácimo (Guazuma ulmifolia)*, *madroño*, cedar (*Cedrela mexicana*), strangler figs such as *Ficus glabrata*, walnut (*nogal/Juglans olanchum*), níspero, guavo (*Inga*), and oaks. Now rare, due to logging, are Spanish cedar (*Cedrela odorata*), spiny cedar (*pochote/Bombacopsis quinatum*) and lignum vitae (*Guaiacum officinale*). Gallery forest, found along streams, includes ceiba, guanacaste, and *ron-rón (Astronium graveolens)*.

Above c1,200-1,500m is cloudforest, which seems to be mainly *Lauracaea, Leguminosae* and oaks, with some *Pinus pseudostrobus (pinabete* — more resistant to cold than *Pinus oocarpa)*. *Pinus caribaea*, the short-needled Caribbean slash-pine, is best suited to altitudes below 1,000m with a short dry season and up to 3,000mm of rain a year; it's found in savanna on the Atlantic plains as far south as Bluefields. This provides excellent timber, so that most of the pine (and mahogany) of the Atlantic plains have been cleared, mostly thanks to US companies who 'mined' the area, taking a billion board feet of lumber over 80 years, and doing precisely no reforestation. However, the Contra war has slowed deforestation by turning many of the wilder parts of the country into free-fire zones and leaving many of them still littered with mines. Sandinista land reform also helped to reduce pressure on the forests. Even so, it's still a major problem. In addition, the government is again granting mining and forestry concessions to largely unsupervised foreign companies.

Climate
Precipitation ranges from 1,270mm in Ocotal and 1,400mm in Rivas to 6,350mm at the mouth of Río San Juan. West of Matagalpa (where precipitation is an average 1,520mm) it's dry from November to mid-May, with the heaviest rainfall in June and September/October and a dry *canicula* of about four weeks from mid-July to mid-August (due to a temporary strengthening of the northeast trade winds). To the east the dry season lasts only two to three months and is less dry. Above 1,200m the hills are often in cloud, with many ridges only visible for a few hours in the early afternoon. From March pastures are burnt, followed in May, just before rains, by the *milpas*. January is the coldest month, but even then temperatures in Managua only range from 21-31°C, only 3°C less than in April and May, the hottest months.

National parks
IRENA, the *Instituto de Recursos Naturales y de Ambiente*, was founded in 1979, when only three national parks existed and nothing had been done in two of them. Volcán Masaya was the only park that existed other than on paper. In 1983, 35 areas (totalling 17,265km², 13% of the national area) were identified as potential protected areas, and some of these are gradually being implemented. In January 1995, IRENA came to an agreement to use the army against animal smugglers, with the help of the World Society for the Protection of Animals: apparently 5,000 birds and animals a *day* are smuggled from Nicaragua and Honduras to El Salvador.

IRENA doesn't have a lot of information on parks other than Volcán Masaya, but if you want to talk to them, the offices are at the terminal of bus 266 beyond the airport. They're open from 08.30 to 15.45 Monday to Friday, but are not geared up for visitors; you should find Señor Castillo in hut 3 — he's the son of the owner of the Hospedaje Castillo in Altagracia. 1995 has been declared the Year of Legislation for Protected Areas, so we may see more progress, although parks are hardly a government priority.

Ecological organisations
JA! (meaning now, at once, although it stands for Young Environmentalists) (Apdo C-101 Managua; tel: 70897/650136; fax: 668 503); lively and noisy, mainly acting to save Lake Tiscapa (a volcanic crater in the capital) from pollution. **Fundación Nicaraguense para la Conservación y el Desarrollo** (Altamira d'Este no 774 (Rotonda), Managua (Apdo 1009; tel: 785 204; fax: 674 021) and at San Carlos); affiliated with Friends of the Earth.

Chapter Fifteen

Central and Southern Nicaragua

MANAGUA

Managua is totally different from any other Central America capital. It's largely free of smog, but instead it's at the mercy of earthquakes. As a result of the 1972 quake, and Somoza's cynical pocketing of all the international aid sent afterwards, the city centre is now almost empty. The city is now very decentralized, with new developments all in the suburbs and around the main markets/bus terminals. In a funny way the centre reminds me of New Delhi, with grassy expanses, beggars, ruins, street-corner comedor stalls, women with bundles on their heads, air-painted billboards, and tortillas that could pass for chapattis; but it's less efficient than India. This may change: since 1990 mayor Arnoldo Alemán has boosted city income from US$6m a year to US$27m, largely by more effective tax collection, and spent a lot on what the opposition calls cosmetic improvements. A more substantial change is that exiles are returning from Miami and opening businesses here.

The cheap hotels are in the Barrio Martha Quezada, perhaps the quietest area in any Central American capital. It's largely traffic-free, although buses 109, 116, 118 and 119 pass nearby — ask for the Hotel Intercontinental. To reach the Mercado Central/Huembes (for buses to Granada, Rivas, Matagalpa, Estelí and Ocotal) take buses 109 or 119; for the Mercado Bóer/Lewites (for León and Chinandega), take bus 118; and for the Mercado San Miguel (for Jutigalpa and Rama) take buses 116, 118 or 119.

Tourist information

There isn't really a properly set-up tourist information centre. At the Ministry of Tourism, one block west of Avda Bolivar, one block south of the Intercontinental, the *Dirección de Promoción y Relaciones Internacionales* office on the first floor mezzanine is helpful and can sell you the odd map.

Museums

The Museum of the Revolution has closed. The *Museo Nacional*, east of the centre on Pista P J Chamorro (Mon-Fri 09.00-16.00), is a disappointment.

SOUTH OF MANAGUA

The most accessible National Park in Nicaragua is also the oldest (founded in 1975), the best organised and one of the most interesting. This is the **Volcán Masaya National Park**, which is at km23 on the main highway to Granada, served by all buses to the towns of Masaya and Granada. Also known as Volcán Santiago, the main complex of craters is low and easily accessible; there's a road all the way to the top, with plenty of traffic, especially at weekends. Entry is from 09.00 to 17.00 Mon-Fri, 09.00-18.00 Sat/Sun, though once you're in you can stay as long as you like; pedestrians pay under US$1 and cars about US$3.

Rather than getting a ride all the way to the top, it's worth going first to the visitor centre 1.5km down the road, where there's a good display about the park, wildlife and volcanism in general. There's a restaurant next door, and a tap and toilets outside. From here it's definitely worth hitching to the top, as it's another 5km of hot dry hiking otherwise. The road ends at 590m at a car park known as the Plaza de Oviedo, where you won't fail to notice the clouds of sulphurous smoke billowing from the crater; amazingly, there are green parakeets (*Aratinga holoclora*) that actually choose to live in the fumes. Here you are looking into Volcán Santiago, composed of the original Nindirí crater at the bottom and the Santiago and San Pedro craters, formed between 1852 and 1859; this caldera covers an area of 52km². Above, to your left, is the higher Volcán Masaya (635m), containing the San Fernando and San Juan craters; this has been inactive for 200 years and is filled with trees. Nindirí was the local chief who brought Fernandez de Oviedo, the first foreigner to describe the volcano, to the top in 1529. To the right of the car park is a large cross, commemorating the one raised by the friar Francisco de Bobadilla, which was already in place when Oviedo came here; Bobadilla thought this was the mouth of hell, perhaps sharing the belief of local Indians who supposedly used to throw children into the crater as sacrifices.

The last major eruption was from the San Fernando crater in 1772, when lava flows reached the lake and the present highway; in 1985 a violent emission of sulphurous gases from Volcán Santiago left a large swathe of land to the west of the volcano uncultivable. Between 500 and 3,000 tonnes of gas are still belched forth daily, making it one of the world's worst natural polluters.

From the car park a path continues to the east of Volcán Santiago to another viewpoint (the *Mirador Boca del Infierno*). Below this (accessible only by guided groups) is the Caverna Tzinancanostac (also known as the Bat Cave), a lava tube 612m long (although see only 150m). Four species of bat live in this cave, including the common vampire. Park staff also lay on free tours of El Comalito, a small cone behind the visitor centre with active fumaroles, where they also discuss the ecology of the pioneer growth on the lava flows.

The habitat is described as tropical dry forest, but most is in fact lava, either bare or in the earliest stages of recolonization by plants. It's not quite a lunar landscape, but it's not far off; there's certainly no shade from the sun. The dominant trees are dry forest species such as guanacaste and indio desnudo; the dry season is when thousands of flowers burst into flower, including 12 species of orchid. The fauna likewise is typical of dry habitats, including magpie-jays, hawks, woodpeckers, coyote, various small felines, rabbits, iguanas, white-tailed deer, and monkeys.

Other than following the road to the top, all that unaccompanied visitors are permitted to do is to follow the Coyote Path (*Sendero de los Coyotes*) down through this scrub to Lake Masaya at the eastern end of the park. On no account drink from the lake, which has been infected with cholera. From the lake it's possible to follow a path to the left to meet the main highway at Nindirí.

Mombacho

From Masaya you can continue to Granada, perhaps the most attractive town in Nicaragua, and the departure point for several places of interest around Lake Nicaragua. The town is dominated by **Volcán Mombacho** (1,363m), immediately to the south. This was once over 2,000m high, but its upper part collapsed in the 16th century, wiping out a village and hurling 300 basalt and andesite blocks, now known as Las Isletas, into the lake. The west end of the present summit ridge is adorned with tens of radio masts, but the higher east end is clear with a good view of the whole coast from Rivas to León. Its tourist potential is virtually untapped, although it is now preserved as a nature reserve. It's covered in deciduous forest, with big trees such as fig (*Ficus ovalis*) and *majagua* (*Heliocarpus appendiculatus*), ceiba and cedar, with dwarf forest above. It's suffering badly from logging; local groups such as *Los Amigos de Mombacho* have begun to take an interest and to campaign for its protection. It's now an isolated island of forest and has just 33 species of mammals (such as howler monkeys, coyote and raccoons) and 70 birds (more green parakeets and parrots, turquoise-browed motmots, and great curassows), as well as black and green iguanas.

To reach the summit you can either take a bus from Managua or Granada to Nandaime and take a road east known as *la chuscada* to the reserve headquarters, 7km away, and from there a track north; or get off a Granada-Nandaime bus at the Diriomo junction and follow a signed track east, forking left after about a kilometre towards *Los Antennas*.

Lake Nicaragua

Lake Nicaragua (also known by its indigenous name, Cocibolca) is by far the largest lake in Central America, a real inland sea. It's now clear that it was never a bay of the Pacific, cut off by vulcanism and sedimentation; rather it was formed by faulting just a few million years ago, filling with rain water and forcing an outlet by the Río San Juan to the Atlantic. This was the competitor to the Panamanian isthmus as a possible route for an inter-oceanic canal. It's well known for its bull sharks (*tigrone/Carcharinus leucas*), and other species such as sawfish and tarpon, which can move freely from the lake to the sea. In preHispanic times this area was one of the main centres of settlement south of the Mayan area, and there are many petroglyphs and other artefacts, especially on some islands which seem to have been used as cemeteries.

The **Zapatera National Park** covers the island of Zapatera (5,226ha), 34km south of Granada, and a few associated islets (18 of them, with a total area of just 18ha). Its main importance is as an archaeological site, with tombs and rock carvings at Sonzaponte and San Miguel Vigil on Zapatera and on the adjacent Isla del Muerto. The large statues found here have been taken to the San Francisco convent in Granada, where they stand under a makeshift shelter; the most interesting ones, carved between 800AD and 1200AD, show human figures with animal doubles on their backs. The island receives an average of 1,475mm of rain a year and is covered with tropical dry forest up to about 400m and with tropical moist forest above that to the summit (625m) of this ancient eroded volcano. This is far richer and more exuberant than the dry forest, with epiphytes including beautiful orchids. The fauna is not rich, with just six species of mammal (including white-tailed deer, armadillos and howler monkeys) and 49 birds (including anhingas, white-fronted parrots, orange-fronted parakeets and grey hawks).

The largest island in the lake is **Ometepe**, now a popular centre for rest and recreation for long-term travellers. It was created by two volcanoes, both in the classical cone shape, which leads to some people describing the island's appearance as 'like a well-filled bra'. The volcanic soil is very fertile and there are plenty of prosperous small farms, although the steeper slopes are still covered in thick forest. The island's isolation and self-sufficiency meant that it was largely unaffected by the turmoil of the revolution and the Sandinista years, and it remains tranquil and restful. People sit around in rocking chairs on the sidewalk, watching the world go by, but also keeping an eye on the TV at the back of their front rooms.

The island is served by occasional ferries between Granada and San Carlos, where the lake flows into the Río San Juan, and by more frequent ferries (six a day) from San Jorge, a few minutes by bus from Rivas. These have an odd timetable, not very user-friendly unless you want to get to Managua very early in the morning. One faster boat charges two and a half times as much as the standard boats, but unless you want to wait five hours, or even wait overnight, you may find you've no choice but to use it. The San Jorge boats dock at Moyogalpa, where buses meet the boats to take you to Altagracia, the best place to stay if you're interested in hiking.

There are many attractive walks along beaches and through farms; the island is also great for mountain-biking — bring your own, no problem putting it on the ferry. There's a road, with buses, all round the northwestern half of the island (Volcán Concepción), and paths around the southeastern half (Volcán Madera), linking many small farms.

The higher volcano, at 1,610m, is Concepción, which is still active and largely covered in lava and ash. It's not an attractive hike, but if you want to do it, head south for about 2km from Altagracia and turn right to go up through a cemetery and then head left to a cinder gully. Volcán Madera (1,334m) is a far better bet: there's plenty of good forest, housing white-faced and howler monkeys and plenty of birds, and a beautiful lake in the crater. All the petroglyphs on the island are in the Madera half, and there are plenty of good ones beside the paths, depicting people, animals and geometrical shapes such as spirals. Señor Castillo, of the eponymous hospedaje in Altagracia, is a great enthusiast for the island and for the petroglyphs in particular, and if you want to see the best you should ask him to arrange a guide for you.

Most people assume you need a guide to hike up Madera as well, but it's really not necessary. From Altagracia you need to take a bus at 05.20, or at a pinch 09.30, towards Balgüe; this passes the Santo Domingo beach area, where there are a few cheap places to stay. Get off after almost an hour at the Balgüe *puesta de salud* — there's a rock here marked 'ATTO Tours' and also a kiosk with a *Helados Eskimo* sign, but, alas, no ices at all when I was there. From here a track runs uphill past banana fields and a few houses, passing through a stile after five minutes and swinging left to reach the Hacienda la Magdalena, a big wooden building with a marvelous large verandah looking out over the lake. A cobbled path goes straight up to the right of the farm, reaching a small house in ten minutes; this is your last chance to fill up your water bottle. Going straight through the yard of this house, the path passes through one more field and enters the forest; just to the left at the top of the field is a petroglyph, portraying a bird swallowing its prey.

It takes about three hours to reach the crater from here; the forest is relatively dry at first, with dry forest species such as magpie-jays, and then gets wetter and wilder, with plenty of mud and fallen trees. Due to prevailing winds, the flora has more in common with the eastern shore of the lake than with the far closer western shore. It's not an easy path, but navigation is straightforward — upwards, ever upwards. Once you reach the crater, it's possible to go down to the beautiful little lagoon, but a rope is useful for this (which is where a guide can come in useful). Returning by the same route, buses head back to Altagracia at 15.30 and 17.30; if you have time and want to get clean, there's a path down to the lake opposite the shop.

Beyond the lake

At the southern end of the lake is the **Solentiname archipelago**, known as an artists' haven; the priest, poet and, later, Sandinista foreign minister Ernesto Cardenal was responsible for creating a school of naïf artists, whose works you can see in the San Francisco convent in Granada. Again, these are Tertiary volcanic islands with petroglyphs, though you'll need local guidance to find the best. There are very simple hospedajes on the two largest islands, Mancarrón and San Fernando. The islands are reached from San Carlos, itself reached either by boat from Granada (via Ometepe) or by bus from Managua along 130km of dirt road.

San Carlos is also the jumping-off point for trips down the Río San Juan to **San Juan del Norte** (Greytown) on the coast. The river roughly marks the border with Costa Rica (although there are disputes about exactly where it is); about a third of the way down is El Castillo (or Castillo Viejo), with the ruins of a fort built in 1675 to stop pirates reaching Lake Nicaragua, and a few hospedajes. Henry Morgan was beaten back, but in 1780 Nelson was able to capture the fort, although he lost his eye in the process. Beyond here, on the

Nicaraguan bank, is the **Río Indio-Maíz Biological Reserve**, protecting a large slice of very wet coastal rainforest. It covers 3,000km² but has only four full-time rangers, so the protection is more theoretical than effective. The reserve headquarters are back in San Carlos, so stop there for information. They may be able to help you with transport downriver; commercial service is irregular and can be very expensive. January to March are the best months for walking; in the driest months, April and May, the river can be very shallow, making it difficult to get through by boat. The landscape along the river is a combination of undulating hills, tangled vegetation and green cliffs rising from the water. There are fincas all along the river, but there's plenty of lush greenery and the area is incredibly rich in birds. White and grey herons and egrets stand on the banks backed by shades of tropical green. There are tanagers, caciques, grackles, plovers, manakins, peppershrikes and hummingbirds.

The place to head for is probably the Río Bartolo, about 20km downstream from El Castillo, where there's a research station with rooms available. There are no tourist trails, but you will be able to get quite a way into the forest. The coastal strip is now part of the **Si-a-Paz** (Yes to Peace) international park, continuing over the border to Barra del Colorado in Costa Rica. This is even more of a paper park than the Indio-Maíz.

From San Juan del Norte it's possible to hike into **Costa Rica** along the coast; be sure to get your exit stamp here, and it's wise to get a Costa Rican visa, even if you don't strictly need one. To get started, you need to take a boat across the Río San Juan to the *barra* or sandbar. Don't listen to stories of a two-hour jaunt; it's a six-hour hike to Boca del Colorado and a further four or five hours from there to Barra del Colorado, and it's also wise to take a break in the shade at midday. You'll probably spend the night at Boca del Colorado, a few fishermen's huts at the mouth of the Río Colorado, which you need to cross at some point. Barra del Colorado is split into two, Norte where most people live, and Sur where most of the facilities are, including the *commandatura*, where you must get your entry stamp. It's also possible to take a boat from San Carlos (one daily, Monday to Friday) up the Río Frío to Los Chiles in Costa Rica; this is a little-used crossing and you may find the Nicaraguan army extracting US$5 from you, due to their border dispute with Costa Rica.

La Flor

As in Costa Rica, turtles lay their eggs on beaches on Nicaragua's Pacific coast, and there are several reserves to protect them. Right by the Costa Rican border, 18km south of San Juan del Sur, olive ridleys and leatherbacks nest at the **La Flor Wildlife Refuge**; between July and January the ridleys come ashore in seven or eight *arribadas* of around 3,000 turtles each, far fewer than in Costa Rica but nevertheless impressive enough. There is some tropical dry forest dominated by tamarind and calabash gourd trees, as well as mangroves. This is inhabited by howler monkeys, raccoons, coyotes and skunks; birds include marine species such as pelicans and magnificent frigate birds, and orange-fronted parakeets. To the north of San Juan del Sur and El Astillero is the similar reserve of **Chococente**.

Chapter Sixteen

Northern Nicaragua

NORTHWEST OF MANAGUA

Beyond Lake Managua lies the Cordillera de los Maribios, a line of mostly extinct volcanoes that continues across the Gulf of Fonseca into El Salvador. The first and most impressive is **Volcán Momotombo** (1,297m), often seen as a national symbol, on matchboxes and so on. It's good to look at, but there are two schools of thought about actually climbing it. Rob made an expedition of it and had a splendid time, camping near the top and enjoying great views at sunset and sunrise. Others say it's unnecessary masochism and if you want to see the inner workings of a volcano you should go to Volcán Masaya. Equally there are two ways up, one easier but more complicated in bureaucratic ways, the other a less pleasant climb but unplagued by permits.

The easier route is from the north, through the premises of a geothermal energy plant that is said to provide almost a quarter of the country's power. Although the volcano can be ascended and descended in one long day, it's preferable to camp near the top: of course you'll have to carry all your water, but the views make it worthwhile. You're required to have a permit from the *Instituto Nacional de Energía* in Managua, which should be a mere bureaucratic formality but is made a pain by the sheer unhelpfulness of their staff. You'll need to take or send a letter of application (giving names and vehicle details) to the INE on Pista de la Municipalidad, at the southern end of the new extension of Avenida Bolivar, and return to collect it a couple of days later.

In Managua take a bus (every half hour throughout the day) from the Mercado Boer (Israel Lewites) bus terminal for La Paz Centro. You need to leave Managua by 08.00 if you want to get to the top the same day, as connections from La Paz Centro to Puerto Momotombo aren't too frequent. These leave from the old train yard; the last one is at about 15.30. Tourists come to Puerto Momotombo to see the ruins of León Viejo, destroyed by Momotombo in 1609, but few stay the night. I believe there's a hospedaje here, and there's certainly a rather poor and noisy one in La Paz Centro. You can swim in the lake, although it's not the cleanest; but it's worth going down to the beach to see Momotombo and Momotombito, which is a smaller but equally perfect volcanic cone rising out of the lake. This is entrancingly beautiful on the night of a full moon.

In the morning start as early as possible by walking northeast along the dirt road around the lake. In just under an hour you should reach a junction from

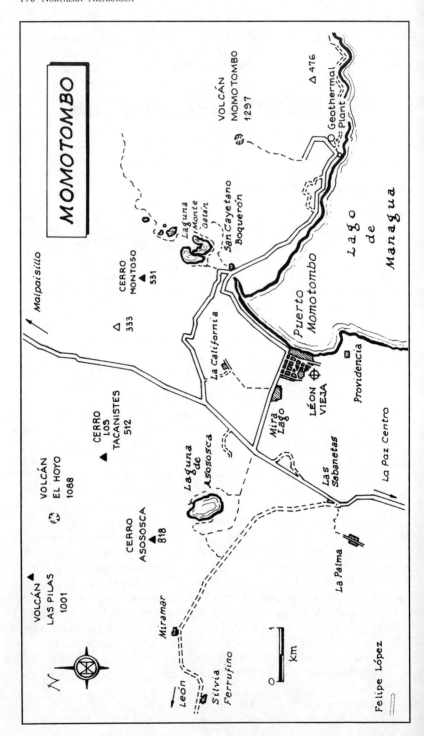

MOMOTOMBO

Felipe López

the left (a more direct route from La Paz Centro) just before a gate and checkpoint at Boquerón (marked as San Cayetano on the 1:50,000 map). The road leads on another 6km to the so-called *Luz y Fuerza* plant (tapping steam from geysers to generate power), where the increasingly rough road swings left and climbs to almost 200m. A rough path heads straight up the volcano from the lefthand side of the parking lot; when Rob was here the first 10m had been bulldozed, so that it was hard to see its start. However, it's then clearer as it climbs steeply through lava vegetation. The wind rustles through the dry trees, lizards slither and iguanas scurry, jays and parrots squawk angrily and butterflies ghost around. It is a little eerie but fascinating. The going becomes harder and soon you are fighting to keep going upwards instead of sliding back on the scree.

After one and a half to two hours the trail becomes somewhat indistinct but by now you'll know that north and up is the direction to the summit. After perhaps two or three hours of walking you'll find yourself on a flattish shoulder (just above the tree line) with superb views of the scree-covered peak and the lake and countryside around. Some protection from the wind can be found and this was where Rob spent the night. From this point to the summit takes one to two hours over loose scree. Lovely!

The summit is exciting. The soft earth is cracked and hot to the touch, puffs of sulphurous gases billow all around you. There is a more or less safe path across the peak which you can follow to look at the gently puffing fumaroles and the garishly yellow-encrusted crater. It smells like an out-of-control chemistry experiment, and a water-soaked bandana (if you have any water to spare) around your mouth helps when the wind blows the wrong way. Use your common sense here, because too much exposure to these gases will damage your lungs and eyes.

The alternative, permit-free, route involves back-tracking for five minutes from the checkpoint along the La Paz Centro road; where the road bends left there's a gate on the right. From here a cattle path leads up to a ridge and down to Laguna Monta Galán; fork left along the lakeside (through dry forest) and then strike off to the right straight up the volcano. The path shown on the map reaching a point just below 200m no longer exists. There is some very, *very* spiky undergrowth here — you absolutely do not want to be wearing shorts here. If this is too tough, you can continue to the northern end of the lake and head a few hundred metres northwest and follow slippery lava scree up the mountain; it's going to be a long hot morning's work whichever way you go. To return to civilization, the workers' buses leave for La Paz Centro at about 16.30, although they don't seem particularly helpful.

The Cordillera de los Maribios continues to the northwest; Volcán El Hoyo (1,088m) and Volcán Las Pilas (1,001m) are easily visible just a few kilometres from Momotombo. They're extinct, but there are fumaroles on El Hoyo, so that no vegetation grows on it. To the north is the village of Malpaisillo, proposed site of a far larger geothermal energy complex. Continuing to the northwest, Cerro Negro appeared in 1850 and remains active; it erupted in 1992, showering ash on León. Volcán Telica (1,060m) has a complex system of craters still pumping out acid rain; next comes Volcán San Cristobal, now the highest volcano in Nicaragua at 1,745m, and also its most 'voluminous'. As mentioned, Mombacho used to be higher; so was **Volcán Cosigüina**, right at Nicaragua's northwestern extremity. Now only 870m, it was over 3,000m high until blown apart in 1835 by one of the most violent eruptions ever recorded, heard in Belize, Jamaica and Bogotá. The caldera, with a clear blue lake at its bottom, is about 2km in diameter. You can hike up from Potosí (reached by bus from Chinandega). There are large areas of mangrove on either side of the road to Potosí; take a bus from Chinandega to Puerto Morazán to hire a boat on the Estero Real (now a nature reserve).

BOSAWAS AND SASLAYA

The best backpacking in Nicaragua (as opposed to day trips) is in the north of the country, above all in the **Bosawas Nature Reserve**. This is 8,000km² of largely untouched primary forest, the home of the Mayangna (Sumo) people. The whole of the Atlantic half of Nicaragua is a largely empty area which has traditionally been seen as fit only for exploitation. In the rubber boom at the end of the 19th century, Nicaraguan *Castilla elastica* trees were the main source of latex north of Amazonia; in the 1880s rubber-gatherers found gold in a place now called Bonanza, just outside the Bosawas Reserve. North American companies moved in to mine for gold, and throughout this century vast amounts of timber were removed as well, both as fuel for the mines and to be shipped to North America, and more recently, Taiwan. Almost all of Northern Zelaya has been stripped of its primary forest and is now a savanna of cattle grazing and secondary scrub; in addition the rivers are poisoned by mercury and cyanide and other waste from the gold mines. Now much of the remaining forest has been protected by the Bosawas Reserve, but it's by no means totally safe: in 1995 a foreign company, Nycon Resource, was allowed to prospect in Bosawas, despite being opposed by the local Sumos, the provincial government of the RAAN, and even the Minister of the Environment and Natural Resources!

The other threat is from the ever-advancing agricultural frontier, as peasants and smallholders from elsewhere in Nicaragua, forced to move by exhausted land and growing populations, clear fields for themselves from the forest. Interestingly, in 1603 the frontier of settlement ran north-south through Jinotega and Matagalpa, and then actually retreated westwards, thanks to attacks by Indians, pirates, and from 1704 to 1781 groups of Miskitos and Zambos (a Miskito-Negro mix) led by British officers, all coming up the Río Grande de Matagalpa and the Río Coco to attack settlements in the interior. In 1789 the mining centre of Nueva Segovia was moved for the second time to the present site of Ocotal; there were further revolts by the Matagalpa Indians throughout the 19th century, and it was only the coffee boom of the 1890s that pushed the line of settlement to Muy Muy. Even in the 1950s the frontier of settlement reached only to Tuma and Matiguás, barely east of its position in 1603. Since then, with the logging boom and the building of a road from Matagalpa all the way to Puerto Cabezas, on the Atlantic coast, settlers have moved into the whole of this area; in all around 100,000 people moved into the agrarian frontier regions between the 1950s and 1970s. From the road you'll see almost no primary forest, and the same applies along the main rivers. The southern fringe of the Bosawas reserve is to be released from the reserve in recognition of the fact that it is past preserving.

About 95% of the Sumo Indians, around 5,000 in all, are said to live within the Bosawas reserve. Miskitos live to the north, along the Río Coco (also known as the Segovia or, in Miskito, Wangki). The Miskito are in general slightly more 'Westernised' than the Sumo and tend to see them as a lower race. It's probably not necessary to say that the Somoza government treated *indigenos* badly, but the Sandinistas aroused, if anything, more ill-feeling at first by their technocratic and centralizing approach to development. Tomás Borge, the Sandinista security chief, was sent in to repress dissent in a rather heavy-handed manner, and when the Contra uprising gathered pace, between 18,000 and 30,000 Miskitos crossed the border to Honduras to join them — not out of allegiance to their political views, but simply because they had been so alienated by the Sandinistas. They began to return from 1985, when the government adopted a more pragmatic approach. In addition, up to 40,000 people were moved out of border areas by the Sandinistas in 1982 to allow a 'free-fire zone' in the war with the Contras. Almost all of these people have now returned, although in some cases villages have been re-established in different positions to those shown on maps. With the creation of the reserve, there is now some establishment support for the *indigenos*, and they have recently been able to obtain court orders against illegal settlers on their lands, something previously unheard of.

The core area of the Bosawas Nature Reserve, the **Saslaya National Park**, was created in the early 1980s, but largely unimplemented; many people in the area have never heard of it. Bosawas was created in 1991 and has far higher name recognition, as it actually has staff, and Peace Corps volunteers, and has been able to do some good work. Saslaya covers the highest peaks of the Cordillera Isabella, Cerro Saslaya (1,651m — or 1,990m on some maps) and Cerro El Toro (1,652m), and some of the wildest forest you're likely to find anywhere. It's a great hike into the forest on Saslaya, but not everyone will manage the final climb to the summit; there's a camping spot just below here which would be a good objective in itself.

Alternatives to hiking are to take a boat trip, either north up the Río Ulí to Palomar, where the Sumo residents are keen to develop ecotourism, or from Musawas, the Sumo capital. To reach the latter, you should continue east (by plane, or by road via Rosita) from Siuna to Bonanza, site of the only operating gold mine in the area, and of another Bosawas Reserve office, also with gringo volunteers. From Bonanza it's at least a day's hike to Musawas, from where you can follow the Río Waspuk deep into the Reserve.

This is tropical moist forest, but in its lower reaches it seems remarkably close to tropical dry forest for somewhere on the Atlantic slope of Central America. There's lots of interesting stuff: in addition to ceiba, Spanish cedar,

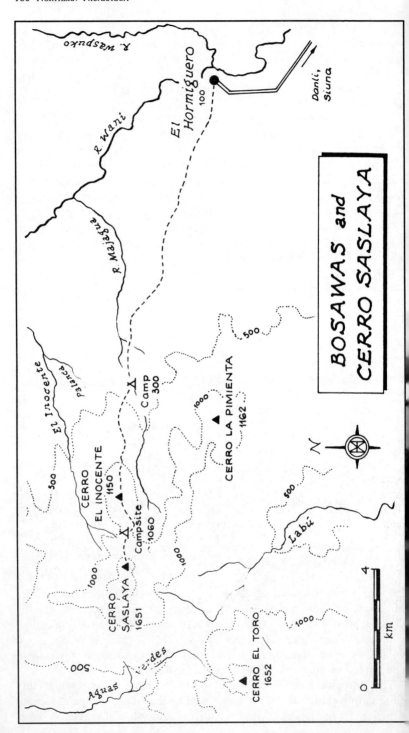

BOSAWAS and CERRO SASLAYA

strangler figs, begonias, *ron-rón (Astroneum graveolens)*, and so on, you can also find rubber trees (*Castilla elastica*), *achiote (Bixa orellana,* used for food colouring and body paint) and *escalera de mico,* a spiral vine whose grated bark is used against foot fungus and arthritis. You may see any of the normal forest mammals, such as howler, spider and white-faced monkeys, felines, peccary, tapir, squirrels, agouti and armadillo, as well as iguanas and snakes. Birds are plentiful: we saw or heard green and scarlet macaws, green parrots, oropendolas, solitaires, crested guan, great curassow, highland tinamou, tanagers and eagles, and relatively few hummingbirds. There are also quetzals and keel-billed toucans.

Hiking directions

The jumping-off point for Saslaya is the gold-mining town of **Siuna**, reached from Managua by a daily plane and a bus on Mondays, Wednesdays and Fridays (returning the next day). The plane is operated by Costeña, and continues to Puerto Cabezas on the coast. From Matagalpa, there is a bad road via Waslala, on which there are trucks but no buses; you're better off taking a bus to Muy Muy and then picking up the bus from Managua early in the morning. Siuna is a town of 9,000 scattered around several hills, with a small market in the centre, an airstrip to the east beside the Puerto Cabezas road, and a large gold mine occupying most of the northern part of town. This is now closed and shut up, but when it was operating there was a type of apartheid here, with Nicaraguans not even allowed into certain areas of town. Even so the town has declined so much since the mine's closure that people constantly ask outsiders if they've come to reopen the mine. The road, never good, is a lot worse nowadays, and there's only enough electricity for three of the town's four sectors to have power each night (and only until 21.00). Plenty of gold is still being found by panners in the area's rivers.

There are several hotels, of which the best is the *Costeña,* near the baseball stadium and airstrip. You can eat in the market or at the *Desnuque,* also by the airstrip; there's a bank (on top of a hill by the mayor's office). The Bosawas Reserve office is just beyond the *Costeña* at house S-30A; staff are helpful, and there'll probably be a Peace Corps volunteer somewhere around.

You need to get to the village of El Hormiguero (meaning 'the antheap'; in full, El Hormiguero Nuevo, as it's only been in its present position since the early 1980s), at just below 100m. It's now at the confluence of the Wani and Waspuko rivers, not 5km west as shown on maps. The farmers' co-operative here is keen to develop ecotourism, mainly by groups, but they'll also welcome individual hikers. Ask for the co-op or at the village kiosk for somewhere to stay and for a guide. A pick-up runs from Hormiguero to Siuna at about 06.00, returning at around 13.00 or 14.00; it takes about an hour, so you won't be able to start hiking before 15.00. If you can manage this, you can reach a hut about two and three-quarter hours away for the night; if not, you're better off waiting till the morning. You should have a guide, both to support their attempts to provide an alternative to further clearance of the forest, and because the trail is unmarked and the forest is pretty wild. The cost is minimal, about

US$8 a day.

The path heads west passing the new Roman Catholic church on your left, then swings a bit right out of the village; you'll see the peak of Saslaya ahead, far more dramatic than anything else in this area. Various paths head out across the fields, but after 15 minutes you'll go to the right through a gate, after the last house, and then swing left towards Saslaya. After ten minutes you'll go to the right across a log bridge and turn left; in five minutes turn left again across another log bridge, and another five minutes later. After another 20-odd minutes you'll move from secondary growth into the true forest, after which the trail is pretty clear for a while. There's no water until a stream an hour and a half away; after crossing this it's another ten minutes to a river, 8km from Hormiguero. The hut is across the river (which you can probably get across without getting your feet wet) and about five minutes to the left. Guides can catch crabs and shellfish for you and boil them up with *malanga*, a yuca-like root.

The path continues beyond the hut; in about 50 minutes you'll cross the Río Majagua, and ten minutes to the left, on the left bank, reach the *campamento*, where there are hammock rails and wooden frames for mosquito nets. This is your last water for many hours. The path heads out from the back of the camp and begins to climb; after about 2½ hours of uphill slog you'll come to a viewpoint of sorts. From here you can look out over the forest, allowing you to see clearings dotted here and there, some even inside the reserve. There's a steep climb for five minutes and an easier 15 minutes to bring you to the top of Cerro El Inocente (1,150m). From here the path is tiny and unclear, but it follows the ridge westwards, so you shouldn't go wrong. Trees here are shorter and much more mossy than lower on the mountain, with lots of palms. It drops steeply to a saddle and climbs briefly to reach the upper campsite at about 1,060m, about an hour from El Inocente. There's just a wooden cross here, a couple of benches and a fireplace; there's plenty of space for tents, but you're better off hanging a hammock and mosquito net from a couple of trees. There's water a couple of minutes below to the left; the second stream is usually better.

The path to the summit climbs steeply up from the camp; at first you have to deal with loose roots and vines, but then the roots become more solid and more like a staircase. After an hour you arrive at the crux: a cliff of about 20m with a fixed rope and some logs jammed across a vertical cleft. It was possible to climb it with no other aids when I was there, but a bad rainy season or just normal wear and tear could bring down one of the logs and make it impossible without a climbing harness or other gear. You should belay yourself by passing the rope around your back, under your shoulders and wrapping it around your forearm. The most difficult stage is moving from right to left across the second log (trying not to put all your weight on the log) and up from there. At the top you need to go left (the path to the right soon reaches a dead end) and then up another bit of cliff, mostly hauling yourself under and through mossy roots. It's not far to the top from here, although you need to take care — your feet barely touch the ground as you climb over the roots and branches, and there are several spots where you could fall straight through the undergrowth and a long way down. Likewise at the summit you have to climb up on branches to get any kind of view. In its way this is some of the densest vegetation I've ever seen. Other than here you have next to no views all day, though the forest and its wildlife are ample compensation. The rope was fixed by an American priest living in the area; I was told that I was the sixth gringo to reach the top, assuming (logically enough) that no-one ever came here before the road was built. I'm claiming it as a probable first British ascent.

Usually you'll return the way you came, although with a good guide you could take a slightly longer and slower route, turning left off the ridge (about half an hour beyond El Inocente) to drop north through generally open forest to the Río Palanca, a tributary of the Río El Inocente. You spend as much time hiking down the river itself as along its bank, until you reach the Río Wani; there's a good path along its right bank, but after 50 minutes or so you should wade across to the left bank — it was thigh-high in March. The next hour and a half's hike was all through hot open farmland, before finally fording the river again to Hormiguero.

If continuing to the coast you should be aware of the Laguna Pahara and Laguna Yulu Karata Nature Reserves, respectively north and south of Puerto Cabezas. Offshore, just to the northeast, is the Miskito Keys Protected Area, one of the main feeding grounds for the green turtles that breed all along the Atlantic coast of Central America. There are also manatees, lobster and shrimp. You'll have to charter a boat to get out here.

MATAGALPA AND THE NORTH

Matagalpa is the best base for hiking in northern Nicaragua, although as mentioned you shouldn't head directly from here to Siuna via Waslala, as this involves a day, or more likely a day and a half, of crashing around in the back of a truck. Instead you should get a bus down to Muy Muy and then pick up the Managua-Siuna bus at some ungodly hour of the morning. Whichever way you go, you need the little-known northern market, not the main bus station at the southern market. There are decent little places to sleep and eat in Matagalpa, and one supermarket, on Avenida Escobar, making it the only place to buy hiking food (including chocolate!) in northern Nicaragua.

The area immediately north of Matagalpa is often said to have the best hiking in Nicaragua, and certainly these are the only easily accessible hills. However, the area is too dry and deforested to be very attractive. The main exception is the **Selva Negra** estate, on a ridge about 8km north of town, where a considerable area of forest has been preserved by the owners of a coffee finca. The place has an interesting history: in the 1880s the Nicaraguan government was encouraging immigrants to come and grow coffee in the then largely unsettled hills of northern Nicaragua. The area of Matagalpa was largely settled by Germans, whose settlements can still be traced in place names such as Alemania and Bavaria; the finca of Selva Negra is called *Hammonia*, the Latin for Hamburg, although the Ineter map gives it as *Armonia*, and of course

Selva Negra itself refers to Germany's *Schwarzwald*. In 1905 a group of the settlers introduced a traction engine known as the *Terrocarril* to take their coffee to La Paz Centro, where it was put on a train to the port of Corinto; this wasn't a huge success, but one of its wheels can be seen here. The present owners, grandchildren of the original settlers, still produce premium coffee, now organically, and also run what may be the country's best hotel (Apdo 126 Matagalpa, tel: 061 23883, Managua tel: 658 342). It has a youth hostel annexe, costing US$10 for those under 26 or thereabouts. One of its key attractions is the forest behind it, much of it secondary but being allowed to revert to a natural state as fast as possible.

To get there, take a bus towards Jinotega from the southern market (you can also catch these at the bridge just west of the cathedral square) and get off just after km140, before the top of the climb. The entry to the hotel is on the right, marked by an armoured car abandoned there when the fleeing commander of Somoza's National Guard in Matagalpa was cut off at the pass during the revolution of 1979. You'll have to walk for 15 minutes along the pine-lined driveway to the entry gate, where day visitors have to buy a 20 Cordobas coupon (under US$3), redeemable for food and drink in the hotel. Turn left up to the hotel (at 1,250m) to pick up a map and find the hiking trails; most of the trails only take a quarter-hour or so to walk, giving you plenty of time to sit and wait for the wildlife. The trails take you more or less to the end of the secondary forest (coffee plantations until 60 years ago), but you're welcome to make your own way onwards into the primary forest. You can even climb in about four hours to the 1,635m summit just east of the road — no machete needed. This is the end of the hotel's land, but forest continues to the Atlantic, so Selva Negra is not the isolated patch of forest I'd expected. It's not a Nicaraguan Monteverde, but there's still a fair amount of biodiversity, with 75 bird species (including quetzals, toucans, hummingbirds, American swallow-tailed kites and boat-tailed grackles), 85-plus orchids, deer, sloths, howler monkeys, puma, ocelot and agouti.

It's possible to hire horses and explore the lower parts of the estate; groups are also given tours of the coffee plant. You could even walk back to Matagalpa; either from Hammonia directly south down the Las Cabañas stream, or following the road on from the checkpoint to the Hacienda San Luis, and then to San José, La Gloria, and down the Molino Norte valley. Nothing wild, just pastoral countryside where you can see people going about their everyday business. In the other direction, it's possible to follow the road over the pass and then turn right to walk downhill through the fincas of La Fundadora (built by Alexander Potter, who also built the road to Matagalpa), La Salvadora and La Sultana, to Las Robles on the Lago de Apanás, east of Jinotega. This is coffee country, green and lush most of the time; but it suffered badly during the Sandinista revolution. There are places to stay in Jinotega, and famous statues in the church. Some people have even walked on along the dirt roads northwest from Jinotega to San Rafael del Norte and Estelí. San Rafael was Sandino's headquarters; there's a museum in his wife's house, and a church with a painting of the devil with the face of Daniel Ortega.

An interesting stroll is to head left down the road from the armoured car, and turn right almost at once to the village of Palsila (or San Simón de Palsila), about 2km away. Many of the inhabitants are blond and blue-eyed, possibly due to an incursion by British pirates, although no-one knows. They are also democratically minded, each owning a couple of hectares of his own land. It's attractive countryside, and there's a good view from the 1,487m hill with a radio mast on top, reached from the road junction.

Salman Rushdie raved "O the beauty of the mountains at Estelí", but I couldn't see it myself. It's hot bare arid country, and I wouldn't recommend hiking here. On the Honduran border, 100km north, the Cordillera Dipilto would be a better bet if it weren't still strewn with mines laid to keep the Contras out. This used to be a very popular area, including the country's highest peak, Pico Mogoton (2,103m), but for the time being you should stay away. This is the best example in Nicaragua of the type of pine-oak forest found almost all over Honduras; it's also the southern limit of many North American bird species. The base is Ocotal, where there are cheap hospedajes, or the better *Las Colinas* hotel, 15km north. A dirt road runs northeast from Jinotega up the Bocay valley into the Bosawas Reserve; there is some settlement along this road, as well as problems with *recontra* bandits.

Howler monkey

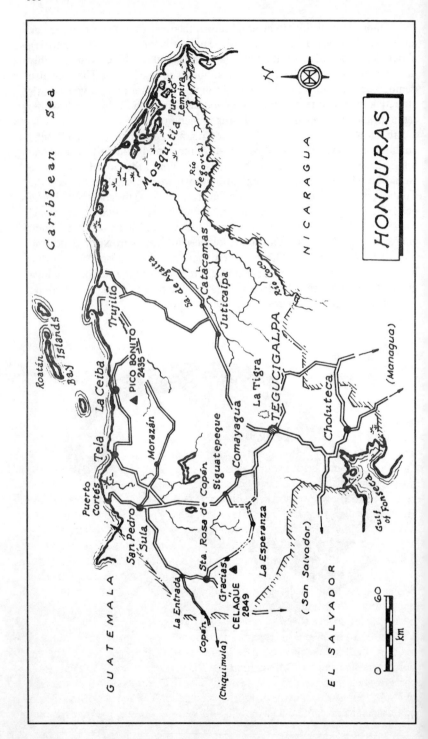

Chapter Seventeen

Honduras
General Information

In 1502 Columbus first made contact with the American mainland; having difficulty in finding water shallow enough to anchor, he named the nearby land Honduras, which is Spanish for 'depths'. Hondurans tell us that the name also refers to the ruggedness of the countryside, with its many deep valleys lined by steep-sided mountains, which provides great backpacking terrain, especially in the west of the country. A population of at most 120,000 was reduced by at least half in the 1530s by measles, introduced by Europeans, and by being taken as slaves to Peru, and didn't recover to previous levels until the early 19th century. However, by the 1880s it had grown to 330,000, by 1935 to 962,000, by 1961 to 1.9 million, and by 1993 it had turned five million and was still growing at 3.3% a year. Not surprisingly land shortage is now a dominant factor in Honduran life.

Another key feature is the way in which the military has a hold on every aspect of life. After decades of propping up, or indeed running, US-backed regimes and serving as a bulwark against communism in Nicaragua and El Salvador, the army now owns a bank (BANFFAA) and Hondutel, the 'state' telecommunications corporation. Officers make money in many other ways and have a say, if they choose, in almost any government decision. Nowadays the current of democratisation that is flowing through Central America is making itself felt here too, but Honduras is the only remaining Central American country whose army insists on absolute freedom to select its own leadership. However, it does see a democratic facade as essential to its own survival, and has almost given up harrassing the populace at checkpoints; Honduran troops are also serving with the UN in Haiti. With murders up from 2,000 in 1993 to 3,000 in 1994, the army has helped whip up a national panic about crime to justify putting soldiers on the streets and keeping military budgets up. President Reina has pushed hard to abolish conscription, against bitter military opposition. Even though, with the end of the regional crisis, the army has been reduced in size to 17,500, its budget has increased from US$42.5m in 1992 to US$45m in 1994. The chief of the armed forces has been accused of making US$32m by corruption: he denies it but is retiring anyway. The Air Force's present and previous commanders have been accused of selling spare parts for their personal profit, with a link alleged to the death in a plane crash of Mario Reina Midence (the president's nephew and counsellor). Meanwhile, conscript soldiers earn US$5 a month (with bed and board), against a national minimum wage of US$77.

The Secret Police (DNI or National Investigation Unit), which had been under military control since 1963 and was linked to 183 disappearances in the dirty war of the 1980s, was closed down in 1994 and replaced by the civilian DIC (Criminal Investigation Unit), with 1,500 FBI/Israeli-trained agents. There's plenty of corruption elsewhere, nowadays mostly linked to the drug trade; the most notorious case was that of a Liberal deputy who 'borrowed' a drug-runner for the weekend from Trujillo jail and never brought him back.

Visitors should know about this, but it's not going to affect you directly. Honduras is the least expensive country in Central America and one of the very friendliest, with a wealth of good hiking and with conservation and ecotourism movements just gathering pace.

Money

Honduras is cheap! The currency is the lempira, named after the Indian chief who rebelled against the Spaniards and now has his head on Honduran coins and the one lempira note.

Transport

Trains are effectively useless as a means of public transport, although tourist trains do run out of La Ceiba (Zona Mazapán edificio 55; tel: 43 3525). School buses go to most places, supplemented by pick-ups which go virtually everywhere else. Half of the buses in Tegucigalpa are worn out, 80% of those in San Pedro Sula, and 100% elsewhere: the operators want to increase fares by 100% on dirt roads, and by 70% on paved roads, to fund replacement. The alternative is the over-priced North Coast Shuttle (run by Aventuras Centroamericas, Edif. Nina 1-6, 1 Calle, 15/16 Avdas NO, San Pedro Sula; tel/fax: 57 2380); they run from Copán to Trujillo on Sundays, Tuesdays and Fridays, returning on Mondays, Wednesdays and Saturdays, and the fare for the full journey is US$32. The main highways are excellent, and unleaded fuel was introduced in 1995.

Many people fly in to San Pedro Sula, where a new US$60m airport terminal was due to open in mid-1995, to handle 800,000 passengers and 38,000 tonnes of cargo a year. The state airline TAN/SAHSA went bankrupt several years ago, and the Salvadoran airline TACA took over many of its flights, which have a reputation for being late.

Maps

The *Instituto Geográfico Nacional* is in SECOPT (the *Secretaría de Comunicaciones, Obras Públicas y Transporte*) at the east end of 15 Calle, off 1 Avenida in the south of Comayagüela. The *Departamento de Publicación* is open Mon-Fri 08.30-11.50 and 12.30-16.30. There are departmental maps at 1:200,000 and hiking maps at 1:50,000, costing about US$2, and there's said to be an excellent new topographical map of the country. Probably the most requested map, of La Tigra, was out of print when I was there.

Food

The *comida típica* is ubiquitous, beans and rice with tortillas, with meat, cheese, yuca, *platano*, avocado or cabbage salad. *Tapado* is a stew, found especially on the north coast, of fish or meat with *platano*, yuca and coconut milk. Good snacks include *baleadas*, beans and cheese wrapped in a tortilla. *Pan* means dry rolls, buns and cupcakes as well as bread; try *pan de coco* (Garífuna coconut bread) and *casaba* (yuca bread) as well.

Cartons of orange juice are ubiquitous, leading to a big litter problem; it's 100% pure, but not 100% orange juice. As everywhere oranges are sold on the street, but here there are machines to remove the peel. Avoid bottled banana drinks, which taste of pear drops. *Salva Vida* (meaning 'Healthy Life', not 'Empty Forest') is an excellent malty beer.

Hotels

They're cheap and friendly here, and any minor inadequacies can be forgiven.

Naturalists' Honduras

The country is for the most part very mountainous, with only the narrowest of level strips along the coast in places. There's flat ground to the east (in the area known as Mosquitia) and the northwest (the Ulúa Valley); the latter continues via the Comayagua valley to the Gulf of Fonseca on the Pacific, a major break that forms the southern limit to the range of many montane bird species, as well as of *Taxus* and *Abies* (yew and fir) trees. The northern ranges are ancient, based on Paleozoic granite, mica-schist, slate, and some gneiss, with Cretaceous rocks (limestone, some conglomerate and sandstone) deposited on top; the southern cordillera is more recent, being formed of Tertiary igneous rock, alternate layers of andesitic tuffs and basaltic lava, over a kilometre deep in places. The coastal plains, north and south, are formed of Pleistocene marine sediments.

The characteristic forest of Honduras is pine-oak forest. Seven species of pine are found in Honduras, each in a specific ecological niche and all in the hills except for *Pinus caribea*, which is found in the savannas of the Atlantic coast. From September until May many birds, mostly migratory species, nest in the pine forest, including nine species of warbler, five woodpeckers, vultures, vireos, the American swallow-tailed kite, white-fronted parrot, green parakeet, toucan, red crossbill, bushy-crested jay (*serenqueque*), magpie-jay (*urraca*), and treecreeper (*trepador*). There's true cloudforest (lower montane moist forest) on the northern and eastern slopes of the southern cordillera, and montane rainforest on the northern slopes of the northern mountains, with more precipitation coming from rain than from clouds. Pure tropical rainforest, with massive buttressed trees up to 60m tall, is found above all in the northeast. In all there are at least 663 (perhaps 710) species of bird to be seen in Honduras, as well as 112 mammals, 89 amphibians, 177 land and freshwater reptiles and seven sea reptiles (six turtles and a snake).

The Atlantic coast is pretty damp all year round, but not as much as further south. The driest season here is from March to May, and the wettest from

September to February, when both road and river travel may be impossible in Mosquitia. To the west the altitude makes the climate pleasant; the dry season runs from December to May, and there is also a dry spell in late July/early August (which produces a partial growth ring in pine trees). The Gulf of Fonseca, on the Pacific, is hellishly hot in the dry season. Maximum annual rainfall is of the order of 5,000mm, and can be below 1,000mm inland. Temperatures can reach 38°C in March and April, and drop to 5°C in December or January. Usually two crops can be raised each year, one of corn, then another of beans or sorghum.

This is a very interesting time in Honduras, with both conservation and ecotourism gathering momentum. Population growth has led to widespread deforestation and exhausted soil, and there is considerable pressure to move into unspoilt areas and work them out as well. Vote-winning means that politicians, and the National Agrarian Institute (INA), in charge of agrarian reform, have tended to back the colonists, but it's now becoming clear that deforestation leads to climatic changes and water shortages. Law 87-87 declared all Honduras's cloudforest as national parks, above all to preserve watersheds; however there's no general sympathy with conservationists — even the Ministry of the Environment calls ecologists 'communists' (one of the worst insults in the Honduran lexicon). The President himself said in 1995 that 'ecological concerns should not slow down a country's development' and did nothing to block an INA scheme to build a road (already shown on many maps) along the Río Paulaya (the border of the Río Platano Biosphere Reserve) and bring 20,000 more settlers into the area. When a scheme of this sort is announced, many people jump the gun and start moving in at once, slashing and burning; in fact most of the useable land is already in use, and where forest is cleared the land will soon be exhausted. Despite the International Labour Organisation's Agreement 169 (ratified by congress in 1994), guaranteeing full consultation with indigenous groups and environmental protection, there has been nothing of the sort. At Semana Santa of 1995 further widespread land invasions were promised by the *Asociación Nacional de Campesinos*, claiming they're trying to reduce grain imports! The INA always claims to be supporting the law, but is easily distracted by the judicious application of money. It can usually be persuaded to give land title to colonists, but has refused 40,000 indigenos title to their land. (The Yoro Xicaques, or Tolupans, now about 20,000 strong, have had title to their land since 1864, thanks to the help of a priest.)

Honduras is the only Central American state with a major timber export industry. In 1974 Cohdefor, the Honduran Forestry Development Corporation, was set up, and soon produced a highly professional corps of foresters. Nowadays, however, Cohdefor has become a byword for corruption and mismanagement, and it has been very resistant to ideas about sustainable forestry. At its best, it's very selective, taking only two or three trees per hectare in broadleaf forests; however, the sawmills are very inefficient, with outdated circular saws that waste much of the wood. In addition many mangrove swamps are being destroyed for shrimp farming (Honduras is now the third largest exporter of cultivated seafoods in Latin America, with sales tripling since 1980 to a total of US$134m in 1994). Shrimp farmers are also accused of shooting birds, but in general there is far less hunting by Hondurans than ten years ago. Honduras was building up a nice line of business from North Americans who came in winter to shoot duck and doves, but this was actually banned in 1995.

The most obvious environmental problem in Honduras is that of fire, which rages all over the country throughout the dry season. Wherever there is forest you're likely, at this time of year, to see plumes of smoke where trees are being illegally cleared for agriculture; and almost all existing fields will be burnt every year or two, supposedly to boost soil fertility and to kill ticks and weeds. This in fact leads to erosion and depletion of water supplies, atmospheric pollution, and deaths of many potentially useful insects and animals. Above all it doesn't work: forest soil will in any case be exhausted within a couple of years. In early 1995 there were 37 fires burning around Tegucigalpa, of which only two were under control, leading to 50% water cuts and the likely closure of the airport. Around 200,000ha a year are lost to slash-and-burn. There's widespread dismay, but no-one seems able to do anything positive about the burning.

Despite all this, Honduras is beginning to catch up with Costa Rica in terms both of conservation and research, and of tourist development. The north coast and the Bay Islands are taking off in a big way, with more and more direct flights from North America, and although much of this is conventional beach tourism, ecotourism is developing too. However, the definition of 'ecotourism' is still rather vague here; most operators are simply offering day-trips for rafting or diving. The best operations are those that go to the Río Plátano in cooperation with the indigenous peoples, and the best of these are as good as any in the world.

More and more scientific research is being done in Honduras, and new species are being found all the time (one or two amphibians each year, for instance). Less exotically, Peace Corps volunteers and others are seeing birds and plants hitherto only known in neighbouring countries.

National parks

The first national park in Honduras was La Tigra, not far from Tegucigalpa, founded in 1979. Others slowly followed, for instance on the Río Plátano, and around the Montaña de Celaque, although they only existed on paper for a long while. The now legendary law 87-87 created national parks of all cloudforests (defining their core or nuclear zones as all areas over 1,800m), and local NGOs have gradually been created to take over their management. Important as this was, it created a rather lopsided park system, and is now being modified to include a broader range of habitats, especially coastal areas. Each is surrounded by a buffer zone, still being defined in some places, and this is where the real struggle against deforestation is taking place.

Information is in short supply; some of the parks have produced leaflets but there's no co-ordinated system for getting hold of these elsewhere in the country.

Your best bet is the *Prolansate* office at Calle 9, Avda 2/3 in Tela (tel/fax: 48 2042). In Tegucigalpa, you can try MIRENA (the Ministry of Natural Resources), immediately north of the Hondutel building by the Miraflores flyover (bus 5); go into the annexe across the side-road from the main building (ie just behind Hondutel), go up one flight and turn left to the *Departamento de Control y Fiscalización*.

Ecotourism companies

Cambio CA, Calle 1, Avda 5/6 SO, San Pedro Sula (Apdo 2666; tel: 52 7274, fax: 52 0529/Trujillo tel/fax: 44 0445).

Explore Honduras, Edificio Med-Cast, Blvd Morazán, Tegucigalpa (Apdo 336; tel: 311 003, fax: 329 800/SPS tel: 52 6242, fax: 52 6239).

La Ceiba Ecotours (not very eco), a half-block north of the Hotel Ceiba, Avda San Isidro, La Ceiba (tel: 43 2371).

EuroHonduras, Edificio Hospital Centro Médico, Avda Atlántida, La Ceiba (tel/fax: 43 0933).

Turtle Tours, Villa Brinkley, Trujillo (tel: 44 4444).

La Mosquitia Ecoaventuras, Col. Walter 1635, Barrio La Leona, Tegucigalpa (Apdo 3577; tel/fax: 37 9398/Apdo 471 La Ceiba; tel: 43 2569).

Adventure Expeditions, 1020 Altos de la Hoya, Tegucigalpa (tel: 37 4793, fax: 37 9953).

Ecological organizations

Almost every actively managed national park or reserve has its own NGO involved with it; these are detailed in the relevant places, as far as possible; there's no national co-ordination, though the Peace Corps may put a list together. Local offices of Cohdefor, the Forestry Development Commission, are always worth a visit.

Asociación Hondureña de Ecologia, Tegucigalpa (Apdo T-250; tel: 32 90180/Apdo 32 Tela).

Fundación de Parques Nacionales, La Reforma, Tegucigalpa (tel: 36 6148, fax: 36 5356) they sell the same map as the tourist office, not much use otherwise.

A perennial problem for backpackers in Central America is the "Cerquita" response. When you ask how far it is to the next village it is always "Cerquita", or in other words "very near". Invariably you walk on and on ... and on. It seems that if the concept of measured time is rare, that of measured distance is rarer.

Chapter Eighteen

Central and Southern Honduras

SOUTHEASTERN HONDURAS

Tegucigalpa

Tegoos, as it is known, is dirty and crowded, but coming from the south it seemed like paradise, with great English-language films, friendly people and lots of cheap restaurants, as well as real bread and the *Pizza Hut* salad bar! The city is divided by a river into Tegucigalpa itself to the north and east and Comayagüela to the southwest; the latter is the rougher area, with most of the budget hotels, but there are cheap places in Tegucigalpa as well, such as the *Hotel Tegucigalpa* at Avda Gutemberg 1645. The city desperately needs a central bus station, but for now Comayagüela is where you'll find most of the bus companies, although they're not obvious.

Tegucigalpa is surrounded by devastated land, stripped bare above all by the city's demand for fuelwood. In particular the peak of El Picacho, overlooking the city, has been turned in five years from a semi-forested ridge to bare rock, as the Barrio Reparto expands ever upwards. The United Nations Park (the 'lungs of the capital') is deteriorating rapidly, although there are plans for reforestation and environmental education to dissuade the populace from destroying what's left.

Tourist Information

The IHT (Honduran Institute of Tourism) has unsigned offices on the corner of Avenida Ramón Cruz and Calle Republica de Mexico, to the east of central Tegucigalpa, and no English is spoken at the front desk. They sell a map of protected areas with limited information on the rear. The Honduras Information Network can be phoned on 1 900 288 6111 in the USA and 43 2762 in La Ceiba.

Museums

Tegucigalpa museums have their opening hours on boards that are taken inside when they're closed — no help at all; when they're open you hardly need to know when they're open! The new *Museo Historico de la Republica* in the former Presidential Palace on Avda 6 (Tues-Sun 09.00-12.00,13.30-16.00) is good.

Gear shops

Adventure Sports Shop, 114 Calzada Cartagena, Blvd Morazán, Tegucigalpa.

La Tigra

The oldest and best-known of Honduras' national parks is La Tigra, just east of the capital. Although it's generally described simply as cloudforest, the reality is rather more complicated. There is primary cloudforest, but much of it is inaccessible to visitors; most of what you see is secondary forest, replacing forest cut for fuel and pit-props by the mine that operated here from 1881 until 1954. The remains of the mine are in fact one of the most interesting features of the park, distinguishing it from all the other cloudforest reserves. The nuclear zone is relatively small at 7,571ha, and only day-hikes are possible here.

The higher forest, above 1,800m, is mostly oak, with cypress and *aguacatillo*, draped in bromeliads, orchids, moses and ferns; the lower slopes are covered with pines, as well as some liquidambar. The area is well studied by scientists and there's plenty of wildlife, although there's been a lot of hunting in the past and most of the animals stay in areas where tourists aren't allowed. They include white-faced monkeys, margays, tigrillos, ringtails, quetzals, mountain trogons, toucans, American swallow-tailed kites, white-tailed hawks, common screech owls, crested guans, slate-coloured solitaires and various hummingbirds; shrewmice and paca have been found as high as 2,200m, agouti at 2,000m, and armadillo also live high in the cloudforest. In the lower parts (subtropical moist forest) you may see white-tailed deer, collared peccaries, agouti, and toucanets. In all there are at least 170 bird species, plus 30 migratory birds.

The most direct access to the park is by the Jutiapa entrance, just 17km east of Tegucigalpa, but there is no public transport here. Most backpackers will take a bus around to the more interesting eastern side and base themselves in the ghost town of El Rosario, abandoned headquarters of the mining company. The main axis of the park is the closed road between these two entrances to the park; it is also possible to walk in or out to the north, through the park's buffer zone (mostly pine forest), though only the more dedicated hikers will choose to do this.

Buses run daily at 07.00 and 15.00 from the San Pablo market in Tegucigalpa's eastern suburbs to San Juancito, passing through the touristy village of Valle de Angeles. From San Juancito you have a steep 4km climb to El Rosario, getting there around sunset (18.00) if you took the 15.00 bus — very convenient. The most rewarding route to La Tigra, however, if you have time, is to combine this bus with the walk described below to the charming village of Santa Lucía.

Getting there

Tegucigalpa city buses 2, 15 and 21 to La Sosa turn sharply left off the concrete road in La Travesía, by a shop and a tree on an island, at the top of a long hill, about 1.5km beyond the new bypass. Just beyond this point there's a junction, with a sign giving the distance to Santa Lucía as 10.8km by the right-hand fork. However, it's only just over the hill by the left fork, which is the old Spanish muletrack to the mines of Santa Lucía. This drops for a couple of minutes to cross a stream, the Quebrada Mololoa, where the local women do

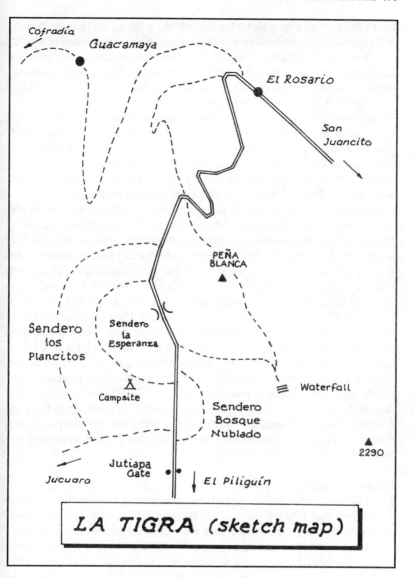

Cofradía
Guacamaya
El Rosario
San Juancito
PEÑA BLANCA ▲
Sendero los Plancitos
Sendero la Esperanza
Campsite
Sendero Bosque Nublado
Waterfall ≡
▲ 2290
Jutiapa Gate
Jucuara
El Piliguín

LA TIGRA (sketch map)

their laundry. From here it climbs steeply, and after half an hour and five turns enters pine trees, near a few shacks, and continues to rise easily. You'll see a lot of people going the other way with big bundles of *leña* (fuelwood), illustrating the environmental pressure on the surroundings of any Honduran city. If the smoke haze is not too bad, there's a good view from here of Tegucigalpa and the huge white three-domed basilica of Our Lady of Suyapa to the south.

Thirty minutes after entering the pine wood, turn left at a junction marked by a white arrow painted on a tree. To the left you can see Santa Lucía, and the path simply drops gently along the side of the valley for ten minutes, turning left across a dry streambed and climbing very easily for 20 minutes to turn left onto a dirt road just before the church of Santa Lucía. This is in a very fine site, looking out over the valley and the picturesque village, with its cobbled streets, whitewashed houses and red-tiled roofs; very much like the villages painted by Velásquez and other famous Honduran artists. There are residential centres both for the blind and for the Peace Corps here; otherwise there's nowhere to stay. There are buses to Tegucigalpa every hour or two, but if you're continuing to La Tigra it's easier to walk the 2.5km down to the Tegucigalpa-Valle de Angeles road. Here you can wait for the 15.00 bus from Tegucigalpa to San Juancito, or pick up one of the hourly buses from the Mercado San Pablo to Valle de Angeles and hitch on from there.

San Juancito is also a former mining town, but not as much of a ghost town as El Rosario. Nestled snugly in the Río Chiquito valley and surrounded by towering forest-clad mountains, it has the atmosphere of an old-style frontier town with its simple wooden buildings and moustachioed horsemen. Here you need to turn right across the bridge, right again past the post office, then left at a sign to climb steeply to El Rosario. Here 30 or 40 huge old three-storeyed wooden buildings, once hotels, a school, a hospital and office buildings, all perch forlornly on the steep mountainside. Cars park here below the visitor centre, which may not be open until the evening. The road continues uphill and turns sharp left to pass above the visitor centre and the lovely wood-panelled buildings that now serve as a dormitory and the Cohdefor office. There's a small *pulpería* a bit further on, and another, where you can get meals from time to time, down the road below El Rosario. To sleep in the dormitory here you need a permit (costing about US$2 per night) from the *Departamento de Control y Fiscalización* at MIRENA (see above); there's nowhere particularly suitable for camping here, but there is a camping site half an hour from the Jutiapa entrance.

Hikes in La Tigra

From El Rosario at 1,580m, the old road runs up past the dormitories, over a pass at just over 2,200m, and down to Jutiapa. Various paths loop off this on both sides; the route I describe uses some of these to make an easy day's hiking to return to El Rosario, although you may of course choose to just go to Jutiapa and from there continue towards Tegucigalpa.

The road climbs steeply, passing a couple of turnings to houses, and reaches a water tank at a crossroads after about 15 minutes; here I turned left on to a good track which runs on the level along the thickly-forested hillside to a waterfall 45 minutes away. This passes some disused mine-workings; first a powder-store, in which you could sleep *in extremis*, and then the Peña Blanca mine, with a good tunnel into the mountain. If you've brought a flashlight you could explore, but remember the risks of poisonous snakes, rabid bats, cave-ins and so on. Ten minutes from here you'll reach a junction by a stream, where you should keep left; you'll pass above a small waterfall and then turn right to climb on a narrower path for ten minutes to the foot of the main waterfall. There's not much to see in the dry season, but it would be good in the wet. This is attractive forest, but it's noticeable that there are no big trees.

From the waterfall you should return for three minutes to a path signposted 'Jutiapa', which meanders to the right for almost ten minutes before climbing relatively steeply for 20 minutes and dropping for five minutes to rejoin the dirt road on a hairpin bend just west of the pass. It takes just two minutes (downhill to the left) to reach the *Sendero Bosque Nublado* (Cloud Forest Path), which turns off to the left on the next bend, at 2,175m. This is a much better path, but the markers do not refer to any particular features, and there's no information leaflet as yet. It drops steadily for 25 minutes to rejoin the road, just 100m above the Jutiapa gate to the park; this is at about 1,900m, at about the upper limit of the pines. In early 1995 a new Visitor Centre was being built just below the present gate, which will probably have better displays than those in the current visitor centres. A pick-up runs from here at 16.00 daily down to El Piligüín (8km, about US$0.60), where you can take a bus to Tegucigalpa; there's nowhere to stay in Piligüín, so catching the pick-up to the park at 07.00 is rather more difficult.

Just below the gate, you could turn right/north on to the *Sendero Las Granadillas*, but this is a very easy loop through secondary forest and is not of any great interest. Returning up the hill, less than 100m above the *Sendero Bosque Nublado* you'll find the Jucuara road to the left, which runs through the buffer zone to join the route out described at the end of this section; this also gives access to the *Sendero Los Plancitos*, which loops around through the northern side of the nuclear zone to rejoin the road above El Rosario. Another three minutes up the road you'll come to the left turn onto the *Sendero La Esperanza*, perhaps the best path for a view of the forest, although it's still secondary growth. After 20 minutes this brings you to a campsite among rather larger trees, all heavily laden with moss and creepers. There's a tunnel here, which soon gets muddy but would be somewhere to cook in the rain; there's a small stream a couple of minutes further on. It's an easy steady climb for 15 minutes to the road at a nice grassy spot on a bend, just on the Rosario side of the pass. Here you can see the old telegraph line to the mine and, above, at least seven radio and TV towers; these can be reached by road from the Jutiapa side, but the road on is impassable.

Heading down to the left, the path runs along a steep slope, with no huge trees but lots of impressive moss and creepers; there are good views south to the even steeper slopes of the highest peak, known simply as *el punto mas alto* (2,290m). After 30 minutes it passes the eastern end of the *Sendero Los Plancitos*, and then winds down past old mine tunnels to reach the water tank again in 15 minutes. From here you can return to El Rosario by the road, as above, in about ten minutes, but I chose to explore the route to the left, which takes a very long easily-graded route around above El Rosario. It drops into the next valley to the north, with a view across to the village of Guacamaya, and after 20-odd minutes reaches the Rosario cemetery, with seven graves with names such as Jenkins and Rounds. From here it takes just five minutes to get back to El Rosario, arriving at the bend below the dormitories.

Hiking out

Most hikers will leave either from Jutiapa or through San Juancito, but it is possible to hike out to the northwest through the pine forest of the buffer zone. This is very different to the cloudforest of the nuclear zone, and might be worthwhile if you won't have any other chance to hike in this quintessentially Honduran scenery. When Rob first hiked this way, it was a pleasant trail leading to the Olancho road; now it is a 4WD road, and the Olancho road has been replaced by a new highway a considerable distance further to the west. If you have to walk all the way, it'll take eight hours or so.

The route leaves El Rosario following trolley lines from below the large stone building at the entrance to town, which is said to have been the first US consulate in Honduras; it can also be reached by a ramp from just below the visitor centre. This track runs on the level around the hillside below the cemetery and up the Guacamaya valley; after an hour it rounds the head of the valley and returns along the other side, reaching Guacamaya in another 30 minutes. Turn left at the school to go over a saddle and into pine trees, and fork left onto another 4WD road after 20 minutes. This soon starts to climb steadily, passing a cleared pasture after 20 minutes and a new coffee finca after 15 more (less if you use the shortcuts). You reach a pass in five more minutes and drop for a while, passing a large *cafetal* on the right after 20 minutes. The path on is grassier and less used, and still very pleasant walking through dry pine forest with plenty of birds. You'll climb for 15 minutes to another ridge, then drop for 20 minutes to a bridge over a stream and climb for 15 minutes. Before the ridge you should fork right off the road onto a well-used path which soon passes through the scattered village of Los Plancitas and, after 20 minutes, continues straight on where a dirt road turns off to the right. After about seven minutes, fork right at the end of the village and drop steeply, turning left onto the road after five minutes. This drops steadily through more scrubby open country, populated by immensely noisy parrots and cicadas; after 40-odd minutes you reach Zapote, where you can take a short-cut to the right after the pig sheds, or carry on along the road to cross a bridge and then swing back. In another ten minutes you'll reach the old Olancho road at a row of *pulperías*, and turn left. There's next to no traffic, so you should keep walking, passing through the *very* quiet village of Cofradía after 20 minutes and then climbing to a ridge from which you can see the new road in the distance. About an hour's walk from Cofradía (through bare limestone dotted with cacti) you'll cross a ridge and turn right, soon turning left and crossing the Río Choluteca after 15 minutes; it's another 20 minutes up to km13 on the new highway. Buses from Talanga and Vallecillo will pick you up here, as may longer-distance buses to and from Juticalpa and Catacamas.

Around Tegucigalpa

Another picturesque colonial mining town within easy reach of Tegucigalpa (reached by regular buses from the Jacaleapa market) is **Yuscarán**, 800m over which towers the mountain of Montserrat (1,891m), with 2,300ha of subtropical moist forest preserved as a biological reserve. A 14km dirt road leads up to the radio masts on the summit, and you need permission from Hondutel or the army to enter their compound. The Yuscarán *Recursos Naturales* (RRNN) office can arrange a visit with a week or two's notice.

The road from Tegucigalpa (the highway to Danlí and Nicaragua) also passes just north of Cerro El Uyuca (2,008ha), where there's a smaller reserve of 234ha of cloudforest; turn south at km14 to get here.

Just over 100km south of Tegucigalpa is the **Gulf of Fonseca**, the country's only outlet onto the Pacific. Disputes between Honduras and El Salvador over ownership of some of the islands in the Gulf seem to have been settled by the International Court of Justice, and the Gulf's environment and development are now supervised by a trinational commission. It's badly deforested and very very hot, so there's not a lot of hiking here; however there are a couple of volcanic islands which offer some possibilities. The largest is **El Tigre**, which has a radar station (built to support the Contras, now used for tracking drug-smuggling planes) on its 760m peak; there's a road up, through subtropical dry forest, but of course you won't be able to get in to the radar compound. Rather bizarrely, the island's main town, Amapala, was the country's main Pacific port for many years, and was of course visited by Drake. To get here you need to take a boat from Coyolito, reached by bus from San Lorenzo on the PanAmerican Highway. Most of the coastline around the Gulf consists of protected mangrove swamps, which can be visited by boat from Amapala or Coyolito.

NORTH FROM TEGUCIGALPA

Heading north on the country's main highway, from Tegucigalpa to San Pedro Sula, you pass through attractive hilly country covered with typically Honduran pine woods; there are enjoyable walks to the right/east at km47, towards some good cliffs and crags, and left at km54, up an attractive valley. At km58.5 you pass the Chuleta Tenampua; any kid from the houses just above this roadhouse can take you up to the **Tenampua Fortress**, about 20 minutes away. Set in a naturally fortified site on the edge of a mesa this is in fact four fortresses on top of each other, and the last (upper) one was the scene of the last stand of the Indians who rose in revolt in 1537-39 (when the dreaded Alvorado was away in Spain). You can also arrange a guided visit through the Archeological Museum in Comayagua, 30km north, as also to lots of other Mayan sites in the Comayagua valley, including an adobe pyramid.

Comayagua was capital of Honduras from 1543 until 1880 and remains an interesting and attractive town, with a fine cathedral and other historic buildings. The Comayagua valley is part of the low-lying channel that runs across the country from Puerto Cortés to San Lorenzo on the Gulf of Fonseca. The flora of the valley itself is dominated by thorn-scrub, largely *Mimosa tenuiflora (carbón)*, with acacias, a tall cactus called *tuna (Nopalea lutea)*, and the gourd tree *Crescentia alata*. Immediately to the east is the **Montaña de Comayagua**, one of the highest in the country at 2,407m, covered in cloudforest, which serves as one of the main sources of water for the huge El Cajón Dam (which supplies 65% of Honduras' hydro-electricity). This is now a national park of about 17,000ha, currently almost totally undeveloped for tourism but nevertheless easy enough to get to. It's been an isolated island of forest for a long time, so that the fauna is somewhat impoverished; nevertheless there are pumas, lots of peccary, paca, agouti, raccoons, quetzals, toucans and toucanets. Monkeys and tapir haven't been seen here since the late 1980s.

Fundación Ecosimco is the NGO that works in the park: its headquarters are at Calle 0 and Avda 1 SO in Comayagua, where you can get some limited information. There are two good ways in: the first involves taking the hourly La Libertad bus north from Comayagua to San Jerónimo, and then a pick-up east to Río Negro, on the northern side of the park. There are plenty of unmarked trails into the park from here, and you can ask around for a guide here. The second heads east from Calle 2 NE in Comayagua and after 13km of 4WD road reaches San José de la Mora (shown on maps as Las Moras), to the south of the park, from where you can follow the line of the ridge to the summit. Further south, Calle 3 SE leads to an old logging road through El Volcán and up to some radio masts, at 2,000m in a fairly deforested area; there's a checkpoint fairly high up but this can easily be avoided if you're hiking. Crossing a footbridge at the east end of Calle 3 NE, you could hike east to El Sitio, where there's an impressive limestone cave.

CERRO AZUL MEÁMBAR

Just 30km north is Siguatepeque, a slightly smaller city at the cool altitude of 1,138m, and another good place to stay — try the *Hotel Versalles* and the *Pizzeria Venezia*, owned by a retired Italian-Canadian. This is the main base for PANACAM, the **Parque Nacional Cerro Azul Meámbar** (not to be confused with the other Blue Mountain, the Parque Nacional Cerro Azul — see below). This stands between the El Cajón Dam and Lago de Yojoa, so it is even more important than other cloudforests as a source of water.

The massif is largely composed of rheolitic and andesitic rocks of volcanic origin, although the oldest rocks in the area are marine sediments. The park covers a total of 25,600ha (256km²), of which 5,600ha covers the nuclear zone. Even on the highest peaks (maximum 2,080m), rainfall is only 2,000mm per year, with a six month dry period, making this pretty dry for so-called cloudforest. Technically it is, in fact, subtropical wet forest, made up of deciduous trees such as maría, *Drymis granadensis*, san juan (*Vochysia hondurensis*), sangre blanco (*Pterocarpus sp*) and sangre colorado (*Virola sp*), aguacatillo (*Persea sp*), and native conifers such as pinotea (*Podocarpus oleifolius*) and cedrillo (*Weinmannia tuerckheimii*), with plenty of tree ferns and palms. The highest parts (closed to visitors) also have small patches of dwarf forest. The buffer zone is largely composed of subtropical moist forest, mainly *Pinus oocarpa*, but with other trees in transition zones, notably oaks such as *Quercus peduncularis* and *Q. oleoides*, and liquidambar, san juan and *Pinus pseudostrobus*. The lowest, flattest areas also have ceiba, guanacaste, indio desnudo and other trees, as well as some epiphytes.

In fact most of the buffer zone, up to 1,500m and beyond, is now occupied by coffee plantations; there's a great deal of settlement pressure on this area, and in 1992 what was then said to be the largest coffee plantation in Central America was being planted above Río Bonito, at the south edge of the park. These plantations are especially damaging, as new strains of coffee need less shade but more fertilisers; because there are no shade trees, birds cannot move so freely, confining them to increasingly small areas, and because they don't eat the insects more pesticides are also needed.

There's been only limited scientific research here, but 64 species of bird have been found, as well as 33 mammals, 15 snakes and 12 other amphibians and reptiles. The birds include quetzals, toucans, parrots, parakeets, hawks, vultures, guans, curassows, hummingbirds, motmots, jays, woodpeckers and tanagers; mammals include howler, white-faced and spider monkeys, two-toed sloths, tamanduas, armadillos, coati, ringtails, skunks, pumas, ocelots, margays, tapir and peccary.

The park is now managed by Proyecto Aldea Global (Global Village Project), whose office is on Calle 3, Avda 1/2 NO — head north three blocks on Blvd Morazán and turn left at Bilares Pimpilon (Apdo 94 Siguatepeque, tel: 73 2741). Their main office is in Tegucigalpa (Apdo 1149, tel: 32 8287). They've been able to raise funds from development agencies and have ambitious plans to find alternatives to continuing deforestation and coffee planting. Ecotourism is a part of this, although there will be few facilities before 1997. Contact them a few days in advance if you want to hire a guide or make other arrangements. There are other ideas, such as farming paca, iguanas and deer for meat and butterflies for export. There is opposition: with foreign money, a North American boss in Tegucigalpa and Peace Corps volunteers all leading to accusations that the gringos have bought the park.

Access to the park

As the Tegucigalpa-San Pedro Sula highway forms the western boundary of the park, it's not surprising that many of the easiest access routes start here. At about km149.5 there's a road east to Cerro Azul, at km158 (El Cacao) another to Buena Vista de Varsovia, and at km162.5 another to San Antonio de Yure; these are all roads recently built with coffee money to villages in the buffer zone at between roughly 800m and 1,000m, all of which are intended to have park information centres. From them trails run uphill and meet to head southeast around the nuclear zone to the park's research station and down to the *aldea* (village) of San José de los Planes, which is at 1,050m, just 4km from a road around the south side of the park. From here a road was built north up to Los Cedros (1,200m); although this was built illegally (as it enters the nuclear zone), it was funded by IHCAFE (the Honduran Coffee Institute), to serve *cafetals* which just happen to belong to the mayor of Meámbar.

The road to the south of the park runs from Jardines de Taulabé, at about km148, east to the town of Meámbar, which would be a good base for the park if it had a few basic facilities — ironically for an area which is so crucial for the nation's hydro-electricity, there is no power here. However, the park's visitor centre is planned to be on the town's southern edge, from 1997. From Maraguai, 3km north, there's a road west to Potrerillos. Another road runs to the east of the park, from Meámbar and Maraguai to San Isidro and west to La Guama at km165.5; just south of this road is the village of Las Delicias, home of the park's chief ranger Teodoro Calles and start of a good hike down to Potrerillos, as well as local day-walks. A visitor centre is planned for La Guama, and an environmental education centre at the Finca Los Piños 3km south of Santa Elena, 2km east of La Guama.

The massif is very steep and rocky, with slopes up to 100% (vertical), and there are many spectacular waterfalls; these are, of course, not so spectacular by the end of the dry season. The best are around Potrerillos and can be seen from paths to Las Delicias and to Los Cedros. Starting from Las Delicias, after about 3km you'll cross the Canchilla valley, once a rare example of subtropical dry forest, but now very deforested. It's about 4km more south-southeast to El Palmital, roughly following the 600m contour through Agua

Fria, before dropping slightly to El Palmital, which can also be reached by a 2km track from the road. From here you need to climb to the right, to a water-tank, then take a very sharp left to pass above an abandoned landing strip. The path crosses a ridge of about 900m and drops to the Potrero de las Flores (on the Quebrada de la Vega), where there are beautiful bathing pools. It's about a kilometre southeast through young pines and over the next hill to the Río del Potrero and the first waterfall. The best is another 1.5km south, on the Quebrada de Las Pavas de la Chorrera at about 730m. This is about 20m high and very impressive in October and November; unfortunately a *campesino* has burned the area just below it to plant his milpa, but he's welcoming and friendly. From here you can either head down the valley for a couple of kilometres to Potrerillos (c500m), passing an ancient sugar cane-mill manufactured in New Orleans, and then descend to Meámbar, as above, or (probably the next day) head west up the right/south bank past the waterfall. This area is largely deforested (due to charcoal-burning) as far as La Crucita, where there are two houses, and then a cairn at around 1,100m; from here you continue uphill to the right to Cerro Las Marías (1,446m), a beautiful area of pine/oak forest with great views to the summit area immediately west. From here you drop about a kilometre west to Los Cedros, where the new road starts at the mayor of Meámbar's front door, quite a way beyond the first house. This is impassable to vehicles for much of the year, but you should be able to hike down to Los Planes in a couple of hours. In Los Cedros you can ask to be shown the way to the 50m waterfall of La Morra. This is a transition zone from pine/oak to cloudforest, with lots of liquidambar, and has as much potential as a base for ecotourism as anywhere in the park. On the one hand the new road has opened this up, but on the other it brings the risk of more settlement and forest clearance.

Lake Yojoa

On the other side of the highway, **Lake Yojoa** has been protected since 1971; it's a natural lake of 90km² and offers the greatest ornithological variety to be found anywhere in the country, being a stopover for many migratory waterbirds and the southern limit of several conifers (*Abies guatemalensis, Cupressus lindleyi, Pinus ayachuite, P. montezumae,* and *Taxus globosa*). However, the natural cover of the surrounding plains is mostly broadleaf forest; annual rainfall ranges from 2,300mm to 3,500mm, but the area also receives plenty of water from the surrounding mountains. It's not hard to see 70 species of bird in a day, and there are 344 in all, as well as 37 mammals and 129 reptiles and amphibians.

The lake is popular with Hondurans and there are many hotels and fish restaurants along the main highway and to the north. Waste from mines and restaurants is polluting the lake, and local landowners have formed the *Fundación EcoLago*, as much to protect their business as for genuinely ecological reasons. They've built a *Centre de Interpretación* and *hotel campestre* (with boat hire) at km161 on the main highway, as well as promoting reforestation and wildlife reserves and putting out a bulletin. Sewage sytems may be installed, but it seems more likely that the fish restaurants will simply be moved elsewhere. As in Lake Atitlán (Guatemala), black bass was introduced to the lake in 1954, for sport fishing, and has decimated the native fish population; in 1964 the fast-growing *Tilapia* was introduced in turn to serve as food for the black bass, but the problem remains.

At the north end of the lake (turn west at km166, through Agua Azul and past the Hotel Brisas del Lago, by the volcanic cone of Cerro El Hoyo) is the archaeological site of **Los Naranjos**. Currently almost unknown, it's intended to turn it into a major attraction and thus generate enough funds to study it properly; the *Musée de l'Homme* of Paris has been working here intermittently since 1967. It's one of the most interesting sites in what has traditionally been thought of as a no-man's-land between the Maya and Inca territories. Inhabited from 900 or 300BC to 200AD, probably by the Lencas, there are nine well-preserved settlements and two deep defensive trenches.

It's also a good area for caves; the best known is **Taulabé**, a Natural Monument back towards Siguatepeque, just below km140. A boardwalk and a string of lightbulbs extend for about 300m, beyond which you're on your own. There are stalactites and stalagmites, bats and swallows' nests; human remains are also said to have been found here. There's a generator but it's in a bad state; mains power is only a kilometre away but they seem incapable of hooking it up. The cave was found in 1969 during road-building and has still not been fully explored. The Masical and Pencaligue caves, nearer the lake, would also be of interest to cavers.

From the highway, you can see the impressive massif of **Santa Barbara** across Lake Yojoa to the west. The summit is (if you count the various peaks of Celaque as one) the second highest peak in Honduras, at 2,744m, and its 130km² of cloudforest was declared a national park in 1987. The lower slopes, up to 1,500m, are very wet subtropical forest, above which there's very wet low montane forest. On the summit there's a rare association of Guatemalan cypress and fir (*Cupressus benthami* and *Abies guatemalensis*) with pine and hardwoods, perhaps the only one in Honduras. Here too there are limestone caves and very steep slopes (easily eroded once the tree cover is removed); the forest is thick and largely unexploited, and it's a venue only for the more self-reliant hiker. If you do get there, you may see deer, collared peccary, tigrillo, howler and spider monkeys, guans, toucanets and quetzal. The easiest access is through the town of Peña Blanca; a visitor centre is being built in Sauce, above Peña Blanca, and you can find a guide there; from the lakeside, access is through San José de Los Andes to Las Vegas. The NGO working in the park is *Corazon Verde* (Green Heart), Apdo 28, Santa Barbara, with whom you should talk before going to the park.

Chapter Nineteen

Western Honduras

The highway from Tegucigalpa ends at **San Pedro Sula**, hot as hell but the country's commercial capital. The airport (east of town; the stopping buses to Progreso will drop you a kilometre away) is increasingly busy with flights from North America, and it's certain that you'll have to pass through the city at some point. It's a good place for feeding up and buying food before heading into the hills.

Overhanging the city to the west, **El Merendón** (1,749m) is seriously menaced by the trade in fuelwood, and the authorities in San Pedro are becoming worried about deforestation and the threat to their water supplies. In 1990 the removal of vegetable material was banned, and its tropical moist forest may yet survive. Right on the edge of town, it's a convenient place to see araçari and toucans.

CUSUCO

A far better bet, if you have a day or two, is the **Cusuco National Park**, one of the best developed parks in the country. This has been protected since 1959, when it was discovered that the pines here were the tallest in Central America; it became a National Park in 1987, preserving part of San Pedro's water supply. It's a massif of Palaeozoic metamorphic rocks such as gneiss and schist, with granitic intrusions from the Tertiary and Cretaceous to the extreme east. There's up to 3,050mm of precipitation a year, and the tree cover is subtropical wet forest and subtropical wet lower montane forest (with patches of dwarf forest in the closed nuclear zone), 72% pine (*Pinus patula and P. maximinoi*) and 28% deciduous — largely liquidambar, limoncillo (*Myrcia splendens*), aceituno (*Toxicodendron striatum*) and *Talauma mexicana*. The wildlife includes 34 mammals, including howler and white-faced monkeys, white-tailed and red brocket deer, tapirs, armadillos, collared peccaries, cats including jaguar, puma, ocelot, yagouraoundi, and lots of smaller beasts such as pacas, agoutis, kinkajou, coati and tayra. Every bird survey reveals more species previously known only in Guatemala; in 1992 a survey counted 100 species on the northern slopes, including quetzals, American swallow-tailed kites, black and crested guans, curassows, trogons, motmots, tinamous, jays, woodpeckers, flycatchers and warblers. The same applies to amphibians and insects, but more so, with species new not only to Honduras,

CUSUCO NATIONAL PARK

but also to science being found every year or two.

Cusuco is managed by the Fundación Ecologista Hector Rodrigo Pastor Fasquelle (or Fundación HRPF), found above the *Pizzeria Italia* at Calle 1/ Avda 7 NO in San Pedro (Apdo 2749; tel/fax: 52 1014). They have a small library and some leaflets and maps. You can also get information from Cohdefor at Calle 4/Avda 10 NO (tel: 53 4959). To get there on your own, take a bus from Avda 5/Calle 11 SO to Cofradía, an hour west; coming from Copán get off at km15¾. Then take a pick-up to Buenos Aires (de Bañaderos), an hour and a half north; there's always one at about 14.00 on Mondays, but there are plenty of others at random times. From here hike 5km west up the Río de Cusuco valley to the park *campamento*, where there's a visitor centre, dormitory and camping space. This is set in pine, but trails run up into the rainforest. To the north, the self-guided Danto (Tapir) Trail (one hour) and the Quetzal Trail (two to three hours) are on the slopes of Cerro Cusuco (2,000m); to the south, the Sierra de las Minas trail (an old logging road) runs south and east to the road south of Buenos Aires in three or four hours. The Golondrinas or Sierra de Cantiles trail runs west and then north, skirting the nuclear zone and continuing for two days to reach Tegucigalpita, where the Río Chiquito meets the coast road; to go this way, head up the Río Cusuco valley (crossing it twice) to reach a superb garden of rainforest plants, from where the little-used path plunges into the primary forest. If you wanted, you could loop back by following dirt roads on the right/east side of the Río Cuyamel and Río Frío to Las Brisas and Buenos Aires. Cambio CA (Calle 1, Avda 5-6 SO, Apdo 2666; tel: 52 7274, fax: 52 0523), one of the best ecotourism outfits in the country, operate overnight tours to Cusuco, as well as hikes along this route to Tegucigalpita. Cerro Cusuco and Cerro Jilinco (the park's highest peak at 2,242m) are covered by the 1:50,000 map 2562-1, but the rest of the park is on adjacent sheets.

Further west along the Sierra del Espiritu Santo, paralleling the road to Copán Ruinas, is the **Cerro Azul National Park**, which also protects 15,000ha of cloudforest, surrounding a peak of 2,285m. Not a lot of information is available, although amateur surveys have shown at least 86 bird species (including crested guans, chachalacas, turquoise-browed and blue-crowned motmots, nine hawks and falcons, three parrots, three parakeets, three jays, three woodpeckers, six hummingbirds, and so on) and 19 snakes. Mammals include paca, collared peccary, raccoons, skunks, dwarf anteaters, opossums, howler and spider monkeys, coati and kinkajou. If you want to explore while in the Copán area, take the main road east to San Antonio, then a dirt road north through El Ocotón and Peña Blanca to the Quebrada El Cañon, and head directly west towards the peak.

COPÁN

Virtually every visitor to Honduras (and many of those to Guatemala too) comes to Copán, the country's greatest Mayan ruins. Although largely overshadowed by the immense sites half-hidden in the jungles of the Petén and Yucatán, Copán is the birthplace of Mayan archaeology. It's notable for the great number of stelae and inscriptions found here, and after more than a century of work researchers can now translate about half of the Mayan glyphs. There's little here specifically for the ecotourist; the nature trail (to the right outside the gate to the archaeological site) is a rare example of subtropical dry forest, but there's litle to be seen except at dawn and dusk. The tame spider monkey and scarlet macaws at the gate do allow you a much closer view than you'll get in the wild. There's no shortage of people offering horse-riding (a good way to see some of the many more Mayan ruins dotted around the valley and its slopes), as well as inner-tubing down the river and bird-watching. It's also possible to visit nearby Chortí Maya villages, in many ways untouched by modern life, but now at risk from insensitive tourism.

Hiking near Copán

There are some pleasant and simple approaches to the Copán area through the Sierra Gallinero, just to the southeast. This is not particularly wild country, and the main attraction is seeing village life and pleasant pastoral scenery rather than lots of wildlife: even so, there's no shortage of birds. The simplest

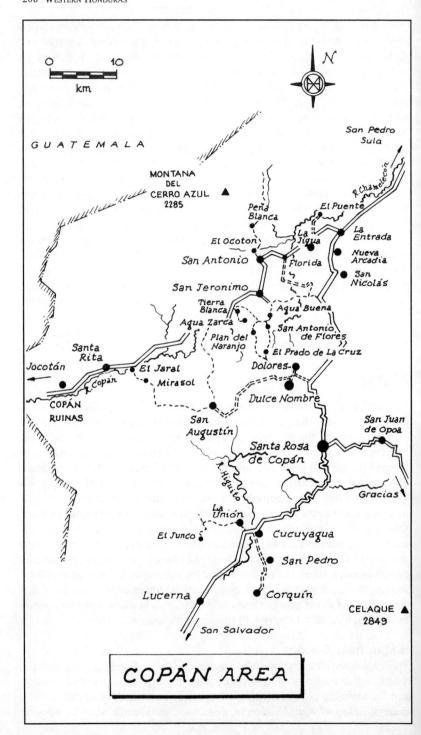

COPÁN AREA

route is to get off a bus about 10km north of Santa Rosa de Copán (on the highway to San Pedro Sula), at the turning west to Dulce Nombre and Dolores; this is poorly signed, so make sure the bus *adelante* knows where you're getting off. Then take a pick-up, or an ancient and overcrowded bus (two daily from Santa Rosa), through Dulce Nombre to San Agustín, 15km west as the vulture flies. Hike straight on past the plaza, forking right in the village, and climb steadily up a dirt road to reach the school in about ten minutes. Roughly five minutes beyond the school you should fork left between two pines onto a smaller path — if in doubt, you need to follow a power line. This path heads around a valley and drops to a stream after ten minutes, and then climbs steadily through coffee plantations, crossing another stream after 30 minutes. You reach the pass in another 45 minutes, where you'll find all that's left of the forest that used to cloak these hills. There are woodpeckers and hummingbirds here, but you're unlikely to see much else unless you head off into the forest along the ridge.

From here on it's all downhill, in principle, for 10km. The path runs out along a ridge between two noisy streams, finally dropping down to their confluence an hour from the pass. From here the path follows the left bank of the Río Mirasol, with just a brief excursion to the right bank; after 45 minutes you'll pass through La Libertad and continue on a dirt road. Again it's mainly coffee, with shade trees and jays, oropendulas, vultures and a pair of toucans. The road follows the right bank for 15-20 minutes and then crosses back to the left side, with easy fords. After about 50 minutes the Quebrada Tepenchín and another track come in from the left, and after 40 minutes more you'll pass through Mirasol, another scattered village. Keep to the right here to follow the valley, and in another 40 minutes you'll reach a new road bridge (and an old pedestrian suspension bridge) where the Mirasol flows into the Río Copán. It's just a couple of minutes up the hill to the road at El Jaral, about 12km east of Copán Ruinas. It can be very hot hiking down the road, and you'll probably be gasping for a drink, but be aware that the restaurant here is aimed very much at the air-conditioned minibus market. Immediately west is the Hacienda El Jaral, which claims to be 'Copán's Mountain Resort' and a centre for ecotourism, although there really isn't much of that sort to do here.

At least 15 years ago, Rob hiked north by a different route from Dolores, through what was then a mix of lush forest and farmland. It's undoubtedly been largely deforested since then, but would still be an interesting hike; there are plenty of friendly people about, so you can manage without maps by asking the way and heading more or less northwest. A dirt road runs from Dulce Nombre and Dolores to El Prado de la Cruz and north up the Quebrada de los Madríles (or Pasquingual) through San Antonio de Flores and Agua Buena to San Jeronimo and the Copán Ruinas highway; from San Antonio take a path to the left, climbing hard to Las Delicias and dropping down to Agua Zarca, from where there's a better track to Tierra Blanca, just south of the highway. A slightly harder variant is to start from El Prado, going 2 or 3km to El Bosque and then climbing onto a knife-edge ridge with spectacular views, known as Cuchilla El Zapotal. This you follow for about a kilometre before dropping down to Plan del Naranjo and continuing over hilly pastureland to Agua Zarca.

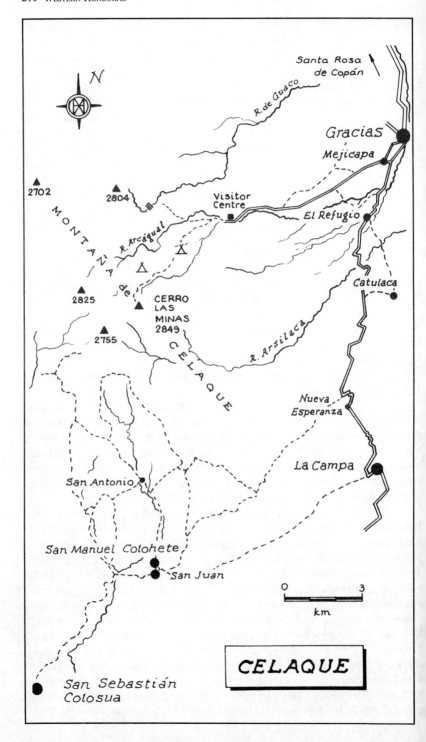

CELAQUE

CELAQUE

From Santa Rosa de Copán, two-thirds of the way along the highway from San Pedro to Ocotopeque, you can take a side trip southeast to Honduras' highest peak, the **Montaña de Celaque** (2,849m). It's not a mountain so much as a volcanic mesa, with a plateau and other peaks of 2,825m and 2,804m. The name is Lenca, translated either as 'frozen waters' or 'box of water', referring either to the waterfalls visible in season from far away or to the 11 rivers born there. It's covered by the largest, highest and least altered area of cloudforest in Honduras, which has been isolated for thousands of years, producing a unique biology with some endemic species. Pine forest continues all the way to 2,000m and higher, with broadleaf forest above; the nuclear zone, above 1,800m, covers 17,000ha, and the buffer zone covers another 10,000ha. There are spider monkeys, tapir, puma, ocelot, white-tailed deer, peccary, coyote, agouti and coati; as in La Tigra there has been a lot of hunting here in the past, so the wildlife tends to stay hidden. There's only one tourist path, so it's easy enough for the animals to stay elsewhere. However, birds are more visible — quetzals, emerald toucanets, trogons, guans, chachalacas, woodpeckers, warblers — over 100 species in all.

At the moment access is only via Gracias, an historic and reasonably attractive town with quite a few places to sleep. It's reached by a good road (with six buses a day) from Santa Rosa; on the other side, the road is dreadful to La Esperanza, La Paz and Comayagua, and there are only three buses a week at best, as well as pick-ups. There are plans to open up a path from Belén Gualcho, to the southwest, which would allow an interesting traverse over the summit to a very picturesque area. The western side is not as steep as the Gracias side, and is much more threatened by ever-expanding coffee plantations. Three hours walk south of Belén Gualcho is one of Honduras' very few volcanic cones, **Volcán Pacayita** (2,516m); this is a biological reserve, theoretically protecting 9,700ha of cloudforest. Six of the seven Honduran species of pine are found here, but the reserve is said to be more corn than pine at the moment.

In **Gracias** there are some decent places to stay (including the *Erick*, by the bus office, and the unmarked *San Antonio* next to the *Merendero Susan* at the northern exit from town) and a good place to eat (the *Guancascos*, on the plaza). There are three historic churches, and a restored fort (open 07.00-17.00) just west of the market. A worthwhile excursion is to hot springs 5km south, one hour by a path turning right after the first bridge on the La Esperanza road, or by road, a more roundabout route.

Hiking in Celaque

From Gracias (at 765m) there's a dirt road to the park visitor centre, 8km away; the *Guancascos* will arrange transport for US$3 (minimum three people). Heading south down any of the main streets you'll meet a road at 45° which you should follow to the right to Mejicapa, 1.5km from Gracias. Turn right past the colonial church of Santa Lucia and follow the road steadily up through fields; after an hour and a quarter you reach the few houses of Villa Verde (1,200m), which is as far as cars can get without four-wheel drive. The track enters the pine forest and climbs more steeply up the valley of the Río Arcagual, reaching the visitor centre (at 1,400m) in 20 minutes. This served as a hydro-electric plant from 1954 to 1981 (you can walk up to the dam, a kilometre away), and now has dormitories, latrines and a caretaker who will store gear and whose mother will cook you *comida tipica* for a dollar. To go with the food, there's a trust-the-hiker supply of *Salva Vida* beer! You should also pay US$2 each to enter the park, plus US$1 each per night.

The open pine forest just above the visitor centre is most attractive, and it's intended to establish a self-guided nature trail here along the river. The only other trail, apart from the one to the dam, leads to the summit, starting behind the visitor centre. There are two campsites on the mountain, at either of which you could leave your gear while you go up to the summit. Ignore the paths left down to the river until you reach a sign after about five minutes, where you do turn left and soon cross the river. After five minutes you'll cross to the left bank of the Quebrada El Mecatal and then start to climb, with a drystone wall to the left. This is easy going for ten minutes until you reach a junction: one is the old route, while the other includes new zigzags, which are almost too easily graded. The two are soon reunited and you continue to zig upwards; after five minutes there's a rock on the right with a good view out over the pine forest, and in another 25 minutes (an hour or so from the visitor centre) you'll reach a sign at 1,800m, marking the start of the nuclear zone. Somewhere just below this a new path turns off to the right/north, marked with plastic tags, and leading uphill for an hour or so to a steep ridge overlooking a giant waterfall. Continuing towards the main summit, the path runs across to the left and down to cross two dry streams and then a good one after 30 minutes; the path climbs past a ruined hut to reach another good stream in another 30 minutes. The pines are gradually thinning out, and there are some big patches of bracken here; after 15 minutes more you reach a poor spring, and two minutes above that (at 2,050m, about two and a half hours from the visitor centre) the Campamento Don Tomás. There's room for a few tents here, a table, latrine and a grotty shack: you can get the key from Miguel, the *vigilante* at the visitor centre, but as it stands it's not worth it. If you don't have a tent the porch would give minimal shelter.

From here on the path is much worse, and the red plastic tags become more and more important as it gets steeper. The climb eases briefly after an hour, but then you have to slog hard again for another 20 minutes before reaching the plateau and the Naranjo campsite (2,560m). There's a loo with a view, levelled space for three to five tents, and just beyond, the Naranjo creek, the last water source. It can be chilly here, with temperatures occasionally as low as 2°C. On the plateau, you'll see some really big cloudforest trees at last, still including quite a few pines, as well as oak and liquidambar; it's very different from any cloudforest you may have seen in Costa Rica, for instance, much quieter, more open, without a solid canopy, although there are some huge rafts of moss. It's only a plateau relatively speaking: as you go on you'll continue to climb quite steeply. After about an hour, you can take a break on a fallen tree on a summit of about 2,780m; five minutes after this you should take a sharp, poorly-marked turn to the left. After five minutes more there's another sharp left turn, just where you get your first view of the summit, and again after five minutes more you need to turn left at some fallen trees. Soon you start to climb, and keep going for 30-40 minutes to finally reach Cerro las Minas, the highest peak of Celaque (2,849m). Views are limited here, with the only opening to the southwest, but there are some attractive stunted trees and bushes.

At the moment you have little choice but to return the way you came, although the trail on to Belén Gualcho may be reopened before too long. You should be able to get down to the visitor centre in under five hours, and to Gracias in one and a half hours from there.

THE SOUTHWEST

Heading south from Santa Rosa, the main road to El Salvador gives access to a few more reserves. The **Erapuca Wildlife Refuge** lies 10km west of La Unión; this is 6,500ha of cloudforest, surrounding a peak of 2,360m, which is one of the best places in Honduras for rock climbing. For information, contact Professor Elmer Rivera at the Institut Marcos Aguirre, Cucuyagua, Copán (about 4km east of La Unión). The peaks of Erapuca and Erapucita are flat on top, so you can camp there, enjoying good views to Guatemala and El Salvador; to the north, east and west the slopes are as steep as 90%, with dwarf forest just 2-3m high. Quetzals, swallows, solitaires, owls, deer, tigrillos, armadillos and foxes can be seen here.

Just before Nuevo Ocotepeque, the last town in Honduras, the highway slogs up and over El Portillo, at 2,010m the highest paved road in Honduras. On the left/south side of the pass a dirt road leads into the **Güisayote Biological Reserve**, the most easily accessible cloudforest in the country. However, accessibility has of course brought people and damage. Even so, it's worth stopping off here, or taking the bus from Ocotepeque (at least hourly — it takes an hour to crawl the 18km) for a day-walk. There's 7,000ha of forest; from 800m to 1,300m it's wet subtropical forest of *Pinus oocarpa* and oak, the 'bosque tipico' of Honduras. Above this there's a transitional forest of *Pinus oocarpa, P. maximinoi*, a hybrid of the two, and liquidambar; from 1,800m is cloudforest of oak, avocado, walnut, cedar, and other broadleaved trees, as well as more pine. At the summit of 2,310m there's the odd patch of dwarf forest. There are still quetzals here (although it's said that they're eaten by the El Portillo campesinos!), and swifts, solitaires, parrots and sloths. The *Asociación Departamental de Ecología de Ocotepeque* has put together a natural history display in the Departamental Government offices on the north side of the plaza (free, open Mon-Fri 08.00-12.00 & 14.00-17.00); for more information contact Professor Oscar Edgardo Urbina V at the *Escuela Normal Mixta* in Ocotepeque.

At the pass you'll find a sign north to a *Sendero Natural*; this has been messed up by roadworks, and is not worthwhile anyway, although it's worth popping up to the viewing platform above the road. If you have time to kill, you could start up the new track and then cut across left to the obvious cattle track, which is soon half-choked by blackberries. Eventually you'll reach a patch of primary forest, and have the choice of turning back or continuing down through secondary growth for 30 minutes to a dirt road; turning right, it's 15 minutes to the highway and ten more back up to the pass. On the other side of the road, there's an obvious dirt track up past a minimalist *pulpería* to some radio masts and on along the side of the ridge. This gives an interesting side-section view of the forest, with good bird-watching potential, as well as plenty of blackberries at the end of the dry season. It takes about an hour to reach a farmhouse, with a turn to the right to the radio tower on top of El Portillo de Güisayote; if you continue along the main track you'll pass through a gate and meet a dirt road across the ridge. This allows access to three new iron ore mines, as well as for logging; the country is pretty degraded, but turning right will bring you down to El Chorro, from where you could walk right across to the main road at El Moral, or continue all the way to Ocotopeque. It's easier to take it easy up here and return to the pass; there's a good grassy shelf just above the track about five minutes north of the farm, ideal for camping if you can get water from the farm.

Professor Urbina can also provide information on the **El Pital Biological Reserve**, just 3km horizontally from Ocotopeque but rising over 2km above it, the largest single mountain in Honduras. There's still 1,500ha of cloudforest, and many waterfalls visible (in season) from the road. The easiest access is along the Río Marchala: take the Pie del Cerro road from the north end of Antigua Ocotopeque (south of the present town). There are plans to link this to Güisayote.

The **Montecristo-Trifinio International Park** is shared with El Salvador and Guatemala and is best visited from El Salvador.

Mayan head from Copán

Chapter Twenty

Eastern Honduras

From San Pedro Sula the other possibility is to head east along the coast and perhaps loop back via the Sierra de Agalta (one of the most interesting national parks in Honduras) to San Pedro or Tegucigalpa. Your first stop should be the town of **Tela**, base of *Prolansate*, the Foundation for the Protection of Lancetilla, Punta Sal and Texiguat. They have an information centre at Calle 9, Avda 2/3 (Apdo 32; tel/fax: 48 2042) which is perhaps the best place in Honduras to look for information about national parks and other conservation matters. There are Peace Corps volunteers here, too, who are a good source of information as well. Tela is a pleasant beach town, mostly frequented by backpackers, although the expensive Villas Telamar (1km west beyond the Río Tela) does have package holidaymakers bussed in directly from the San Pedro airport. However, this may change if the Tela Bay Development Project goes ahead; a Mexican company plans to invest at least US$500m in tourist facilities to attract 36,500 'ecotourists' (not what I call ecotourists) and 20,500 'traditional' (beach) tourists each year (and 8,500 Honduran tourists — almost forgot them!). Inevitably this will cause massive disruption to the delicate ecosystems of the area. Tela Bay is beautiful, with undeveloped beaches and mangrove-lined lagoons on either side of the town, and simple villages of Garífuna (Afro-Carib) fisherfolk, some reached only by boat.

To the west the **Punta Sal National Park** is now seen as one of the jewels of the Honduran park system, an area of 1,300ha boasting 14 separate ecosystems, including coral reef, tropical moist forest, mangroves, beaches and salt lagoons. There are manatees, turtles and caimans here, and in total 83 bird species, 72 fish, 37 mammals, 30 reptiles and 4 amphibians. Most of it is too swampy for hiking, but you can walk in along the beach — although you'll be told in Tela that you should take a tour. The best operators are Garífuna Tours (Calle 9, Avda 4/5), who go daily by boat, with snorkelling and a fish roast for US$13, and Cambio CA (Calle 1, Avda 5/6 SO, San Pedro Sula; tel: 52 7274, fax: 52 0529) who take the banana railway (the outer boundary of the park's buffer zone) to km22 at Puente Martinez, and then a boat north along Canal 32 and Canal Martinez to the largely Garífuna village of Río Tinto; this is a better bet if you want to see the swampland birds.

To do it yourself, take a bus (every half hour) 9km to Tornabé and then a pick-up onwards for 8km along the coast to Miami, on the Laguna Quemada. From here it's three hours' walk (or one hour by boat) to the Punta Sal headland,

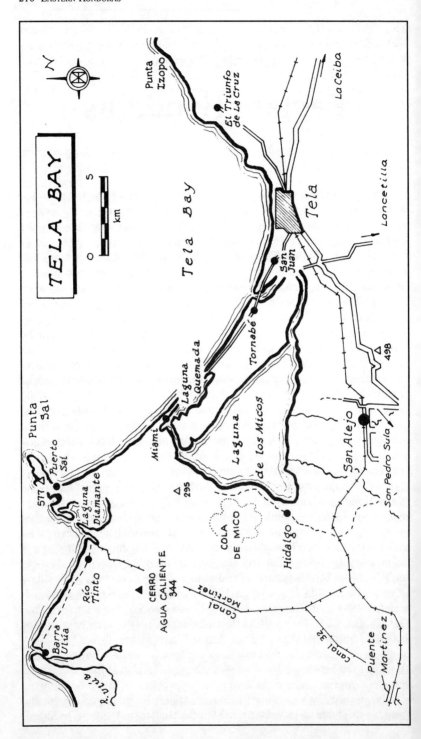

which rises to 176m. There are four trails through its forest, where you can see both sea and forest birds and howler and spider monkeys. You can camp on the beach, but beware the sandfleas! Immediately west is the small Laguna Diamante; if you can get a boat ride past this to Río Tinto (where there's a hospedaje), you should find it easier to hitch a boat ride south from here to Puente Martinez than the other way. You can also walk west along the beach to Bajamar (crossing the Ulúa and Chamelecón rivers) and take a bus from there to Puerto Cortés.

Although generally known as Punta Sal, the park has officially been renamed after Janeth (or Jeanette) Kawas; she was president of Prolansate and was murdered in February 1995, two days after leading a demonstration against INA plans to give national park land to *campesinos* who were almost certain to sell it at once to the company behind the Tela Bay Development Project. She also antagonized African oil palm farmers who want to dig a new canal west of the Canal Martinez, and Colonel Mario 'El Tigre' Amaya (a notorious figure from the 'dirty war' of the 1980s) who claims to own land in Punta Sal, on which he says he plans to set up a school of maritime science. The director of Prolansate now carries a pistol, although this is hardly unusual here.

The eastern side of Tela Bay is marked by **Punta Izopo**, not quite as striking a headland, and not quite as important as a nature reserve. There are no trails, making boat trips the best option. Garífuna Tours operate these, travelling by road to Atenas de San Cristobál, then by *burra* (pushcart) along a banana railway for 5km to Puente Léan, and then by boat down the Rio Léan to Colorado, on the coast. Again there's a coastal trail, starting from the village of El Triunfo de la Cruz; this can be reached by bus from Tela or by walking along the coast through La Ensenada and south of Cerro El Triunfo de la Cruz. From here it's 60km to El Porvenir, where you can find a bus to La Ceiba; there are rivers to cross, although you should be able to get a canoe across the two deepest. This route passes through the Cuero y Salado reserve.

While in Tela you should certainly get out to the **Lancetilla Botanical Gardens**, founded as a United Fruit research station in 1926, but run by Cohdefor since 1975. Prolansate is involved as a support group, but isn't actually running the place; there's also input from the Peace Corps, the National Forestry School (in Siguatepeque) and CATIE in Turrialba (Costa Rica). Not surprisingly, there's a marvellous collection of fruit trees from all over the world, as well as a visitor centre, an orchid garden and a large area of untouched tropical moist forest; being on coastal migratory routes, this has attracted up to 250 bird species, and these attract many more bird-watchers. The best birding is at dawn and dusk, so it's worth sleeping at Lancetilla; there's a dormitory and *comedor*, and you can camp on the football ground. Official visiting hours are Tues-Sat 07.30-15.30, Sun 08.30-16.30, and in any case it's unwise to walk up in the dark; buses heading southwest to San Alejo or El Progreso will drop you at the turning about 5km from the entrance to Tela, and it's another 3.5km south from here.

Prolansate's other responsibility is **Texiguat** wildlife reserve, in the Cordillera Nombre de Dios; much of its 10,000ha of cloudforest is secondary

BANANA REPUBLICS

Along the coast you'll be passing through mile upon mile of bananas (and increasingly pineapples, coconuts and African oil palms as well), with plantation buildings reminiscent of those of the Panamá Canal Company: white-painted, louvre-windowed and on stilts. Every guidebook talks of how United Fruit and Standard Fruit dominated the economies and politics of most of Central America for so many years, but it's hard to connect this with the present. Bananas are still North Americans' favourite fruit — they eat an average 27lb pa, or half a pound a week — so maybe we should sort out the labels. The United Fruit Company became United Brands in 1969, and is still present in Panamá, Costa Rica, Honduras and Guatemala under the name Chiquita Brands. Standard Fruit, now part of Castle & Cooke, is the largest supplier of bananas and pineapples in the USA, and operates as Dole in Honduras and Costa Rica; they pulled out of Nicaragua in 1983. The third main player is Del Monte, the largest US producer of canned fruit and vegetables; they operate in Costa Rica, Honduras and Guatemala. These companies have massive power, but even in Costa Rica (the world's second largest producer, with sales of US$560m in 1994) they account for less than half of production.

Central American production is far cheaper than in the West Indian islands, and Britain set up quota schemes to protect its former colonies; these were replaced in 1995 by EU agreements that include Costa Rica and Nicaragua. Panamá and Honduras, excluded from Europe, are instead flooding the US market and driving prices down. The US companies are complaining bitterly, while islands such as Dominica are facing economic collapse.

growth, and Cohdefor is working with a Canadian team on forestry management here. There may be good hiking, but I haven't heard a lot about it.

The trail east along the coast from El Triunfo de la Cruz to El Porvenir passes through the **Cuero y Salado Wildlife Refuge**, which claims to be the largest manatee reserve in Central America. Its 13,225ha contain 8,500ha of tropical moist forest, as well as mangroves, but it's estimated that 46% of the area is now used for cattle pasture or rice farming. Even so, there are 196 bird species, most of them very visible, including hawks, eagles, toucans, trogons, spoonbills, anhingas, jabirú, pelicans, egrets and boat-billed herons. In addition to the hundred-odd manatees, mammals include howler and white-faced monkeys, jaguars, anteaters and raccoons, and there are crocodiles, iguanas and turtles here. In July and August the beaches are alive with crabs coming ashore.

The reserve is managed by FUCSA (Fundación Cuero y Salado), in the old Mazapan rail station in La Ceiba (Apdo 122; tel: 43 0329, fax: 43 1391), and Cambio CA and EuroHonduras (Edificio Hospital Centro Médico, Avda Atlántida, La Ceiba; tel/fax: 43 0933) operate tours. They drive west to La Unión and then take a *burra* (pushcart, poled along the rail line) north to Salado Barra, at the mouth of the Río Salado. You can do it yourself by taking a bus to La Unión (every two hours or so) and then either renting a *burra* yourself (about US$9) or hiking the 9km to Salado Barra. This is where you'll find the FUCSA base and a small dormitory, as well as camping space, and you can arrange a boat to visit the mangrove-lined channels or the Bancos Salmedina coral reefs 4km offshore. You'll need to get permission from FUCSA and pay US$10 per day.

Pico Bonito

La Ceiba, about 23km east of La Unión, is the major city on the northern coast, with many people passing through, especially to the Bay Islands. Other than the Cuero y Salado reserve, the main attraction is the **Pico Bonito National Park**, towering up behind the town. This massif (mostly Cretaceous and Eocene limestone) boasts the highest peak on the Atlantic coast of Central America, and one of the largest and wettest expanses of cloudforest in Honduras. Behind Pico Bonito (2,435m) is the slightly higher Pico Corozal (2,480m), but much of this area is virtually unexplored. With 22 ecosystems this is the most valuable national park in Honduras, with everything from dry and very dry tropical forest (up to 1,400m in the Aguán valley, to the south) through various types of very wet subtropical forest (in the higher parts) to wet tropical (transition to subtropical) forest, from 50m to 600m on the coastal side. The subtropical or cloudforest is made up mainly of pine, oak and avocado trees, with lots of epiphytes, ferns and mosses; the wet tropical (rain) forest is mainly caoba, cedar, false laurel, San Juan, and along streams ceiba, guanacaste and figs. Rainfall varies from 920mm a year on the southern side to 4,300mm on the coast. Wildlife includes jaguars, ocelots, margays, spider and howler monkeys, tapir, collared peccaries, white-tailed and red brocket deer, ringtails, otters, coatis, armadillos, kinkajous, pacas, opossums, iguanas, harpy eagles, quetzals, guans, curassows, scarlet macaws, yellow-headed parrots, and toucans. The deciduous tropical forest of the upper Aguán valley (mainly trees such as indio desnudo, ron-rón and raintrees, under different names here) is home to motmots, woodpeckers, rabbits, opossums, armadillos and coyotes.

The NGO working in the park is FUPIB (Fundación Pico Bonito), based in office 3, Edificio Reyes, 695 Avda San Isidro (on the north side of the *Carrion* store) in La Ceiba. You can also inquire at the Cohdefor office, on the Tela highway about 2km east of the airport (tel: 43 1033). The Silviculture department of CURLA, the University of the Atlantic Coast, is involved too, and their *campamento* is as far as most visitors go. La Ceiba EcoTours and EuroHonduras both operate day trips here for about US$35, and there are plans to further develop it for ecotourism.

It's not easy to get into the nuclear area; traditionally, a group of CURLA students goes to the top of Pico Bonito every year, but very few others go this way. It's a very muddy rough path, totally unmarked and not at all easy to follow; the slopes are so steep that only hammock camping is possible above the *campamento*. You should allow three days to get up and one to come down, and carry all your water. Assuming you'll use the *campamento* as a base, you need to take the '1 de Mayo' bus from Avda República right around the airfield to Armenia Bonito. The CURLA campus is on the south side of the airfield, and you can also take the students' bus there, then walk on along the south side of the runway for about ten minutes to meet the bus route. Turn left over a bridge and cross another after five minutes to pass the *pulpería* where the bus terminates. The dirt road continues, turning left after five minutes, right after five minutes and right again after five more. You'll cross the dry Quebrada Manga Seca creek after a couple of minutes and pass through a

La Ceiba

CUERO y SALADO

Visitors' Centre

El Porvenir

Danto

Trujillo

CURLA

Armenia Bonito

La Union

El Pino

Camp

Cascada

PICO BONITO
2435

La Masica

San Francisco

R. Bonito

Tela

R. Perla

MONTAÑA DE COROZAL
2480

R. Cuero

N

O   10
km

PICO BONITO
and
CUERO Y SALADO

gate, and turn left after ten minutes; this passes a last couple of houses and reaches the Río Bonito in under ten minutes. Although the river may be dry where it passes under the coastal highway, there'll be plenty of water here, upstream of the plantations; it's a lovely spot, with rocks strewn across the clear fresh water.

Tearing yourself away, the track, now pretty basic, swings left, and then right by the forest edge at last; after 15 minutes it swings up in a hairpin bend, and in five minutes reaches a sign on what is to be a visitor centre. A few minutes later the track enters the forest, and 15 minutes later reaches the *campamento* clearing, at all of 200m altitude. There's a large hut on stilts, with three totally bare rooms, and dirty latrines out the back. Otherwise it's a beautiful place: from the balcony there's a view right up to Pico Bonito, and a path leads down to the Quebrada Grande, with wonderful rocky pools in pristine forest.

From here a path heads into the foothills, continuing up the valley behind the latrines, past a few trees labelled for the benefit of the forestry students.

After 30 minutes this reaches a ridge with a junction. The path to the right climbs along the ridge for ten minutes and then drops west into the valley of the Quebrada Quilina, to return to the airfield. To the left the path drops (most of the time) to the northwest, reaching a hilltop, marked on the map as 403m, in 20 minutes. To the right here there's a fenced but very basic viewpoint north over wild forest towards the airfield, while to the left the path drops to the southwest and emerges after 30 minutes into a field with the foundations of the visitor centre just to the left. The forest is pretty dense around the *campamento* so there's not a lot else you can do without a machete and serious jungle-bashing, which in my experience is generally more effort than it's worth.

One alternative is to go a way up the path towards Pico Bonito, which starts across the Río Bonito, on a zigzag track that's easy to spot. To get here you can fork right as you enter the field at the top of the hairpin five minutes north of the visitor centre site; where this reaches the forest edge one path heads left to the *campamento*, parallel to the track described above, and another heads down some steps to the right to the rivers, which you need to cross to the west. Alternatively, if you want the most direct route, you should take the main highway west across the Río Bonito at Colonia 1 de Mayo and then take the first track left/south up the left bank through Montevideo and on to the zigzag track up to the last house. Once on the ridge, you basically have to follow it all the way to the top.

The Río Cangrejal flows past the east side of the park and the town of La Ceiba, and is followed by an attractive dirt road (the old road to Olanchito or *antigua carretera a Olanchito*), which gives views of fine waterfalls. There are several good bathing places, the first at Playa del Venado, just 2km south of the coastal highway. Buses go most of the way along this road to Yaruca, an historic town from where you could walk 20-odd km down to San José, west of Olanchito. Most of the tour companies in La Ceiba offer rafting trips on the Cangrejal; the specialists are Ríos de Honduras, in the Caribbean Travel Agency, Avda San Isidro (tel/fax: 43 0780). The trip is possible all year round, though a little unexciting by April, the driest month. It's easy to get to another waterfall, on the Río Zacate; get off a bus at the river 2.5km west of El Piño (itself 6km west of Colonia 1 de Mayo) and it's about 2km south along the right/east bank.

For most purposes, 1:50,000 map 2863 III (La Ceiba) is fine; the next sheet south, 2863 IV (Pico Bonito) is only necessary if you're going to Pico Bonito or elsewhere in the heart of the park.

The Bay Islands

The Bay Islands (Islas de la Bahía) have for many years been the epitome of small-scale, locally-based tourism, but big business is moving in, with more direct flights from North America. Utila in particular is one of the cheapest places in the world to learn to scuba dive, and many travellers set aside time and money for this. Coral reefs also allow great snorkelling; there are ten reserves, mostly underwater. Reserve or not, don't touch the coral: it's very delicate, but at the same time it can cut you badly. Utila is on the continental shelf, with waters no deeper than 10m, while you can go as deep as 275m around the others. There are many fish, and dolphins and whale sharks. The Roatán agouti (*Dasyprocta ruatanica*) is an endemic species, now threatened. The Bay Islands Conservation Association (Edificio Cooper, Calle Principal, Coxen Hole, Roatán; tel: 45 1424; or c/o Robinson Crusoe Tours on Utila) is very active.

The **Swan Islands** (Islas Cisne), a third of the way to Jamaica, are not easy to get to without your own yacht, although there is a US weather station there. There's a National Marine Park protecting turtle-nesting beaches, and tropical moist forest with endemic flora and fauna, such as the rodent *Geocapromys brownii thoracatus* or *hutia*.

Closer to shore, between the Bay Islands and La Ceiba, the **Hog Islands** (Cayos Cochinos) are so called because of the feral pigs that kept the buccaneers in salt pork in colonial times. The islands are private property, but there are diving resorts: contact Hondu-Tours (9 Calle, Avda 14 de Julio; tel: 43 0457) or Sea Safaris (Avda 14 de Julio, Calle 1; tel/fax: 43 2272) in La Ceiba. There are places to camp, if you ask permission and bring all your food and water. Hire a boat in Nueva Armenia, east of La Ceiba, for the 17km trip.

Around Trujillo

The last of the major towns along the north coast is **Trujillo**, founded in 1525 and the first capital of Honduras. There are beaches, an old fort and an engagingly haphazard museum. Immediately behind the town rises the peak of Cerro Calentura (1,235m), part of the **Capiro y Calentura National Park**. This is 50km² of tropical moist forest or low elevation broadleaf forest, boasting 18 species of mammals (including plenty of howler monkeys), 64 reptiles and amphibians and 58 families of birds. The NGO working here is FUCAGUA, to be found on the first floor of the *Biblioteca Municipal* in Parque Colón, the central plaza (tel/fax: 44 4294); there's been little tourist development, although there are guided walks during *Semana Santa* (Easter week). The main ecotourism outfit here is Turtle Tours (tel: 44 4444), at the expensive, but pleasantly tatty, Hotel Brinkley, above the town in Buenos Aires. To get here, simply walk south on the road that leaves the plaza to the east and curves south; this road continues all the way to the Hondutel radio towers at 1,200m on the western side of Cerro Calentura. There's also a US radar station here, tracking drug flights. You need permission to get to the top; ask for the *guardebosque* (forest warden) at the *Municipalidad*, or let Turtle Tours take you up in their 4WD jeep, for US$15-20 (minimum two persons).

Turtle Tours also operate three-hour trips into the park up the Río Negro, but it's easy enough to do this alone. From the plaza, take the main road east, past the prison sponsored by Pepsi (these guys would put their logo on a hearse) to the Río Negro bridge and on for another ten minutes to turn right on to a dirt road. After about seven minutes fork right by a new housing development and follow a grassy track between hedges, to ford the river after five minutes. A good path goes up through shoulder-high scrub and forks left; in just a couple of minutes you're back at the river, by a good pool with log frames set up on the far side from which you can sling hammocks or mosquito nets. Continuing up the path you'll see quite a few of these frames, in fact set up for sawing logs. There are also scattered clearings with banana and palm trees, which offer good viewpoints over the forest and the coast. You can take paths up through the plantations to climb up the mountain side, or follow the river to more bathing pools and a waterfall.

FUCAGUA also works at the **Laguna de Guaimoreto**, a wildlife refuge 5km east of town. This is a mangrove lagoon of 50km², with caimans, turtles, white-faced monkeys, fish and lots of birds. You can get here with Turtle Tours, by renting a boat at the Bahía Bar (on the beach east of Trujillo, near the airstrip and posh hotels) or by taking a bus either towards Puerto Castilla (getting off at the bridge over the channel that links the lagoon to the sea) or towards Durango (getting off after the army base, at a sign left to the *Hacienda Trubador*, where there's a crocodile reserve).

As elsewhere along this coast, there are pleasant walks along the beach to small Garífuna fishing villages. To the west, a dirt track (with occasional transport) runs 10km to Santa Fe, and a similar distance on to San Antonio and Guadalupe.

The Río Plátano Biosphere Reserve

The term **Mosquitia** applies to the whole area of lowland rain forest on the Atlantic coast between Trujillo and the Nicaraguan border. Quite a bit of it is protected in various ways, but almost half its area now forms the **Río Plátano Biosphere Reserve**, which offers perhaps the most exciting prospects for genuine ecotourism in Central America.

For a good example of small-scale sustainable tourist development, controlled by the indigenous inhabitants, the place to head for is **Las Marías**, a day by boat up the Río Plátano. With the help of MOPAWI (the NGO working in the area) and the Peace Corps, the Pesch villagers have set up a co-operative (*Asla Takanka Kupi Kuni* or United Heart) to share the work and profits and to lay down strict regulations for both guides and tourists. It is decreed that each *pipante* will take only two tourists and will have a crew of three, and forest trips will have two guides, unless it's a group of less than three tourists on a day trip. Prices are fixed at 50 lempiras (US$5.50) per guide per day, plus meals, and 30 lempiras per day for a *pipante*. Accommodation costs 15 lempiras (US$1.60) each; camping is negotiable. Guides are required to elect a leader (as are the tourists), and are not allowed to bring weapons or dogs or to do any hunting or fishing. It's to everybody's benefit to stick to these norms. You can get more information from MOPAWI in Tegucigalpa (Apdo 2175, tel: 37 7210; tel/fax: 37 2864) or in Puerto Lempira. In addition, I was amazed to find an *Ecotourism on the Río Plátano* page on the Internet!

The park covers no less than 525,000ha of largely virgin tropical lowland rainforest, a mix of mangrove swamps, marsh and pine forest. There's a wealth of birds (especially during the migratory season, September to February), including scarlet and green macaws, toucans, parrots, harpy eagles, crested guans, curassows, roseate spoonbills, herons, egrets, kingfishers, tanagers and oropendolas. This is also a good place to see mammals which are more or less invisible elsewhere, such as jaguars, ocelots, margays and tapirs, as well as howler monkeys, pacas, agoutis, peccaries, giant anteaters, and in the coastal channels manatees. There's a local sub-species of the white-faced monkey, *Cebus capucinus limitaneus*. You should also see iguanas and crocodiles.

The human interest is as great; the bulk of the populace are Miskito or Pesch *indigenos*. Along the coast and into Nicaragua live the Miskitos who gave the area its name, and inland live the Pesch (the common name Paya is seen as pejorative), who, if left to themselves, can still live in sympathy with the rainforest. It's said that they numbered over a million before the Spanish Conquest, but there are now only 3,000 in the Biosphere Reserve; their language is said to be related to that of the Chibchans of northern Ecuador and Colombia. Immediately south of the Biosphere Reserve is the Tawahka Anthropological Reserve, home of the last 780 of the Tawahka group of the Sumu people. They have been consistently driven downstream along the Río Patuca by forest clearance and the advance of the agricultural frontier, and their future is not yet assured. Nevertheless they preserve more of their cultural identity than any other Sumu group. There are also Garífuna villages along the coast.

Access to the Río Plátano

Many maps show a road from Dulce Nombre de Culmí up the Paulaya valley to Sico, which doesn't exist; nevertheless a track does go far enough north from Dulce Nombre for this to be the bridgehead for fast-spreading colonization of the southern part of the reserve. Pesticides and cattle manure from this area, and sediments released by deforestation, are fast washing down the Paulaya and Patuca rivers, threatening to wipe out the *cuyamel* fish, which needs very pure water. A few ecotourism companies do bring groups in from Tegucigalpa by this route, but it's not ideal for solo travellers.

It's more rewarding in any case to enter from the north: as a rule this involves flying (daily, US$25) from La Ceiba to Palacios, near the mouth of the Río Tinto (the united Sico and Paulaya rivers). There are two ways to get in overland, firstly by taking a bus or pick-up east from Tocoa or Trujillo via Bonito Oriental and Limoncito to Iriona, then following the beach through Garífuna villages such as Sangrelaya to Batalla and taking a boat to Palacios, or secondly by getting off the bus at Icoteya and then taking a boat down the Río Sico. Palacios was the British Black River Colony from 1699 to 1782, with cannons and a cemetery still to be seen, and you can take boats up the Sico or Paulaya from here. There's a hospedaje and restaurant. Normally though, you should go, immediately on landing, to the *Isleña* office to catch the *lancha collectiva* (ferry) to Payabila, via a canal parallel to the coast and the Laguna de Ibans (about an hour, US$3). From Payabila walk along the coast through Belén (hospedaje) and Kuri (Biosphere Reserve headquarters) to Barra Plátano, about two hours walk. You may be able to get a ride in a truck.

In Barra Plátano you should get to work at once to find a boat to take you up

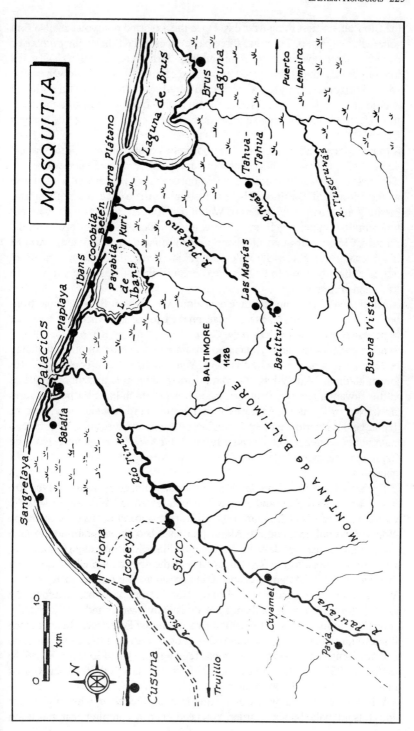

the Río Plátano first thing next day. Once this is sorted out, you can also find somewhere to sleep. There are three basic types of boat here: the *pipante* or *cayuco*, a dugout which is poled or paddled; the *tuk-tuk*, what the Thais call a longtail boat, a dugout powered by what is essentially a lawnmower engine with a horizontal shaft; and a version powered by a more powerful outboard engine. To get to Las Marías takes about eight hours in a tuk-tuk and costs from US$70 return for a boatload; an outboard does it in six hours and charges from US$90.

In Las Marías (28 Pesch and Miskito families strung out over 5km of river) you can camp or stay in hospedajes or homes, and arrange guided walks into the forest or *pipante* trips upstream. Ecotourism groups usually go a bit further to the village of Batiltuk. There's a popular trip to see the preHispanic petroglyphs (*piedras pintadas*) of Walpulbansirpi, three hours upstream, but you can also make much longer trips into the depths of the forest, up the Plátano, Cuyamel or Sulawala rivers. On returning to Barra Plátano, you need to go to Kuri (or Nuevo Jerusalem) to radio *Isleña* and confirm your flight out; next day the ferry to Palacios leaves Payabila at 05.30, and you'll be in La Ceiba around noon.

Alternatively you can continue east along the coast to Brus Laguna, from where another channel leads to Ahuas, on the Río Patuca, where is a hospital; light planes operated by *Aerolineas de Socorro* often fly out to remote villages to bring patients in, and if you talk to missionaries, doctors or pilots you may be able to go along, for about US$30. You can also take a boat up the Río Patuca to the Miskito village of Wampusirpi and on to Krausirpi or Krautara in the Tawahka reserve. Brus Laguna and Ahuas both have hospedajes, and airstrips from which you can fly to Puerto Lempira and from there to Tegucigalpa. Puerto Lempira is the largest town in Mosquitia, with hotels, restaurants, a bank, and the head office of MOPAWI. It lies on the Laguna de Caratasca, the largest lagoon in Mosquitia, where a 120,000ha reserve protects manatees.

Tours to Mosquitia are operated by three main companies. Adventure Expeditions (1020 Altos de la Hoya, Tegucigalpa; tel: 37 4793, fax: 37 9953), Cambio CA and Turtle Tours in Trujillo (see above) all use the standard itinerary via Palacios and Las Marías, as described above. Cambio CA also operate a far wilder ten-day trip, driving from Tegucigalpa through Catacamas, then taking mules to the Río Cuyamel (not the one mentioned above), and then boating via Matamoros and Krautara down the Patuca to fly out of Wampusirpi. From October to February Ríos de Honduras operate a four-day raft trip down the Río Sico; there's not a lot of white water and the Sico valley is hardly untouched by colonization (it's not in the Biosphere Reserve), but it's an enjoyable trip. You could also contact La Moskitia Ecoaventuras, Colonia Walter 1635, Barrio La Leona, Tegucigalpa (Apdo 3577; tel: 31 4628, tel/fax: 37 9398), or Cecilio Colindres of Limi Mina, at the Hotel San Carlos in La Ceiba (tel: 43 0330) or at Brus Laguna.

When to go? The rainy season is from May to December, when high water and flotsam make boating harder. You need to bring camping gear, mosquito netting, repellent and medication, flashlight, water purification and large water containers. Bring *lots* of food — you have to feed your guides, and it's not at all ecofriendly to clean out the village supplies, even if you pay through the nose for them. The locals are allowed to hunt for their subsistence, but they shouldn't have to feed you on iguana or peccary, and after all you came here to see the wildlife alive, didn't you? Bring lots of rice, pasta, beans, powdered soup, and plenty of coffee and sugar. They'll have pots and pans, but if you have a stove bring that. You'll be in and out of the water every day, so have dry shoes and clothes for the evenings; you'll also be in the sun whenever you take a boat ride, so bring long trousers, a long-sleeved shirt and a sun hat.

The Sierra de Agalta

From Trujillo there are two routes to Tegucigalpa, either via Olanchito and La Unión or via Juticalpa. The latter route is slower, on a poor dirt road from Bonito Oriental over the Sierra La Esperanza to El Carbón, San Esteban and Gualaco in the upper Sico valley. To the left is the Cordillera de Agalta, a long ridge dividing the Sico from the Paulaya; its northeastern end is the Sierra de Río Tinto National Forest, then there's the Montaña El Carbón Anthropological Reserve, protecting Pesch people driven from the Dulce Nombre de Culmí area by settlers, and their holy mountain of Cerro del Diablo. Then comes the Montaña de Malacate Wildlife Reserve, and then, southeast of Gualaco, the **Sierra de Agalta National Park**. Together these reserves form a crucially important wildlife corridor linking the Río Plátano Biosphere Reserve via northern Olancho (where the Olancho Forest Reserve protects 1.5m ha of pine forest) to the Pico Bonito cloudforest of the Cordillera Nombre de Díos. Due to the great altitudinal range, there's a very high degree of biodiversity and endemicity here, and it's now evident that Agalta is the northern limit of range of many bird species, as of the two-toed sloth and the glass frog.

Protecting this has been a major saga: Olancho is cowboy country, with a redneck attitude to conservation. To the northwest of Juticalpa deforestation is total, while near Catacamas it's reached to above 1,500m on the south side of the Sierra de Agalta. The biggest problem at the moment is the 1,200m pass on the trail across the Sierra de Agalta from Dulce Nombre de Culmí to San Esteban, where forest has been cleared for fields leaving a corridor of forest presently just two or three kilometres wide; if this is cleared, the link from Mosquitia to the Cordillera Nombre de Díos will be severed, with devastating long-term effects on biodiversity and genetic vigour. There's already a 3km gap in the forest where the Trujillo-Gualaco road crosses the Sierra la Esperanza.

However, no-one can fail to notice the growing lack of water and the rising temperatures — in 1992 it hit 44°C in Juticalpa. The longer-established ranchers and timber barons have now been convinced that preservation of the forest is essential to preserve their water supplies. They're also quite keen to stop new challengers moving in to their territory; now that some of them are parliamentary deputies, there is hope that they may take effective action. Even in San Esteban, which has the reputation of being the wildest of wild east

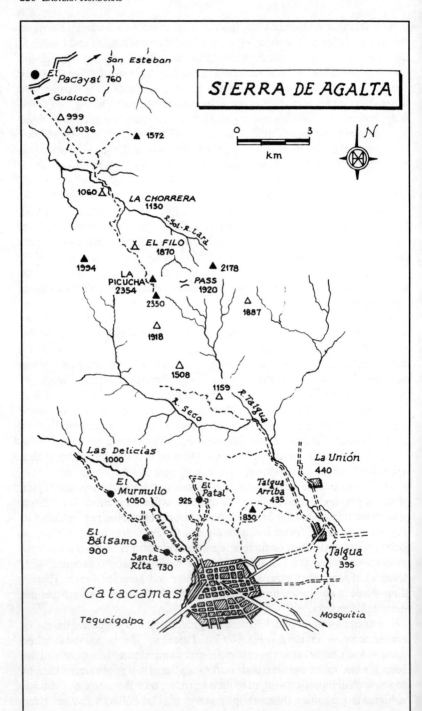

towns (just about every man carries a gun stuffed into his jeans, though visitors are in no danger here), there is plenty of enlightened interest in the national park. IHCAFE, the Honduran Coffee Institute, has since 1991 ceased building roads and promoting forest clearance for coffee-growing in the park buffer zone. Even some army officers have seen the light, with patrols intercepting illegal logging and smuggling of exotic animals. At the southwestern corner of the Sierra de Agalta, between Catacamas and Juticalpa, is a spectacular canyon called El Boquerón, and intensive PR work here, with school trips, volunteer groups and so on, has led the way for public acceptance of the national park as a whole.

To the southeast of the Cordillera, the Guayambre, Guayape and Patuca rivers mark the line of the Guayape Fault, the longest in Honduras, which produces occasional slight tremors. West of the Gualaco-Catacamas line the rock is mainly limestone, with spectacular canyons and caves (some still only seen from the air); to the east the mountains seem to be mainly Paleozoic granites, with some very old volcanic rocks around Dulce Nombre de Culmí. It's fortunate that, for much of the range from 1,000-2,000m, rivers are relatively level and slow-flowing, allowing lots of aquatic life and a complex food chain.

The valleys are ideal cattle country, with pools that rarely dry out; they are mostly open savanna, with native grasses such as *Paspalum sp*, and thorn-scrub dominated by *espino blanco (Acacia farnesiana))*. There are a few remaining patches of tropical dry forest (especially along streams), with trees such as guanacaste, indio desnudo, gourd tree, pine, fig, *Cedrela mexicana* and guapinole (*Hymenaea coubaril*), and animals such as opossums, raccoons, armadillos, and a few surviving bands of monkeys. There are lots of raptors circling above the savannas, and the ponds attract a wide range of waterfowl, such as plovers, sandpipers, fulvous and black-bellied whistling ducks, masked ducks, Muscovy ducks, rails, crakes and jacanas, as well as occasional roseate spoonbills and even brown pelicans.

The lower slopes, up to about 1,300m, are covered with wet subtropical forest of pine and oak, with thick broadleaf growth along streams. On steeper slopes and up to 1,500m you'll find very wet subtropical (or rain) forest, with liquidambar, caoba, cedar, oak, palms, and on limestone the endemic Olancho walnut *Juglans olanchanum*. The pine/oak forest is patronised mainly by migratory species such as warblers and vireos, as well as guans, toucans and trogons. The upper slopes, from about 1,800m (30% of the park's area, but almost all of the nuclear zone), are subtropical low montane wet forest, mostly oak, with *Pinus oocarpa*, *P. ayacahuite* and *P. pseudostrobus*, cedar, avocados and liquidambar, with lots of epiphytic bromeliads, ferns, cacti and orchids, and an understorey of spiky terrestrial bromeliads and bamboos. It's very windy above about 2,000m, keeping trees to a maximum height of 5m, and from 2,200m to the summit of La Picucha at 2,354m there is a dwarf cloudforest of stunted *Pinus maximinoi* and *Podocarpus sp*, covered with up to a foot of moss, with *Vaccinium* (blueberry) and terrestrial bromeliads (in which lives an endemic *Hyla* frog). There's an endemic moss species too, and others only found many miles away to the south (the spores are wind-borne, and this is the highest point between Costa Rica and Pico Bonito).

Due to the steep slopes and thick forest, the massif's role as a corridor, and to its high altitudinal range (1,900m from Catacamas to the summit), there's a wealth of wildlife here; and thanks to its also forming a high barrier it forms the limit of the range for many species. Thus it's the southeastern limit for 14 birds, and the northwestern limit for five antbirds and the three-wattled bellbird. In all 418 species of bird have been seen here (217 above 1,000m), with another hundred rated as probables; however this list includes six species not seen since the 1960s, and five very rare migrants. There are 33 species of hummingbirds, 8 orioles, 17 tanagers, 13 woodcreepers and 42 warblers. On the 12km trail to La Picucha 175 bird species have been seen. Sixty-one species of mammals have been seen: all the possible large mammals except the giant anteater and including the mantled howler, spider and white-faced monkeys, tapir, jaguar, puma, margay, ocelot, yagouaroundi, opossum, raccoon, paca, agouti, coati, tamandua, white-tailed and red brocket deer, white-lipped and collared peccary, and the common and Deppe's squirrels. There are plenty of bats as well, notably the common vampire. There are 300 species of butterfly, including blue *and* white morphos.

The highest part of the Cordillera has been protected since 1987 by the Sierra de Agalta National Park, the third largest park in Honduras (behind the Río Plátano and Pico Bonito), with a buffer zone of 35,700ha and a nuclear zone of 25,500ha (over 610km²). There's no single NGO working there: in Catacamas you can get information from the *Grupo Ecológico de Olancho* in the Barrio San Sebastian, or in Juticalpa from the regional offices of Cohdefor. In Gualaco there should be a visitor centre at the Cohdefor offices; or ask around for the Peace Corps volunteer.

Hiking directions

Given the widespread deforestation in the Catacamas area and along the Dulce Nombre-San Esteban trail, it's best to enter the park from Gualaco, at 640m to the northwest; there's a path from here to La Picucha, at 2,354m the highest peak in the Montaña de Babilonia. This requires at least one night's camping, although at a pinch you could make a day-trip in to a waterfall. From Tegucigalpa, take the hourly bus to Juticalpa, then a local bus to Gualaco (the last may leave at 14.00). From Trujillo, a bus leaves at 04.00; you can leave at a more civilized hour, but may have to spend the night in San Esteban (where the bus will leave you at an unmarked hotel by Vaquero's Bar).

Gualaco is a small, quiet town, the kind of place where kids follow you around saying 'Hello grreengo, what is my name?" and the day's biggest thrill comes when the dogs chase a donkey down the road again. It's actually a major centre for logging in the huge pine forests to the north. You should buy all hiking supplies before you get this far, but there are some good and *very* inexpensive places to sleep — try the *Hotel Calle Real* on the road into town from the bus stop, where they'll gladly look after your bags. At the moment there is officially no electricity supply, although there are street lights, but in

1995 everyone was just tapping in and helping themselves; either it'll be regularized or everyone will be cut off. By now there should be a park visitor centre open at the Cohdefor offices, on the left/north as you head east on the main road (before the petrol station).

There should be a bus east at about 07.00; in any case you should be able to get a ride 12km east to the start of the trail at El Pacayal (750m); coming from Gualaco (but not the other way) there is a sign on the right reading 'PNSA, Entrada a La Picucha'. It's at the top of a rise on a broad straight stretch of road: you should find it OK. A 4WD track heads into open pines to the right, climbing easily for 20 minutes past some reedy ponds, then passing through a gateway and climbing a bit more steeply. After another ten minutes the track swings left while a path goes straight ahead to follow the ridge; you can go either way, as they meet up again after 25 minutes walking where the track ends at a gate. Continue straight uphill on the obvious path: after ten minutes at most (at about 1,100m) you need to fork right onto a new park-built path, replacing one that follows the ridge northeast almost to a 1,572m peak and then drops to a valley. In 1995 the junction wasn't very obvious, due to burning; it's just above a big ants' nest, by three oaks and a pine tree.

The new path is obviously purpose-made rather than something that evolved over years; it follows the contour for about 15 minutes before dropping to cross two streams (almost dry in April), then climbing to reach the nuclear zone boundary sign after 45 minutes. This lists all the usual prohibitions — hunting, building, litter, soap. It's just above a good stream; after crossing this you need to climb for about ten minutes and drop for ten more to reach the Río Sol (or Río Lara). Head upstream to an arrow sign, and follow the path on the right/north bank; you'll ford the river and reach the lower *campamento* in ten minutes (2½-3 hours from the road). You're still at 1,100m, the same altitude as the start of the new path. Here there's just a latrine and a tin roof on four poles, with a ladder up to platforms at roof level.

Continuing upstream, you cross the river four times in 15-20 minutes to reach La Chorrera waterfall, pride of the park, although by April it may only be flowing on one side. You'll recognise the liquidambar trees here by the ugly holes cut near the ground to collect sweetgum; there are plenty of lovely butterflies and tiny frogs here. Particularly above the waterfall, there are birds such as sun bitterns, American dippers and water thrushes, and a very lively ecosystem based on plentiful water life and its primary and secondary predators; you can see a lot of pawprints even if you don't see the animals. Above here, from 1,100-1,400m you may find ten of the 14 possible woodpecker species and five of seven possible Furnarids, including the rare tawny-throated leaftosser. The only common snake on this trail is the cloudforest viper *Bothrops godmanii*, from 1,200m to the summit.

Many people only come this far; if heading on to the top camp in the dry season you should take plenty of extra water, as there may be no more above here. The path starts with some steps and then zigzags steeply up through palms, then climbs on through young cecropias and then denser forest. After an hour or more (you'll need a few rests on the way) you'll have to skirt to the right where the path is blocked by fallen trees, then turn left onto an easier ridge at 1,600m. The path passes through a couple of clearings in pine forest (alive with mosquitoes and horseflies, strewn with creepers that clearly evolved specifically to catch feet) and then heads into thicker broadleaf forest, with a dense layer of dwarf bamboo, as well as lots of ferns and epiphytes. It's very attractive where it's not too steep! There are plenty of monkeys here, as well as guans, chachalacas, trogons, hummingbirds, and tapir droppings on the trail. After an hour you'll reach the upper campsite at El Filo (about 1,870m), just to the right, with no facilities other than a few poles to hang things on. There's a saddle five minutes further on, below which you can find water for most of the year.

You should camp here, and then go to the summit in the morning, and down and out the same day if you want. Continuing from the saddle (without your backpack), you need to head slightly to the right before heading uphill — the path's clear enough once you find it, and may be marked with plastic tags. It climbs steeply for almost 20 minutes before suddenly emerging into a patch of dwarf forest with a view ahead, then continues as a narrow path ducking and twisting under very mossy branches. There's another view to the summit after 20 minutes, then again you plunge into the dwarf forest, over damp mossy roots and under similar branches. It's rather easier than Saslaya (Nicaragua), where you may have to climb under the roots or over the branches as well. There are cliffs to the left, and good views along the cordillera; below you can hear monkeys and three-wattled bellbirds calling. The last section is rather steeper, and after 20 minutes you emerge on the summit of La Picucha (2,354m). There's only low undergrowth here, including bromeliads with tightly bundled leaves holding water that in need you could drink with a straw. Butterflies fly over the peak occasionally, as well as king vultures, red-tailed hawks and warblers.

It's worth going on another 20 minutes to where the path ends, about a kilometre southeast, at two abandoned radio towers on a second summit (2,350m). Bizarrely, there's the body of a VW microbus here, presumably helicoptered in to house radio instruments. You can easily climb the larger tower, although it was misty when I got there. There's no way on, attractive though the idea of descending directly to Catacamas might be; the east-west ridge of the cordillera is also too thickly forested to be passable. So you'll have to return the way you came.

If you do pass through Catacamas, or even not, it's well worth stopping off at **El Boquerón**, just north of the highway from Juticalpa. There's very mixed flora here, with abrupt changes from tropical dry to tropical wet forest, tropical dry forest again on the upper side of the canyon, subtropical wet forest above that, and a stunted cloudforest-like habitat at the top of Cerro Agua Buena (only 1,433m, but 1,000m above the canyon floor). So there are emerald toucanets as low as 400m, and mixed flocks of trogons at 600m, including elegant trogons (usually found in dry forest), violaceous trogons (rainforest) and collared trogons and quetzals (cloudforest). The elegant trogons and other birds from the Pacific lowlands are beneficiaries of deforestation, extending their range this far east relatively recently. It's said to be easy to see a hundred bird species in a day, with 175 recorded in all. There are also plenty of mammals, with many living in dens in the karst cliffs, such as collared peccaries, porcupines, agoutis, pacas and spotted skunks. There's also no shortage of tropical pit vipers (*Bothrops sp*).

Another excursion from Catacamas is to the **Talgua Valley**, just northeast. This is largely deforested, and there have been fatal landslides as a result, but it's worth asking about visiting caves. The Talgua cave, about 3km up the valley, contained bones, jade and other items dated 980-770BC, which showed (by bone protein analysis) that the inhabitants did *not* eat corn, which has always been seen as the cornerstone of settled life in this area. The remains of a village, found by chance in 1994, may turn out to be larger than those of Copán at the same period, and as important.

La Muralla

One of the best organised of Honduras' protected areas, and the one where you can see most wildlife for least effort, is the **La Muralla Wildlife Refuge**. It's particularly known as a good place to see quetzals, although I saw none. There's road access to the visitor centre, and an easy network of trails nearby. It's close enough to Tegucigalpa for day-trips by those with a car: turn off the Juticalpa highway at the Los Limones police post at km125.5 — it's only signposted once you've made the turn. From here it's 58km on a good dirt road to the town of La Unión; buses from Tegucigalpa to Olanchito and Trujillo use this route.

La Unión is a town which has really seen the benefits of ecotourism: the amount of new business can be gauged from the three new hospedajes, where previously there was just one unnamed dive. The *San Carlos*, on the north side of the plaza, is friendly and understands the concept of vegetarianism; the *Hotel La Muralla*, just south, has better rooms. Cohdefor has a *campamento* about 4km out of town, where groups may be able to stay; book this through Danilo Escoto in Tegucigalpa (Proyecto de Desarrollo Forestal, Apdo 1378; tel: 22 1027). Cohdefor is working closely here with US AID and producing a cadre of good forestry officers who understand the need for sustainable management and conservation; this is one of the few places in Honduras where the Protected Areas Programme has had real support from the Cohdefor hierarchy. La Unión has gained a fine civic hall, and lots of 'Protect the Trees' signs in the plaza!

While Olancho is dominated by low pine-covered hills, La Muralla is relatively high and covered in deciduous cloudforest. The south side is steep; a large area to the north was recently added to the reserve; it's less hilly, but is almost entirely unknown (although there is illegal logging there). The visitor centre is in the extreme southwest corner of the reserve, below the peaks of La Muralla (1,981m), Los Higueralles (1,985m) and Las Parras (2,064m). There are three life zones: subtropical low montane wet forest (pine), transitional subtropical low montane wet forest (pine and liquidambar), and subtropical moist montane forest (oaks, *maría, Lauraceae, Dendropanax, Miconia*, and cecropias). There's a great variety of ferns, as also of orchids, *rubiacea* and *piperacea* bromeliads. There are 37 species of mammals, not counting bats (including all five Honduran felines, both types of deer, tapirs, collared peccaries, white-faced and howler monkeys, raccoons, kinkajous, and grey foxes). More than 150 species of bird have been seen, including king vultures, owls, collared and mountain trogons, great kiskadees, American swallow-tailed, black-shouldered and plumbeous kites, crested and black guans, emerald toucanets, hummingbirds, tanagers, woodcreepers, woodpeckers and flickers.

From La Unión (700m) it's 14km north to the visitor centre at about 1,400m, on the good dirt road to El Dictamo. You should be able to get a ride (or arrange one in La Unión); but on Good Friday (the Honduran Ramadan) I had to walk up (in three hours) and down. The visitor centre has a good display and fauna lists, as well as an audio-visual show (presumably only in the evenings when the generator is running). To use the dormitory you need permission from Tegucigalpa, as above; if they won't let you in without permission, there are nice simple campsites in the forest, and you could probably sleep on the visitor centre porch. Bring some cookies for the rangers, who live up here for a week at a time. From the porch it's possible to see quetzals feeding early in the mornings from March to May.

The basic loop is the narrow and pleasantly rustic Pizote trail (3.7km), starting behind the visitor centre; after 30-40 minutes you reach benches at a junction — the path left is closed after five minutes, but would otherwise just bring you down to a dirt road back to the visitor centre. Continuing, it's 15 minutes up to cross the Jaguar trail, which continues for a couple of kilometres to the left; the bizarre hut just right is a latrine. It's another 15 minutes down to the Cuatro Pavas campsite, but another three minutes down the main path is a left turn to the better Monte Escondido site, about a kilometre away; from here an unmarked trail heads uphill to almost 2,000m. Continuing downhill on the Pizote trail, just a minute below the exit from the Cuatro Pavas you need to turn sharp right; the trail on is now closed. The newest route is the Liquidambar trail, which starts from the track up to the visitor centre and at once crosses the road and heads down into the lower forest; an interpretative leaflet should be available by now.

To the south of La Unión, the **El Armado Wildlife Refuge** protects a karst landscape with big caves, including one containing a large lake. There's a lot of farming here, even in the 34km² nuclear zone, and almost all the forest is secondary growth. It's 60-70% broadleaf, mostly tropical wet low montane forest, largely oak and liquidambar, as well as walnuts, maría, avocados, caoba and cedar. The balance of 30-40% is of course pine. Mammals include howler and white-faced monkeys, pumas, paca, agouti and coati; birds include black-shouldered and American swallow-tailed kites, blue-throated motmots, toucanets, hummingbirds, woodpeckers, kiskadees and roadrunners. The refuge is managed by Cohdefor in La Unión and shares the same ecotouristic goals; ask at their offices before heading out here.

Yoro and Pico Pijol

To get from La Unión to San Pedro Sula you must either get a ride on a pick-up (from the junction at the start of the road to La Muralla) to Yoro or, by bus, take the very roundabout route via Olanchito. Yoro is the chief town of its department and base for the **Montaña de Yoro**, another area of cloudforest created a national park by Law 87-87 where very little has happened since. Of a total 30,000ha, about 15,500ha are cloudforest (rising to either 2,245m or 2,383m) and about 12,000ha form the nuclear zone. The forest is a mix of pine with broadleafs such as liquidambar, cedar, caoba and fig, with wildlife such as cats, deer, armadillos, quetzals, toucans, guans and curassows. However, the chief interest may be the indigenous Tolupans living in the park. Before visiting, contact AMY (the Asociación Ecologica Amigos de la Montaña de Yoro), Apdo 23, Yoro (tel: 67 2227, fax: 67 2460), or through Cohdefor, the Peace Corps volunteer, or the library in the centre of the plaza, where they hold about two meetings a month.

The Yoro valley is perhaps the worst area in Honduras for field burning in the dry season, with up to ten fires burning at once on a single hillside, producing palls of smoke, itching eyes and degraded water sources. The remaining forests are, of course, vanishing, and the savanna is now being invaded by a thorn-scrub of *Acacia farnesiana*.

And finally, between El Progreso and the El Cajón reservoir, you come to the **Pico de Pijol National Park**. Again this is cloudforest created a national park in 1987; it's crucially important as a source of water for El Cajón, so being left alone is in many ways the best thing for it. There's a logbook at the summit (2,282m), but no other infrastructure, not even a clear path to the top (although campesinos are willing to act as guides). The lower slopes are very steep, so it's easier to camp higher up. For information, contact DRI Yoro, at the east end of the main street of Morazán beyond where the buses park.

There are three ways in: to head for the peak, take a bus from Morazán to Nueva Esperanza (240m) and head south from the central park across the football field; it's about 12km and just over 2,000m climb from here; the first half of the route is pretty deforested and can be very hot. It's 6km to Cerro de Pajarillos (1,575m), overlooking the Río Pijol to the south; here you swing left/east, with a path to about 1,700m. It's also possible to head east from Morazán on the main road to the Chankaya *desvio* (turning) and then take a pick-up south through Sobirana and El Cedrito to Tegucigalpita (1,200m); where the dirt road turns left/southeast here, you can continue ahead on a track up the Jacagua valley. In about 5km you'll reach the altitude of 1,600m, only 3km east of Pico Pijol. If you don't want to hike up into the cloudforest, it's possible to take a bus from Morazán (via the La Regina *desvio*, on the main road west) to Los Murillos, and walk south for half an hour down the dirt road to El Ocotillo. Ask people here for the path to the Poza Las Piratas, a beautiful bathing place with a fine waterfall, and some other pools further upstream.

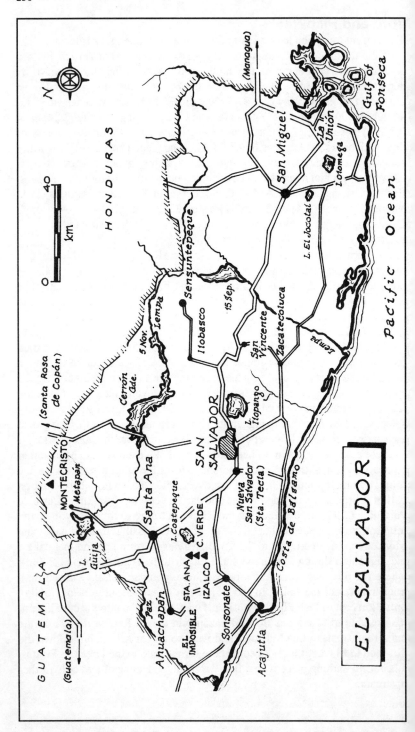

Chapter Twenty-one

El Salvador
General Information

HISTORY

The civil war that tore El Salvador apart for over a decade really does seem to have ended at last, with both sides too tired to go on. At least 50,000 (1% of the population) were killed, and a million fled abroad. However, Salvadoran history has been interrupted by wars at regular intervals, such as in 1932 and 1969, and their causes can all be traced back to over-population and land shortages. When the Wall Street Crash led to a collapse in coffee prices, Farabundo Martí led a peasants' revolt, joined by Indians who were constantly being uprooted from their lands by coffee plantations; 30,000-50,000 were massacred, and Indian culture was virtually wiped out. Since then El Salvador has been almost wholly *mestizo* in culture, and the least diverse of the Central American states. In 1969 the famous 'Soccer War' arose from chronic land shortage; illegal immigrants who had been on Honduran banana plantations for many years were deported, leading to riots at El Salvador-Honduras soccer matches in Tegucigalpa and then in San Salvador. Bolstered by this, the Salvadoran army attacked Honduras; in four days nearly 2,000 died, mostly Hondurans, but at the end of it all El Salvador lost 400km² of territory.

In 1979 yet another military coup led to the formation in 1980 of the Farabundo Martí National Liberation Front (FMLN), who rose in rebellion inspired by liberation theology, the example of the Sandinistas in Nicaragua and the murder of Archbishop Romero in March 1980. Some limited attempts at land reform were foiled by the military's insistence on the most ferocious repression, which soon led to death squads piling up the corpses of almost anyone who wasn't devoted to the regime. The Sandinista success led to the Reagan government pumping huge quantities of military aid into the army, but the war soon became unwinnable by either side. The failure of the Christian Democrats led in 1989 to the election as president of Alfredo Cristiani, of the extreme right-wing ARENA party which had done much to stir up the war in the first place. However, this did actually lead to peace talks, even though these soon ended in failure. The FMLN launched a desperate offensive in the capital, which the army crushed bloodily, while also murdering six Jesuits, their housekeeper and her daughter.

After this, peace talks had to succeed, although they took some time to come to fruition. US military aid was cut from US$207m in 1984 to US$11m in 1993, convincing the army that it would have to end the war. Deaths actually rose after a human rights agreement was signed in July 1990; in June 1991 UN human rights observers arrived, and a peace deal was finally concluded on New Year's Eve 1991, as UN Secretary-General Javier Pérez de Cuellar's term of office ended. In the next year the army was reduced from about 54,000 to 30,000 (though the officer corps was hardly touched) and brought to a certain extent under civilian control, with the death squads, Treasury Police and National Guard abolished. The National Intelligence Directorate, which supplied a list of victims to the death squads, was replaced by the State Intelligence Organisation, under presidential control. In return the FMLN disarmed and recognised the legitimacy of the Cristiani government.

However, not everything has gone smoothly; those named by the UN Truth Commission as having been involved in death squad killings and disappearances were granted an amnesty by the national assembly, and indeed the death squads have reappeared, with a trade union organiser, a lawyer and three FMLN leaders being killed. The Truth Commission report accused Mauricio Gutierrez Castro, president of the Supreme Court, of blocking investigations into massacres such as that at El Mozote in 1981 (when over 500 were butchered, including 131 children); he retired in June 1994, and the entire Supreme Court was replaced. The new Supreme Court is the best El Salvador has ever had, even if it overwhelmingly reflects the political line of ARENA, the parliamentary majority. The National Civil Police is also being slowly reformed; there are only 7,700 police but 15,000 are needed. 75% of prisoners (down from an amazing 90% in 1989) are awaiting trial or sentencing.

Changes are supervised by the National Commission for the Consolidation of Peace (COPAZ), which has two members from the government (one military), two from the FMLN, and one from each of the six political parties in the Legislative Assembly. Its National Reconstruction Plan is based on traditional concepts of export-driven growth and large infrastructure projects, and depends on US aid; the Bush government insisted that all aid be channelled through the central government, thereby continuing its policy of using aid to legitimize the government rather than facilitating new ways of doing things. Many people would prefer to see small-scale local community enterprises rather than continuing emphasis on cash crops; in any case most people feel that the USA, having poured US$6,000m into the war, is not putting nearly enough into the peace.

Both the main opposition parties, the Christian Democrats and the FMLN, are split and ineffective; in elections in April 1994 ARENA's Armando Calderón Sol was easily elected president, and ARENA won 39 of the 84 seats in the national assembly (although the left wing's 21 seats allow them to block constitutional changes).

By 1995 the government was gathering confidence and proposing radical economic reforms, with privatization of telecommunications, electricity generation and ports, import tariffs cut from 20% to 15%, then to 6% over three years or so, and sales tax up from 10% to 14%. Since January 1992 the economy has grown at 5% pa (with 7% expected in 1995), and the 1994 public sector deficit was a mere 1% of GDP. Inflation was 8.9% in 1994, the lowest in Central America (excluding Panamá), and exports in the first four months of 1995 were 48% higher than in the same period of 1994. The government of El Salvador wants the other Central American states to follow suit, but they are currently unable or unwilling. Even if it has to go it alone, El Salvador is, with Chile and Trinidad & Tobago, seen as one of the most likely candidates for entry into NAFTA. Nevertheless, although El Salvador is one of the most prosperous countries in Central America, with a large middle class, 70% still live in poverty, and half are underemployed.

Nevertheless, the fundamental cause of the civil war remains unsolved, as there are still too many people with too little land. In 1980 3% of farming families had 80% of the land, 60% of farming families had none, and 35% had too little for subsistence. During the 1980s some large estates were broken up and over 300,000ha redistributed to 80,000 *campesinos* (*indigenos* have generally been excluded); 45% of this land was 'non-productive' but most of it was cleared anyway. But demobilised combatants have received only 40% of the 10,000ha promised in 1992, and partly as a consequence crime is soaring (in 1994 there were 500 crimes a day, and 9,135 murders in all, making this one of the most dangerous countries on earth; in the first 15 days of 1995 the murder rate was double that for the same period of 1994). A vigilante group called *Sombra Negra* (Black Shadow) has killed at least 20 'delinquents' since January 1995 in San Miguel, and moved on to threaten corrupt judges, and there's also a plague of kidnappings; foreign visitors are most unlikely to be affected by this, but there's a risk of mugging after dark. Hire-cars may be held up, especially on the airport highway, and embassies are very keen for all visitors to register with them.

PRACTICAL INFORMATION

Money

This is the only Central American country where one has to show proof of purchase to cash a travellers cheque. Mail is more expensive than in neighbouring countries, but otherwise costs aren't high; this might change if El Salvador succeeds in linking its economy to NAFTA.

Transport

El Salvador is a small country and nowhere is far from anywhere else. There are no longer any passenger rail services, but buses go everywhere at frequent intervals. They're pretty old and tatty, but are at least painted pretty colours rather than being left school-bus yellow. In San Salvador you have to pay on entry; there are in theory two classes of buses, the regular blue ones and the *preferencial* red ones. It's hard to see what the point of the red ones is, except in the rush hour when they may be slightly less crowded, but you may have no choice; some buses charge a round colon (12 US cents), which is neither one thing nor the other.

Buses out of town each have a route number, uniquely in this region. As usual at this end of Central America, there's plenty of space for baggage on the roof-rack. Those to the east of the country leave from the *Terminal de Oriente*, east of the centre (reached by buses 7, 29, 33, 34), and those to the west leave from the *Terminal de Occidente* (buses 4, 27 and 34). There's also the relatively new *Puerto Bus*, at Alameda Juan Pablo II and 19 Avda Norte (tel: 22 2158), used by almost hourly buses to Guatemala City, and two a day to Tegucigalpa.

Maps
These are available from the *Instituto Geográfico Nacional* at Avda Juan Bertis 79, northeast of the centre by buses 4, 43 and B; follow yellow arrows to *Relaciones Publicas*. There's no need for bureaucratic permission, but you will be sent downstairs to the archive, back upstairs to pay, then downstairs again to collect your maps. Being a small country, maps are at 1:25,000 rather than the normal 1:50,000, with contour lines every 10m, and it can be hard to adjust to the extra detail. The tourist office's free map of San Salvador is the same as the IGN's 2357 II SW; for city centre details you'll have to rely on a guidebook.

Food
You can eat well here; the national speciality is the *pupusa*, a tortilla stuffed with cheese, beans or sausage-meat (*chicharrón*); this should be made to order and served mouth-burningly hot, with coleslaw. It's messy, but you'll always get a paper napkin afterwards. It's often accompanied by hot chocolate, which looks disgustingly black and grainy but is really not bad. *Comedors* always have plenty of platano, avocado and tomato, to go with the rice and beans (usually refried here), and foreigners are usually offered bread (*pan frances*) as an alternative to the thick doughy tortillas. Tetrapak drinks are available everywhere, with more variety than in Honduras. In San Salvador there are good vegetarian restaurants, but the macho culture means that they have to make everything with soya dressed up to look like meat.

Hotels
There are plenty of cheap hotels much like those everywhere else in Central America, except that here many charge separately for the day and for the night. You can either pay extra for the day or remove all your luggage; you should be able to leave it at reception. Despite their daytime use, the rooms are usually perfectly clean and decent; soap, towel and toilet paper are often provided, but a lock may not be.

El Salvador is the only Central American country with anything like organised camping sites; these are the *Turicentros*, 14 recreational parks at pools, beaches and other beauty spots, used mainly by day visitors but (apart from Parque Balboa south of San Salvador) also available for camping; ISTU has an information sheet. Another almost socialist feature of El Salvador is the workers' resorts on the coast and Lake Coatepeque, where you can actually stay for free, as long as you apply in advance at the *Ministerio de Trabajo*, in San Bartolo, in the eastern suburbs of San Salvador (bus 29).

Naturalists' El Salvador

El Salvador is the most overpopulated country in the mainland Americas and the most environmentally degraded. Although most of the land is mountain and unsuitable for farming, it has nevertheless been almost entirely deforested, and there is not a lot of scope for hiking or ecotourism. In the late 19th century El Salvador became the largest coffee producer in Central America and by the late 1920s had built an excellent road system with the proceeds, allowing easy access to the forest; by 1946 erosion was becoming a problem and now affects 77% of the country. The northern mountains are largely bare of topsoil, wells are drying up, and sedimentation is threatening hydro-electric power generation. Likewise, the 1950s and '60s cotton boom virtually eliminated the dry tropical forest on the coastal plains. Now just 240,000ha (under 3%) of original forest cover is left, and none may be left outside national parks by 2005. In the 20th century El Salvador's population has grown from one million to five million and, as mentioned, over-population and land shortage have led to war throughout the century.

While the Contra war in Nicaragua was actually beneficial environmentally, delaying deforestation and other exploitation, this was not the case in El Salvador. When guerrillas based themselves in the forest around Volcán Guazapa, north of San Salvador, the army's response was to destroy 70% of the forest with white phosphorus and other defoliants. Now there's a plan for a Forest of National Reconciliation here, with 75,000 new trees (one for every victim of the war), then campsites, a restaurant, museum and a zoo, all paid for by a debt-for-nature swap. In the Morazán, Cabañas and Chalatenango departments (along the northern border) the army likewise unleashed scorched earth tactics, and now there's a shorter rainy season and worse crops.

The country's geography is dominated by two roughly parallel rows of volcanoes, of which the highest is Volcán Santa Ana at 2,381m; however, the country's highest peak is El Pital (2,730m), on the Honduran border. Predictably this is one of the world's most active earthquake zones, and you may well feel the odd tremor. The volcanic soil is very fertile and used largely for export crops such as coffee and cotton. Almost the entire interior of the country is drained by the Río Lempa, which runs from the Guatemalan border into the centre of the country, up to the Honduran border, and then to the Pacific.

Because of its degradation, it's really not worth describing the natural flora of El Salvador other than under the specific national parks: suffice it to say that in places there are quite a few conifers. This marks the southern limit of cypress (*Cupressus*) trees in the Americas.

Climate

The weather is humid but not too hot, with temperatures ranging only from 25° to 31°C. The wet season is from May to October; November to February are the most pleasant months, then it's hot till May. Average precipitation is 1,830mm a year.

National parks

The National Parks Service, known as PANAVIS (*Parques Nacionales y Vida Silvestre*), dates back to 1974, and about 7,000ha are effectively protected, although other reserves exist on paper. Some reserves are owned by ISTO, the Salvadoran Institute of Tourism, which confuses things somewhat; some protected areas in fact came out of the land reform programme, resulting in some still being disputed. There are now four national parks (El Imposible, Cerro Verde, Nancuchiname, and Deininger), two wildlife refuges (Barra de Santiago and El Jocotal), and the Montecristo International Park.

El Salvador is the main destination for the exotic birds and animals illegally captured in the forests of Nicaragua and Honduras, and you'll see plenty of tame parrots in hotels and restaurants. One of PANAVIS' main activities is intercepting smuggled wildlife and where possible returning it to the wild; this is more complex in the case of birds not naturally found in El Salvador, such as the keel-billed toucan and red-lored parrot. Macaws have been extinct in El Salvador for 40 years, and while there is as yet no habitat fit to release them into, PANAVIS is breeding them for sale, as well as iguanas and butterflies.

For more information, contact PANAVIS at MAG (the Agriculture Ministry), Apdo 2265, Cantón El Matazano, Soyapango, San Salvador (tel: 277 0622 x69, fax: 277 0490), or take bus 33A east to El Matazano and get off where it turns left by a blue sign on the right reading '*MAG Conservando y Protegando los Recursos Naturales*'; it's a relatively busy stop.

Ecological organisations

AMAR (Amigos del Arbol), Calle Los Granados 9, Colonia Las Mercedes (tel: 225 6176).

ASACMA (Salvadoran Association for Environmental Conservation), Calle Maquilishaut 208, Urb. Buenos Aires 3, San Salvador (tel: 226 5514).

Audubon Society of El Salvador (tel: 298 0811).

Fundación Ecológica Salvadoreña, Paseo Gen Escalón, Condominio Balam-Quintze, 2° planta (floor), local (office) 8 (Apdo 3409; tel: 298 0500).

Unidad Nacional Ecologica Salvadorena (tel: 226 7165).

Chapter Twenty-two

Guide to El Salvador

SAN SALVADOR

I've rarely been in a more polarised city than San Salvador: the centre and the eastern side are noisy, lively and more than a bit dirty, with the only blatant sex industry I've seen in Central America, while the west end is the home of the middle classes (not just a morally repugnant elite), with expensive shops and restaurants set on clean, broad streets. Most budget hotels are to the east, but there are a few affordable ones by the western bus terminal and just west of the *Ciudad Universitaria*. The centre is swamped by about 12,000 stalls (only 3,000 of which are authorised), so that it's hard to cross the road, or even to stop, catch your breath, and look at the sights. The traffic is awful, too.

Sights are few and far between; the cathedral is ugly now and will be far uglier if it is ever finished, the archbishop having said 'we must stop building the cathedral and start building the church'. The El Sol supermarket on Avda 4 Norte, between Calles 1 and 3 Oriente, is central and convenient for hiking fare, but check your bill.

Tourist Information
ISTU's main office is at Calle Rubén Darío 619 (9/11 Avda Sur; tel: 222 8000); they also have branches at most border crossings and the airport.

Museums
The National Museum has closed, with no new home for the collection identified as yet. The Natural History Museum (Wed-Sun 09.30-16.00) is in the Sabura Hirao Park, at the south end of Calle Los Viveros, south of the centre beyond the zoo; it's not at all bad, with plenty of labelled plants and trees outside.

Around San Salvador
There are various parks and suchlike in the immediate area of San Salvador, of which the most obvious is the Boquerón volcano; however, the best known and most accessible is the **Parque Balboa** at 972m in the hills to the south of town, reached by bus 12 'Mil Cumbres' from Avda 29 de Agosto and Calle 12 Poniente (east of the Mercado Central). This was the first *Turicentro*, opened

in 1949, but doesn't have camping facilities. It's a good and popular place for a day out and a picnic; if you feel more energetic you can walk 1km south to the Puerta del Diablo (Devil's Doorway), a huge split boulder on the summit of Cerro Chulo, with great views. This is also reached by the Mil Cumbres bus; there have been muggings here. There's little natural forest, but there are oaks and liquidambar trees as well as planted trees and gardens; animals include rabbits, agoutis and sloths.

In the western outskirts of San Salvador are two new and virtually undeveloped parks which may become invaluable as the green lungs of the city. The **Parque de los Pericos** lies just south of the Masferrer roundabout, at the west end of Paseo Escalón; it's partly an ex-military area, which has preserved a forest corridor to Boquerón. The *pericos* (parakeets) move gradually uphill during the year to breed high up in September and October. There are four species, of which the most important is the green parakeet *Aratinga strenua*, as well as the orange-fronted and orange-chinned parakeets (*A canicularis* and *catalnica/Brotogeris jugularis*). **El Espino** lies just south and is bisected by roads from the Escalón area down to the PanAmerican Highway; it's well used, both by strollers and by fuelwood-gatherers. It's also important as a water source, and as an absorber of air pollutants for the area. Thousands of parakeets nest here too; other birds in these parks include toucans, owls, jays, solitaires, orioles, yellow warblers, and the blue-gray tanager (*azulejo/Thraupis episcopis*), yellow-winged tanager (*tangara ale amarilla*), great kiskadee (*cristofue/Pitangus sulphuratus*), rufous-naped wren (*guacalchia/Campylorhynchus rufinucha*), clay-coloured robin (*sonsontle/ Turdus grayi*), laughing falcon (*guatze/Herpetotheres cachinnans*), the woodpecker (*cheje/Centurus aurifrons*) and hummingbirds such as *Anthracothorax prevostii*.

Boquerón

Also known as the Volcán de San Salvador, **Boquerón** rises to 1,893m to the west of San Salvador and makes a good day trip. The name means 'big mouth', a fairly common name for volcanoes, but it's really justified by this 1.5km wide crater. First you need to take bus 101 (every few minutes from Calle 1 Pon. at Avda 3 Norte) to Santa Tecla (at 924m, officially known as Nueva San Salvador); pick-ups from the villages on Boquerón come into Santa Tecla early in the morning and start returning (at roughly hourly intervals) from about 10.00. You can easily get here by then from San Salvador or the Los Chorros *turicentro* and campsite (4km west on the PanAmerican), but I preferred to base myself in Santa Tecla, where there are a few cheap hotels, in a rather more peaceful atmosphere than the capital.

The pick-ups and the occasional bus 103 leave from Avda 6, north of Calle 2, and head north up Avda 7, a broad tree-lined road on the other side of town — the road shown on the map has been buried by new housing. You're soon climbing up through coffee plantations on a very rough road, and after 7km reach a junction at the Finca Altamira, marked by a Coca-Cola sign left to Boquerón; you may be dropped off here, but buses terminate at the last *pulpería* before the summit. The volcano's outer slopes are intensively cultivated, and there are houses and shops everywhere; on the rim there are at least 30 TV and radio aerials. It takes 30-odd minutes to walk from the junction up to the rim of the crater; here you're at 1,874m (according to the map), directly east of the cone in the bottom of the crater. The view east over San Salvador is usually pretty smoggy, although if it's clear you can see all the way to the twin peaks of Volcán San Vicente (Chinchontepec), 60km east of the capital; views to the west are generally more reliable, especially in the dry season.

The main path leads south past a forest of aerials; at the last one it continues around the rim while another drops into the crater; there are small fields on the inner slopes too, but for the most part they are wooded, with local people coming to take fuelwood. There are two routes down; the most direct turns right after two minutes and is marked with painted directions in English. To return by the other, easier route, look slightly to the west, before a thatched shelter; this route incorporates some wooden staircases and takes long, level traverses across the slopes. The bottom of the crater, at about 1,350m, is black sand and gravel covered in grass, and there's not a lot to see beyond another sandy cone and crater in the middle. It's a humid, enclosed space, and after climbing back up (at least 40 minutes) you may not feel too excited by the prospect of continuing around the rim of the main crater, especially as it takes almost two hours. It takes 30 minutes on a good path to reach the highest point (marked by an inconspicuous survey point), and another hour before you enter woods, where soldiers and guerrillas played hide-and-seek for years. The path is alright, but there are no views until you reach a viewpoint (with a concrete pillar, marking a departmental boundary) after 15 minutes. The path on is rather messed up by cultivation, and it takes a good 45 minutes to get back to your starting point — it's further than it seems.

Returning to the road junction at Finca Altamira, it seems tempting to go on to climb the higher peak of **El Picacho** (meaning simply 'The Peak'; 1,960m), just to the northeast; however I found all the possible routes from this side had been closed by the coffee growers. There is a route up from San Salvador; take red bus 46 to the end of the line in San Ramón and head west. The first kilometre or so is on a very poor road, but then it gets better.

Instead I returned to San Salvador by a direct path; this starts by the cemetery, a few hundred metres beyond the road junction, more or less on the pass at 1,570m. Heading down to the right, this cart-track soon becomes a horse-track; after about 20 minutes two paths come in from the right and then one from the left, just before a good viewpoint. The main path soon hairpins down to the left, to the San Antonio Abad suburb, but I continued along the open grassy ridge of El Castillo (1,270m). After ten minutes this swings right to drop into some trees, then turns left to run into a sunken path; after five more minutes you'll pass to the north of a graveyard for roadplant and reach asphalt. You'll pass some new houses, turn right over a watercourse and then left onto Avenida Republica Federal Alemana; at the end turn left onto Calle del Mirador and at once you're at the Lomas Verdes roundabout, from where bus 52 takes you into town.

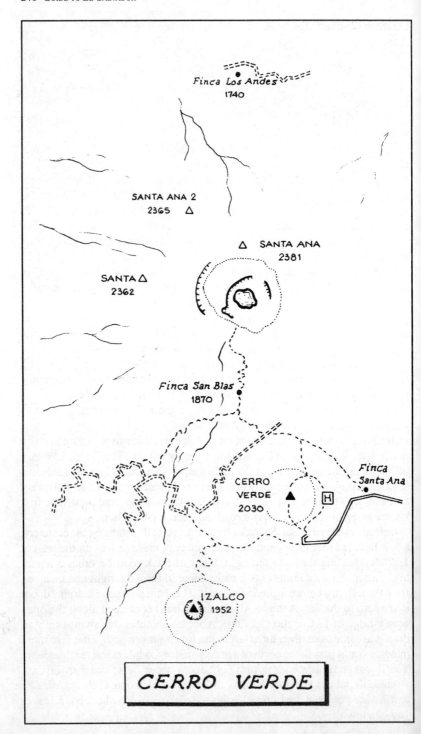

Finca Los Andes
1740

SANTA ANA 2
2365 △

△ SANTA ANA
2381

SANTA △
2362

Finca San Blas
1870

Finca
Santa Ana

CERRO
VERDE
2030 ▲ H

IZALCO
1952

CERRO VERDE

CERRO VERDE

Perhaps the most scenic area in El Salvador is **Lake Coatepeque** and the three volcanoes to its southwest. The lake is in a deep caldera and is very popular for sailing, fishing and swimming, as well as just hanging out in hotels and restaurants along its shore; as a lake without an outflow, it is, naturally, beginning to suffer from pollution problems. Bus 220 runs hourly to the lake; to visit the volcanoes you need to take bus 248 (five a day) along the ridge to the east and south of the lake (with great views), to the top of Cerro Verde. Both these buses run from Santa Ana; coming from San Salvador, take the 201 for Santa Ana but get off at the El Congo flyover and pick them up there. Coming from the south, bus 209 from Sonsonate to Santa Ana takes the same route east of the lake and will drop you at the turning to Cerro Verde, 14km from the summit.

Of the three volcanoes, the oldest is **Cerro Verde**, now just an eroded and forested hill; **Volcán Santa Ana**, to the north, is younger and higher, with a huge crater still belching smoke, and the youngest is **Izalco**, still bare rock and rather ugly. Together they offer an interesting lesson in the stages of volcanic evolution. Izalco erupted out of nowhere in 1770 and grew and grew and grew to its present height of about 1,952m; its permanent column of smoke and flame led to its being known as 'the lighthouse of the Pacific'. The Salvadoran Institute of Tourism built a fine hotel on Cerro Verde specifically to allow tourists and conventioneers to look down into Izalco's active crater; as soon as the building was done, in 1957, the eruptions ceased! Even so, it's a popular resort, if mainly with day-trippers. Above the coffee plantations there's mature forest, largely oak with 58 species of orchids, which harbours 127 species of birds, including 17 hummingbirds, toucans, solitaires, and rufous-naped wrens (*Campylorhynchus rufinucha*), as well as deer, rabbits, armadillos, pacas and raccoons. Volcán Santa Ana is at an earlier stage, with lava slopes beginning to be colonised by cactus and other pioneer species; it boasts the largest agave association in El Salvador, but was scarred by fires in February 1995 which destroyed 60ha.

The buses bring you to the top of Cerro Verde, where you'll have to pay about US$0.80 entry fee. The *Hotel de Montaña* (tel: 217 2434, fax: 222 1208) is to the right beyond the car park, and you can camp by the entrance gate. To the left, on the 2,030m summit, are radio masts and the park buildings. Straight ahead is the start of the *sendero natural* or nature trail which loops to the left around the hilltop, with viewing platforms towards Lake Coatepeque and Volcán Santa Ana. This takes a minimum of 15 minutes, although you won't see much wildlife at this pace; just a couple of minutes beyond the second platform you need to turn right by a bench to come up to the rear of the staff accommodation. The aerials on the summit are just to the right; to the left are toilets and a small path right which brings you to a *pupusería* (where you can get food and drink until at least 19.00) and back down to the car park.

If you go straight on past the bench you'll find the path soon ends at a power line, but it's possible to find the tiny path to the left which takes you under the power line and then up to the right to the start of the *sendero natural*; although some informal paths have been fenced off, others are open and clearly well used. If you want to look for birds and animals, this is the way to go.

For a more rewarding hike, you'll have to head across to **Volcán Santa Ana** (or Ilamatepec); start off along the *sendero natural* and after ten minutes turn right at the power line to a *mirador* towards Volcán Santa Ana. The Finca San Blas (or San Bla', as the locals say) is not far below at 1,870m on the saddle between the two mountains, and it takes about 10 or 15 minutes to follow the power lines down to emerge at a T-junction on a dirt road (this can also be reached from the road up to Cerro Verde, turning off at the Finca Santa Ana, just above a *Pro Familia* family planning sign). Cross over and follow a track past a football pitch, through the finca and up to the right to pass above the finca. After about five minutes, turn left on to a grassy track, rising gently, and after about ten minutes (a couple of minutes before it ends) turn left on to a small path, marked in paint 'Mario 25/12/94'. The woods have been pretty badly mauled, but there are still a few hummingbirds and squirrels in residence. The path winds easily uphill then traverses to the left; after 10-15 minutes, just as you're beginning to wonder if it'll ever go uphill again you'll come to a bit of wall and a gully. Here the rocks are marked 'Chocoyo Arce 7/3/95' at the start of a very small steep path up over rocks and through cactus; keep going upwards where the path again turns left, and in a half-hour or so you'll be at the southern rim of the crater. The last stage of the climb is relatively easy, on black lava, with black crickets to match.

Santa Ana has four craters inside each other, with a very green sulphurous lake at the bottom, and fluffy white clouds of steam venting from beside the lake. There are a couple of radio masts on the far side of the crater, at the highest point of the mountain, and presumably a track to them from the northeast. To the north, about 2.5km beyond the summit, the **Finca Los Andes** has been taken over and is to be run as a national park by PANAVIS, almost in competition with Cerro Verde (which is owned by ISTU, remember). At the moment there's free entry but no infrastructure; accommodation and camping facilities are planned, as well as horse trails to Lake Coatepeque and Volcán Santa Ana.

From Cerro Verde your other option is to climb **Izalco**, although being the lowest of the three and nothing but rough lava scree, this is not the most alluring of prospects. The path starts from the road just 150m below the car park, where there's a new gate; the path down is well made and has recently been fenced with barbed wire on the downhill side of each zigzag to prevent shortcuts. At the moment it seems rather oppressive, but may mellow with age. It takes 20-30 minutes to drop to the saddle at about 1,630m; here you emerge to find a bare mountain of raw lava in front of you, in total contrast to the forest behind you. You have over 300m to climb at an angle of about 55°; it shouldn't take more than an hour. There have been muggings here, with people being stripped of everything down to their shoes; beware of strangers asking for water!

Izalco is in the top righthand corner of map 2257 II NW (Nahuizalco), Cerro Verde in the top lefthand corner of 2257 II NE, and Santa Ana in the bottom righthand corner of 2257 I SW (Juayúa) — but you don't actually need any of them.

MONTECRISTO AND THE NORTHWEST

Santa Ana, the crossroads of western El Salvador (at 776m), was for Paul Theroux:

> 'the most Central American of Central American towns... perfect in its pious attitudes and pretty girls, perfect in its slumber, its coffee-scented heat, its jungly plaza, and in the dusty elegance of its old buildings whose whitewash at nightfall gave them a vivid phosphoresence.'

It's still a great place for an evening stroll, with a relaxed feel and attractive buildings, notably the neo-classical Calvario church and the neo-Gothic cathedral, with a stucco facade over rough brickwork, although many of the commercial and public buildings are good too. There are quite a few cheap hospedajes south of the centre, towards the market and bus station, though some are pretty rough; there's also a *turicentro* at the 'Place of Beautiful Women' (Sihuatehuacán, the Nahuatl name for Santa Ana), reached by city bus 51. However, the Apanteos pool is far more attractive, a free 50m pool fed by springs and in turn feeding a public laundry below the outlet; it's just north of town, at the end of the second road to the right after the junction of 9 and 11 Avdas Norte.

A bypass is being built to the northeast of town; if you're driving up to the northwest of the country you'll probably come this way, though if you travel by bus you'll take the 201 into Santa Ana and then the 235 to Metapán (there are also a few through services). This passes Lago Güija, on the Guatemalan border, and Volcán San Diego, where some of the only dry forest left in El Salvador can be found, and where the country's last scarlet macaws were seen 40 years ago. The objective is the **Montecristo-Trifinio International Park**, shared with Guatemala and Honduras (the Trifinio being the point where the three borders meet). It's been aptly said that Montecristo 'resembles more an integrated rural development project than a protected area'; it's a response to deforestation that led to frequent flooding in the Metapán area from the 1930s to the 1960s. From 1971 there's been extensive reforestation, with pines and *Cupressus lusitanicus*, and the wildlife has been protected since 1974; the international park was set up in 1986, and in 1992-97 is receiving 7.5m ECUs (US$9m) from the EU. They plan to plant 2.3m trees, improve 100km of roads and provide drinking water, alternative sources of income, and education. The highest parts are still largely untouched cloudforest, well worth visiting but closed to visitors from May to October (the breeding season). There are good day-walks possible, but as a rule no longer hikes. At the moment mountain bikes are not allowed in Montecristo, although they'd be ideal for reaching the new campsite in particular; but this may change.

Precipitation is only 2,000mm a year (though more than anywhere else in the country), but relative humidity is an average 100%, with temperatures

MONTECRISTO

between 10° and 15°C, producing real cloudforest above 2,100m. This is largely oak, with pines, cedar, liquidambar, mountain avocado and other deciduous species, and tree ferns up to 8m in height; wildlife includes birds such as the quetzal, emerald toucanet, various hummingbirds (notably *Atthis ellioti*), orioles, slate-coloured solitaire (*Myadestes unicolor*), chachalaca (*Ortalis vetula*), striped and mottled owls (*Strix fulveus* and *Ciccaba virgata*), blue-crowned and blue-throated motmots (*Momotus momota* and *Aspatha gularis*), cinnamon-bellied flower-piercer (*Diglossa baritula*), white-faced quail (*Oropelia silvestris*), buffy-crowned wood-partridge (*Dendrortyx leucophrys*), hepatic tanager (*Piraga flava*), chestnut-capped and yellow-throated brushfinches (*Atlapetes brunneinucha* and *A. gutturalis*), Vaux's swift (*Chaetura vauxi*), black guan (*Penelopina nigra*), ivory-billed woodcreeper (*Xiphorhynchus flavigaster*), laughing falcon (*Herpetotheres cachinnans*), and rufous-browed peppershrike, and mammals such as the spider monkey, puma, collared peccary, white-tailed deer, rabbit, paca, raccoon, armadillo, silky anteater, porcupine and squirrels.

To visit you should have permission from PANAVIS, or from the MAG office in Metapán (tel/fax: 42 0475), but their policy is to let gringos in anyway (though excluding the cloudforest in the closed season). If you don't have your own 4WD vehicle, you should wait for a pick-up on Calle San José, by the Hotel San José at the south end of town, to get to the park headquarters at the *Casco Colonial* (Colonial Compound); this should cost less than a dollar. At the park gate, about 5km along the road, you'll almost certainly not be allowed in on foot, and it would be a tough hike anyway. The *Casco*, at 870m, is a really beautiful place, built in 1783 as an ironworks. Check in here, then return a few hundred metres to the main dirt road (at about km7.5) and get a ride on up; the whole buffer zone is inhabited, so there's quite a bit of traffic. The road ends at about km21 at Los Planes (1,820m), the main tourist centre, where you'll find a camping site, latrines, a automatic weather station and a small shop; the main attraction is the *Jardin de los Cien Años*, where you can see all 250 varieties (of 149 species) of orchids found here. This is a beautiful display in a well-kept garden; if there's a ranger around, he'll be bound to also show you the 'Trees of Love', one penetrating the other. From the fork, the left-hand track runs up into the cloudforest to reach Cerro Montecristo itself, on the border to the north.

The right-hand track drops into the valley of the Río de la Hondurona and climbs to the settlement of Honduritas, at 1,980m; just beyond here it joins an old pilgrimage route to the shrine of Esquipulas in Guatemala. There's no doubt that Honduritas is Salvadoran, but the whole area to the east is in dispute and it's wiser not to hike here. The Salvadoran map 2359 III SE shows the border well to the north of that shown on Honduran map 2359 III, leaving many small settlements in limbo. Although 220km of the Honduran-Salvadoran border were defined by the treaty after the Soccer War, and the remaining 140km by the International Court of Justice in 1992, only 80km have actually been demarcated, with another 50km planned for 1995. The problem is complicated by many of those living in the 300km^2 allotted to Honduras refusing to accept Honduran citizenship, and Honduras refusing to accept dual citizenship.

There's a beautiful new campsite deep in the forest down a track to the left (heading uphill) from km18¾; this is intended for groups but the track in is very rough and it's hard to see it being crowded. At km19¼ another track heads left/north to reach a height of 2,270m on the slopes of Cerro Miramundo (the peak visible from Metapán); you can walk into the cloudforest in any direction, although there are few distinct paths. At km18 a 4WD track turns right/east, though pine/oak forest following a ridge to its end at Cerro la Joya (1,814m); there's a fence here overlooking cleared land (now being reforested), with a view all the way to Boquerón. You can drop down to the right (either along the fence or on an overgrown logging track) to the corner of the field, and return in about ten minutes to the main track (km16¾, at 1,720m) by a small footpath. It's planned to build some tourist cabins in the cleared field (part of the Finca El Mirador), which could be a very attractive proposition.

EL IMPOSIBLE

The greatest biodiversity in El Salvador, such as it is, is found in the El Imposible National Park. It owes its name to its rugged karst landscape, which certainly used to make access very difficult, but nowadays coffee is planted in many places, and 70% of the forest cover is secondary growth. The primary forest is what used to be the typical forest of the Salvadoran hills, but it's now found hardly anywhere else; indeed at least two tree species (*Guapira witsbereri* and *Parathesis congesta*) are found nowhere else. There are around 300 other tree species (notably *níspero, caoba* and cecropia), 120 vines and 180

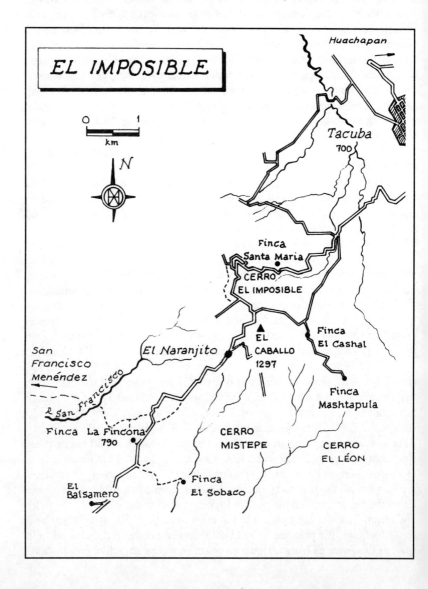

herbaceous plants, as well as ferns and mosses.

There are 250 or so bird species, of which the most abundant are the elegant trogon (*Trogon elegans*), blue-crowned and turquoise-browed motmots (*Momutus momota* and *Eumomota superciliosa*), yellow-olive flycatcher (*Tolmomyias sulphurescens*), long-tailed manakin (*Chiroxiphia linearis*), rufous-and-white wren (*Thryothorus rufalbus*), yellow-green vireo (*Vireo flavoviridis*), and Tennessee warbler (*Vermivira peregrina*). Also common are the mottled owl (*Ciccaba virgata*), white-collared swift (*Streptoprocne zonaris*), Vaux's swift (*Chaetura vauxi*), berylline and cinnamon hummingbirds (*Amazilia beryllina* and *A. rutila*), white-tipped dove (*Leptotila verreauxi*), ivory-billed woodcreeper (*Xiphorhynchus flavigaster*), greenish elaenia (*Myiopagis viridicata*), brown-crested, social and sulphur-bellied flycatchers (*Myiarchus tyrannulus, Myiozetetes similis* and *Myiodynastes luteiventris*), banded and plain wrens (*Thryothorus pleurostictus* and *T. modestus)*, Swainson's thrush *(Catharus ustulatus)*, lesser greenlet (*Hylophilis decurtatus*), fan-tailed and rufous-capped warblers (*Euthlypis lachrymosa* and *Basileuterus rufifrons*), blue bunting (*Cyanocompsa parellina*), and thicket tinamou (*Crypturellus cinnamomeus*); there's a great variety of raptors, notably the black hawk-eagle (*Spizaetus tyrannus*), white-necked hawk (*Leucopternis albicollis*), black-and-white owl (*Ciccaba nigrolineata*), and the king vulture (*Sarcoramphus papa*) found only here in El Salvador. Mammals include puma, ocelot, margay, taira, white-tailed deer, silky anteater, kinkajou, raccoon, coati and paca.

Since 1991, El Imposible has been managed by an NGO, on the Honduran pattern; this is *SalvaNATURA*, as they style themselves. To visit you must get permission at their office at Avda 77 Norte and Calle 7 Poniente, Escalón, San Salvador (tel: 298 4001); foreigners are almost sure to get permission, although there are limits on numbers admitted. The park is in two halves, with the wilder eastern half (west of Concepción de Ataco) closed, except to researchers.

The centre for the western half is the Finca La Fincona, on a dirt road from the coastal highway north to Tacuba; to get there take bus 498 from San Salvador towards the Guatemalan frontier at La Hachadura (or the far more frequent 205 to Sonsonate and then the 259) and get off at the San Francisco Menéndez turning, at about km117, 4km west of Cara Sucia (where you can stop in the *hospedaje Mary*). From the turning there are pick-ups for the 5km to San Francisco, and there may be occasional buses (286) from Sonsonate. There's nothing much in San Francisco beyond a few simple *comedors*, so get all hiking supplies before coming here.

The park gate is at the north end of the village; the guard may be working in the tree nursery but will come out to check your permit. A very rough road leads on into the buffer zone, with quite a few huts hidden in the scrubby forest; it climbs steadily up the right bank of the Río San Francisco, and ends after 45 minutes (3.5km) when a path drops down to cross the river by stepping stones. From here, at 450m, the path climbs steadily; after 20 minutes keep on to the left where a path comes in from the right, and after 15 minutes turn right and cross a stream, still dry at the start of the rainy season. It's just five minutes more up to the finca, at 790m. The first building, the *casita*, was being rebuilt in 1995 to serve as a visitor centre, and perhaps in time a bunkhouse; the *guardebosque* lives immediately above, the latrine is along a path behind the *casita*, and there's a spring three minutes below (forking right almost at once). It's easiest to camp here, but accommodation is also available about 1km south at El Balsamero, a larger building over 100 years old.

The dirt road to Tacuba is just 100m or so further east (beyond a huge and spectacular ceiba tree); you can head north on the dirt road (blocked by logs, but passable to bicycles) for a couple of kilometres before entering an area of coffee plantations. The road goes on rising for about 3km to the El Imposible pass at about 1,270m, just below the peak of El Caballo (1,297m); there are good views and tracks through the plantations on either side, but rather less wildlife. You should be able to get a ride to Tacuba before the pass. Starting from La Fincona, there's a path to the right on the first left bend (seven minutes up the road), which is a shortcut, bringing you back to the road after 15 minutes; it takes you through secondary forest with lots of cecropia trees and plenty of birds. Continuing along the road, there are plenty of birds in the forest to the west, while to the east you have good views of the rugged ridges and forest beyond Cerro Mistepe (944m), immediately southeast. In ten minutes you'll reach a fenced embankment (resembling a bridge) where the road crosses through a gap to the west side of the ridge. Beyond here you get into the coffee, but it's still a nice walk.

To get deeper into the forest and to visit a few caves, you should head south down the road for about five minutes and take a path to the left by an obvious tree (!) on a right bend. Turning left at once brings you in about five minutes to a viewpoint (with well-made bamboo benches) looking out to Cerro Mistepe and beyond it Cerro El León (1,110m), with the park's radio relay on top; to the left there are good limestone cliffs around the head of the Quebrada El Jutal. Taking the right-hand path, you'll cross a dry stream after ten minutes and then climb to another *mirador* with a better view of the Cueva El Altillo. A minute below this is a right turn to the Cueva del Cal, a small cave with a fern-fringed entrance and bats. Continuing down the main path, after 8-10 minutes there's a vague junction among some biggish boulders where we turned left to cross the dry Quebrada El Jutal to reach the Río Mistepe. The path continues above the boulders along the right bank, then crosses after five minutes (although a path continues up the right bank towards Cerro El Caballo). It takes five minutes to follow a vague path up to the Cueva El Altillo, the last bit being a bit scrambly and requiring hands in places. This is a smaller cave than the Cueva del Cal, but with a good view out across the densely-forested valley; it's strewn with *jutal* snail shells and what may be human bone shards. There's a good display of phallic 'organ' cacti here.

Heading back to the Quebrada El Jutal, you can head down its left bank and then the left bank of the river, hopping from boulder to boulder before turning left into an overgrown coffee plantation to the ruins of the Finca El Sobaco. There's not much to see here, but in theory you can still find an overgrown path up the ridge to Cerro Mistepe; in the next valley east is the Río Mashtapula, which marks the boundary of the closed zone; if this is ever opened up there would be a great long-distance hiking route from east to west across the park. For the time being, however, all you can do is to return up to the dirt road, about 40 minutes from the river.

To leave, it may be easiest to head south down the dirt road; it takes almost an hour to enter El Caroso, where you'll see the first sign of vehicles using the road (there's a bus to Sonsonate at about 04.30), and another quarter of an hour to reach the main village where you will, in time, find a pick-up. This will take you down to Cara Sucia, where you can eat and sleep and take a bus to the border or to Sonsonate. There are archaeological remains in the Cara Sucia area, but they are being left unexcavated at the moment due to lack of funds for protection and security.

On the coast immediately south of El Imposible, and perhaps to be linked to it one day, is the **Barra del Santiago Wildlife Refuge**, protecting mangroves and breeding grounds of the olive ridley turtle. To get there, get off the bus at Guayapa, east of Cara Sucia, and ask the way; you'll probably have to take the *lancha* (boat) to the refuge's scientific centre, where you can camp or may be able to find a bed. The most interesting wildlife is the *machora* (*Atratosteus tropicus*), a fish with a forked tail that it can use to support itself as it comes out of the water to feed.

To the northeast of El Imposible in the Cordillera de Apaneca are the lakes of **Laguna Verde** and **Laguna de las Ninfas**, in volcanic craters which are now very slowly drying out and becoming clogged by reeds. They're still very popular with visitors, especially the Laguna Verde, in which you can swim. They can be reached from Apaneca, about 20km from Sonsonate (bus 285 towards Ahuachapán). The most interesting wildlife here is the endemic frog *Hyla salvadorensis*, and both species of salamander found in El Salvador. Mammals in this area include coyote, armadillo, grey fox, tigrillo, paca, agouti and opossum; birds include toucanets, herons, and the clay-coloured robin (*Turdus grayi*).

NORTHERN AND EASTERN EL SALVADOR

The **Deininger National Park** lies virtually due south of San Salvador, to the north of the coastal highway east of La Libertad; it's owned by ISTU but hasn't been developed much for tourism or anything else, although nearby villages hunt, farm and take wood from within the park. It's a 732ha triangle, with its base formed by a 3.15km stretch of the highway (providing easy access), composed of broken blocks of limestone with a maximum altitude of just 280m. It's covered with tropical dry forest, made up above all of *Bursera simarouba* (known here as *jiote*), with guanacaste (known here as *conacaste negro*), *Pithecellobium saman* (*zorra*), fig, ceiba, and the palm *Bactris subglobosa*. There are 87 species of birds, notably the laughing falcon, chachalaca, turquoise-browed motmot, collared araçari (*Pteroglossus torquatus*), rufescent tinamou (*Crypturellus cinnamomeus*), and flint-billed woodpecker (*Campephilus guatemalensis*). Mammals include typical dry forest species such as coyote, white-tailed deer, yagouaroundi, armadillo, silky anteater, porcupine, opossum and four-eyed opossum, raccoon, agouti, paca, hooded skunk, pocket gopher and neotropical fruit bat (*Artibeus jamaicensis*).

On the coast just to the east, near the relatively new international airport at Comalapa, the **Santa Clara Regional Park** protects more dry forest and mangroves, although much of the latter has been lost, leading to problems of coastal erosion.

South of the coastal highway west of Usulután, where it crosses the Río Lempa (on the left/east bank), is the **Nancuchiname National Park**, which has greater problems than any other park in El Salvador, with many conflicts with the local populace. There are plenty of demobilised guerrillas and soldiers, all in need of land. The park is open to visitors, but there's no wildlife yet; the park authorities want to repopulate it with macaws and monkeys, but they haven't yet managed to persuade the locals not to kill them at once. The Río Lempa is linked by channels to the Bahía de Jiquilisco, a huge area of mangroves and backwaters. A big and totally unsuitable tourist development is planned on the eastern end of the western spit closing this bay, the Peninsula de San Juan del Gozo.

Near the eastern end of the coastal highway, east of Usulután, the **Laguna El Jocotal Wildlife Refuge**, to the south of the highway, is the best place in the country to see waterfowl, particularly ducks such as *Dendrocygna autumnalis*, the black-bellied tree duck. The coastal highway ends on the Gulf of Fonseca at the port of La Unión (bus 304 from San Salvador, 320 from San Miguel). This is just north of **Volcán Conchagua** (1,243m), which is worth climbing (take bus 382 to Conchagua) because of the range of habitats from sea to summit, as well as the views over the islands of the Gulf. Los Farallones, the islands in the mouth of the Gulf, were claimed by El Salvador but have now been allotted by the International Court of Justice to Nicaragua; Meanguera and Meanguerita have, however, been confirmed as Salvadoran. Meanguera has fine beaches, and migratory birds from North America spend time in this whole area.

There are no reserves or parks in the north of the country, which was the guerrillas' stronghold; but in fact there's still lots of pine forest here due to the war, and the area is seen as having considerable potential for ecotourism. The most interesting base would be **Perquín**, which was the 'capital' of the ERP (Revolutionary Army of the People, now renamed Popular Expression of Renewal) guerrillas and now boasts a Museum of the Revolution. There's plenty of evidence of fighting in the surrounding countryside, but it's now possible to take very enjoyable hikes. The green hills of Morazán department were described by Jeremy Paxman as 'as rich as spring in County Wicklow'. According to the Hondurans, the border is immediately north of Perquín, while according to El Salvador it's further north at Sabanetas; most of the area has been allocated to Honduras by the International Court of Justice, but there's still scope for confusion. You can get here by bus 332 from San Miguel (the main town of eastern El Salvador), and can stay in a basic *Casa de Huespedes* or with locals.

Since the end of the civil war, refugees have been returning from camps in Honduras and rebuilding their villages and their lives. Along the road from San Miguel you can stop in **Segundo Montes**, one of the most successful resettlement projects, with housing provided by Oxfam and aid from other organisations. They're well organised, with agricultural and craft co-ops and groups working in health, education and even conservation. Again, there's good walking in the area.

Segundo Montes is named after one of the six Jesuit priests killed by the army in San Salvador in November 1989; it's a group of villages, and you should stop first at the Cultural Centre in the main one, San Luis (about 8km north of San Francisco Gotera), to get information and a dormitory bed.

To the north of San Salvador, on the road to the El Poy border crossing, the Embalse Cerrón Grande is a huge artificial lake on the Río Lempa, which it's proposed to develop for windsurfing and ecotourism. The surroundings are currently very deforested, silting up the dam and reducing its power-generating capacity.

258

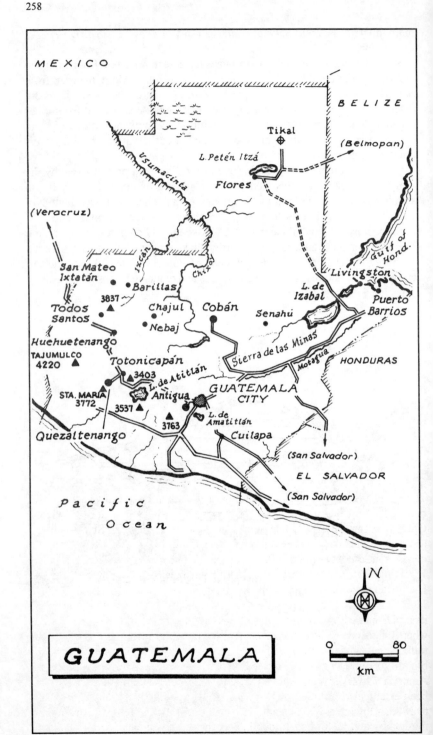

Chapter Twenty-three

Guatemala
General Information

HISTORY

Guatemala is just emerging from 30 years of civil war, and the situation is still so unusual that I make no apologies for giving a more detailed historical background. Until recently the human rights situation was so appalling that I was uncertain whether I could in conscience go to Guatemala (or El Salvador), but as things improve I think it's OK; and it really is well worth visiting. You should make an effort to show solidarity with the oppressed rather than endorsing the oppression, although of course this can be an easy way to justify your holiday to yourself. You must be aware of the massive divide between the *ladino* and *indigeno* populations: these are not so much racial as cultural definitions, as the term *ladino* includes not just *mestizos* and Europeans but also those Indians who have adopted a Latin culture. The *indigenos* cling defiantly to their Mayan languages and culture; *indio* is a demeaning term. While we're on the subject, it's not an insult to describe someone as a peasant or *campesino* — this is a simple factual description. The best academic estimates are that about 47% of the population are *indigenos*, and these are the poorest and worst educated people in Guatemala, living on an insufficient area of its worst land.

The country's story is simply appalling, and things are only slowly getting better. Having been conquered by the psycopathic Pedro de Alvarado, Guatemala lost 80-90% of its population in the first century of Spanish rule, to diseases such as measles, typhus, smallpox and plague. In Totonicapán department a population of 60,000-150,000 in 1520 fell to nearer 8,000 in 1689, and returned to preHispanic levels only in the mid-19th century; in Huehuetenango department a minimum of 260,000 in 1520 was reduced to 16,162 in 1664-78, and was only double that in 1825, though it's now twice its preHispanic level. Many of the survivors were enslaved, and in later years when indigo, cocoa and cotton plantations dominated the economy the colonists took the land and relied on semi-slave labour. Many uprisings were put down bloodily. From 1837 to 1865 the country was ruled by Rafael Carrera, Central America's first dictator, who abolished elections almost as soon as they'd been established. Another dictator, Justino Rufino Barrios, ruled from 1872 to 1885, allowing coffee plantations to take over much of the best land in the mountains and instituting forced labour for the inhabitants. From 1898 to

1920 a similar tyrant, the paranoid Manuel Estrada Cabrera, held power, followed from 1931 to 1944 by Jorge Ubico, 'the kind of man who made the trains run on time'; between them they allowed the United Fruit Company to take over vast areas of the lowlands, linking Guatemala's fortunes intimately to the USA. Ubico reintroduced forced labour and passed the *ley fuga,* or law of flight, which allowed the police to kill at will.

However, in 1944 a revolution led to the election as president of Juan José Arévalo, ushering in the only ten years of real democracy Guatemala has known. Arévalo encouraged private investment, agricultural diversification, and the formation of trade unions, and tried to limit foreign influence over the economy. He devoted a third of the state budget to social spending, but unfortunately gave the armed forces legal autonomy (as the officers who had helped bring him to power wanted economic but not social reform). The traditional elite saw all this as socialism; Arévalo survived 32 conspiracies against him, and was succeeded in due course (in 1950) by Jacobo Arbenz Guzmán. In 1951 he legalized the communist Guatemalan Labor Party (PGT) and the next year began to tackle one of Guatemala's most fundamental problems with a moderate programme of land reform (distributing 800,000ha to 100,000 families). He also built a hydro-electric plant and a highway to a new Atlantic port, all in direct competition with US monopolies, and announced plans to expropriate 150,000ha of unused UFC land, paying compensation at its declared taxable value (a fraction of the true value). This outraged John Foster Dulles (US Secretary of State) and his brother Allen (director of the CIA), both intimately tied to United Fruit, and in 1954 a potentially farcical US-backed invasion overthrew Arbenz and replaced him with Colonel Carlos Castillo Armas.

With the army filling the power vacuum, the course was set for decades of military repression and the guerrilla struggle against it. Castillo disenfranchised the illiterate three-quarters of the population, reversed land reform, revived the secret police and so on. The USA praised Guatemala as 'the first nation ever to return from communism' and invested heavily in new roads and electrification. Castillo Armas was murdered in 1957; elections in 1958 were annulled by the army, which imposed General Miguel Ydigoras Fuentes (Ubico's police chief) as president. After two years of incompetence and corruption, reformist junior officers, led by Marco Antonio Yon Sosa and Luis Turcios Lima, attempted a coup, and in 1962 Yon Sosa and the PGT launched the FAR (Rebel Armed Forces) guerrilla movement in Baja Verapaz. In the Sierra de las Minas, Turcios Lima launched the Edgar Ibarra Front, for a while one of the continent's most effective guerrilla forces. Once bitten by the Cuban revolution, the USA was highly alarmed: in 1963 J F Kennedy installed General Enrique Peralta Azurdia; he introduced a new constitution allowing 'limited democracy', which banned even Christian Democracy and Social Democracy as 'exotic ideologies'. However, Arévalo's old Revolutionary Party was allowed, and won the 1966 election, bringing Julio Cesar Mendez Montenegro to the presidency. Despite supposedly reformist views, he offered the guerrillas an amnesty, and when they refused it invited in US military advisers (bearing napalm, night-sights and other hardware) and unleashed a spectacularly effective campaign in the eastern mountains which virtually wiped out the guerrillas, and also killed around 8,000 peasants. Despite the government's reformist inclinations, power was now really held by the military, allied with right-wing factions; 'disappearances' were invented in Guatemala in this period, and death squads operated with impunity. The economy did well, with 5% annual growth and inflation below 0.5%, until the oil crisis spoilt things; the boom was export-driven, so there was never any need to develop a local consumer market.

During the 1970s corruption was institutionalised and the army moved into business in its own account, even setting up its own bank, the *Banco del Ejercito,* in 1972. It also took control of Guatel (the state telecommunications company) and Channel 5 TV, as well as of other bodies, giving it clear control of the state. In 1975-81 US$175m was spent on arms, but $425m was reported, the balance going into the generals' offshore accounts. There were some strikes in this period, and several times the government gave in, but the death squads soon settled accounts with the strike leaders. The 1970 elections were won by General Carlos Arana Osorio, who remained the power behind the throne of the next two general-presidents, Kjell Laugerud García (1974-78) and Romeo Lucas García (1978-82). Each promised change, but maintained the farce of elections which only the right could contest, and only the army could win ('it's not winning the election that matters, it's winning the count'). In 1971 guerrillas operating in the Petén were defeated and moved east to the Sierra Madre, where they stayed silent and built local support (previously neglected). In 1979 they unveiled themselves as ORPA, the Revolutionary Organization of the People in Arms. Likewise in 1972 survivors of the Edgar Ibarra Front returned from Mexico to the Ixcán and formed the EGP (the Guerrilla Army of the Poor), opening a new campaign in 1975.

The 1976 earthquake killed 22,000, and left at least a million homeless; little aid reached those in need. In 1977 the US State Department named Guatemala 'a gross and consistent violator of human rights', and in 1978 President Carter cut off military aid. From 1978, Lucas (generally regarded as the most stupid and brutal president the country has yet had) unleashed the worst terror yet, with death squads now wiping out centrist politicians as well. When Guatemala City bus fares were doubled in 1978 there were riots in which 31 were killed (although the fare rises were replaced by a government subsidy to bus operators which is still in effect). Over 100 Kekchí were killed by the army at a meeting in Panzós (Alta Verapaz). In January 1980 the Spanish embassy was occupied by *campesinos* protesting against atrocities in Quiché department; police immediately burnt it down and killed all 40 (including Rigoberta Menchú's father).

In 1982 the last openly rigged elections in Guatemala were won by another general, Anibal Guevara, but he was soon toppled by a reformist group of officers who installed General Efraín Ríos Montt as president. Remember this name, he's still one of the most intriguing and important figures in Guatemala. He announced an intention 'to put an end to corruption, guarantee human rights and revitalize our institutions', and a bemused Ronald Reagan called him 'a man of great personal integrity, totally committed to restoring democracy'; however, he started by instituting a state of siege and censorship, and suspending congress. There was a reduction in murders, corruption and other abuses, but in the highlands a campaign was launched to deal with the guerrillas by the year's end. The army turned to a crucially important new strategy, known as *fusiles y frijoles* (bullets and beans). Having successfully terrorised the indigenous population, the army now told them that anyone who wasn't with them was against them, and would be killed as a *subversivo*. However, those who co-operated would be housed and fed. In 1981 the army set up the first Civil Defence Patrols; by 1985 these numbered a million, armed with 12,000 old Remington rifles (supplied by Israel), with membership virtually compulsory for all men in the highlands. They were expected to patrol the area and to pass on any information about guerrilla movements, but the real intention was to polarize society and cut the guerrillas off from their support.

Ríos Montt was only in power for 18 months before being overthrown for planning land reform, or because of his religious evangelicalism. He was replaced by his Minister of Defence, General Oscar Humberto Mejía Víctores, known as *Sapo* or Toad due to his good looks. The new military strategy gained momentum, with mass relocation of highland *campesinos* to model villages, each with an army post, and the destruction of their old homes; massacres became less common, but still many died in the forced relocation, and many more fled into exile. Ríos Montt had counted on at least US$10m

---

EFRAÍN RÍOS MONTT

Efraín Ríos Montt had a model career in the army, rising from private to general and Chief of Staff. In 1974 he ran against Laugerud for a coalition of Christian and social democrats, took 45% of the vote, but lost on a 'recount' and was possibly paid off to go to Spain as a diplomat. He reappeared, to general surprise, as leader of the *junta* that took over after the 1982 coup. By then he had been born again as an evangelical Christian, and presidential sermons on Sunday-night TV were a feature of his time in power. He later became pastor of the *Iglesia del Verbo* on Avenida de la Reforma in Guatemala City, but increasingly came to be seen as something of a saviour himself. In the highlands, despite the bloodshed of his period in power, he's credited with bringing peace, by giving them an alternative to accepting the guerrillas' rule. He was debarred from running for the presidency in 1990 by a law prohibiting anyone who had been brought to power in a coup from becoming president. However, he is contesting this for the 1995 elections, claiming the law can't be retroactive, and that he was in any case not involved in the coup that resulted in his taking power.

It seemed clear that if allowed to run he would sweep the opposition aside, until he called for 'popular resistance' to attempts to stop him running and foolishly released tapped phone calls by his opponents, and then fell sharply back in the opinion polls behind Alvaro Arzú of the Partido de Avanzada Nacional, a former mayor of Guatemala City. A grenade attack on Ríos Montt was blamed on the army, where he's still seen as stepping out of line, but may have been set up to boost his popularity. His party, the FRG, will remain the dominant force in the congress.

from Evangelical churches in the USA, but in the event there was almost no money for building new homes. The death squads returned (killing 200 a month), but it transpired that the military really did mean to return to democracy. (This was partly to allow Reagan to force military aid through the US Congress.)

Elections in 1985 were won by the Christian Democrat Vinicio Cerezo Arévalo, who took a calm and realistic view of what he could achieve with all the levers of power still held by the army, in alliance with landowners and the business community. Leftists saw him as having sold out, while the right wing of course saw him as communist, and sent their death squads out as usual (by the end of Cerezo's term murders were up to 200 a month again). What's more, export prices slumped and the quetzal (until now tied at parity to the US dollar) fell to a quarter of its value. At the end of the day, it was enough of an achievement for Cerezo to achieve a peaceful transfer of power in 1990 to another civilian, Jorge Serrano Elías, who had served under Ríos Montt. In March 1990 talks began with the URNG (the guerrillas' umbrella group), but progress was slow. The demand for change grew, boosted by the award in 1992 of the Nobel Peace Prize to Rigoberta Menchú, a Mayan activist living in exile. In mid-1993 student riots led Serrano to suspend the constitution; the USA suspended aid, and Serrano was ousted by the generals. After a period of confusion, Congress elected the human rights ombudsman, Ramiro de León Carpio, president: this surprising choice produced a short-lived optimism, but he too has found that the head of state has little real power.

Real democracy remains impossible without economic reform, but this has been resolutely blocked, although Guatemala's tax levels are among the lowest in the world. The army may have been converted to the need for change (Guatel is to be privatised), but the business community has not. When De León proposed a unified 10% import tariff in 1995, CACIF, the employers' forum, threatened a total industrial shutdown and sued; they also filed a suit of breach of professional ethics (as a lawyer) against the president. He backed down but then claimed the proposal had been a 'political tool' to get other changes accepted, such as a 1.5% tax on net assets. In other respects society is far more open, with extensive press coverage of various legal scandals. Predictably, the two most discussed involve US citizens, Mike DeVine, murdered by the army in 1990, and Jennifer Harbury, 'wife' (they were judged common law spouses in absentia, although there's no proof he was ever in Texas) of a guerrilla leader, Efraín Bámaca Velasquez, killed by the army in 1992. It's claimed that Colonel Julio Roberto Alpírez (then commander of the *Kaibiles* (elite forces) school in Poptún, and implicated in both deaths) was a CIA agent; he was released by a military court on his own recognizance. After three years' delay six soldiers were sentenced for the DeVine killing; the officer, Captain Hugo Roberto Contreras, escaped within 24 hours and has not been seen since, but the five others are serving 30 years. Colonel Mario Roberto García Catalán (then commander of the Flores base) has also been suspended, although he claims, illogically, that he 'never met DeVine and therefore could not have ordered his execution'. Clinton is opening CIA files, which should liven things up. There's also the case of the US archaeologist, Peter Tiscione, killed by four machete blows in his hotel in 1992; it was announced that he had committed suicide, but it seems more likely that he stumbled across a gun- or drug-running operation. Some domestic cases are also receiving attention, such as the murders of Jorge Carpio Nicolle (leader of the National Centrist Union, who lost the 1990 election), in 1993, Epaminondas Gonzales (President of the Constitutional Court) killed in 1994, two days after approving the extradition (quickly reversed) to the USA of a colonel on drugs charges; suspects are in jail but seem unlikely to be the real killers. In 1995 the army Chief of Staff, Colonel José Luis Fernández Ligorría, was accused of drug-trafficking, running a car theft ring and murder — the case was dismissed by a military tribunal in two weeks. In 1994 de León replaced all the Supreme Court's judges as 'hopelessly corrupt': its president Juan José Rodil Peralta is accused of fraud and embezzlement (his secretary was a former Miss Guatemala, whom it's said accompanied him on trips at state expense): although he's now a presidential candidate he's gone missing. Another presidential candidate, General Hector Alejandro Gramajo (Minister of Defence in 1987-90 and architect of the return to civilian rule), was fined US$47.5m by a US court in 1995 for human rights violations (the warrant was served when he was briefly at Harvard).

Negotiations with the guerrillas have produced agreements on human and indigenous rights, and a ceasefire may be achieved in time for the URNG to participate in elections in November 1995. There's little fighting now, but the guerrillas are extorting money from ranchers and trucking companies. Elections in 1994 saw a clearing out of congress, with only 18 of 88 members being re-elected, and Serrano's MAS losing all its seats; the winners were the Guatemalan Republican Front (FRG), led by Ríos Montt, who became president of congress; by mid-1995 the FRG and its allies held more than half the seats in the congress, as the traditional parties continued to fall apart. At the end of 1994 there was a resurgence of death squad activity; as in El Salvador they have claimed to be removing 'delinquents', but victims have also included a university lecturer, a public prosecutor, a Belgian priest, a journalist and students. A UN commission accused the government of not investigating or controlling the military and the USA suspended military training for the rest of 1995, also refusing visas to URNG leaders, except for visits related to the peace process. Various human rights organisations have concluded that 1994 was little better than 1993, with between 1,056 and 1,950 reported human rights abuses, and between 138 and 322 extra-judicial executions. The police force is thinly spread, due to all resources having been diverted to the army; there's only one officer per 3,000 people, and until 1994 there were no radio-linked patrol cars. There's an epidemic of common crime, notably kidnappings for ransom. Precise figures for the entire civil war period are, of course, unobtainable; it's estimated that between 100,000 and 150,000 have died, with perhaps 25,000 killed in the four years of Lucas' rule (though Arana and Ríos Montt were almost as bloody). In addition, over 400 villages were eliminated and up to a million people displaced; now the refugees are returning and, on average, one village is resettled each month.

PRACTICAL INFORMATION

Money

The Guatemalan unit of currency is the Quetzal, long tied to parity with the US dollar, but now worth far less; it's divided into *centavos*, but I didn't see a one-centavo coin until my last day in the country. It's not easy to change quetzals back into dollars other than at the airport.

Transport

Inter-urban buses in Guatemala are the most overcrowded in Central America; it's illegal to carry standing passengers, so therefore (presumably) buses have 3+3 seating instead of the 3+2 layout (with a wider aisle) elsewhere in Central America. Nevertheless, there are always people standing, and whenever the bus passes a police checkpoint they all squat down and hide. Presumably this means it's semi-illegal to give up your seat. The driving in Guatemala is the most dangerous in Central America, and the unmade roads are also the worst.

I was warned about tourists being charged about 30% extra on buses, and about bags being stolen, but in the event I noticed absolutely no problems. Baggage does go on the roof, but seems to be no more at risk than anywhere else, except perhaps on the long haul to Flores. On the other hand tourist minibuses in the Lake Atitlán area do get held up, and I did find that truck drivers asked extortionate rates. One phenomenom of the Mayan highlands is the departure in the very early hours of buses into the main towns; you may be able to sleep on board from c22.00, but it's no way to keep fit for hiking — though sometimes I think it's the buses one has to keep fit for.

In the capital you need to pay on entry, with green and white *preferencial* buses costing more; the cheapest (at about 10 US cents) are the *MuniTrans* trailerbuses, basically articulated trucks. These were introduced after riots in 1994 forced the withdrawal of a 50% rise in bus fares; it remains to be seen how long they'll last. The main bus routes are very smoggy.

The Maya didn't invent the wheel, and it's hard to imagine them on bikes even now (the hills are too steep, the roads too rough) — but it's great mountain-biking terrain. Antigua is the best place for bike hire or repairs; in Guatemala City, try Supercicles at 19 Calle 1-58, Zona 1 (tel: 300 991 5, fax: 301 005) and 3 Avda 1-22, Zona 9 (tel: 342 960).

The Aurora airport is to be replaced at some point, as planes crash occasionally, and residents suffer hearing damage; it's disconcerting to see a 747 coming in to land so low over the city. It now handles 608 flights in all and 18,000 passengers per week, and is to receive a Q20m facelift.

Maps

Maps are marked IGN, but it really is the Military Geographical Institute, at Avenida de las Americas 5-76 (buses pass a block or so to the west, but it's easier to walk from the Obelisco). The maps are relatively expensive, and the new series of 1:50,000 maps (started in 1988 but not yet complete) more so at US$5; you can buy adequate photocopies from *Casa Andinista* in Antigua. It's all done in the IGM foyer, with no bureaucratic obstacles.

Food

Guatemalan food has surprisingly little in common with that of Mexico, although you'll find tortillas and *guacamole*, and the beans are more likely to be refried (reduced to a pulp so that what goes in looks like what comes out). An Antigua speciality is *pepian*, stewed vegetables (and meat) on rice. In the highlands people eat beans and tortillas; try *mosh*, a sweet milky porridge, for breakfast, and *atol*, a drink of rice or maize with sugar. *Pan* or bread is routinely offered to foreigners instead of tortilla; it's OK in restaurants but in shops is often stale. You can also buy factory-made bread preserved in plastic packaging, as well as *roles de canela* (cinnamon rolls), favourite fodder for hiking. Sandwiches are available in some places, although they may be spelt *sanchéz*.

Soft drinks are called *aguas* here; at the opposite extreme *Quezalteca* and *Venado* are fearsome firewaters — *Venado Libre* (Venado and cola) is sold ready-mixed in cans. There's a decent dark beer, *Moza*, as well as the ubiquitous *Gallo* lager, and Israeli imports.

Hotels

These are all pretty decent, the only budget places in Central America to provide loo seats. Your own padlock may be useful in some cheap joints.

INDIGENOUS CULTURE

It used to be taken as read by outsiders that the Maya of the highlands supported the guerrillas against the dreadful repression of the army and Ladino society; but recently this view has been undermined. It's clear to those who know the Maya that all they want is to be left alone to lead their own lives. *Between Two Armies* by David Stoll (Columbia UP 1993) is the best account of their situation in the Ixil area. The Mayan Unity and Consensus Group, an umbrella for 76 organisations, and the newsletter *Rutzijol,* are now achieving some recognition, and there's a possibility that some kind of self-determination and autonomy can be achieved in the future. With mechanisation, Maya labour is less important, and most landowners would be happy to leave them to themselves in the hills. Some villages, such as Santiago Atitlán, have even convinced the army and police to withdraw from their bases altogether, with petitions, blockades and civil disobedience.

Although no-one could miss the amazing costumes of Mayan women, and in some areas, men, much of Mayan culture is kept intensely private, especially details of their religion, a hybrid of Catholicism and animistic shamanism. Mayan women in particular have an intense aversion to outsiders, and girls seem to be programmed more or less from the age they can walk to run away from any outsider. In part this is because of a belief that gringos want to steal indigenous children for adoption or to take their organs for transplant; this myth is supposed to have been spread either by the Russians (for their own peculiar purposes) or by the Guatemalan army (to keep tourists away and allow them to get on with their dirty work, while deploying more troops 'to protect tourists') but it seems to me that it's a more ancient memory dating from the Spanish conquest, when girls were raped and boys were taken to work in the gold mines. In 1994 there were mob attacks on female gringos suspected of wanting to steal Maya children, and one American journalist is still in a coma. That this ancient memory still has so much force says a lot about the Mayan culture and the power of history and tradition in it. You are now unlikely to be attacked (but be careful about talking to kids), but being constantly shunned and ignored by the women can be very wearying (the men are fine). The problem is worst in the resettled villages, where the people have returned from exile with radios, T-shirts and a distrust of the outside world, which after all has done them little but harm. It's a small comfort that the women distrust buses and jeeps almost as much as gringos, retreating up the verge until a bus has definitely stopped, and often huddling together near the door rather than separating to sit down.

In the more established tourist areas you'll immediately see why the Indians are Guatemala's number one tourist attraction. Nowhere else in Latin America will you find such diversity of native costume: over a hundred villages have their own distinctive dress, and variations within the villages make up about 500 different costumes. One glance at the Mayan goddess Ixchel hard at work on her back-strap loom shows that weaving is one of the oldest Indian crafts. Indian textiles, and the traditions and customs associated with them, make a fascinating study. We hope the following information will get you started, but also that as soon as possible you will visit the splendid new Ixchel Museum in Guatemala City with its marvellous collection of regional costumes.

In preHispanic times, every colour and symbol woven into the clothing had a meaning. If you ask an Indian today the significance of a particular design, he may shrug his shoulders and say: *Es el costumbre*. But you can be sure that the origin of the design goes back to the time of his Mayan forefathers. In those days the main colours used were red, yellow, black, blue and green. Red signified blood, yellow meant maize, black was the colour of war and weapons, because it's the colour of obsidian, of which spearheads were made; blue was the colour of sacrifice, and green was the royal colour (quetzal tailfeathers were woven into the warp). The points of the compass were also represented by colours: white — north, black — west, green or red — east, and yellow — south.

Symbols woven into or embroidered on the cloth usually had connections with the various Mayan gods. The plumed serpent, Gucumatz, Kukulcan or Quetzalcoatl, was a popular theme, representing the creator of the world from darkness and silence. This was often stylized to an S. The sun was often portrayed, as it still is, in the neck openings of *huipiles*, the women's blouses. The animals most often depicted are the sacred ones who brought man news of the existence of maize — skunk, coyote, parrot and crow. The double-headed eagle is also a ancient design motif that found favour with the Spanish: 'Oh, how jolly,' they thought, 'these savages already know the royal insignia of Carlos V!'.

Nowadays, Indian costumes are more likely to denote class and village rather than deities. There are three social classes in each village: the nobles (*principales*), middle class (*media clase*) and labourers (*plebeyos*).

Even the wearer's virility may be incorporated into the designs. For example, in Chichicastenango, a male elder has a large, elaborate 'sun' embroidered on his trousers. A younger adult has a simple sun under an elaborate one to indicate his social inferiority. A young boy also has two suns, the top one simple, the lower a mere +. Rays are added when he reaches puberty. A sterile man may never use a full sun.

Textile design has inevitably fallen victim to fashion. Only older people wear simple, 'tasteful' designs, while the youngsters' clothes have broken out into riots of crude colours and chaotic patterns.

Older Indians may still maintain an anthropomorphic regard for their clothing, as described by Lilly de Jongh Osborne. When she bought a particularly fine *tzut*, the vendor wept bitterly, caressing the material and apologizing to it for the sale, explaining that she needed the money. Such women often think their clothing has a soul of its own, needing to be cherished, amused and entertained like a child. On another occasion, a couple came to the house to sell a beautiful old *huipil*. Before parting with the blouse the man thoroughly beat it, to prevent his wife's soul from being sold along with her clothing.

(Ronald Epstein adds: It is very inappropriate to suggest buying a piece of clothing that an Indian is wearing. The clothing not only reflects a personal creativity and imagination, but is a strong force in unifying the Indian culture. You are essentially undermining the indigenous culture by buying such personally valuable items: for gringos to wear Indian clothing cheapens their expression.)

Sadly, and inevitably, more and more Indians are abandoning their customs and clothing. The amazing thing is that so many, particularly women, continue to wear their costly native dress. Perhaps tourism has had a hand in this, possibly because the wearer realizes the commercial value of remaining visibly indigenous.

Few people leave Guatemala without buying some woven or embroidered material. The best places to do your shopping are the big markets (Chichicastenango, Huehuetenango, the capital's *Mercado Central*) or from individuals who approach you in the streets of smaller villages. Bargain seriously, but don't be *too* tight.

Indian markets and fiestas

In any country with an indigenous population, markets and festivals play a prominent part in rural life. Weekly or daily **markets** are held in almost every town and village throughout Central America, and it is here that each place displays its individuality. One morning in a market will teach you a great deal about the place: the produce grown in the area, the traditional costumes worn by the women (and some men) and the town's facilities. Although Ladino markets sell useful or tasty goods, it's the Indian village markets that attract

WOMEN'S CLOTHING

Huipil	a loose blouse dating from preHispanic times.
Corte	a simple wrap-around skirt, usually made from tie-dyed material. The number and position of the folds, the length, and size are all determined by local tradition.
Faja	the sash securing the *corte*. The manner in which it is worn may indicate rank.
Perraje	has a variety of uses, as a shawl, a baby carrier or as protection from the elements.
Cinta	a belt or elaborate head-dress as worn by the women of Santiago Atitlán. *Listón* refers to other styles of head-dress, and *Tzut* is a headcloth.
Servilleta	napkin used to cover a basket, or to wrap goods.

MEN'S CLOTHING

Shirts and trousers were introduced to the Maya by the Spanish. Each village has adapted the basic articles to the local climate and occupations.

Camisa	shirt, in varying lengths.
Pantalón	trousers vary from knee-length cotton pants, worn in fishing villages, to ankle-length woollen ones found in the highlands.
Banda	belt securing trousers.
Capixaj	an overtunic, probably inspired by European greatcoats.
Chaqueta	often an official garment to show authority. It's a woollen jacket worn by middle or upper class men. Marital status may be indicated by black braid.
Ponchita	a little apron or kilt, usually just a rectangle of cloth.

tourists. For the inhabitants, it's the most important day of the week and they make the best of it, walking in from the neighbouring areas carrying the goods they wish to sell and walking unsteadily out again (men, that is) after some cheerful hours of drinking with friends. The women enjoy their traditional pursuit of gossiping as they sit beside their little pyramids of tomatoes, lemons, tangerines and so on. Everything is conducted quietly; no voices are raised except for those of tourists conducting a bargain. There is no striving to sell, and indeed I've heard a story of an Indian woman refusing to sell her last few lemons because then she would have to go home and it was still early.

If you go to markets to buy Indian handicrafts you will be expected to bargain. There is no rule as to what fraction of the first price quoted you can expect to pay. Don't be rude with your bargaining or denigrate the product; this is not the Indian way. Much better to praise it but regret your lack of money. One dark note: be very wary of pickpockets and thieves in all markets.

Whilst markets are a quiet hum of activity, **fiestas** explode with sound. There is music and dancing, and often a display of fireworks in the evening.

Firecrackers are let off all day in a nerve-shattering way, particularly in any village with a lot of ladinos, who always love noise.

Indian fiestas are always a fascinating blend of Christianity and paganism. Feasts and ritual dances were being held long before the conquest, and early Jesuit missionaries prudently kept the festivals but exchanged the idols for saints. It has worked ever since. Fiestas are held on religious and patriotic holidays, but it's only the religious ones that are of interest to tourists (any country's Independence Day, for instance, is a tedious blend of closed shops and military parades). In Guatemala there are national fiestas, such as Holy Week and All Souls' Day, and village fiestas when the patron saint is honoured. Go to any village named after the saint whose day it is, and you'll find a fiesta. Both national and local festivals are fascinating, but a small village fiesta is probably the most delightful, with all the local people dressed up to the nines, dancers in incredible costumes and unbelievable masks (of which only that of the conquistador is easily identifiable).

Ritual drunkenness is another cheerful hangover from earlier days, so to speak; it's still very popular. After a few days of fiesta you can see the long-suffering wives and daughters bearing their hung-over menfolk home. There are lots of pre-conquest features in modern fiestas. Dances, for instance, often symbolize the Four Cardinal Points sacred to the Maya.

Feasting is still a major part of any fiesta, and there is always a great selection of local dishes to whet the appetite. And scenes to whet the photographer's appetite, too. In both markets and fiestas you can usually take photos without upsetting anyone, and in fiestas you'll sometimes be invited to join in the fun.

NATURALISTS' GUATEMALA

The basic layout of the country is similar to that of those to the south, with a thin but fertile plain along the Pacific coast, a chain of volcanoes bordering this, rather more rugged mountains in the centre of the country, and a broader plain on the Atlantic coast. The volcanic chain begins at the Mexican border with the Sierra Madre, ancient igneous and sedimentary rocks containing the country's highest peak, Volcán Tajumulco (4,220m). It continues past the huge caldera of Lake Atitlán and south of Guatemala City to El Salvador and also along the Honduran border to the Atlantic. To its north, beyond the PanAmerican and Atlantic Highways, the T-shaped Sierra los Cuchumatanes and its eastern extensions in Alta and Baja Verapaz are largely formed of Paleozoic and Mesozoic sediments on a crystalline base, all very folded and uplifted. To the north lies the tableland of the Petén, largely limestone; this ends at a fault line to the north of Lake Petén and the Sierra del Lacandón, which marks the boundary of the Yucatán.

The Pacific plains are largely given over to cotton and other export crops; likewise the hills, to 1,500m or above, are dominated by coffee, above which wheat, corn and beans are grown for subsistence. The native flora is not particularly similar to that in the rest of Central America, with many North America species at their southern limit here — juniper *(Juniperus)*, bald cypress

(*Taxodium*), hop hornbeam (*Ostrya*), American hornbeam (*Carpinus*), box elder (*Acer negundo*), supplejack (*Berchemia scandens*), Virginia creeper (*Parthenocissus quinquefolia*), Carolina/yellow jessamine (*Gelsemium sempervirens*), wallflower (*Erysimum*), cinquefoil (*Potentilla*), beard tongue (*Arbutus, Penstemon*), and snowberry (*Symphoricarpos*). There are at least 8,000 species of plants, including 17 conifers, of which nine are pines (compared to 38 in Mexico). Perhaps the best-known Guatemalan flower is *Cattleya skinneri*, one of the first orchids to be hybridized commercially. There are 600 species of orchids, of which 200 are endemics — it's a national joke that the national flower, the white nun orchid (*Monja blanca/Lycaste virginalis alba*) is a parasite.

There are 600 species of birds, 250 mammals, and 200 reptiles and amphibians. The national bird is the quetzal, and there are still about 45,000 in Guatemala (40,000 of them in the Cuchumatanes and the Sierra de las Minas). It really isn't hard to see them here. You can buy bird checklists for the *Biotopo del Quetzal* and for Tikal, at about a dollar apiece. Two interesting large birds, both found only in Guatemala and the neighbouring parts of Mexico are the horned guan (*pavo de cacho/Oreophasus derbianus*) in the highlands of western Guatemala and Chiapas, and the ocellated or Petén turkey (*pavo petenero, pavo ocelado/Agriocharis ocellata*), in the Verapaces, Petén and Yucatán, recognised by eye markings on its tail.

Guatemala is gorgeous for hiking. With a predominantly Indian population, who still travel as their ancestors did, on foot, there are paths everywhere, and beautifully costumed people to share them with. Although we give some specific trails to inspire confidence, you can hike anywhere that's above the treeline. But do check the security situation (the *Casa Andinista* bookshop in Antigua is the best starting place), check that there are villages in the area, and bear in mind that if you go across the grain of the country you may find yourself having to cross valleys perhaps 1,000m deep.

If **volcanoes** are your thing, buy the *Guia de los Volcanes de Guatemala* by Carlos E Prahl Redondo (Club Andino Guatemalteco 3/e 1992), which gives an outline of hiking on 37 volcanoes, as well as lists of those in El Salvador, Honduras, Nicaragua and Costa Rica. The 1:250,000 map of Guatemala department (ND15-8) covers all the volcanoes around Guatemala City, Antigua and Lake Atitlán. Information on current volcanic activity can be had from the Seismological and Vulcanological Institute (tel: 314 986). You'll need to carry plenty of water, especially if you want to camp and enjoy the marvellous dawn views. Nothing is worse than running out of water on a hot dry volcano. Oranges and lemons seem to last longer than plain water, and are more refreshing. In these circumstances there's no point in carrying dehydrated food, as you'll have to carry the water to rehydrate everything anyway. You might as well carry cans, but don't forget the can-opener (I always do) and bring all cans back — empty or full.

It's best to climb in the afternoon or even by the light of the full moon, but be sure to bring warm, windproof clothing — it's surprisingly chilly on those bare summits. The best time of year for volcano climbing is from November to January; other months are very hazy or rainy. Loose scree is tiring and very slow going; beware snakes, and the vicious spines of the *chichicaste* plant.

National parks

Environmental protection in Guatemala dates from 1892, when a forestry law banned clearing land for agriculture; this has been utterly ineffective. In the 1950s a new forestry law created 14 protected sites, ten of which are currently still protected as national parks by DIGEBOS, the state forestry enterprise; these are little known and almost undeveloped. Article 97 of the 1985 constitution obliged the state to protect the environment; in 1987 CECON (the Centre for Conservation Studies of USAC, the University of San Carlos) was put in charge of 'biotopes', of which the best-known are the *Biotopo del Quetzal* and Monterrico, as well as the university's Botanical Garden on Calle Mariscal Cruz, east of Avda Reforma in Guatemala City's Zona 10. In 1989 President Cerezo announced plans for 52 protected areas, and the next year for two large biosphere reserves in Petén (1.4m ha) and the Sierra de las Minas (236,000ha), leaving 16% of the country's area protected. Cerezo claimed that he planned to ban timber exports and to dedicate himself to ecotourism promotion on his retirement, but he was unable to provide any funding for protected areas. International pressure and aid have begun to make a difference since then. There's still very little protection of the highlands, with unique environments in the Cuchumatanes mountains notably at risk.

Ecotourism companies

Maya Expeditions, 15 Calle 1-91, Edificio Tauro #104, Zona 10 (tel/fax: 374 666); established in 1987 and easily the biggest in the country, offering rafting, hiking, bird-watching and bungee jumping.
Mesoamerica Explorers, 7 Avda 13-01, Zona 9 (2nd floor) (tel/fax: 325 045).
Panamundo, 3 Avda 16-52, Z10.
Adventure Travel, 4 Calle Oriente 14, Antigua (tel/fax: 323 228).
Aventuras sin Limites, 11 Avda 9-30, Zona 1.
Ultra Ilimitada, 4 Calle 3-11, Zona 2, Apdo 10-16901 Cobán, Alta Verapaz (tel: 511 547, fax: 511 268); they work with Adventure Travel Centre in Antigua (4 Calle Oriente 7; tel/fax: 323 228), who run a minibus to Cobán on Fridays and back on Sunday evenings).
Epiphyte Adventures, 2 Avda/2 Calle, Zona 1, Apdo 94A, Cobán (tel: 512 169).

Ecological organizations

Direción General de Bosques y Vida Silvestre (DIGEBOS), 7 Avda 6-80, Zona 13 (tel: 735 212). It's proposed to merge this with **CONAP** (*Consejo Nacional de Areas Protegidas*) and **CONAMA** (*Comisión Nacional del Medio Ambiente*) as **IRENAM** (*Institut de Recursos Naturales y Ambiente Medial*), which will be dominated by logging interests.
Centro de Estudios Conservacionistas (CECON) & **Fundación Mario Dary**, Avda La Reforma 0-63, Zona 10 (tel: 310 904, fax: 347 664).
Tamandua, 2nd floor, edif La Cúpula, 7 Avda 13-01, Zona 9 (tel: 232 2690), or

ask at the cafe on the ground floor.

Asociación Guatemalteca pro-Defensa del Medio Ambiente, 20 Calle 19-44, Zona 10 (Apdo 1352; tel: 681 327, fax: 372 084).

SOME FIESTA DAYS IN CENTRAL AMERICA

January 15	Feast of the Black Christ of Esquipulas
January 20	Day of San Sebastian
March 19	Day of San José
April 25	Day of San Marcos
June 13	Day of San Antonio
June 24	Day of San Juan (note: being John the Baptist's day, festivities may take a rather wet form)
June 29	Day of San Pedro and San Pablo
July 25	Day of Santiago (St James)
July 30	Day of San Cristobal
August 4	Day of Santo Domingo
October 4	Day of San Francisco
November 1-2	All Saints' and All Souls' Days (day of the dead — surprisingly festive)
November 11	Day of San Martin
November 25	Day of Santa Catarina
November 30	Day of San Andres
December 4	Day of Santa Barbara
December 25	Christmas Day (services only)
December 28	All Fools' Day. Beware!

Movable

Carnival	The week preceding Ash Wednesday and Lent.
Palm Sunday	The Sunday before Easter.
Holy Week	All week, but mainly on Thursday and Friday.
Holy Saturday	The day before Easter Day. Effigies of Judas are hanged and burnt.
Easter Day	Religious services rather than fiesta.

Note: Fiestas are often held on the Sunday nearest the saint's day.

Chapter Twenty-four

Central and Southern Guatemala

GUATEMALA CITY

Maps show it as *Ciudad de Guatemala*, bus *adelantes* call it *Guate'*, but most others call it 'the capital'. It's the largest city in Central America, and, in parts, one of the noisiest and dirtiest. When Aldous Huxley came here in the 1930s it was a sleepy town with a population of less than a quarter of a million, just a tenth of the country's population, but now almost 2m of the country's 9m people live here. My first impressions (on the Friday evening of the May Day weekend) were of fumes, heavy traffic heading west, long queues outside banks (and cars lining up at arrays of autobanks a dozen wide) and every tree with a man leaning on it; it didn't seem so different on later visits, either. It's not a particularly bad place to stay, but it's wiser to set up base in Antigua. Most affordable hotels are in the central Zone 1, handy for buses but not for the airport; hotels around the Trebol junction are *very* sordid, with a couple of marginal exceptions (right on the PanAmerican Highway from Antigua) — you're only 3km from the airport here, with buses 63, 83 and 85 to take you most of the way, but from Antigua it's really easier to take the airport shuttle.

Tourist information

INGUAT, the national tourist board, is at 7 Avenida 1-17, right by the railway bridge in Zona 4 (open Mon-Fri 08.15-16.00, Sat 08.15-13.00; tel: 311 333, fax: 318 893). From 06.00-08.00, 16.00-21.00 and at weekends you can also get information by phoning 314 256. They have maps and lists of hotels and main bus routes; if you need more detailed information ask for the library. There's also a very helpful office in Antigua.

Museums

The two best museums in Guatemala are both associated with the private *Universidad Francisco Marroquín*. The *Museo Ixchel* has moved to the university campus, at the east end of 6 Calle, Zona 10 (open Mon-Fri 08.00-16.50, and Sat 09.00-12.50); it's devoted to indigenous textiles, and is a riot of colours, patterns and information (some even in English). This is the place to go to help you recognize and appreciate village costumes. The *Museo Popol Vuh* (Avda La Reforma 8-60, 6th floor) deals with archaeology, and is just as impressive (open Mon-Sat 09.00-17.00). There are two natural history museums in the capital, neither very special. The better is the one at the

Botanical Garden (Calle Mariscal Cruz 1-56, Zona 10; Mon-Fri 08.00-12.00, 14.00-18.00); the National Museum of Natural History in Parque Aurora (7 Avda 6-81; Tues-Fri 09.00-16.00, Sat-Sun 09.00-12.00, 14.00-16.00) is full of rather tatty stuffed animals. The latter is opposite the National Museum of Anthropology and Ethnology, which has a pretty amazing collection of Mayan artefacts, including some surprisingly naturalistic stelae.

Gear shops

Second-hand hiking gear can be found at Mayan Mountain Bike Tours, 6 Avda Sur 12B, Antigua.

ANTIGUA

Just an hour from Guatemala City, the former capital makes a better base for most purposes, and especially if you want to take trips up any of the surrounding volcanoes. If Panajachel is the gringo resort of Guatemala, Antigua is the gringo capital, where people actually live and work: writing, researching anthropology PhDs, attending language schools, running hotels, bookstores or tour companies, as well as theatre groups, Jewish groups and HIV support groups. The town usually seems swamped by gringos except at weekends when it's full of real Guatemalans — the middle-class from the capital, who come to stroll and dine, and the highlanders who sell their *cosas tipicas* here. Then the plaza is jammed with cars (chauffeurs cleaning some and drunks peeing on others), while *mariachis* tout for business (is it a Composers' Union requirement that every song should contain the word '*corazón*'?).

Although many of the churches are still awaiting restoration, the town is still a beautiful place, with elaborate doorways, and windows often covered by metal grilles or harem-style wooden versions, which look especially good on street corners. Above the single-storey houses you can always see a volcano, not exactly casting a shadow over the town, as writers tend to claim, but impressive anyway.

It's a great place to watch video films and feed up after a spell of unrelieved rice, beans and eggs in the backcountry; but when you want to get back to rather less costly food, you'll find the only *comedors* are in the market, behind the bus station. There's a decent supermarket nearby at Alameda Santa Lucia 5, and a VISA cash machine in the *Banco Industrial*, just south of the plaza. The main plaza is always busy, but it's also worth finding the quieter Plaza San Pedro, where the vendors set up their backlooms, tied to the palm trees, and may even let gringos try their hand. The Tourist Office is now in 'Tropical Jades' at 4 Calle Oriente/3 Avda Norte, next to Doña Luisa's famous café. There are two excellent bookshops on the west side of the plaza, and the *Casa Andinista*, opposite *Doña Luisa's* at 4 Calle Oriente 5A, which is best for hiking guides and photocopied maps. Owner Mike Shawcross is planning to move away from Antigua, but the shop will remain the best source of information on the highlands; you can also hire tents and sleeping bags here. *The Rainbow Café* (7 Avda Sur/6 Calle Poniente) has the best choice of second-

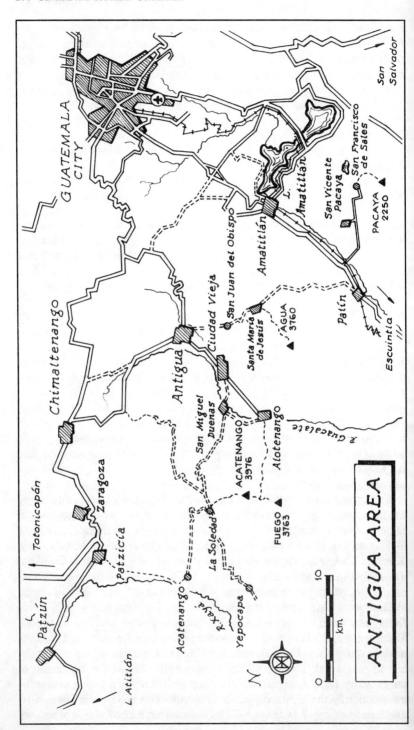

hand books. There's a public library on the plaza, the new *Biblioteca Internacional de Antigua* at 5 Calle Poniente 15, and at 5 Calle Oriente 5, CIRMA (the *Centro de Investigaciones Regionales de Mesoamérica*) houses an excellent academic library (open Mon-Fri 08.00-18.00, Sat 09.00-13.00).

Hiking around Antigua

Hikers will probably want to tackle one of the volcanoes around Antigua; in fact, almost all visitors end up taking a minibus trip to **Volcán Pacaya**, which in fact lies south of the capital and is not visible from Antigua. This is because it's active and can usually be relied on to put on a good show, and because it's relatively low at 2,550m, with a road to within 1½-2 hours of the top. The catch is that it's all too common for people to be mugged on Pacaya, and there have even been rapes and murders. Most of the tour operators claim that they will provide an armed guard and a flashlight per person, but in the event these hardly ever materialize; nor do the minibuses always get you all the way there and back. The problem is that competition is so intense that prices have fallen from around US$25 per head to US$6 in 1995, a price at which it's impossible to provide a decent service. If you think about it, the operators actually need a few robberies to dissuade tourists from going it alone, so there's a strong suspicion that they simply pay off the robbers to persuade them to hold up someone else's group. The price is of course very tempting, so if you do want to see the volcano the thing to do is to go to the plaza in Antigua at 13.45 and join the largest group; all tours leave at 14.00 and return at about 23.00. In fact most robberies seem to occur earlier in the day. Juancho, Popeye, and Quetzal Volcano Expeditions have all been mentioned as companies to avoid, but they can easily change their names. It's also risky to go to the Cerro de la Cruz, immediately overlooking the town of Antigua from the north.

It's quite easy to do it yourself; buses run from the capital's Zona 4 bus terminal at 07.00 and 15.30 to just beyond San Vicente Pacaya; alternatively take any bus towards Palín or Escuintla to the Pacaya turn and get a pick-up or one of the four daily buses. The road ends at San Francisco de Sales (1,900m), about an hour's walk from San Vicente; a 4WD track continues to the right/ south almost all the way to a TV tower on a ridge of Cerro Chino, which offers the best views of the black active cone. Circumstances permitting, it may be possible to follow the ridge up to the left to the foot of a dormant cone which you can climb to look down on the activity. What you're seeing is typical of a strombolian volcano, with steam, gases, ash, rock, lava, volcanic bombs and other sorts of pyroplastic materials.

Of the three volcanoes around Antigua, **Volcán Agua** (3,760m) is the easiest to climb and also one of the most beautiful mountains in the world, an almost perfect cone. There are some organised tours, but it's quite easy to do it yourself, and it's particularly popular with parties of young Guatemalans, who like to see the sunrise from the summit at weekends. The mountain was so named for the lake in its crater; in 1541 an earth tremor following heavy storms caused a massive landslide from the volcano's flank which drained the lake and flattened the original city of Santiago de los Caballeros, near what is now known as Ciudad Vieja de Antigua (Old Antigua). Other than this there has been no activity in historic times.

Buses (every hour or so, more on Mondays, Thursdays and Saturdays, market day in Antigua) will take you to Santa María de Jesús at 2,080m; there's a hospedaje here, and women wear fine *huipiles* with a purple diamond motif that symbolizes the volcano. Nowadays Santa María, Ciudad Vieja, and Antigua all have populations of about 25,000, although Antigua covers a much larger area and had a population of 60,000 at its peak. A rough 4WD road, starting about 1km before the entrance to Santa María, runs up to the radio masts on the rim; you can get to it from the village plaza by taking a road between two ancient columns (opposite the church) and turning right to pass the cemetery. This path intercepts the road after about a kilometre, and you can either continue along the road or look for short cuts. You'll end up crawling up scree on hands and knees in any case. It takes between three and six hours to reach the top, where you can camp either on the soccer field or on the summit; chilly, but you'll have a good view of any eruptions of Fuego. It's possible to make a day trip from Santa María, or even (with the 05.00 bus) from Antigua, but the views are likely to be poor.

When John Lloyd Stephens went up Agua in the late 1830s, his party entered thick forest 45 minutes after leaving Santa María, and gradually 'the path became steeper and muddier, the trees were so thickly crowded together, their branches and trunks covered with green excrescences, that the sun never made its way through them'. After two hours struggle they emerged exhausted from this jungle, and reached the top an hour later; in the crater they found inscriptions dating from 1548, and 1834 when a Russian, an Englishman and an American drank a bottle of champagne there. I don't believe these are still visible. Nowadays I gather it's just about possible to pedal a mountain bike to near the top of the forest; you can also hire a mule in Santa María.

The next easiest to reach is **Acatenango** (3,976m), to the west of Antigua; this and the adjacent Fuego are the least visited in the area and thus the safest from robbery. Buses run occasionally from Antigua towards Acatenango village or Yepocapa, on a poor road west from Ciudad Vieja; alternatively, take one of the far more frequent buses to San Miguel Dueñas and then hike or take a pick-up onwards. You need to get off at the Finca La Soledad (2,400m), where the trail starts just west of a soccer field (about 1,500m west of the trail shown on the 1:50,000 map). The trail starts off in fields and then enters pine forest; there's no water along the trail but there are two good camping sites. The first, about two hours up, is a grassy clearing at about 3,100m, where you need to keep left: the larger trail to the right soon peters out. Another hour or so up is another clearing, on a flat shoulder of the volcano at about 3,350m, known as La Meseta or El Conejo. This is about halfway up; it's another three or four hours to the top, almost all in forest (so not too hot). It's only about 70m climb from the treeline to the first, lower, summit, Yepocapa (3,800m); you can save some energy by skirting around this cinder cone to the saddle between the north and south peaks, from where it's a slow, tiring climb of about 200m past the crater to the higher summit, Pico Mayor. The *Club de Andinismo Guatemalteco* has a shelter on top of Yepocapa.

The last of the peaks around Antigua, **Volcán Fuego** (3,763m) is usually reached via Acatenango, camping and leaving packs at the saddle known as La Horqueta (3,250m) between the two. There's a 5m tree dahlia (*D. maxoni*) growing on this saddle, as well as fuchsia and salvia. Fuego is still active, and a plume of smoke is often visible from Antigua; when there was ice on Acatenango in March 1995 there was none on the warmer rocks of Fuego. The last major eruptions were in 1962-63, when the cone was destroyed, in 1973 and in 1974. Allow a couple of hours from the saddle, and take *plenty* of water. It's best to return to La Soledad and not by the tempting route directly down to the east to Alotenango (1,388m), unless you have a guide. (It can take ten hours to reach Fuego from Alotenango, so a day trip is impossible.) The same applies to the very difficult descents from Agua west to Alotenango or east to Palín. It is in fact possible to make a circuit of the three peaks: the best time so far is 52 hours, although it should be possible to improve on this.

LAKE ATITLÁN

From Acatenango there's a great view of another group of three volcanoes immediately to the west, around Lake Atitlán. In 1934 Aldous Huxley wrote: 'Lake Como, it seems to me, touches the limit of the permissibly picturesque; but Atitlán is Como with the embellishment of several immense volcanoes. It really is too much of a good thing.' Few other gringos, however, share these qualms, and the main town, **Panajachel**, has become a sort of gringo haven ('Gringotenango', as the *Mexico and Central American Handbook* christened it), with health food and ice cream shops, and even fax/email agencies. There's plenty of inexpensive accommodation, but camping is not as safe as it was. The regular guidebooks give exhaustive information on the fleshpots of Panajachel.

The lake is surrounded by charming indigenous villages, and there's now a fairly well established hiking route around the lake, particularly along the north shore. If you head up into the hills, you'll immediately leave 'Gringotenango' behind you and find villages where the locals are still surprised and pleased to see you. Mountain-biking is particularly rewarding on these tracks: if you hire a bike in Panajachel, check the brakes carefully.

Buses from Guatemala City follow the PanAmerican Highway to the Los Encuentros junction, south of Chichicastenango, and then loop around through Sololá, the departmental capital (with a notorious army camp and a large market) and down to Panajachel. The more direct route through Patzicía, Patzún and Godínez is narrow and little-used and recommended only as an adventurous cycle route; however, this area has a record of armed robberies — check before you take this route. The same applies to walking southeast from Panajachel through Santa Catarina Palopó and San Antonio Palopó (where the men wear kilts); from San Antonio you can take a bus or pick-up back, or take a steep path up to a *mirador* on the road northwest of Godínez. From Godínez you

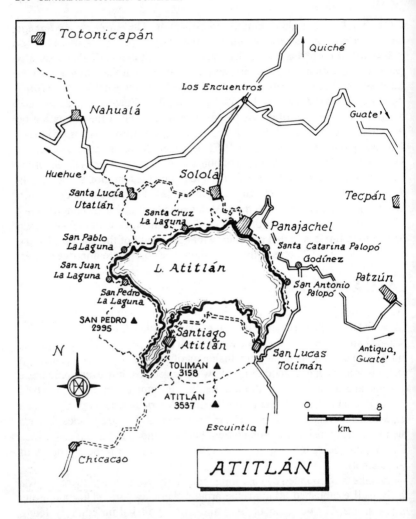

can take a bus to San Lucas Tolimán, at the southeastern corner of the lake, an unattractive place where you can change for **Santiago Atitlán**, the second largest town on the lake. Buses from Santiago all run south from San Lucas to the coastal highway; Santiago is linked to Panajachel only by boat (about six a day). It's the capital of the Tzutuhil Maya (whose men wear long purple and white shorts, while the women wear halo-like head-dresses of wound ribbon), and is probably the most traditional of the lakeside towns; in the middle of the day it's full of daytrippers, plagued by child vendors from hell, but at other times it's very peaceful. However, it had an 'unrivalled reputation for violent nastiness' until it persuaded the army to withdraw in 1990. Make a point of seeing the image of Maximón, the evil saint who drinks, smokes and wears ladino clothes: he moves from house to house, so you'll have to ask to be led to the presence. Take a bottle or some cigarettes as an offering.

The so-called **Atitlán National Park** lies about 5km northeast of Santiago; this was set up as a reserve for the *poc* or giant pied-billed grebe, which was found only on this lake. This flightless bird, twice the size of the common pied-billed grebe, was identified only in 1929, and was protected from 1959; in 1960 the airline PanAm and the tourist board introduced 2,000 largemouth bass into the lake for sport fishing, and these insatiable carnivores soon decimated the fish and crabs that both the *poc* and local *indigenos* depended on. The fishermen couldn't afford the tackle to catch bass, and couldn't spearfish because they couldn't swim. In addition, the *Thipa dominguensis* reeds in which the *poc* and its food lived were being cut faster than ever as the local human population grew. In 1968 a National Wildlife Refuge (the first in Guatemala) was set up, and by 1975 the population had risen to 232 from a minimum of about 80 in 1964. However, the 1976 earthquake opened fissures in the lakebed, so that the water level fell by 5m in the next ten years. A local coffee farmer, Edgar Bauer Ordoñez, acted as a part-time ranger for 14 years, moving 75,000 reed clumps to deeper water, until he was murdered in the early 1980s. However, the population never recovered; the earlier problems were joined by gill-nets and pollution. By 1980 the number of grebes was below 100, by 1989 there were only four, and by 1991 they were extinct, despite desperate efforts. The visitor centre, on a small island, remains open and can be a nice place to camp.

The lake has other problems: in 1965 there were just 28 weekend chalets on its shore where now there are 500, not to mention tourist developments. Off Panajachel in particular the water, which was clear to a depth of 12m, is now clouded by pollution, especially from laundry detergents.

Towering 1,600m over the village is the twin-peaked **Volcán Tolimán** (south peak 3,158m), and just south of it, the perfect cone of **Volcán Atitlán** (3,537m). They are most easily climbed from the Chanán saddle (just over 2,500m) between them; from Santiago head south and fork left along a track to the Quetzal Reserve, 54,000ha of wet premontane forest preserved since 1974. This has been described as an area of almost unnatural quiet, as though the birds had fled the war — ORPA guerrillas were based here and may still be present. It's best to check at the Municipalidad in Santiago. You can equally well go to or from San Lucas, an equal distance to the east of the saddle, via the Finca Pampojilá. Tolimán *could* be climbed in a long daytrip, if fit, but as usual it would probably be cloudy by the time you got up. Certainly to do both you'd have to camp at the saddle.

From Santiago a rough road continues around the far side of **Volcán San Pedro** to San Pedro La Laguna, the third biggest of the lakeside villages. At 2,995m this volcano is the easiest of the three to climb, but it's heavily forested and offers fewer panoramas; on the other hand it's well shaded. From San Pedro you'll need to ask to find the way through the coffee plantations, but the way is clear after an hour or so. Allow a full day for the trip, and get away by dawn if you want any views.

San Pedro itself is like Goa 20 years ago, as the 'hippies' have fled here from the commercialisation of Panajachel. It remained relatively peaceful throughout the civil war, as the villagers refused to denounce each other to the authorities. It's best reached by boat (about six a day from Panajachel, and a few from Santiago), although there is a daily bus. The local *cayucos* (dug-out canoes) are famous and can be hired.

You can walk from San Pedro back to Panajachel in a day; the road runs through San Juan La Laguna, San Pablo La Laguna (known for its bags of *maguey* fibre) and San Marcus La Laguna, and continues as a rough track to Tzununá. A path continues to Santa Cruz La Laguna, from where it's easiest to take a boat on to Panajachel; the path along the shore is precipitous and not easy to follow, although a better one climbs 600m to Sololá, from where there are plenty of buses to Panajachel.

SOUTHERN GUATEMALA

Jutiapa Department, by the Salvadoran border, is not the most exciting or visited of areas, but it does boast quite a few relatively low volcanoes which can be hiked without the crowds or robbery problems of more touristy areas. Perhaps the most attractive is Volcán Ipala (1,650m), which holds a beautiful lake of clean water in its crater, surrounded by thick forest of oak and cypress, laden with epiphytes, where you can swim and camp safely. From the El Progresso junction on the PanAmerican Highway (northeast of Jutiapa) you should head through Santa Catarina Mita and Agua Blanca to Julumichapa (35km), from where you can hike up in 2½ hours. On the other side of Agua Blanca, to the south, is Volcán Ixtepeque (1,292m); turn right off the Santa Catarina road 6km from El Progreso for the finca La Tuna, from where it's three hours to the top — the big attraction here is the large lumps of obsidian that you can pick up. To the west of Jutiapa is Volcán Amayo (or Las Flores, 1,544m) where you can see interesting caves formed by lava flows; turn left at km111 on the PanAmerican for Amayo Sitio and El Aguacate (7km), from where it's a two hour climb. Finally Volcán Chingo (1,775m) is right on the Salvadoran border and is the venue of a rally of Guatemalan and Salvadoran climbers on the Sunday before 15 September, to celebrate Central American independence. Take the PanAmerican all the way to San Cristobal Frontera, turn right/south and then left 4km after Atescatempa, to San José Contepeque, from where it's three hours.

Esquipulas, just to the north of Jutiapa, is one of the longest-established and most important pilgrimage centres in Central America, possibly dating back to the preHispanic cult of the 'Puma of Black Rain'. The Spaniards carved a Black Christ of dark liquidambar wood, which has always struck a deep chord with the Mayans. Pilgrims (mostly women) come here all year round, perhaps a million in all, but the peak is on January 15, with a lesser one on March 9. The interest for hikers is that, as with Canterbury and Santiago de Compostella, traditional pilgrim routes still run across the country to the shrine, and can be recognised by wooden crosses and by massive piles of stones known as *piedras de penitencia*, up to 20m in height and 30m in circumference. The road from Guatemala City was via San José Pinula, Mataquescuintla,

Jalapa, Ipala and Quezaltepeque, though almost all traffic now runs via the Atlantic Highway. The Piedra de los Compadres, 2km north of Esquipulas, is two rocks on top of each other, supposedly two pilgrims turned to stone for having sex while on pilgrimage. Esquipulas is also headquarters of the tri-national Montecristo-Trifinio Park.

The best known reserve on the Pacific coast is **Monterrico**, a 2,800ha *biotopo* managed by CECON to protect mangroves and turtle-nesting beaches. Its highest point is only 6m, and precipitation is just under 2m a year, so it seems implausible that this could be wet low montane forest, but that's what it is, it seems. In fact many of the trees are introduced fruit trees, such as mangos. The only mammals here are anteaters, raccoons, opossums and weasels; birds are more numerous (around 300 species), with herons, ducks, kingfishers, grebes, ospreys, Inca doves, ruddy ground-doves, and orange-fronted, orange-chinned and green parakeets. Olive ridley turtles nest from July to December, while leatherbacks nest from October to February, and the young are born around two months later. CECON has been incubating and releasing thousands of turtle eggs a year for over 15 years, as well as green iguanas and alligators; DIGEBOS also has the 3.1ha Hawaii National Park and breeding station here.

The best way to get here is to take a bus to Taxisco and then another 17km south to La Avellana (there are also three through buses a day from the Zona 4 terminal in the capital), and from there a boat for 2km through lagoons and inland channels (created in 1895). The alternative is via Iztapa (south of Escuintla): take a boat across the Río Naranjo to Puerto Viejo and then a bus (three a day) along the coast to Monterrico. The best place to stay is the *Baule Beach Hotel* (*baule* meaning leatherback turtle), next to the CECON station. If turtle-watching, swimming, surfing and taking boats through the lagoons begin to pall, there's a 1.3km loop walk which offers excellent bird-watching.

At Tilapa, near the Mexican border, the **Reserva El Manchón** (or Mangrove Park) is another turtle-nesting site, also boasting waterbirds such as egrets, blue herons and kingfishers.

Carved motif on dugout canoe, Lake Atitlán

Chapter Twenty-five

The Western Highlands

This is undoubtedly one of the best areas in the world for hiking through largely unspoilt mountains inhabited by colourfully dressed indigenous people. It was, of course, ravaged by the civil war in the 1980s, but is now happily returning to something like normal. Embassies and so on still advise against coming here, but in fact it's safer than anywhere in Guatemala City. Just be sure you are properly equipped and carry enough food.

Here follows an account (written in 1978) by Mark Fischer of hiking and staying with villagers in this area:

'The terrain in the northwest corner of Guatemala is varied and mountainous. Near the Mexican border is low, hot and dry country where peanuts and maize are the chief crops. The north face of the Cuchumatanes mountains is lush and green, receiving copious rainfall from the Caribbean, and is drained by parallel rivers cutting deep canyons in their northerly course towards Mexico and the Caribbean. These drop steeply, giving way to low, flat, hot, tropical jungles where tall trees, monkeys and mosquitoes abound. Between the canyons on the north slope of the mountains are high ridges, populated wherever the land offers a combination of sufficient flat space and an adequate source of water. Deep in the tropical gorges are occasional fincas where ladino landlords grow coffee, bananas, cardamom, maize and sugar cane. The indigenos slash and burn the forested slopes to plant their milpas of maize and beans. Along the high summits are found wheat fields, occasional potato patches and herds of sheep and goats tended by barefoot girls. To the south of the ridge, in the rain shadow, the valleys are dry, almost desert-like, and dominated by cactus and mesquite except along the valley bottoms where fruit trees and greenness prevail.

'Thus there is incredible variety and it's possible to choose and change habitats with facility. The low tropical canyons generally offer hot humid days and warm nights, an abundance of greenery and lazy bathing by the raging rivers in the blazing sun. A soothing torpor is created by the hot sun and air, the timeless, continual roaring of the river, the background symphony of insects and birds, and the womblike enclosure amongst the towering trees. Not even the mosquitoes seem able to arouse much indignation from the hiker.

'The middle altitudes present a variable and more bracing climate. The hot sun is tempered by cool, pleasant breezes; sunbathing and washing by mountain streams are joyful. But there are days when the weather turns sour. Dense overcasts loom lower and lower over the slopes until all is obscured in an opaque fog known locally as *nublina*. So moist is this fog that should you venture forth into it you will be soaking wet within five minutes. It comes in the form of a fine spray, which can travel horizontally as well as vertically, forcing people to close the doors and windows of their already gloomy and smoky houses.

'Nublina and rain have disastrous effects on trail conditions, turning the narrow paths into seemingly bottomless mud-bogs known locally as *fangas*. These are worst in jungle stretches of trail where tall trees and hanging vines prevent the entry of sunlight and drying breezes. Sloshing up a steep, dark, damp jungle mud-pit in the cool, humid, close air, with fantasies of snakes stimulated by the sinuous tree roots undulating through the mud of the trail, can be a strenuous and frightening experience. The mud can also be hazardous on heavily travelled trails leading to and from the roadheads. Numerous pack-animals knead the mud until there is no passage for the pedestrian except through the squishy *fanga*. Sometimes the trail is like a washboard with semi-solid ridges alternating with abysmal bogs; at other times, it resembles a steep ski slope in spring, with hardened moguls amidst yucky muddy troughs.

'The summits are covered with pine and oak forest which in turn are covered with iridescent mosses and clinging orchids. The rainfall is less heavy, but periods of bright sunshine are also rarer. Clouds are continually forming as mists rise up the slopes from the valleys below. One minute finds you blissfully soaking up brilliant sunshine in the clear mountain air, the next finds you putting on your warmest coat as the clouds envelop you and the air is piercingly cold. At night temperatures drop to near freezing point. Expansive views of distant ranges, volcanoes and valleys, and cool clean air heighten your consciousness and the enjoyment of your hike.

'The people are almost entirely indigenous, speaking their own languages, of which the most important are Chuj, Kanjobal, Mam, Ixil and Quiché. Most of the men have picked up Spanish from their fathers or in school (taught by *maestros* imported from more developed parts of the country), and use it when in town to buy supplies or visit a doctor. The women almost uniformly cannot speak any Spanish beyond the simplest greetings.

'This makes things difficult when in search of food, shelter or advice about trails. Often the people are quite shy, even fearful. During the day many of the men are away working in the fields and forests, leaving the women and children at home. They may hide, and dogs will bark and menace you with bared teeth. It helps to pick up a few pebbles, or at least pretend to do so. I would look for huts where a man was at home, relaxing on the patio or chatting inside, or where the children showed a friendly response instead of fleeing.

'Within minutes of arriving in a village, most of the population was aware of my presence through their rapid word-of-mouth communication system. In many cases you will be taken to sleep in the school building; otherwise the villagers know which of their neighbours is the most accustomed to strangers, who is the most intrepid and who is sufficiently dominant in the village hierarchy to receive the honour of the unexpected guest. Be aware that the villagers are helping in the choice of an appropriate house, watch for subtle and indefinable cues, and you will usually find yourself with a family who will treat you well.

'There are, of course, all kinds and degrees of hospitality. A host family may smother you and question your every move and every possession, or may ignore you, giving you a separate space, possibly in a separate hut. The golden mean between these extremes results in a delightful experience. The family receives you warmly, but respects whatever amount of space you require; they take great interest in you but do not change their daily routine. In continuing with their own affairs, they allow you to continue with yours. When I find this, I often stay several days. (We would stress that even if you leave your tent behind, you should always carry enough food; the people and the land are poor and there is barely enough food for all.)

'Travelling far with brief overnight stops can give you a broad overview of a region. Staying in one place for longer periods gives a deeper appreciation of the life going on there. The people are early risers and early retirers. Women are often up at the first cock-crow, a couple of hours before dawn, grinding corn on the stone *metate*. Men rise at dawn to drink home-roasted and home-ground coffee sweetened with black sugar and to eat the freshly cooked *tortillas*. They then set out with machetes and hoes to tend fields, make fences, drive cattle, etc. The women keep the kitchen fire going on the floor all the time, boiling maize and ashes in pots to be later ground into *masa* and patted into *tortillas*, and cooking vegetables and beans. They must also go out for fuelwood or water, which they carry on their heads, walking barefoot with fine posture on muddy, slippery paths. When not cooking, washing clothes, nursing babies or gossiping, the women are usually weaving or embroidering. Then there is drying and shelling of coffee and *frijoles*, basket-making, and shooing invading chickens out of the kitchens and gardens.

'Life seems continuous and slow. There are no great variations in seasons, only more or less rainy to more or less dry. The oranges become ripe, then bananas and mangoes. There are no long-range divisions of time or plans; it becomes time to fence that field, to harvest that corn, for this daughter to take a husband, and so forth. Many people have never heard of the USA or Europe or of languages other than their own and Spanish (known as *castil'*). They may ask if the USA is bigger than Guatemala, or if it is a state in Mexico. People are generally interested in the simple facts of family life — are you married, how many brothers, sisters or children you have, and why your parents let you go so far from home. They cannot conceive how families can split up, with parents and children living in separate houses and even in separate villages.'

I describe hikes in three separate areas of the northwest, first a very short but superb walk right by the PanAmerican Highway, then others around Todos Santos Cuchumatán, where you'll find men and women in wonderful costumes living beneath the highest limestone peaks in the country, and lastly a big sweep right across the much emptier area to the north, from Cotzal all the way to Nentón on the Mexican border.

November to March are the coldest months (with frequent frost above 3,000m), and April to October are the wettest; above 2,300m there's up to 1,000mm of precipitation pa. From 1,000-2,000m there's a mixed forest of conifers, oaks, *Compositae* and legumes, with shrubs and flowering herbaceous plants. Above 2,000m you can find five species of pine (*Pinus oocarpa*, *P. montezumae* up to 2,700m, and *P. ayachuite*, *P. rudis* and *P. pseudostrobus* to 3,400m), with *Arbutus xalapensis* up to 2,750m, oaks (*Quercus acatenangensis* and *Q. pilicaulis*) and cypress (*Cupressus lusitanica*) to 2,850m, and yew (*Taxus globosa*) to 3,000m. From here up to 3,400m you can see fir (*Abies guatemalensis*), and stunted frost-resistant trees such as *Alnus arguta*, *A. firmifolia*, *Baccharis sp*, *Buddleia nitida*, *Acaena elongata* and *Pernettya ciliata*, with smaller plants such as *Chiranthodendron pentadactyla* (little handflower tree), *Oreopanax capitatum*, *Rubus trilobus*, *Muhlenbergia macroura*, *M. nigra*, *Trifolium amabile*, *Geranium alpicola*, *Arenaria sp*, *Viola sp*, mallow, and fuchsia.

Above these are bare alpine heights, with festuca grass, and Pleistocene relics such as *Draba volcanica*, *Arctostaphylus sp*, *Geranium alpicola*, *Aplopappus stoloniferus* and *Weldenia candida*; just about the only trees are junipers (*Juniperus standleyi*). You'll also see *milpas* of mixed corn, squash and beans up to about 2,200m, with corn fields up to 3,100m, and wheat, barley, and beans above. Sheep (raised for wool, not meat) graze above 2,800m.

Nahualá to Totonicapán

The first hike is from **Nahualá** to **Totonicapán** (or the other way — both towns are at about 2,500m, so it makes no odds). The lower slopes are very fertile, with up to a metre of good volcanic soil; higher up the soils are thinner, with rhiolitic lava exposed in many places. The department of Totonicapán is one of the most densely populated in the highlands, but until recently it managed to preserve large areas of forest with traditional communal management. The white pine (*Pinus ayachuite*) is ideal for furniture-making, and fortunately the joiners of Totonicapán and Quetzaltenango have for a long time recognised the need to conserve their prime resource. Unfortunately civil war, evangelical religion and other influences of the modern world have undermined respect for the traditional structures, and now many families disregard the limit of two trees a year. Between 1964 and 1990 the department's population increased by 70% (120,000), and the demand for fuelwood by at least as much. In addition armed gangs come in at full moon to strip pine bark, used in the tanneries of Huehuetanango to replace expensive imported dyes: this kills *Pinus ayachuite*, which is replaced by coloured pine (*Pinus rudis*), which is more susceptible to the pine-borer beetle (*gorgojo del piño/Dendroctonus sp*), resisted by the healthy mixed forest until now. On the main Cordillera María Tecún, north of Totonicapán, only 7% of the forest cover was lost between 1954 and 1972 when the neighbouring departments of Quiché and Sololá lost 60% of their forest, but 14% was lost between 1974 and 1979. Since then things have got

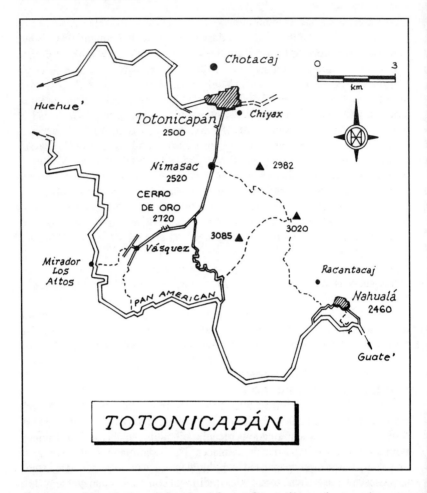

far worse, although there are at least four reforestation projects under way; however, the route described takes you through largely traditionally managed fields and woods.

The older Quiché men of Nahualá wear tweedy kilts, which can only be described as cute, with faded orange shirts and straw hats; the women are shy, and wear dark blue skirts with rainbow-coloured shawls. Their long *huipiles*, worn tucked inside their skirt due to the cold climate, are unique due to the deliberate choice of colours that will run onto the white base. The town is not unattractive, with vendors in front of a good colonial church, but few visitors stop, due to lack of accommodation. However, its Sunday market is very lively. It lies just a few hundred metres from the PanAmerican, and any bus passing by will drop you at the *puente* or bridge, at km156.5 (2,450m), from where a path leads in about ten minutes past the cemetery and soccer field to the east end of the town.

If you can get off the bus almost a kilometre further west you can cut across the fields to the start of the trail and avoid the town altogether. Otherwise, follow the road west from the plaza, cross a bridge and swing left (that's the gate to another cemetery ahead) and take a short cut down to another bridge to the right. Turn right just two minutes beyond this bridge, onto a track which soon climbs up a couple of hairpin bends and ends after 20 minutes, just after a *pila* (laundry basin) which is your last source of water. The next stretch is a hellishly steep climb straight up the escarpment, although it only lasts 10-15 minutes — I took the direct route, although there's an easier one to the left. After this the path climbs more easily up and around to the right, above some cliffs; after five minutes the higher route is the better one. In another ten minutes you reach the plateau and pine-trees at about 2,800m; fork right in another ten minutes above a very rocky eroded section. The next stretch is delightful, a sunken track lined with cactus; swing left and in just over 15 minutes you'll reach the head of the valley to your left, and turn 90° left across it. In five more minutes you'll reach a junction just west of a hill of 3,020m; the path ahead continues pretty much on the level for 5km to reach the highway again at km167, which would also make a good circuit. This stretch of road at 3,000m-plus is known locally as Alaska, due to the regular frosts, and haze permitting has superb views; it's a great bus ride.

Turning right, you can fork left almost at once onto a narrow but well-used path down a valley lined with beautifully-made terraces. After ten minutes turn left down the valley of the Río Samalá (if you're coming the other way, the turning is three minutes after a good little stone bridge). Follow the path over a low ridge, with what seems to be a disused dam to the right, and then drop steeply on a stone-flagged track into a dramatic gorge. After 15 minutes you reach a bridge built in 1991; the track is far older, but I really have no idea quite how old. It drops for another ten minutes, and you then have a level walk-out of another 15 minutes to reach the road in Nimasac (2,520m), 2.5km south of Totonicapán. There are regular buses along this road until 18.00; to the right as you head north are a couple of nice old colonial bridges. Toto' itself has some excellent food shops, and would be a great place to stock up before hiking. Most of the machine-made *huipiles* seen across Guatemala are manufactured here. There are plenty of buses to Cuatro Caminos, the junction for Quezaltenango on the PanAmerican Highway, 14km from Totonicapán.

THE CUCHUMATANES

Huehuetenango is also a good base, with buses to everywhere in the northwest of the country from the new terminal 2km southwest, on the road to the PanAmerican Highway (reached by buses 1 and 11). It's a mining centre at 1,902m, and a relatively cosmopolitan place, in total contrast to the highland villages. Girls whizz around on scooters, while Maya women come in from the hinterland with huge baskets of produce on their heads (and a huge polythene sheet over everything when it rains).

Immediately north is the wall of the Cuchumatanes, schists and serpentines

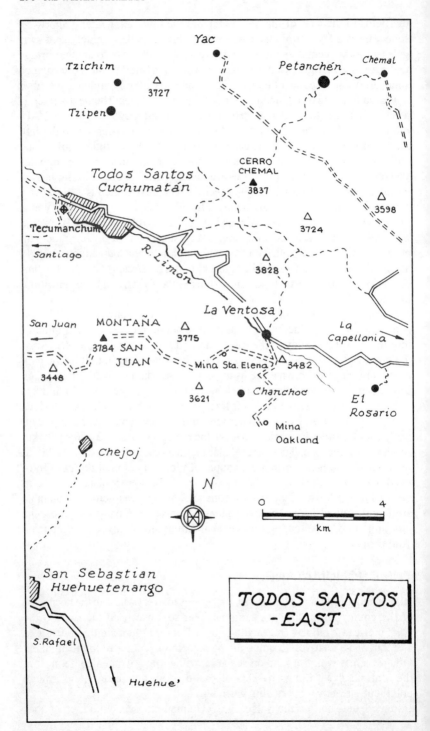

Yac

Tzichim

Tzipen

△ 3727

Petanchén

Chemal

Todos Santos
Cuchumatán

CERRO
CHEMAL
▲ 3837

△ 3598

Tecumanchum

△ 3724

Santiago

R. Limón

△ 3828

La Ventosa

San Juan

MONTAÑA

△ 3775

La
Capellania

▲ 3784 SAN
JUAN

△ 3448

Mina Sta. Elena

△ 3482

△ 3621

Chanchoc

El
Rosario

Mina
Oakland

Chejoj

N

0   4
km

San Sebastian
Huehuetenango

TODOS SANTOS
-EAST

S. Rafael

Huehue'

with Palaeozoic shales and sandstones above, all capped with Mesozoic limestones and very small patches of Tertiary sandstone and marl. There's great hiking here, and some wonderful villages. The place not to miss is **Todos Santos Cuchumatán**, where men as well as women wear *traje* or traditional costume. Men wear striped red-and-white trousers, short black *sobre pantalones* to protect the trousers from wear, and shirts with long brilliantly embroidered collars, always displayed over anything they may be wearing over their shirt. Their leather sandals with large heel cups are unique, and they also carry crocheted bags which they make themselves. Women wear dark blue skirts and gorgeous red *huipiles*. There are two or three buses a day from Huehue', but I describe a route in from the main road north, which takes you over the highest peak in the Cuchumatanes; you can then continue south all the way to the PanAmerican Highway.

Buses towards Todos Santos Cuchumatán, Soloma, San Miguel Acatán and Barillas crawl up in second gear to crest the hill at km281, just before La Capellaria, the junction east towards Salquil Grande. Now you're on a limestone plateau that looks bizarrely Irish, with turf hedges, sheep and stones scattered or in piles, yet with 3m-tall phallic cacti. There are a couple of comedors, where buses may stop, and then Paquix (km288.5), the junction left/west to Todos Santos Cuchumatán, after which the kilometre posts disappear. You need to get off at Chemal, the junction for Petanchén; bus-drivers have a vague idea where this is, but Chemal is more an area than a specific spot. The bus runs up a rocky valley and then drops a bit; just after two tracks turning right you may spot, to the left, a stream going underground, just on the right-hand edge of the Todos Santos map (no 1862-1). Just beyond this, you should stop the bus and get off at a track to the left/west, at the point marked as 3,387m on the map. Chemal means 'the windy place' and gives its name to a fascinating anthropological account of life in Todos Santos: Maud Oakes' *Beyond the Windy Place*.

It's under 3km west to Petanchén; the track can be vague in places, so follow the bicycle tracks and keep asking the way. Before long you'll cross the head of a valley and climb southwest into the scattered settlement. Following drystone walls (of a sort), you'll soon cross a 4WD road from Yac, which soon doubles back and comes in from the left. After ten minutes turn left onto a better road which winds up to a minor ridge, less than half an hour after entering the village. Five minutes beyond this, by a breeze-block house, you'll reach a dirt road from Yac to the main road, about 5km southeast. The highest peak in the Cuchumatanes, Cerro Chemal, is in front of you, and you can strike out towards it across the dry, peaty turf, following a side ridge and climbing over a few walls. There are houses here and a field just below the summit, although little but stones and a few cypress seem to grow here.

It was an easy 35 minutes wander up to the 3,837m summit, where there's a superb example of limestone pavement, slabs of rock eroded into weird (and sharp) shapes and patterns. On the far side of the ridge there are big but easy limestone steps; heading southwest you'll cross a featureless grassy dip and find a path continuing onto a minor ridge and to the left. About ten minutes from the summit you'll cross a path by a pond, and if you continue straight on you'll reach a shepherd's hut on a ridge overlooking the Todos Santos (or Río Limón) valley. I must admit that I had some navigational problems here, due to rain, fog and a misbehaving compass (there's a large hunk of iron somewhere in these mountains!), and the path I ended up taking down into the valley is pretty poor, in fact it's hardly a path at all. What you should do is to follow either the ridge or the path by the pond southeast for 4km, beyond a peak of 3,828m, to a broad gentle shoulder which leads more or less south to the pass of La Ventosa (3,405m) where you can pick up the road to Todos Santos.

What I did, briefly, was to pass to the north of a peak marked as 3,798m, and head downhill on a well-used path which turns out to be used only by fuelwood cutters; this descends steadily enough at first but then traverses right before dropping down below scree — straight ahead are some good cliffs and caves. The path is more or less swallowed up by undergrowth, but gradually revives as signs of wood-cutting reappear; it follows a steep watercourse, and at one point I had to drop my backpack down out of sight and climb down. However, there's a way around all other obstacles; at a clearing above an impassable dry waterfall a good path goes uphill to the left, traverses across and soon drops out of the forest. At once a good dry path became a nightmare of slippery mud through fields, but eventually (after a net minimum of an hour or so) I emerged on the road at 2,780m, just above a sign giving the distance to Todos Santos as 6km. The village is down at 2,470m, with three cheap but cheerful hospedajes; there's also a language school, so the Mam people are not bothered by the sight of gringos. The *Hospedaje Casa Familiar* is the one to head for if you want to learn about weaving (or the *chu* or sauna). The atmosphere is delightful and it's well worth staying a full day here; there is even a museum now, on the south side of the plaza.

Traffic is not plentiful on this road, but it shouldn't matter too much in this direction. Returning up the hill is another matter, and it's well worth catching the bus at about 05.30 if you want to do the fairly long and strenuous hike described here; a shorter and easier variant starts from Todos Santos itself, and there's a bus at 11.30 if you want to return to Huehue'. To see more of the high country, get the bus back 12km to La Ventosa (this is definitely not a place you want to sleep, especially with the option of stopping in Todos Santos) and turn right/south onto a 4WD road right at the pass.

It's an easy 15 minutes climb to a ridge at 3,482m where the road swings sharply right and climbs easily another 100m; you're on sandstone here, and there's even water to prove it — quite unlike the limestone all around. After 30 minutes you'll pass the Mina Santa Elena, a nice grassy site, although there's little left of the mine, and after another five minutes you'll pass an impressive limestone dyke (a long outcrop marching in a straight line across the country) and fork right into a broad grassy valley, with sheep grazing. In 15 minutes you'll reach one ridge and continue up to the next (at 3,650m) in another 15 minutes; a path goes straight up the 3,700m hill to the left, but you should keep to the right and then turn left behind the hill after ten minutes, at the end of the meadow. A minor path heads into the pines, passing along the left/south side of a ridge; after ten minutes this drops down to the left, leading to the village of Chejoj, but I took a very small path onwards, dropping down to get around a thick patch of juniper and then climbing steadily through open pines to reach a grassy saddle in 30-40 minutes. From here it takes under ten minutes to reach the summit of the Montaña San Juan (3,784m) immediately to the left/west. There are a few metal poles marking the summit, and wide views when the weather is clear.

The descent to the west is not easy, and should not be undertaken alone or by anyone without experience of scrambling. There is a path for much of the way, but it's not used by big people with backpacks. Going down a firebreak west to the nearest saddle, you'll find a vague path left around the hilltop; keep above a flat grassy shoulder, and then (after about half an hour) drop down into the trees towards the pass — which should by now be visible. Soon you're out of the trees scrambling down limestone blocks again: beware their sharp edges, which might lead you to think that neolithic man had chipped millions of arrow-heads off these rocks; but no, this is entirely due to the action of water. It should take about 40 minutes to clamber down to the pass (3,250m), or the huts just to its south. The route through the pass, from Chejoj to Todos Santos and Santiago Chimaltenango, is just a sheep-track at this point, but easy enough going.

From here you still have around 11km to cover if you want to go to Santiago, but it's pretty easy going, following an open ridge almost all the way. From the pass the path traverses along the south side of the valley; after ten minutes keep to the bottom of the patch of pines, and you'll come to a break in the ridge and a junction left to San Juan Atitán, about 3km away. This is a very scattered village, with its centre at about 2,440m, and is linked by road to the PanAmerican Highway. There's nowhere to stay and, predictably, the bus to Huehuetenango leaves at 05.30 — but there are pick-ups to San Sebastián Huehuetenango, on the Highway (km276.5) at 1,715m, at other times. However, it's worth seeing as it's a very traditional village where men wear red shirts, white trousers and long wool coats based on a Spanish pattern.

The main path continues westwards along the ridge, and forks left where it splits after 12-15 minutes, just before the first path comes in from San Juan. The path drops more steeply, and after ten minutes reaches the pass (at 2,800m) where the path from Todos Santos to San Juan crosses. It's far simpler to come this way from Todos Santos, so here's Hilary's 1978 description of the route:

'It only takes about five hours from Todos Santos to San Juan, so your best plan is to arrive in Todos Santos in time for the Saturday market, enjoy that scene until after lunch, and then set off up the mountain. This way you can camp at the most idyllic spot, about 2½ hours after you set out. Equally, if you left early in the morning you could get to the PanAmerican and be back in Huehue' by nightfall. It's a rugged walk, steeply up and down all the way, but worth taking time over.

'Take the wide trail that starts uphill opposite the church in Todos Santos. It is broad and winding all the way to San Juan. A few minutes after starting your walk, look out for a path leading back to your left. Does that hillock look like a familiar shape? It's a Mayan pyramid, Tecumanchum, and a lovely spot to take your last look back at Todos Santos. Nearby are two charred crosses, where we saw the ritual sacrifice of a turkey (remember the cross was also a Mayan symbol for the Four Ways). Even if you aren't as lucky as we were, you will see the remains of burnt offerings, blood and candles.

'The climb to the top of the pass will take at most two hours, and you will find water along the way. At the top of the ridge (2,800m) the trail forks and you should take the path to the left for San Juan, the one that descends into a valley with a small cluster of huts. There are several smaller trails that branch off, but you should stay on the wide, rutted main trail which crosses four streams. Each of these provides an excellent campsite, but the first is perfect: flat ground, clean water and splendid trees.

'After the streams you climb up to the top of a ridge where the trail splits into a confusion of six alternatives; the second from the left is probably the best choice to bring you into the centre of the village.'

To reach **Santiago Chimaltenango**, you should turn west along the ridge at this junction; this passes springs and after 15 minutes crosses a 4WD track south of Coltón and passes north of a craggy limestone peak of 2,835m. After 20 more minutes the path runs into a half-built 4WD road from the left, below Cerro El Pichón (2,838m); in 1995 this came to an end just seven minutes further on, with a pony track continuing. In 20 minutes this reaches Bella Vista, with a houses, a kiosk and a hilltop cemetery, and crosses to the south side of the ridge. Santiago is soon visible below to the left, but it's still a way to go. The path continues along the ridge, up as much as down, for ten minutes, then zigs down, continues along the hillside, zigs down, continues along the hillside and finally, after 30 more minutes, enters Santiago (2,260m) by a very small path arriving at the rear of the church.

This is an attractive village, little visited by gringos, where the women wear very attractive costumes. At the moment the only place to stay is a basic room in the *Minitienda La Benedición*, down the hill below the market and church, but the municipality is said to be building its own visitor accommodation. The only buses to Huehue' leave at 05.00, and there's little other traffic. You can walk down the road through San Pedro Necta to the PanAmerican Highway (km301¾) in about three hours, or through the Río Chanjón gorge in about 2½ hours. To go this way, you need to follow the dirt road west past the village cemetery for 50 minutes, turning left (just below 2,200m) onto a good path to the left. There are various routes down through the village of Ixconlaj, but the one I took seems as good as any. This forks left after eight minutes and zigzags down; after five minutes left I turned right into coffee bushes. This is just a small path, but after five more minutes it turns left onto a better one and heads down to the right across a stream, before zig-zagging down from the end of the ridge, to reach the Ixconlaj bridge (built in 1993) at 1,700m in 20 minutes.

The track on follows the left side of the Río Chanjón, rising and falling

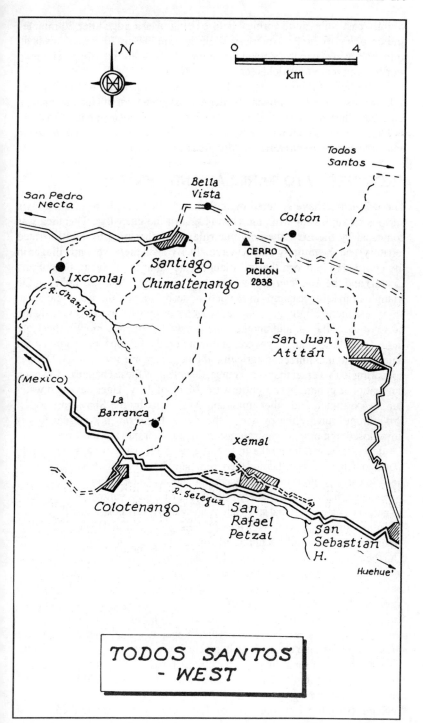

TODOS SANTOS
- WEST

slightly past some good springs, before rising over a ridge after 30 minutes and dropping to the PanAmerican Highway (km294) in 20 more. This is an enjoyable walk, passing donkeys bringing loads up to the village and men working in precipitous fields (dreadful trade...).

The Highway follows the lovely Saleguá valley, which climbs 1,000m in its 65km course from the Mexican border to a pass just west of Huehuetenango. Like the other east-west valleys of Huehuetenango department, it has thin soil and a semi-arid climate, supporting only *Pinus oocarpa*, *P. montezumae* and *Taxodium mucronatum*, the Montezuma bald cypress.

FROM NEBAJ TO BARILLAS AND NENTÓN

The Ixil people have suffered more than any other people from the army's various strategies for winning the war against the guerrillas. This area was contested by the EGP, the only guerrilla group that tried to hold liberated territory, and the military reacted violently. By 1988 there were no villages in the entire area between the Ixil triangle (the villages of Nebaj, Chajul and Cotzal) and the Mexican border, and the entire population was either in the triangle or in refugee camps in Mexico, or dead. Nor was there a single priest anywhere in the region to denounce what the army was up to. Now there are 60 resettled villages, and another one is established each month; these are more centralised than they were, and more on the hilltops, not so much for defence as to maximize the agricultural land. There are also new 4WD roads appearing in this area; maps, of course, do not show these changes. However, navigation is generally straightforward. Many of the villages have had water supplies installed and other important work done by the Shawcross Relief Programme, run by the owner of the *Casa Andinista* in Antigua; this is now closed, but other organisations are taking over most of the work.

I describe here a long hike in two stages of at least two days each, from Cotzal or Chajul to Barillas and then from San Mateo Ixtatán to Nentón. You'll need to carry all your food, but accommodation can be found in schools and so on along the way. The scenery is fantastic, with huge valleys and long steep ridges, and some forest that still shelters quetzals. Hourly buses from the capital, and others from Xela, will take you to **Quiché** (Santa Cruz del Quiché, 2,020m), where the asphalt ends. Kumarcaaj (or Utatlán), the ancient capital of the Quiché Maya, lies 3km west along 10 Calle, surrounded by gorges, and makes a good outing. This is in fact the road to Totonicapán; if you hiked there from Nahualá (see above), you might be tempted to hike the 37km on to here. It's very rough and there's not a lot of traffic. Otherwise Quiché is a quiet place except on market days (Thursday and Sunday), but you're bound to pass through. Three buses a day head north to Nebaj; it's a bad road through steep hills, and buses take about five hours. However, it is spectacular, especially where the road drops down to Sacapulas (crossroads with the Huehue'-Aguacatán-Uspantán-Cobán road) and then climbs about 1,000m out of the valley of the Río Negro.

Nebaj (strictly Santa María Nebaj, 1,907m) is the gateway to the Ixil land,

and the best place to base yourself: inevitably travellers gravitate to the *Pensión Tres Hermanas* (although only two sisters are now alive). We'd heard that the Nebaj *huipiles* are some of the most beautiful in all Guatemala, but nothing could have prepared us for their astonishing colours, geometric design and embellishments. Women wear bright red skirts and long red, purple, green and yellow *huipiles*; for festivals men may still wear scarlet jackets with white trousers. There's no craft co-operative, but plenty of people are keen to sell their wares. The *Rough Guide* gives details of walks west past preHispanic archeological sites to Acul (the first 'model village', set up by the army in 1982, mixing Ixil and Quiché people in order to undermine their cultural identity) and, about 2km beyond, the Hacienda San Antonio, where an Italian family make great cheese. Anthony Daniels described this as 'a lost valley of paradisiacal beauty, in a glorious stadium of mountains'. You can walk on in a day from Acul to Aguacatán; turn left after crossing the bridge, pass the cemetery on your right, and follow the obvious trail. You'll cross a very rocky and rutted section of path, made from sun-baked red sand, and pass two small red lakes, meeting the road a few kilometres before Aguacatán. There's also a walk from Nebaj to a waterfall: take the road north to the bridge (20 minutes) and then a track left along the river for 40 minutes.

However, there's no need to stop in Nebaj; the last bus from Quiché, at 14.00, continues to Cotzal and the Finca San Francisco. The only bus to Chajul seems to be on Sundays, leaving Nebaj at midday, but there are trucks and vans to both villages. There's no hospedaje in either, but you can ask for a room at the *farmacía* in Cotzal or the post office in Chajul. It's a nice enough walk from Nebaj to either village, taking about four hours; there's also a new road from (San Juan) Cotzal (1,797m) north to (San Gaspar) Chajul (1,991m). **Cotzal** in particular is a rather odd place, where people are distrustful of outsiders: the first Civil Defence Patrol was set up here and it's felt the effects of a great deal of violence over the years. **Chajul** is more attractive; the women wear red skirts, red or blue *huipiles*, and a head-dress with huge pompoms, and you'll be met by young girls with these for sale. In the barnlike church, look at the statues flanking the altar: they were dressed in police uniforms, to help them protect the patron, the army dressed them in military uniforms, perhaps to improve their own image, and when I saw them they were in the local men's *traje*.

To get from Cotzal to Chajul, head out of town on the Nebaj road, which rises and takes 90° turns right and left; the new road heads right signposted to a cafe. If you continue across the bridge and go straight ahead after two minutes where the road takes another right-angle turn to the left, you can take a footpath over the hills and due north to join the road about half way along.

From Chajul the route north starts on the north side of the church, turning left at the top and then forking right above the wash-house, climbing to a pass in 15 minutes. This is a dirt road which takes a big sweep to the left to climb onwards; hikers can take an obvious short cut right, parallel to a power line, rejoining the road ten minutes from the first pass. The road continues across a karst plateau for 6km to Juil (after 3.5km ignore the right turn to Xetenam);

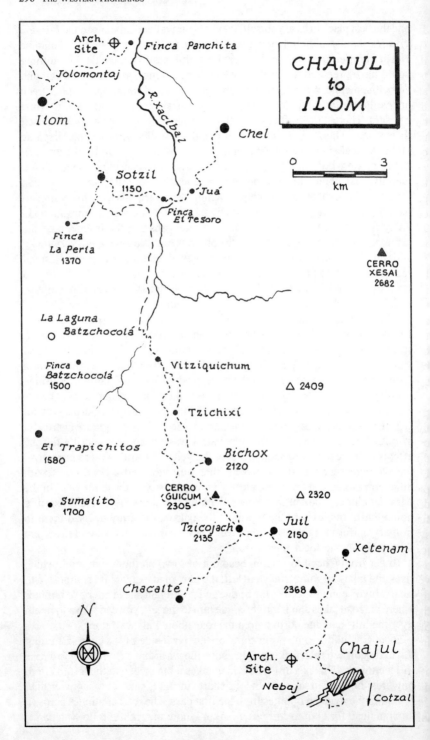

Juil is just to the right off the road, which continues to a junction at Tzicojach (2,135m), about 800m further on. There's now only one house here, although the map shows it as a more sizeable village; you should turn right here to take the highest route to Vitziquichum. The new road to the left is supposed to be a through road to Ilom and the Finca La Perla, passing a spectacular waterfall, but there are so many geological problems that it seems unlikely ever to be opened; an older track swings left from this to Chacalté, 3km southwest, which is the only place where a massacre by the EGP guerrillas (in 1983) has been confirmed.

The dirt road to the right climbs for 20 minutes and then swings left to traverse along the side of Cerro Guicum at about 2,100m; after 30 minutes it passes through the hamlet of Bichox (shown on the map as Xecanuleu). You can take a short cut across the mouth of this valley, but it's not really worth it. The road begins to drop steadily, through some remnants of good cloudforest, where I saw my first quetzal. It's 4km as the quetzal flies from Bichox to **Vitziquichum** (pronounced Vitzi-kechung), but rather more through the hairpin bends, a good hour's walk. The road ends here, faced with the well-nigh impassable obstacle of the Xaclbal valley; if you got a ride this far, you could then hike to Yula San Juan, where you can get another pick-up onwards, in about ten hours. A path turns off to the right across a grassy promontory with two roofed graves and drops steeply down through pines to reach a covered bridge in 25 minutes (at about 950m). This is not impassable to mountain bikes, although you'd have to wheel them down this path. There's a good spring on the far side, so it makes a good place for lunch.

There's a steep climb for at least 20 minutes to a makeshift stall and a parked bulldozer — this must have come in from the north, but, as you'll find, there's certainly not a passable road now. Over about 3km the track drops only from 1,100m to 1,000m, and it's easy to make good speed in either direction. After 40 minutes you reach a point at which you can look over the Finca El Tesoro and Juá and up the Río Chel, to the northeast. As with most places in this area, there were massacres at Juá and Chel, as at Amajchel, a dozen kilometres beyond, one of the EGP's last strongholds. Ten minutes further on a path drops down to the right, leading to Chel, and the main track swings to the left and up a side valley, the Río Ixtapil. After ten minutes it joins a good dirt road coming up from El Tesoro and climbs steadily, reaching a kiosk in the middle of nowhere after 15 minutes. Three minutes further on you should turn right onto a small path: the road continues for a kilometre to the Finca La Perla, where the EGP opened their campaign in 1975 by killing the finca's owner. Anthony Daniels came here (by plane), and Chapter 17 of *Sweet Waist of America* is devoted to understanding what happened here and in the mountains.

The path crosses a good cascade and again becomes a 4WD track, but again after a few minutes you should turn right onto a path down the hill to head directly for Sotzil (1,170m), across the valley. After 15 minutes you'll cross the river on a good log bridge, and then climb hard for 15 more to reach the village; the path dips to a *pulpería* and a footbridge, after which you should

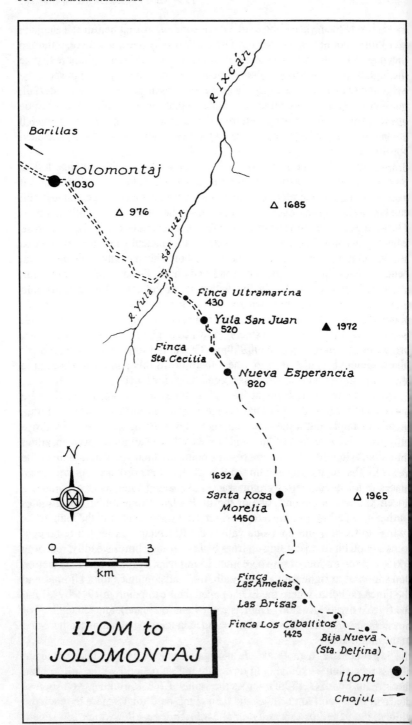

turn right and follow the obvious main path zig-zagging up the steep hill. It takes about 15 minutes more to reach the ridge, where you should turn left onto a better path. After some pretty level going, this begins to rise gradually towards what seems a very obvious pass; after ten minutes there's a soccer pitch above a stream, which is flat enough to camp on if not to have a fair game. The path zigs up for 15 minutes, and then continues to climb more easily for ten minutes to reach the true pass at about 1,350m. To the left/west are big hills, up to 2,365m, and to the north is the deep valley of the Río Xamalá. After five minutes the path meets a 4WD track from the left, and drops steadily to enter the large hillside village of **Ilom** after 15 minutes; it takes another ten minutes to reach the plaza, where there's an agricultural extension building where you might be able to sleep, a kiosk and an unmarked comedor. This is a good place to take a break, about 23km from Chajul.

The track continues downhill, and five minutes below the plaza you can take a short cut left just after a gate, to head across the valley (at about 920m) and up to the Bija Nueva coffee works (shown by its former name of Santa Delfina on maps) after 15 minutes. The village lies another ten minutes on, after which you really start to climb out of the Xamalí valley, taking at least 45 minutes to reach the pass at 1,440m. Here you cross from the Ixil to the Ixcán, with the headwaters of the Río Yula San Juan (which becomes the Río Ixcán) below you. There are a couple of ponds on the ridge, but only scrubby vegetation and corn fields. Turning right at two junctions, in 20 minutes you'll reach a duck pond at the centre of Las Brisas; a 4WD road continues to the left of the hill ahead and traverses around, slightly higher than the path shown on the map, to pass a stream and climb more easily for 45 minutes. The village of Santa Rosa Morelia sits right on this ridge, at 1,450m, and from here the track, almost certainly too rough in places for 4WD vehicles, drops steadily into the valley of the Río Tzanixlac; this would be a long, gruelling climb in the other direction. After 40 minutes passing coffee and bananas, some pine and cecropia and remnants of lusher forest, you'll pass some houses, and five minutes later the village of Nueva Esperanza. These are all resettled villages, and each one has a kiosk (selling drinks, junk snacks and batteries) and an evangelical chapel; few women seem to wear traditional *traje*.

Five minutes beyond Nueva Esperanza you'll pass a stream flowing over calcified rocks, and five minutes further on cross to the left bank of the river (there's a footbridge hidden just to the right). From here on there's general deforestation: in ten minutes you pass through the Finca Santa Cecilia, and then in about 20 more the scattered village of **Yula San Juan**. Pick-ups run from here to Barillas in the early morning, especially Thursday to Sunday; it's not worth hiking the 16km and climbing 600m, but it is worth walking on for 15 minutes through the Finca Ultramarina to the broad gravel floodplain of the Río Yula San Juan (400m) where you can camp near the new bridge, cooled by the breeze off the water. On either side the river flows through steep limestone gorges, and the 6km-long one to the north is covered with particularly dense forest. From the back of a pick-up you can really appreciate the fantastic views as you climb up to the 1,000m karst plateau around Jolomtaj, looking across to faraway peaks and down on patches of cloud in deep valleys.

There are half a dozen places to stay in **Barillas** (1,450m), all pretty affordable, a fairly large market, and other shops and restaurants; there are also three or four buses a day to Huehuetenango. It's a largely ladino town, which serves as the springboard for the colonization of this remote frontier zone. From the 1960s settlers from Quiché and Huehuetenango began moving into this area, and the government was happy to encourage this as an alternative to agrarian reform, producing the *Franja Transversal del Norte* (Northern Transversal Fringe) plan in 1976. A road was built west from the Petén to the army base of Playa Grande, on the Río Ixcán, and a dirt road now exists from there to Barillas, which may be the final nail in the coffin of the guerrillas still hiding in the jungle here. The *Franja* was to be a place to dump peasants driven off land to the south, but it's poor limestone land, only 7% of which is viable for crops, and 35% for cattle. In any case much of the land was bought by colonels and generals, who then sold it at hugely inflated prices, making vast profits and diverting most of the resettlement funds.

The second stage of this hike starts about 18km west at San Mateo Ixtatán and runs down to Nentón, by the Mexican border. Again there's fantastic scenery, and in fact the views are even better, as the trail follows the 2,800m contour high on a ridge for a considerable way. This track is being improved to act as an extension of the Playa Grande-Barillas road, but it's not going to be used much for many years; there's great potential for touring by mountain bike up here. San Mateo is reached by buses to/from Huehue' or by trucks which take a couple of hours to climb the 18km from Barillas. There are great views along the way, even though it's largely deforested except on the hilltops; look out for the cemeteries, which look like allotments, with little sheds over the graves. These are not resettled villages, with their shiny metal roofs, but older wooden houses with shingled roofs.

You need to get off at the obvious junction soon after coming into sight of **San Mateo Ixtatán**, on the other side of the Chexjoj valley, about 2km away by road. There are hospedajes and Mayan ruins here, and a colourful market on Thursdays and Sundays. From the junction, at about 2,540m, take the good new dirt road which climbs steadily up onto an attractive karst plateau, where the road has brought the inevitable deforestation; the pines are being cleared mainly for cattle grazing, but there's also potash burning and fuelwood collection here. You may as well take any lift that's available, at least as far as the col, about 4.5km along at about 2,980m. From here it takes five minutes to drop to Chibazalum, the first of the resettled villages (not shown on maps), and then five more to rise gently above the head of the Pacumal valley. From here the road drops steadily along the north side of this valley, more or less all the way to the plains. It passes through the villages of Yalantán, Ocanté and, after 35 minutes, **Patalcal** (2,660m), the metropolis of this district, with an EU-funded school, water taps, a kiosk and even a truck.

If you want to take the most easily-graded route possible you can swing left as you enter Patalcal to follow the ancient track along the hillside, but the dirt road continues for 20 minutes to Jolomquisis and then climbs up to the right

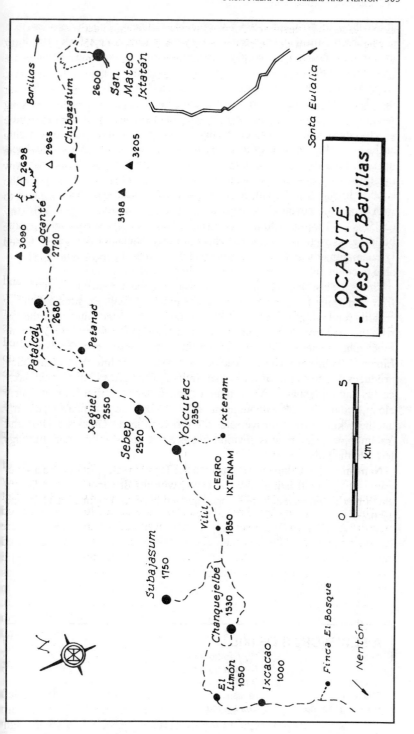

OCANTÉ
- West of Barillas

above the cemetery and onto a flat, open karst plateau. The obvious shortcut leads directly to an old pony track on very rough limestone, which runs along the edge of the plateau and after 15 minutes rejoins the road just before a junction at 2,860m. The road to the right runs northwest to Yalambojoch, where you can catch buses south to Nentón and Huehue'; the road left follows the edge of the plateau onwards, dropping slightly. It's a poor sub-alpine habitat, with long reedy grasses, shrubs, some pine, and the odd cactus, used only for grazing sheep and goats. After 15 minutes you should take a path to the right, as the road takes an unnecessary hairpin down to the left and then climbs back up; there are two more hairpins (switchbacks), with shortcuts, before the road meets the old track at 2,590m just before the ridge of Peñasco Pacumay, after another 30 minutes. The village of Xegual lies five minutes further on, merging with Sepeb, just beyond. The road continues below limestone cliffs to **Yolcutac** (2,350m), 40 minutes further on, where there's a new school and market building, as well as water taps. There are great views of the craggy Cerro Ixtenam immediately south, and beyond that across the huge valley — I was able to count eight separate ridges receding into the distance.

This is the last sizeable village; the missing section of road on to Vilil (24km from San Mateo) was being completed in mid-1995 (with EU funds). It drops steadily for 45 minutes to Vilil (1,850m) and a junction ten minutes further on with the road from Subajasum, 3km north. Taking the left fork, it's 3.5km to Finca Chanquejelbé (1,530m), where the road swings north for 4km to El Limón (1,050m); from here it heads south across an arid limestone plain which produces a better crop of rocks than Ireland; little grows but stunted oaks, cactus and rattlesnakes. You should definitely take the first lift that comes along, and don't walk without plenty of water. Ixcacao is 2km away, and it's another 7km to the Transversale (the dirt road up to Gracias a Dios and Yalambojoch); the road is obvious, but as a rule you should ignore turnings left into the hills.

Nentón is about 4km left/south down the Transversale, just beyond a small gorge. It's a small ladino town at 780m, with the decent *Comedor Lety*, a small market on Sundays, no hospedaje, and buses to Huehue' at 11.30 and 12.00.

A FEW WORDS OF IXIL

Hello	*Tishpap* (to a male)
	Tishnan (to a female)
Goodbye	*Orash*
Thank you	*Tantish*
Have a good trip	*Ona bemba*

THE SOUTHWEST

In the southwest of Guatemala you'll find the Sierra Madre, including the highest peak in Central America, **Volcán Tajumulco** (4,220m). This is only just west of the twin towns of San Marcos and San Pedro Sacatepéquez, the main towns of San Marcos department, and is easily climbed as long as you are acclimatized to the alitude. You should take a Tacaná bus (three a day) from San Pedro and get off a few kilometres beyond San Sebastián at the entrance to Tuchan village, to the left/west. From here a dirt road climbs to a pass of 3,655m before the settlement of Los Romero; fork right at the pass to head straight up the mountain. The lower, left-hand, peak (4,100m) is used for animistic rituals and may be best avoided; from the right-hand one you'll be rewarded (weather permitting) by a spectacular view along a chain of volcanoes stretching as far as Volcán Agua near Antigua, as well as to the Pacific and deep into Mexico.

The ascent from the road takes about four hours, so this trip can be done in a day. It's well worth camping below the summit, however, for the superb dawn views. There is no water above Tuchan.

Returning to Tuchan, the road continues across this high grassy plateau, where sheep and goats graze and little but potatoes and stunted pines grow, and crosses the Cumbre de Cotzil, the highest road pass in Central America at about 3,400m. This was the domain of ORPA, the Revolutionary Organization of the People in Arms (led by the son of the Nobel Prize-winning novelist Miguel Angel Asturias), who had a better reputation than the EGP, and who never tried to hold 'liberated' territory; therefore the area was not ravaged as badly as the Ixil and Ixcán, although the people undoubtedly did suffer. Two or three buses a day run to Sibinal, from where you can climb **Volcán Tacana** (4,093m), which straddles the border with Mexico. Mexican and Guatemalan climbers meet on the summit every Good Friday, which would be a great time to be here. It's a far longer tougher climb than Tajumulco; from Sibinal ask for the trail northwest to La Haciendita, three hours from town, from where the path up the cone is clear. It takes up to seven hours more to climb to Laguna Seca, on a small shoulder just north of the summit, where the climbers camp, although there's no water up here. It's only 45 minutes more to the summit, where there's a crater 400m across.

The main city of western Guatemala is **Quetzaltenango**, usually known by its Mayan name of **Xela**; it was the home of many of the 19th-century coffee planters, but it's no longer a rival to Guatemala City, though still the home of the country's only university outside the capital. It's at an altitude of 2,335m, but is dominated by the 3,772m-high **Volcán Santa María**, a perfect cone immediately south of the city. This can be done as a day trip, but again it's recommended to camp near the top, to enjoy the dawn views. Take the bus to Llanos del Piñal (at least hourly, taking 20 minutes for the 7km), or walk south down Avenida 20, turn right on Diagonal 11 and left at the hospital, and hike on for 5km. Buses will drop you at a crossroads, from where you should follow the road directly towards the right-hand side of the volcano; where this swings right after about 40 minutes, turn left onto a very rocky trail called the *espina del diablo* and follow the arrows painted on the rocks. Climb through rough pasture to a saddle with a flat grassy area the size of a football field, about one and a half hours from the start; you can camp here, but should otherwise turn right, straight up the mountain, *before* entering this area. It's heavily wooded and thus cool enough; it takes two to three hours more to the top, and is rough, rooty and very slippery during the rainy season.

The bare andesite cone is a site for ritual Indian sacrifices of chickens and so on, and you may be lucky enough to witness such an event, especially on a Sunday. The view is stunning, as is the pre-dawn cold. On the southwest shoulder of Santa María is the active Santiaguito (2,488m), born in 1922. You should stay away from this one, as poisonous gas and lava can belch forth without warning. Another volcano that can be climbed from Llanos del Piñal is Volcán Cerro Quemado (3,197m), to the east, although it's covered with spikey *chichicaste* shrubs.

Another volcano close to Xela is **Volcán Chicabal** (2,900m), about 22km west. As Simon Carter told us, the walk itself is nothing special, but the goal is really worthwhile, a really beautiful forest-fringed crater lake called Laguna Chicabal (c2,700m). The starting point is San Martín Sacatepéquez (also known as Chile Verde), an isolated village of Mam people with a beautiful and unusual costume; buses from Xela to Coatepeque pass through regularly. From the far end of the village a path leads up to the right of the church and soon meets the main trail where you turn right. The path soon forks, after a bridge: take the smaller path to the right. Go straight on over the first ridge and down, bearing round to the left. After coming out of the woods you pass near a house and go through a *milpa* before ascending the forested slope to the crater's edge, reached in two or three hours. From here a path leads down to the turquoise lake, and another to the right takes you to a superb viewpoint. There are many crosses around the lake shore and offerings of flowers on a wooden trellis in the water; on Ascension Thursday and May 3 in particular there are important ceremonies here, which should not be disturbed. The scene is really tranquil and beautiful, an unexpected jewel.

Relief on Mayan tripod bowl

Chapter Twenty-six

Eastern and Northern Guatemala

EASTERN GUATEMALA

Heading east from the capital, the Atlantic Highway runs through arid mountains and down to the long straight rift of the Motagua valley. Fast-draining gravel and under 500mm of precipitation per year makes this an inland desert, hot and dry, with several endemic species. The flora is dominated by *Acacia farnesiana*, organ cacti, yucca and calabash-gourd trees.

The Sierra de las Minas

To the north the valley is dominated by the **Sierra de las Minas**, one of the country's two Biosphere Reserves; in theory the whole length of the massif is protected, but in practice only isolated patches are really safe. It's little known, and almost totally unvisited. These are some of the oldest rocks in Central America, Permian sediments above older metamorphic rocks, granites to the north, serpentine and marble to the south. It's misnamed, as there's been very little mining here. The valleys on either side are virtually at sea level, while the highest peak, Cerro Raxon, is 3,015m; this altitudinal difference is very important for wildlife diversity. Above 1,400m there is cloudforest, of which there are three types here, determined largely by rainfall, which varies from 1,000mm above the dry Motagua valley to over 4,000mm per year on the densely forested northern slopes. There's subtropical low-montane moist forest up to 2,200m, dominated by oaks, *Pinus oocarpa*, *Alnus jorulensis* (alder) and the orchid *Encyclia selligera*; subtropical low-montane wet forest, higher and wetter, is dominated by *Clethra sp (zapotillo)*, *Persea donnell-smithii* (a type of avocado), *Pinus maximinoi* and liquidambar; and subtropical low-montane rainforest, the wettest and highest, with the walnut *Alfaroa costaricensis*, *Brunili sp (cedrillo)*, *Gunnera sp* (giant begonia) and *Magnolia guatemalensis*. Below 1,400m there's subtropical premontane dry forest (with 500-1,000mm precipitation) with *Ceiba aescutofolia (ceibillo)* and the orchid *Encyclia diota*, and the wetter subtropical premontane wet forest, with corozo palm (*Orbignya cohune*), mountain guayabo (*Terminalia amazonia*), *Pinus caribea* and sapodilla (*Manilkara zapota*). The forest is rich in epiphytes, including endemic bromeliads, ferns, and 47 species of orchids; there are spectacular examples of coexisting neoarctic (North American) and neotropical (Central/South American) associations. *Acer saccharum var Skutchii*, a variant of the standard North American maple, can be found at its southern limit here between 1,600 and 2,500m (its leaves turn red in late October/early November, before falling and being replaced in March and April); other species at their southern limit include *Acer negundo* (box elder) and an isolated patch of *Mitchella repens* (partridge-berry).

You can find 33 species of mammals here (including howler and spider monkeys, tapir, jaguar, puma, ocelot, tamandua, red brocket and white-tailed deer, peccary, squirrel, armadillo, paca, raccoon, opossum, coati, kinkajou, Eastern grey fox, weasels, rabbits, skunks, and spiny pocket mice), 219 species of birds (including hawks, herons, parrots, orioles, doves and jays, and the quetzal, toucan, chachalaca, curassow, tinamou, clay-coloured robin, grackle, cayenne pigeon, gold-fronted woodpecker and road-runner) and 110 reptiles and amphibians. The horned guan *(pavo de cacho/Oreophasus derbianus)* is a form of wild turkey found only in southern Mexico, Petén and this area of Guatemala, Alta and Baja Verapaz.

The Biosphere Reserve is managed by an NGO, *Defensores de la Naturaleza*, at Avda de las Americas 20-21, Guatemala City Zona 14 (tel: 373 897/370 319, fax: 682 648). They are not the most hands-on of conservation groups, spending most of their energies on producing reports and leaflets and relatively little on supporting the people on the ground. They are building an Environmental Education Centre across the junction of Avenida 7 and Calle 5 from the Archaeological Museum in the capital, which may be worth a visit. To visit the reserve you should have permission from Defensores, either in the capital or their local office in Salamá (about 1km west along the Rabinal road).

The park is long and thin, and a hike along the length of the cordillera would be an amazing expedition; however there is no access to the nuclear zone at the moment, while much of the lower part of the park has been deforested or planted with coffee, especially on the southern side, which is mainly populated by ladinos. The northern side is inhabited by Kekchi Indians and is far less developed — two-thirds of their communities are only accessible by foot. At the moment the best access is from the west end, through the village of **Chilasco** (c2,000m). To get here you should take a Guatemala-Cobán bus and get off at km145, from where it's 12km east up a decent but steadily climbing dirt road. All buses stop at La Cumbre, just south at km132, where there are shops and comedors; if you need a room you'll have to head 17km west to Salamá, the capital of Baja Verapaz department, in a hot, dry basin at 920m. The only buses to Chilasco leave Salamá at 12.30 on Sundays and Thursdays, returning for the market at about 02.00 on Mondays and Fridays, taking people home to Chilasco at 12.30 and returning to Salamá at about 15.30. At other times you may have to wait a while for a pick-up, but you should get a ride in the end. The Cobán highway climbs through pretty impressive pine forests (although afflicted in patches by pine-borer beetle) to the watershed at La Cumbre; the Chilasco road is also very attractive, through pine, cypress, maple and oak. However, once you reach the village you'll find that much of the area around has been deforested in a very unattractive way.

Chilasco is an unusual place; it has done very well out of growing broccoli for export to the USA, and is now producing three crops a year, with liberal use of chemicals. They now have electricity, new homes, and lots of trucks, but it won't be long before the soil is exhausted. The chief *guardeparque* is Don Esteban, whose house is on the main road halfway along the soccer pitch; he's the man to ask about accommodation. There may also be Peace Corps volunteers here, who are usually pleased to see a fresh face. The Biosphere Reserve office is half a block to the left at the end of the soccer field.

From here you can hike in a few hours to a *refugio* just inside the cloudforest; the path continues to the south side of the mountains, but in 1995 it was definitely inadvisable to go this way, as armed men and army trucks were engaged in illegal logging in this area. Continue straight along the side of the soccer field, bearing slightly left to cross the bridge after a couple of minutes, and then turn right to follow a 4WD track up the valley. Where this first splits you can take either route, as they're soon reunited; ten minutes further on ignore the right turn to Santa Cruz. For the first hour the track is well shaded by fairly young pine, cypress and maple trees, but then it runs through open fields and can be very hot, although it's also lined with fantastic blackberries. These are harvested for export, but as the pickers are short and there are no birds that eat the berries there are lots of huge juicy specimens waiting to be picked (in May) at gringo head height and above.

It takes about two hours to reach the Finca Miranda (two concrete huts); at the second gate a track turns left to the Kekchi village of Vega Larga, in a beautiful setting but said to be less than friendly. They make *canasto* reed baskets; the Defensores worker in the village is Juan Ichix. For the *refugio*, swing right, cross a stream and then start climbing up to the left and into the forest. It's pretty steep for 35 minutes, then a bit easier along the ridge for ten minutes. The Louisiana refuge is a simple thatched wattle hut, with a latrine across the track; you can get the key from Don Esteban, or sleep behind it under a thatched shelter (you'll need a mosquito net). If you go on, turn right onto a small path and right again, you'll find water not too far away. It doesn't look like much, but I saw quetzals just 50 metres along the track, as well as plenty of hummingbirds. The main path continues across the mountains to Los Albores, where the logging was happening, and from there down through hot bare country to San Agustín Acasaguastlán, where there's an archaeological site, just north of the Motagua valley road.

There's also a half-day's walk from Chilasco to a spectacular waterfall; most of the way is through deforested terrain, but it's worth it for the waterfall, especially if you keep your gaze focussed on the blackberries. Carry on past the Biosphere Reserve office and fork left after ten minutes (immediately after a house on the left) to climb uphill for a couple of minutes; at the top go straight across a dirt road and then at once turn right into a lane lined with a hedge of ferns and blackberries. After ten minutes this drops down from the ridge to cross a stream and fork left after a couple of minutes to cross a better bridge; there's plenty of deforestation all around, but the path and stream are pretty enough. The path turns right at a gate after five minutes, climbs for five minutes, then passes through another gate and follows a fence for ten minutes.

Three red ties mark the spot at which you can at last turn right and head down into degraded primary forest for 15 minutes. There are some decent steps at first, but the path deteriorates before finally emerging at the foot of the waterfall. It's a big enough fall (with lots of water even late in the dry season), but the valley is still a long way below, so there must be some more good cascades further down. There's one on another stream on the other side of the path down — there's a small path to the left about five minutes below the three red ties. It's hard to get a clear view of this one, but the forest is excellent.

There's also a Biosphere Reserve office in Jones ('Ho-nez'), just north of the highway east of Río Hondo, but this is a very degraded area. However, it should in theory be possible to hike north through the Finca Alexandria and over the ridge to San Lucas, Finca Río Zarco and the town of Panzós in the Polochic valley. To the east of Panzós the main road crosses the Río Cahabón (from Cobán and Semuc Champey) at Cahaboncito; 25km to the north up the river at **Finca Paraíso** there's a thermal waterfall, no less! I gather it's 60°C and 10m high. Apparently you can also swim into caves with waterfalls inside. All the rafting trips on the Cahabón stop here, and there are also boat trips from Río Dulce; you could probably hitch a ride. There's food and accommodation when you get there, and I'm sure you could camp.

The Quetzal Reserve
Continuing northwards up the Cobán highway you'll come to the **Purulha Quetzal Reserve** in the Sierra de Chuacús: this is one of the *Biotopos* administered by CECON and probably the most visited nature reserve in the country. The entrance is at km160.5; there's an overpriced hospedaje immediately to the north, and the luxurious *Posada Montaña del Quetzal* to the south at km156; you can also camp just inside the reserve.

Altitudes range from 1,500m up to 2,348m, with a (relatively) cold wet subtropical climate: temperatures range from 4° to 29.4°C with an average of c16°C, and there's an average of 2,600mm precipitation per year (spread over 245 days). Most of this comes as a mist known as *chipi-chipi*; February to April are the driest months and July to October the wettest, and in November/ December there are cold winds bringing fog from the northeast. Not surprisingly, the mountain is covered with cloudforest, mostly broadleaf trees (*Fagaceae, Lauraceae*) up to 30m tall — figs, walnuts (*Alfaroa costaricensis*), avocados, oaks (*Quercus purulhana*) and *Magnolia guatemalensis*, as well as *Pinus oocarpa* and *P. pseudostrobus* in the higher parts. The understorey includes *Cyathea* ferns, *Chamaedorea* palms, guava (*Inga sp*), as well as bromeliads, orchids, ferns and mosses. There are 80 species of mushrooms, of which 28 are edible, and three toxic.

The fauna is relatively poor, with only 25 species of mammals (howler and spider monkeys, red brocket deer, margay, Northern opossum, Deppe's squirrel, armadillo, long-tailed weasel, hooded skunk and pocket gopher — not an exciting selection), 20 species of amphibians (including the endemic *Eleuthodactylus daryi*) and 28 reptiles, including 19 snakes. Of course, it's the quetzals you've come to see, and the rangers will tell you where your chances are best. Undoubtedly, your best bet is to get up by dawn and simply stand by the road near the hospedaje; they move up the hill as the day passes. They feed on cecropia (*guarumo*) and mountain avocado (*aguacatillo*) when their fruits are in season. Other birds include the mottled owl (*lechuza/Ciccaba virgata*), emerald toucanet (*tucan esmerelda/Aulacorhynchus prasinus*), white-eared hummingbird (*Amazilia cyanocephala*), pale-billed woodpecker (*trepador/Campephilus guatemalensis*), solitary vireo (*anteojudos/Vireo solitarius*), Eastern bluebird (*azulejo/Siala sialis*), indigo bunting (*ruice/Passerina cyanea*), rufous-collared sparrow (*sabanero/Zonotrichia capensis*), black-throated green warbler (*chipe/Dendroica virens*), common yellowthroat (*Geothlypis trichas*) and rufous-capped warbler (*Basileuterus rufifrons*).

The *Biotopo* is named after Mario Dary Rivera, the leading Guatemalan conservationist, who was instrumental in setting up the reserve in 1977 but was murdered in 1981. There are no fees, but donations of a few dollars are requested.

There are two main trails which start together at 1,620m; the lower one, the *Sendero Helechos* (Ferns Path) turns right at 1,770m, while the *Sendero Musgos* (Mosses Path) climbs on to 1,940m and then heads to the right across the hill. There's a trail to a waterfall at 1,865m: it's not very big, but there's a good view, and it's a good example of a geological fault. This longer trail is 4km long and might occupy you for a couple of hours.

Cobán

The capital of Alta Verapaz department is the attractive town of **Cobán**, where you can rest, feed and do your laundry at the comfortable altitude of 1,320m. The *Hostal Acuña*, at US$4 per head, is not quite the cheapest place in town, but it's easily the best value, with great food and atmosphere. It's at 4 Calle 3-11, Zona 2 (Apdo 10.16901, tel: 511 547, fax: 511 268); the owner's son Seán Acuña runs Epiphyte Tours (2 Avda/2 Calle, Apdo 94A, tel: 512 169), operating tours to many caves in the area, including those described below.

The **Parque Las Victorias**, at 3 Calle/11 Avda, Zona 1, is a former private estate managed as a National Park by DIGEBOS since 1980. It's been planted with a wide variety of trees and plants, most of them labelled, so it's very educational, as well as being relaxing. The paths wind to and fro, so in fact it's possible to tot up quite a few kilometres if you want to.

A FEW WORDS OF KEKCHI

Hello	*Chuqwa*
Goodbye	*Inquambi*
Thank you	*Mantiosh*
Where is the path to ...?	*Bar quanlibe ...?*

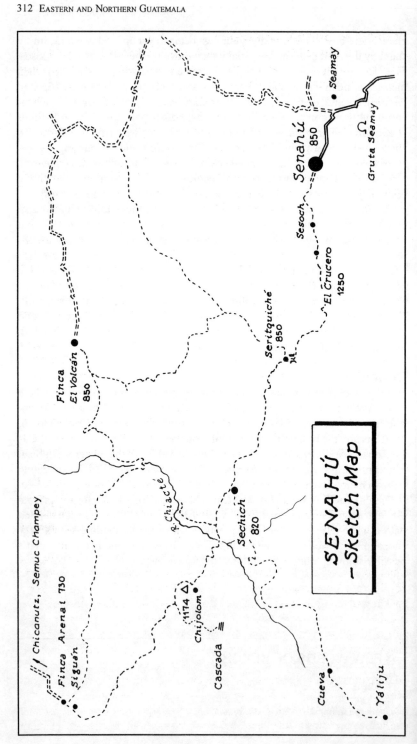

SENAHÚ
– Sketch Map

Senahú to Semuc Champey

According to Mike Shawcross, **Semuc Champey** is the 'most beautiful place in Guatemala', and he should know. These beautiful rock pools in the gorge of the Río Cahabón are well known and visited by everyone who comes this way, but it's also possible to make a very enjoyable hike in from the south through mountains that are rarely visited by outsiders. The starting point is the town of **Senahú**, well worth visiting in any case for its great setting and the fantastic scenery along the road up. There are two buses a day from Cobán to Senahú; if coming from the south, get off the Cobán highway at San Julian, at about km181, a couple of kilometres south of Tactic. Here catch any bus heading east along the Polochic valley to El Estor (four or five a day), get off at the Senahú turning 1.5km west of Telemán and wait for any vehicle heading up the hill.

The route starts virtually at sea level, and climbs steeply before winding up, down and around over several ridges and eventually to Senahú (850m). The hills are covered with coffee, which seems bizarre as this normally grows best on volcanic soils, while these hills are limestone, with spectacular karst cliffs and gorges. In places there is still some forest clinging to the precipices, producing images like those in classical Chinese painting. From a junction 2km before Senahú (between two churches overlooking a soccer field) a dirt road continues north to Finca El Volcán, from where it's a relatively short hike west to Finca Arenal, although there can be a fairly difficult crossing of the Río Chiacté. A path leads 1km south to the Seamay cave, just west of the road, which is worth exploring if you have a flashlight.

I continued the 2km west to the town, where there are some pretty inadequate comedors but a decent cafe in the *Hotel Senahú*, the best in town. The trail starts by heading straight on up the main street to the west, leaving the chapel to the left. After 15 minutes it feints to the right and then climbs steeply to the left for ten minutes; from the pass (1,140m) it's pretty well level for 30 minutes across the karst plateau of El Crucero, before beginning to drop into the valley of the Río Seritquiché. Taking three obvious short cuts as the 4WD road descends more gently, it takes under 40 minutes to reach the Seritquiché school, at 880m, opposite the soccer pitch. The village itself is five minutes further on, across a bridge to the right.

Turning left at once, follow a small path across the fields (although it is cobbled in parts) and fork left after ten minutes to head on down the valley. You'll cross a concrete bridge over the Río Sepec and then follow a pony track above the right bank of the Seritquiché; after 30 minutes there's a gate and then three streams, of which the third is the largest but probably not the purest. It's all cleared land or secondary growth, but wonderfully lush for all that. Climbing steeply to the right/north, you'll cross a ridge at 1,000m after 15 minutes more and then descend, turning left after five minutes into Sechich. To drop down to the river you can take either of two small paths to the left between the houses, or if you miss these turn left a few minutes beyond the last houses (just as the trail starts to head north up the valley), onto an initially overgrown path that swings back below the houses and then across a stream and down to a good suspension bridge at 600m.

The Río Chiacté is a beautiful clear stream here, and there's a good shelter, in which you could sleep, by the bridge. Rest well, because there's an absolute stinker of a climb ahead. Only the shortcuts seem to be in use, and the longer, easier hairpins are rather overgrown. After almost half an hour you'll reach the top of the steepest section, but continue climbing up the obvious path for 15 minutes to the Finca Chijolom. Beyond the drying floor the path swings left below a school and soon crosses a stream. It's pretty much level for ten minutes, so enjoy the break; there's another very hot steep climb ahead. Forking right below a new house, there's a ten to 15 minutes climb before you can finally swing to the right for ten minutes, crossing below a side ridge, above the last house in the village and across a field to the pass (1,170m). Fork right just before the top, drop down into the next valley, cross the stream and head up to the right below houses, through coffee and cardamom plants, turning left onto a ponytrack after 15 minutes.

This crosses another karst plateau, with plenty of fields being burnt and then tilled with pointed sticks: there are no aid programmes here, no tourists, no gringos at all (other than you!). Keep right, and in under 15 minutes you'll reach a col just south of a hill marked as 1,299m on maps. Surprisingly enough, there's a water tap on the far side. The obvious main path runs down along the left side of the next valley, then swings right and heads left through a narrow gap between two hills; turn left after 20 minutes at a tree and drop steeply into a large basin. After another 20 you'll reach the canalized Quebrada Arenal, rushing down from a waterfall to the left to power the finca's hydro-electric plant. The easiest way on is simply to walk along the aqueduct to the right for ten minutes, and then go through a gate to the left and turn right onto a dirt road, which brings you in ten minutes (past a junction left to the Hacienda Yalipur) to the shops at the centre of the Finca Arenal.

From here there's a dirt road for about 12km to Semuc Champey, which is pretty easy to follow. It heads north from the finca and soon swings right to climb to a pass, and then passes through Chicanutz, a coffee-growing area that seems to have no specific centre. It's very lush, covered in all sorts of vegetation, but where fields have been burnt you can see it is in fact very rocky indeed, with limestone outcrops everywhere. From here there's an immense drop in just a couple of big hairpins to the area of Chipoc, before winding slowly down the valley to the car park-cum-soccer field above the Semuc Champey bridge. It's just five minutes along the path at the far end of the car park to the pools (at about 260m).

It may not be immediately obvious, but these beautiful pools are on top of a natural bridge, with the Río Cahabón plunging underneath at the west end in a fury of white water. The pools themselves are fed by side-streams, which are reportedly getting smaller due to burning and farming above. This has mercifully been spared from the curse of safety rails, but if your legs are a bit wobbly after a long, hot hike you should definitely keep well clear. Crazy as it seems, cave-divers have been in; there's an impassable sump in the middle, but it's been fully mapped on either side. There isn't a *mirador* at the exit from the cave, but you can get down through the woods if you want; it's also pretty impressive.

There's a large enough tin-roofed shelter here, but the latrines have clearly never been cleaned: whatever you decide to do, keep well away from the water and don't pollute these lovely pools. There are some good places to stay in Lanquín, 10km to the north, and there's quite a bit of traffic. Cross the relatively new suspension bridge just below the car park, and if you want, ask at the shop, about three minutes further on, to be shown a short-cut up the hill. In any case it's an attractive walk on up the dirt road (with some obvious shorter short-cuts), along the lush Rubella valley to the pass at about 650m. It took me 90 minutes to walk the 7km to the pass, and 30 minutes to walk the 3km down to Lanquín (350m).

There are three fairly similar hospedajes in town, and the much more expensive *Hotel El Recreo* on the road west towards Cobán; just a bit further west there's a path signposted north to the reason for all these hotels, the **Lanquín caves**. These stretch for at least 3km, but only a few hundred metres have been equipped with walkways and electric lights; the latter are unlikely to be on unless there's a tour group going through, but you can ask at the *Municipalidad* for the lights to be switched on at a specific time, which should only cost you a couple of dollars. It's possible to camp at the caves, allowing you to watch thousands of bats flying in and out. About three buses a day run to Cobán from here.

NORTHERN GUATEMALA

The Petén is covered in detail in Jim Conrad's *The Maya Road*, also published by Bradt, so I'll just outline the national parks and other key attractions along the way. Just about all traffic to Petén continues along the Atlantic Highway down the Motagua valley, turning north at the La Ruidosa junction near Morales: it's 34km to the bridge over the Río Dulce, at a place known as Fronteras, El Relleno, or just Río Dulce. This is a centre for boating on Lago de Izabal, immediately upstream, and there are plenty of hotels, restaurants and weekend cottages here; it can be pretty busy at weekends, and there are plenty of minibuses running down to La Ruidosa. There are some cheap places to sleep, and you can camp 1km upstream at the El Tortugal Backpackers' Retreat; another kilometre or so west, at the mouth of the lake, is the Castillo San Felipe, built around 1600 to keep English pirates out. You can go horse-riding, canoeing or windsurfing here, take yacht trips around the lake or down to Livingston at the mouth of the Río Dulce, or even try bungee-jumping from the bridge!

The cheapest way to get to Livingston is by the mail boat, but if you hire a *cayuco* you can stop to swim in hot springs and visit the **Biotopo Chocón-Machacas**, on the north shore of the El Golfete lake. This is one of the reserves run by CECON, to protect the manatee; these are best seen from a rowing boat in the lagoons, but there is also a trail of under 1km, on which you may see tapir droppings. With a rainfall of 5,700mm per year and an average temperature of 27°C, this is definitely tropical rainforest, with big trees such as caoba or mahogany (*Swietania macrophylla*), *palo sangre* (*Pterocarpus officinalis*), wild nutmeg or *cacao volador* (*Virola koschnyi*), breadnut (*Brosimum alicastrum*), *san juan* (*Vochysia hondurensis*) and sapodilla (*Manilkara zapota*). Smaller trees include *Bactris, Chamaedorea* and *Orbygnia* palms, as well as mangroves and a great variety of aquatic plants. Mammals are mostly relatively small, including collared peccary, margay, agouti, kinkajou, raccoon, four-eyed opossum, and three species of squirrel; in addition there are turtles (*Kinosternum acutum, Staurotypus triporcatus*) and iguanas. There are 300 species of birds (180 migratory), including anhingas, neotropical cormorants, herons, Montezuma oropendolas, chachalacas, red-lored and green parrots, keel-billed toucans, collared araçaris, turkey vultures and, in winter, ospreys.

From Livingston you take a boat to the coral cayes off Belize, or across the bay to Punta Manabique, a 12km peninsula with no facilities other than a very simple resort with camping and cabins. Although there are no roads or electricity on the peninsula, it's said to be targeted for development for 'ecotourism': the Fundación Mario Dary is seeking protection for it. There are sandy beaches, plenty of fish, and mangrove swamps (*Rhizophora mangle, Avicennia nitida, Languncularis racemosa*, and the button tree *Conocarpus erecta*).

Both the *Rough Guide* and the *Mexico and Central American Handbook* describe the 'Jungle Trail' from Puerto Barrios to Corinto in Honduras, and give far more detailed accounts than we can here.

Lago de Izabal is surrounded by wet lowlands with many endemic plants, as well as cabbage trees (*Andira inermis*), figs, palms, creepers and epiphytes. Bullsharks and sawfish swim up the Río Dulce to Lago de Izabal (and up the Río Motagua), as they do up the Río San Juan to Lake Nicaragua. Continuing northwards the road passes through low savannas dominated by sedges and grasses, *Pinus caribea, Curatella americana* (sandpaper tree), and *Compositae* (like daisies and dandelions).

The Petén

Petén contains half of Guatemala's surviving forest; it accounts for a third of the country's area but less than a thirtieth of its population. Even so, the population has increased at least tenfold since 1964, and 250 immigrants are said to arrive every day. It's seen as a land of unlimited opportunity, but in fact it's largely infertile. Oil has been found, but for the most part the forest is being cleared for cattle-grazing. Studies have shown that income from sustainable use of the forest is triple that from logging and grazing — products include *xate*, a type of *Chamaedorea* palm used in floral arrangements in the USA and Europe, allspice (*pimiento*), and *chicle*, the gum of the sapodilla (*Manilkara zapota* or *Achras zapota*), a small evergreen found in disturbed forest, such as in Mayan ruins. This gum is still exported to Japan, although it's been supplanted by synthetic chewing gums elsewhere. With Mayan ruins still being unearthed in the forest, there's also massive potential for ecotourism here. All of the Petén north of Lake Petén Itzá (at least a third of its rainforest, no less than 1.4m hectares) has now been preserved, in theory, as a Biosphere Reserve, but much of it is, realistically, zoned for 'controlled extraction'. Only the most important areas, including the main Mayan sites, are receiving real protection. The guerrillas in this area are the FAR (Rebel Armed Forces), of whom it's been said that you have nothing to fear but dying of boredom: they sometimes stop buses to deliver political lectures (especially to North Americans) but do little else.

The centre of Petén is Flores/Santa Elena, from where you will doubtless be visiting the Mayan ruins of Tikal; there's plenty of wildlife here, described in depth in guides that you can buy here and in Antigua. About halfway to **Tikal**, at El Remate, a road turns left/west along the north side of Lake Petén Itzá to the **Biotopo Cerro Cahuí**. This can be reached by walking 2.5km from El Remate, by the Jobompiche minibus (11.00 from the Santa Elena market) or by (expensive) boat across the lake. This is a karst area, rising only to 360m and covered with wet tropical forest; rainfall is a mere 1,416mm per year, but there are still plenty of 30m trees, including local species such as *Haematoxylum yucatanum, Alseis yucatanensis* and *Platymiscium yucatanum*, as well as caoba and oak, and plenty of palms, *Tillandsia* bromeliads and *Epidendrum, Trigonidium* and *Maxilaria* orchids. There are 28 species of mammals, including howler and spider monkeys, red brocket deer, ocelot, collared peccary, paca, agouti, coati, armadillo, weasels and three species of squirrel. In the lake are 24 fish species, as well as the Petén crocodile (*Crocodylus moreletti*) and turtles (*Kinosternum acutum, Claudius angustatus, Staurotypus triporcatus* and *Rhinoclemmys areolata*). Birds include the hookbilled and double-toothed kites (*Chondrohierax uncinatus* and *Harpagus bidentatus*), the crane hawk (*Geranospiza caerulescens*), ocelated or Petén turkey (*Agriocharis ocellata*), buff-bellied hummingbird (*Amazilia yucatensis*), Yucatán flycatcher (*Myiarchus yucatensis*), rose-throated tanager (*Piranga roseogularis*), the Petén sparrow (*Aimophila petenia*), the parakeet (*Aratinga astec*) and the pigeons *Columba nigrirostris* and *C speciosa*, none of which I've seen any references to further south; birds seen elsewhere in Central America include the snail kite (*Rostrhamus sociabilis*), the red-lored, green, white-crowned and brown-hooded parrots (*Amazona autumnalis, A farinosa, Pionus senilis* and *Pionopsitta haematotis*), the Yucatán jay (*Cissilopha yucatensis*) and the vermiculated screech-owl (*Otus guatemalensis*), as well as herons, toucans and kingfishers.

There are two fairly short paths, both leading to the viewpoint on Cerro Cahuí; camping is allowed, and there are hospedajes in the neighbouring villages. The reserve is managed by CECON, with the Mario Dary Foundation, with the aim of creating a model for low-impact ecotourism in this area.

Abutting the Tikal National Park to the west is the 42,000ha **El Zotz** reserve, which it is intended to expand to 49,300ha and upgrade to a National Park. This is hot, wet subtropical forest, home to cats such as jaguar, puma, ocelot, margay and yagouaroundi, red brocket deer, both types of peccary, and howler and spider monkeys. There are literally millions of bats here, and birds such as king vulture, bat falcon (*Falco rufigularis*), curassow, Petén turkey, and crested guan. Its centre is San Miguel La Palotada, due north from Flores by the dirt road (no buses) towards Carmelita (for the fantastic hike, two days each way, to the El Mirador ruins); El Zotz is a small Mayan ruin on the dirt road from San Miguel to Uaxactún, where you may camp although there are no services.

Right up in the northwestern corner of the Petén, 274km northwest of Flores, is the **Laguna El Tigre** (or Río Escondido), a 42,500ha wetland reserve. This too only rises to 100m above sea level, and includes natural savanna and subtropical forest. There's very little protection in this area, which is effectively controlled by poachers, loggers, smugglers and guerrillas. Access is only by boat on the Río San Pedro northwards from El Naranjo. If you get this far, you may see howler monkeys, jaguars, white-tailed deer, white-lipped peccary, Petén crocodile, and white turtle (*Dermatemys mawii*). Birds include the king vulture, scarlet macaw, wood stork (*jabirú/Mycteria americana*), black hawk-eagle (*Spizaetus tyrannus*), snail kite (*Rostrhamus sociabilis*), orange-breasted falcon (*Falco deiroleucus*), and the Petén turkey.

West of Flores and south of El Naranjo along the Mexican border is the Sierra de Lacandón, no less than 255m high; you should know that a hiker was killed by a mine here in 1995. There's a 6,100km² forest reserve, but nine sawmills are planning to illegally cut the last mahogany, ceiba and cedar trees here; in 1995 army trucks taking wood out were blockaded by CONAP and Greenpeace activists in San Andres. The El Ceibal ruins, east of Sayaxché, are in an 809ha reserve, in which the Exxon oil company planned to drill test wells in 1989: the Ministry of Energy and Mines supported them but CONAMA and the Ministry of Culture staff physically blocked Exxon trucks moving gear in, and eventually persuaded them to stay out of the reserve.

Petén is great caving country: the place to enquire (after the *Casa Andinista* in Antigua) is probably the Finca Ixobel, just south of Poptún, where you can walk, swim, ride horses and pig yourself, as well as visiting nearby caves. The Posada Ixobel, in Poptún village, is a more economical alternative. There are also plenty of caves in the limestone hills behind Santa Elena; the best known is Actún Kan (Cave of the Serpent), which has lighting.

APPENDIX ONE

Hikers' Spanish

There are plenty of places, particularly in Guatemala, where you can stop for as long as you want to study Spanish with more or less professional teachers. But however competent you become with the language there are certain words and phrases that are essential for hikers or 'ecotourists' but are unlikely to form part of your language course. Just to confuse you, there are many variations in vocabulary from country to country, which we have indicated below in brackets (CR — Costa Rica, G — Guatemala, H — Honduras, P — Panamá). Note that in rural parts of Nicaragua and El Salvador any 's' is likely to be dropped, so you get *gracia', ma', bo'que', ba'tante* (thanks, more, wood, enough) and so on.

Pronunciation is fairly straightforward, and more so than in Castilian (European) Spanish:
'**d**' is like English 'th' except when it's the first letter in the word, when it's 'd';
'**g**' is as in English except before 'e' or 'i' when it's 'h'; 'h' is always silent;
'**j**' is a guttural 'h';
'**ll**' is like 'y';
'**ñ**' is like 'ny';
'**v**' is like 'b' (and words can often be spelt either way);
'**x**' is 'sh', especially in Mayan words.
'**r**' is rolled, and throughout the region football commentators can be heard on the radio competing in rolling 'r's more absurdly than their colleagues, and yelling 'Goooooooooooal!!' for longer without drawing breath.

The most common word for 'hello' throughout the region is *Adios* — not just in Costa Rica, as many books say. 'Goodbye' is usually *hasta luego* (see you later) or in Guatemala *para servirle* (at your service), or just occasionally *adios*.

PHRASES

You can't get lost	*No puede pedirse*
What's this place called?	*¿Como se llama esta lugar?*
What village is this?	*¿Que aldea es est?*
Where does this trail go?	*¿A donde va este camino?*
Where are you coming from?	*¿De donde viene?*
Where are you from (your country)?	*¿De donde es?*
How far is it to... ?	*¿A que distancia...?*
May I... ? Is it possible... ?	*¿Se puede... ?*
I would like (to eat)	*Quisiero (comer)*
Without meat	*Sin carne*
Bon voyage	*Vaya bien*

WORDS

Left/right	*izquierdo/derecho*
North/south	*norte/sur*
East	*este* or *oriente*
West	*oeste, occidente* or *poniente*
Northeast/northwest	*noreste/noroeste* (easily confused)
Straight ahead	*todo recto*
Backpack	*mochila*
Boat or motorized canoe	*chalupa* (P), *lancha* (CR, G), *tuk-tuk* (H)
Bridge	*puente*
Campsite	*camping, campamento*
Cave	*cueva*
Cloud	*nube*
Crag	*despeñadero*
Crossroad	*cruce*
Dugout canoe	*piragua* (P), *cayuco* (G), *pipante* (H)
Environment	*medio ambiente*
Farm or ranch	*finca, hacienda, caserío*
Farmer or peasant	*campesino*
Field	*campo, milpa*
Forest	*selva, montaña, bosque*
Frontier	*frontera*
Gorge	*desfiladero, garganta*
High	*alto*
Hill	*cuesta, cerro*
Junction	*cruce, desvio* (H)
Lake	*lago, laguna*
Landscape	*paisaje*
Lookout, viewpoint	*mirador*
Marsh	*pantano, marisma*
Meadow	*llano, llanura*
Mountain	*cerro, pico, montaña*
Mountain hut	*refugio*
Mountain range	*cordillera, sierra, fila*
On vacation	*paseando*
Pass	*puerto, paso*
Pasture	*pasto*
Path	*camino, sendero, troncha* (P), *vereda* (G and CR)
Peak	*picacho, pico*
Rain	*lluvia*
Restaurant	*restaurante, comedor*
Ridge	*cumbre, cadena*
River	*río*
Rock	*roca*
Saddle	*puerto, paso*
Shop	*tienda, pulpería, kiosco*

Slope	*cuesta, vertiente, ladera, falda*
Spring	*fuente*
Steep	*abrupto, escarpado*
Stream	*arroyo, chorro*
Summit	*cima*
Tent	*carpa, tienda de campaña*
Tired	*cansado*
Valley	*valle*
Village	*aldea, pueblo, poblado, comarca* (N), *caserío* (G)
Wandering	*errante*
Wood (material)	*madera*

APPENDIX TWO
Selected Reading
Health
The best books we've seen are:
Healthy Travel: Bugs, Bites and Bowels by Jane Wilson Howarth (Cadogan 1995).

Wilderness Medicine by William W. Forgey (Indiana Camp Supply Books, USA).

The Tropical Traveller by John Hatt (Penguin, 1993).

More general are:
Health Guide for International Travellers by Thomas Sakmar *et al* (Passport 1994) and the

International Travel Health Guide by Stuart Rose (Travel Medicine Inc, Massachusets, 6/e 1995).

You can also contact:
MASTA (Medical Advisory Service for Travellers Abroad), at the London School of Hygiene and Tropical Medicine, Keppel St, London WC1E 7HT (tel. 0171-631 4408), or any of the travel clinics run by British Airways, Thomas Cook, Trailfinders and others.

In North America try IAMAT (the International Association for Medical Assistance to Travellers) at 417 Center St, Lewiston, NY 14092 (tel 716 754 4883) or 40 Regal Rd, Guelph, Ontario N1K 1B5 (tel 519 836 0102), or the Center for Disease Control in Atlanta, GA 30333, USA (or by their automated hotline on 404 332 4559, fax: 404 332 4565); their annual bulletin *Health Information for International Travel* is also available from the US Government Printing Office, Washington, DC 20422.

Natural History
The books listed here are all published in the USA. UK readers might like to contact the Natural History Book Service (tel 01803 865913) for the latest catalogue.

Jungles by Edward S Ayensu (Crown, New York, 1980).
An abundantly illustrated book covering all aspects of jungle ecology.

Central American Jungles by Don Moser (Time Life, 1979).
A photographic record; beautiful and informative.

Portraits of the Rainforest by Adrian Forsyth (Camden House, Ontario, 1990).
Beautiful photos and a fascinating ecological overview.
Also *Tropical Nature* (Scribner's, 1984), older and drier.

A Neotropical Companion by John Kricher (Princeton UP, 1989).
An excellent overview of ecosystems and evolutionary processes in the American tropics.

Tropical Rainforest by Arnold Newman (Facts on File, New York, 1990).
A blueprint for rainforest survival, and a standard reference already, with 200 superb colour photos.

Costa Rican Natural History edited by Daniel Janzen (Chicago UP, 1983).
Although specifically concerned with Costa Rica (with detailed coverage of La Selva, Corcovado, Monteverde, Palo Verde and Santa Rosa), this very detailed yet user-friendly guide is full of information on species throughout the region, with full checklists.

Birds of Guatemala by Hugh C Land (Livingston, Pennsylvania, 1970).

Field Guide to Mexican Birds, including Guatemala, Belize and El Salvador by Roger Peterson & Edward Chalif (Houghton & Mifflin, Boston, 1973).
Still in print, a very handy pocket guide.

A Guide to the Birds of Panamá by Robert S Ridgley (Princeton UP, 1989).
Heavy and expensive, but very comprehensive. It now includes the birds of Costa Rica, Honduras and Nicaragua, perfectly complementing Peterson.

A Guide to Birds of Costa Rica by Gary Stiles & Alexander Skucht, (Cornell UP, 1989).
This gives all names in English, Latin and Spanish, which makes it ideal for discussing birds with locals.

A Guide to the Birds of Colombia by Steven Hilty & William Brown (Princeton UP, 1986).
Nearly 1,700 species, half of all those in South America — ideal if you're going through the Darién Gap, though too big to carry.

Neotropical Rainforest Mammals — a Field Guide by Louise Emmons (U Chicago Press, 1990).
Dry, but detailed and authoritative.

Field Guide to the Orchids of Costa Rica by R L Dressler (Cornell UP, 1993).

The Butterflies of Costa Rica by Philip DeVries (Princeton UP, 1987).
These two guides to Costa Rican species can at least provide a sample of those in the region.

Crafts

Indian Crafts of Guatemala and El Salvador by Lilly de Jongh Osborne (University of Oklahoma Press, 1975).

Embroidery of Mexico and Guatemala by Frances Schaill Goodman (Scribner, New York, 1976).

The Highland Maya: Patterns of Life and Clothing in Indian Guatemala by Roland and Roger Bunch (Indigenous Publications, California, 1977).

Guidebooks

Central America on a Shoestring (Lonely Planet, 1994).
Is pretty much in tune with the needs of most of its readers and covers the basics well. Most backpackers will use this.

Mexico and Central American Handbook (Travel and Trade Publications, annually in September).
This is the one to take if you're planning to get well off the beaten track, but it has few town plans and relies overmuch on readers' letters — this means that whereas new hotels and so on get added quickly, dead information is not weeded out. The Handbook also covers the needs of business travellers and those travelling by car. More experienced travellers, who can cope with the risk of information overload, may prefer this to the Lonely Planet guide

There are other general guides:

The Berkeley Guide: Central America on the Loose (Fodor, 1993) is hip and readable, as well as being informative.

The Traveller's Survival Kit: Central America (by Emily Hatchwell and Simon Calder, Vacation Work, 1991) is useful.

The Cadogan Guide to Central America (by Natascha Norton and Mark Whatmore, 1993) provides a more cultural view of the area; there's also a Cadogan Guide to Guatemala and Belize alone.

Adventure Travel in Latin America by Scott Graham (Wilderness, California 1990) covers all of Mexico, the Caribbean and Central and South America, with just a couple of pages per country; it's also a bit dated, writing off El Salvador as war-torn.

The Rough Guides and Lonely Planet both have guides to Costa Rica (the Lonely Planet by our own Rob Rachowiecki) and to Guatemala and Belize (with the Yucatán, in the case of Lonely Planet). Again, Lonely Planet aim firmly at the budget traveller, while the Rough Guides are a cut above them in style and attention to detail, and also in their target market. Frommer and Fodor each put out a guide that covers Guatemala, Belize and Costa Rica, if you can handle their approach.

Costa Rica is well served with at least eight other books devoted to it alone, of which the most relevant to you may be:

Adventure Guide to Costa Rica by Harry Pariser (Hunter, New Jersey, 2/e c1992),

Costa Rica — Natural Guide (3/e John Muir, New Mexico) by Ree Strange Sheck (both Costa Rica residents), or

Costa Rica's National Parks and Preserves — A Visitor's Guide by Joseph Franke (The Mountaineers, Seattle/Cordee UK 1993)

Of the general guides the most up-to-date is:
New Key to Costa Rica by Anne Becher and Beatrice Blake, now in its 12th edition (Ulysses, 1994),

and the most detailed is the
Costa Rica Handbook by Christopher Baker (Moon, California 1994).

Others are:
The Costa Rica Traveler — Getting Around in Costa Rica, by Ellen Searby (Windham Bay Press, California, 1991)
Guatemala Guide, by Paul Glassman (Open Road, Washington DC, 5/e. 1994) and
Insight Guide Costa Rica, by Harvey Haber.

Panamá is covered by:
The Panamá Traveler by David Dudenhofer's (Windham Bay Press).
Panamá, by Marc Rigole and Daniel Desjardins, (Ulysses, Montréal, 1994) and
Getting to know Panamá by Michèle Labrut (Focus Publications, Panamá, distributed by Bradt).

Bradt also publish:
The Maya Road by Jim Conrad, which covers ecotourism in Eastern Mexico, Belize and lowland Guatemala, and

Guide to Belize by Alex Bradbury (1995).

Guatemala as a whole is covered by:
Guatemala Guide by Paul Glassman (Open Road, 9/e 1995).

Guatemala, a Natural Destination by Richard Mahler (John Muir, New Mexico, 1993).

Guatemala (2/e) and *Henry's Hints* by Henry Gall (both from Zotz Press, Antigua, Guatemala).

Honduras is covered by:
Honduras (4/e, by Henry Gall , Zotz, 1992).

Honduras and the Bay Islands by Jean-Pierre Panet and Leah Hart (Passport, New York).

Many of these are most easily obtained after arrival in the country.

Traveller's tales

Guatemala and the neighbouring countries are far better served with travel literature than those further south. Easily the pick of recent books is *Sweet Waist of America* by Anthony Daniels (Arrow/Hutchinson, 1990), which deals mainly with Guatemala but also ventures into El Salvador, Honduras and Nicaragua: it's informative, up-to-date, unbiased but appropriately appalled by abuses committed on all sides, and above all a joy to read. If you're planning to travel along the Caribbean coast (not an area covered to any extent by this book) Peter Ford's *Around the Edge* (Viking Penguin, 1991) is good value, although he was unable to spend much time in Panamá. Salman Rushdie's *The Jaguar Smile* (Cape/Pan, 1987) is an enjoyable snapshot of Sandinista Nicaragua. Mary Morris' *Nothing to Declare, memoirs of a woman travelling alone* (Hamish Hamilton, 1988) is an annoying book with far too much about the inane author; the first 145 pages are spent in Mexico. Older but better are Patrick Marnham's *So Far From God* (Penguin, 1985) and Jeremy Paxman's *Through The Volcanoes* (Michael Joseph/Paladin, 1985), covering all the Central American countries. Older still, but entertaining in its tetchy way, is Paul Theroux's *The Old Patagonian Express* (Penguin/Pocket Books, 1979, now also in Picador), which uses rail travel, then still possible, as a peg to hang his tale upon. Going yet further back in time, *Incidents of Travel in Central America, Chiapas and Yucatán* (Dover/Century) is John Lloyd Stephens' classic 1841 account of the discovery of the great Mayan ruins and much more; *Incidents of Travel in Yucatán* is the 1843 follow-up.

For a more factual view of Central America, see *Central America Inside Out* by Tom Barry (Grove Press, USA, 1991); Barry is also author of *Inside Guatemala* (The Inter-Hemispheric Education Resource Center, Albuquerque, USA), one of a series on all the Central American states. *Roots of Rebellion: Land and Hunger in Central America*, also by Barry, (South End Press, 1987) and *The Pacification of Central America 1987-1993* by James Dunkerley (Verso, 1994) both provide analysis of the current political situation in the region.

The Latin American Bureau (1 Amwell St, London EC1R 1UL; tel: 0171 278 2829) publishes books on society and politics in the region, as well as a quarterly review, *Latin American Outlook*, free to members. A similar service is provided by the Latin American Travel Advisor (PO Box 17-17-908, Quito, Ecuador; fax: +593 2 562 566), who put out a very detailed quarterly guide to travel risks in the region (US$15, or US$39 for a year's subscription). The South American Explorer's Club (126 Indian Creek Rd, Ithaca, NY 14850, USA; tel: 607 277 0488; or through Bradt in the UK) has a wealth of information (for members) on hiking in the Darién Gap and points south; it also has clubhouses in Quito and Lima.

Index

Notes:
1 Where necessary, we have indicated the relevant country (CR — Costa Rica, ES — El Salvador, G — Guatemala, H — Honduras, N — Nicaragua, P — Panama).
2 The diversity of wildlife in Central America and the lack of space in a book of this kind conflict; index entries have been reduced to avifauna, fauna, flora and natural history.
3 Similarly, various struggles, wars and revolutions may be found only under history.
4 There are no people listed in the index.
5 V = Volcán; L = Lake, Lago or Laguna